FORGOTTEN LONDON

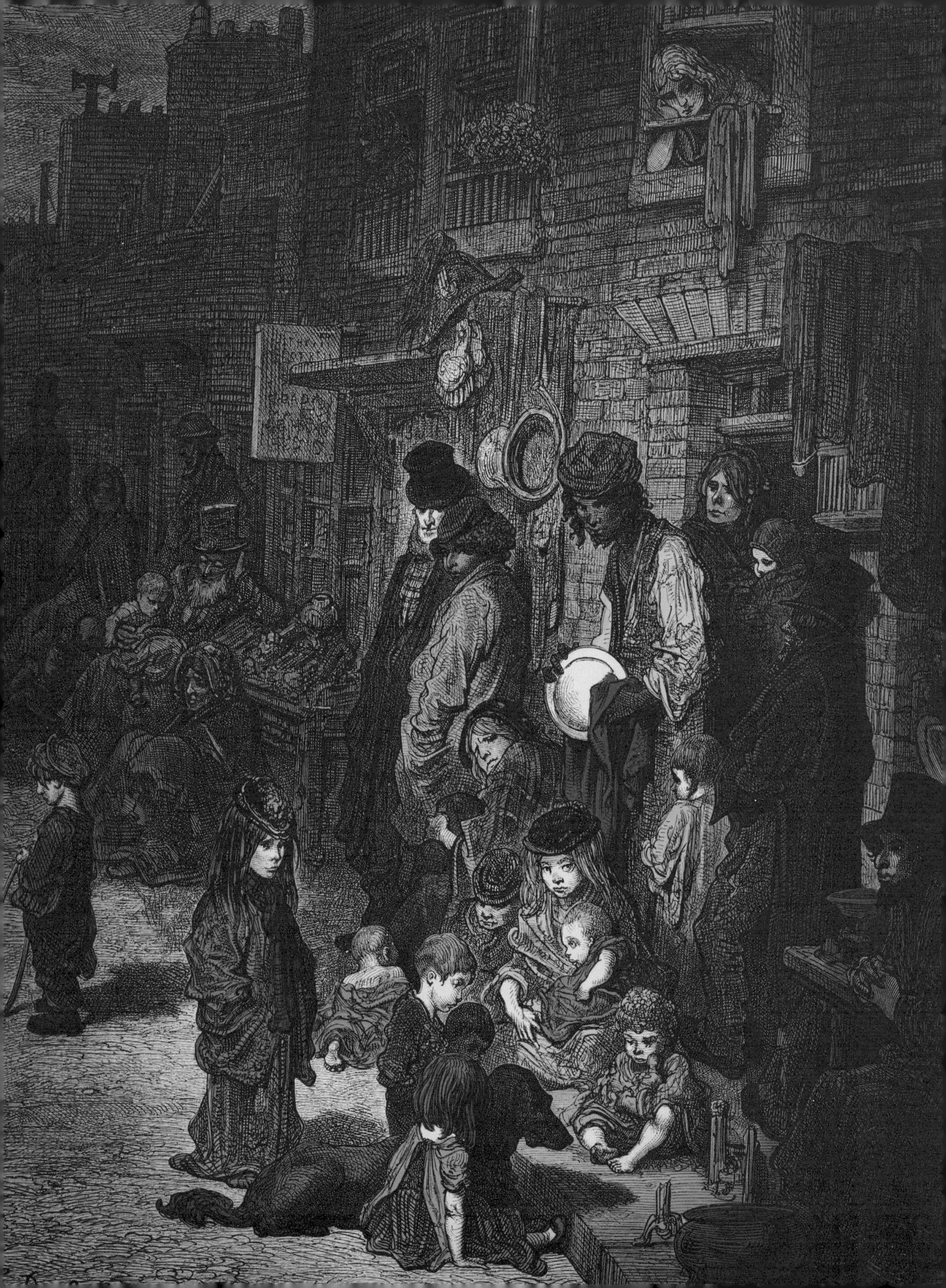

PETER ACKROYD

FORGOTTEN LONDON

EXPLORING THE HIDDEN LIFE OF THE CITY

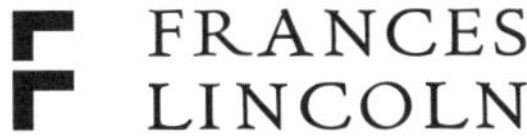

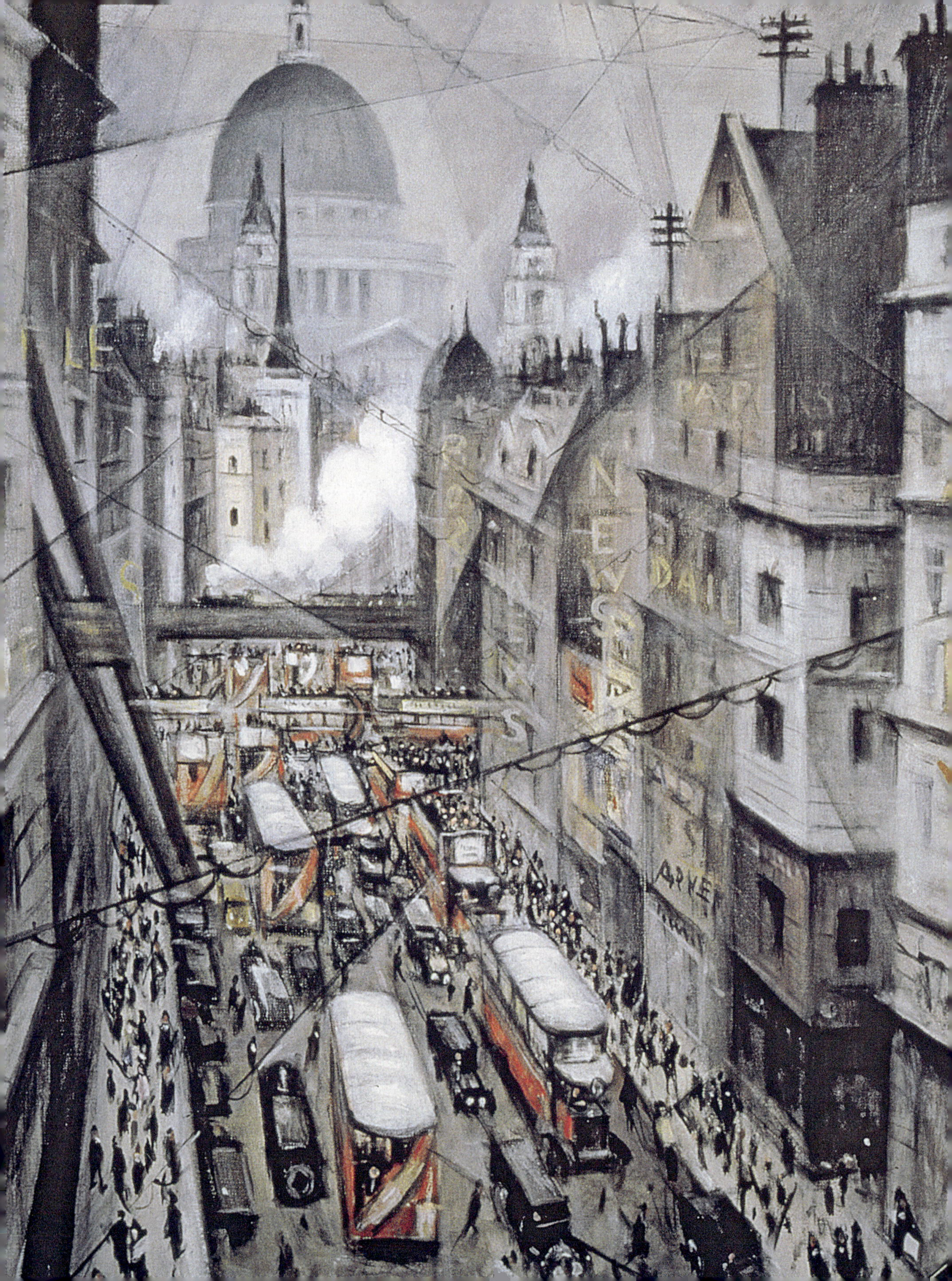

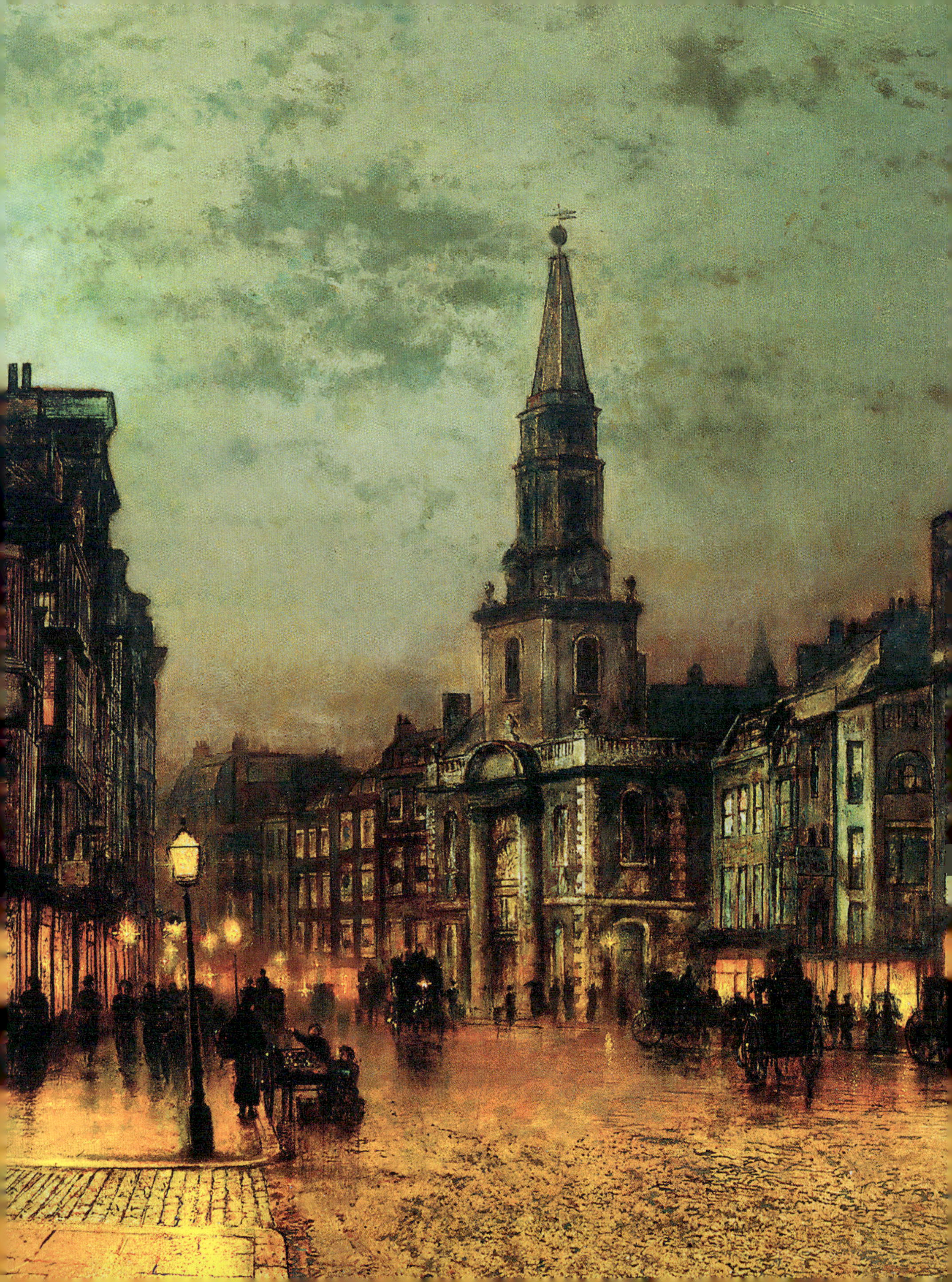

INTRODUCTION

In a century of change and turmoil, London was born again. That has been the secret of the city for two thousand years, ever since its inception. It has always been a place of money and of power. It has never stopped growing and has expanded in an unconstrained and unmanageable way. For many centuries it has been impossible to see it as a whole and could only be understood as a congregation of various disparate areas. Until recently, Londoners only knew the districts in which they lived and worked. Throughout its expansion, it has attracted millions from various cultures, distant lands and alien religions. It has been the haven for the poor, the unwanted and the dispossessed. But it has also been the home of the affluent and the powerful. Rich and poor live side by side in a common embrace, so that London has become an arena for contrasts and oppositions. It is the sum of its differences. For most of its history it has also been a harsh city, and has been described as 'a great sea' in which its inhabitants are always in danger of drowning.

Despite its rebirths, or reincarnations, its fundamental identity – its spiritual and historical character – has remained the same. The crowds of London have always been its life, and make up the immensity. They also suggest the weariness and forgetfulness that the city induces in the anonymous flow of traffic and of people. There are other symptoms of urban life. Its din, its everlasting noise, has been a matter of astonishment to the rest of the country. That noise has been compared with thunder and earthquake but, essentially, it is an emblem of human energy and the spread of human power. It embodies mobility, change and speed. The streets, the courts and the alleys have become ever more crowded. In the process London has created a new form of human energy and, over the centuries, new ways of living and of working. But there are other symptoms too. London has, for example, always been the nucleus of disease. It was known as a place in which no one was ever wholly well. It crushed the poor, exploited women and harboured violence. This is its story from the nineteenth to the twentieth centuries.

'Londoners live in the crowd, and can
hardly be said to know themselves
outside it.'

1837–1850
SMOKE, FILTH AND FOG

The great city still retains the shape and atmosphere of eighteenth-century London. It is comprised of a thousand different territories, of streets and parishes which are only brought together by crowds and mobs which can sometimes dominate them and spill over their borders. Each district, from Holborn to Clerkenwell, has its own trades and its own shops, its own styles of building and its own street markets. It will have its own street traders, going from house to house, and its own street entertainers. It will have its own particular smell. And then of course it will produce its own particular people. The inhabitants of one parish are subtly different from those of another. There will be eccentrics in dress and behaviour all over London, but each area has its own customs and trades which determine appearance and character. But despite that diversity, there are other forces that are beginning to form urban life. London is now more controlled, with the advent of Peelers rather than beadles and night watchmen. It is slowly becoming brighter, and more anonymous. Gaslight is replacing oil lamps and candles. Gin shops and taverns are being supplanted by the glittering gin palaces. In the more affluent neighbourhood the shops, and shop windows, are more colourful and more ornate. London is becoming a spectacle. The city is also becoming faster. The streets are still filled with horses but the hackney coaches and cabriolets are now rivalled by the new omnibus. These 'omnis' now join the outlying villages, such as Acton and Kensington, with the centre so that London is ever expanding. The advent of speed and brightness seems to be marking a great transition in urban life.

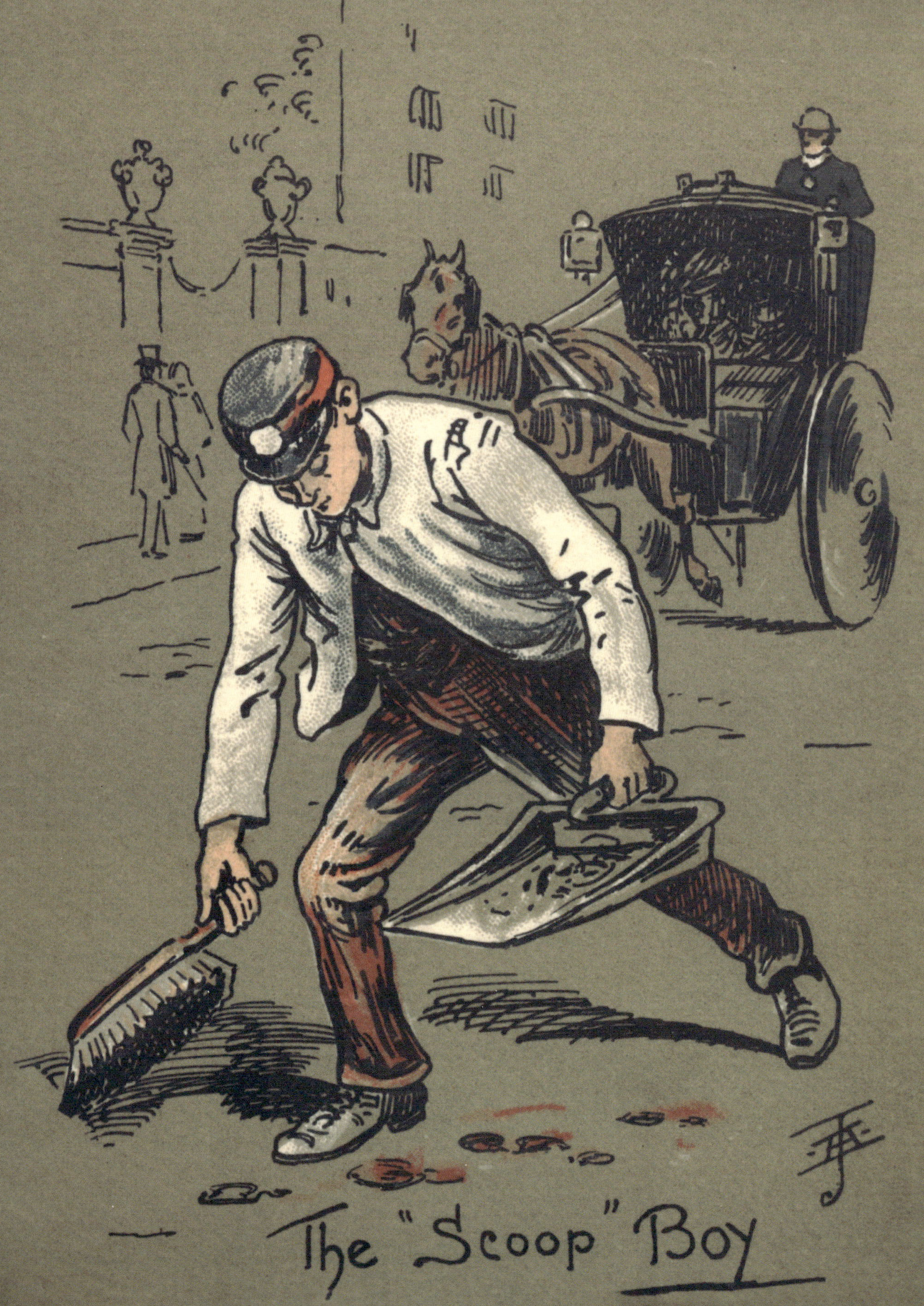

The "Scoop" Boy

There is a smell or – should I say? – the traces or the
suspicion of a smell, so familiar that it is rarely noticed.
It is the odour of urine and excrement mixed with
decaying refuse and damaged fruit, of fried fish and damp
corduroy, of a chimney on fire, of dead cats and bad eggs, of an
open drain or two; it might come from old clothes and old shoes
laid out for sale, from barrows offering cat meat or hare skins,
from the cesspools to be found in every lane or alley. Thousands
of cows are kept in the makeshift dairies, while pigs and other
animals are to be found in the cellars or ground-floor rooms.
The droppings from the chickens, kept in cages or in yards, have
the sharp perfume of ammonia. More obtrusive is the dung from
the many thousands of horses which make up the traffic of the
roads; despite the efforts of the 'orderly boys' in red uniforms
who run into the street to sweep it up, it is scattered and spread
everywhere. It has a penetrating odour which settles within
unventilated rooms or shops. As a result, the thick layers of mud
in the streets, in wet and humid weather, have a foul stench.
Household refuse and slops, thrown from windows or out of
doors, contribute to the general atmosphere.

It is rivalled only by the smell of the people. Each person
has his or her own particular odour, which is sometimes masked
by bergamot and lemon oil or by eau de cologne – but these
are reserved for the affluent. Too much washing is generally
considered to be unhealthy and the poor do not wash at all.
Cleanliness is distasteful to many and is considered to be 'stuck-
up'. The smell of the children in impoverished areas, half-naked
or dressed in rags, is taken for granted. You know your neighbour
or acquaintance as much by his distinctive smell as by his face
or clothing. In the poor districts the air is musty or mouldy, with
the penetrating sweet and sour scent of human decay. When this
is combined with the stench of the homeless and the vagrant, it
can become overpowering. Since it is considered that all smell
harbours disease, and that it creates the conditions for the onset
of fever, of malaria and cholera, a hot summer or a strong wind
from the east of the city is a cause for anxiety among Londoners.
The east is a darker region.

Yet in general all smells are accepted and familiar, part of
the atmosphere, to be recognized only in unusual circumstances.
Close to the river, for example, the combined stench of the sewers,
whose waste is emptied into its waters, is scarcely to be endured
even by those accustomed to it. The putrescence is not confined to

A postcard scene of
an orderly or 'scoop' boy
at work, c.1903.

the Thames. The Serpentine is said to be 18 inches of water above 9 feet of mud. By meat markets or fish markets, all conducted in the open air, the atmosphere is polluted. Gasworks and manufactories rival the older stench of the knackers' yards, even if all of them are kept away from the centres of the city.

Each district has its own peculiar and distinctive odour, from the piggeries of Shepherd's Bush to the street markets of Seven Dials, from the tanneries of Bermondsey to the shambles of Smithfield. In Shadwell it is the sharp scent of the sugar manufactories. Long Acre smells of onions and Southampton Row of antiseptic. Tower Street has the pungent odour of wine and tea. The neighbourhood of Temple Bar is suffused with the stink of stale brown stout. However, there is also a general city scent. Any room that becomes warm begins to smell. The perfume of damp stone and old wood is pervasive along the streets. So, of course, is the constant presence of fresh horse dung.

The streets of London are individual and particular, little territories with their own borders and customs. They lie beside rolling streams of carts, coaches, wagons, trucks and barrows. Some have a row of posts to separate them from the road, but

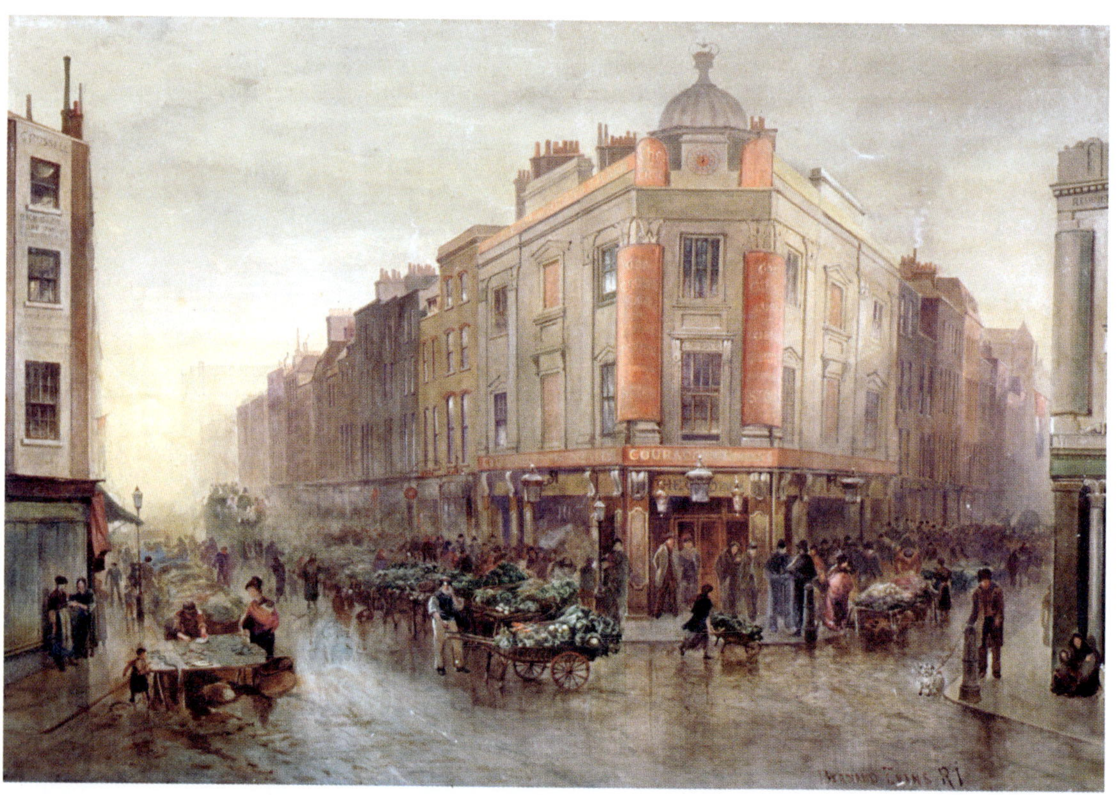

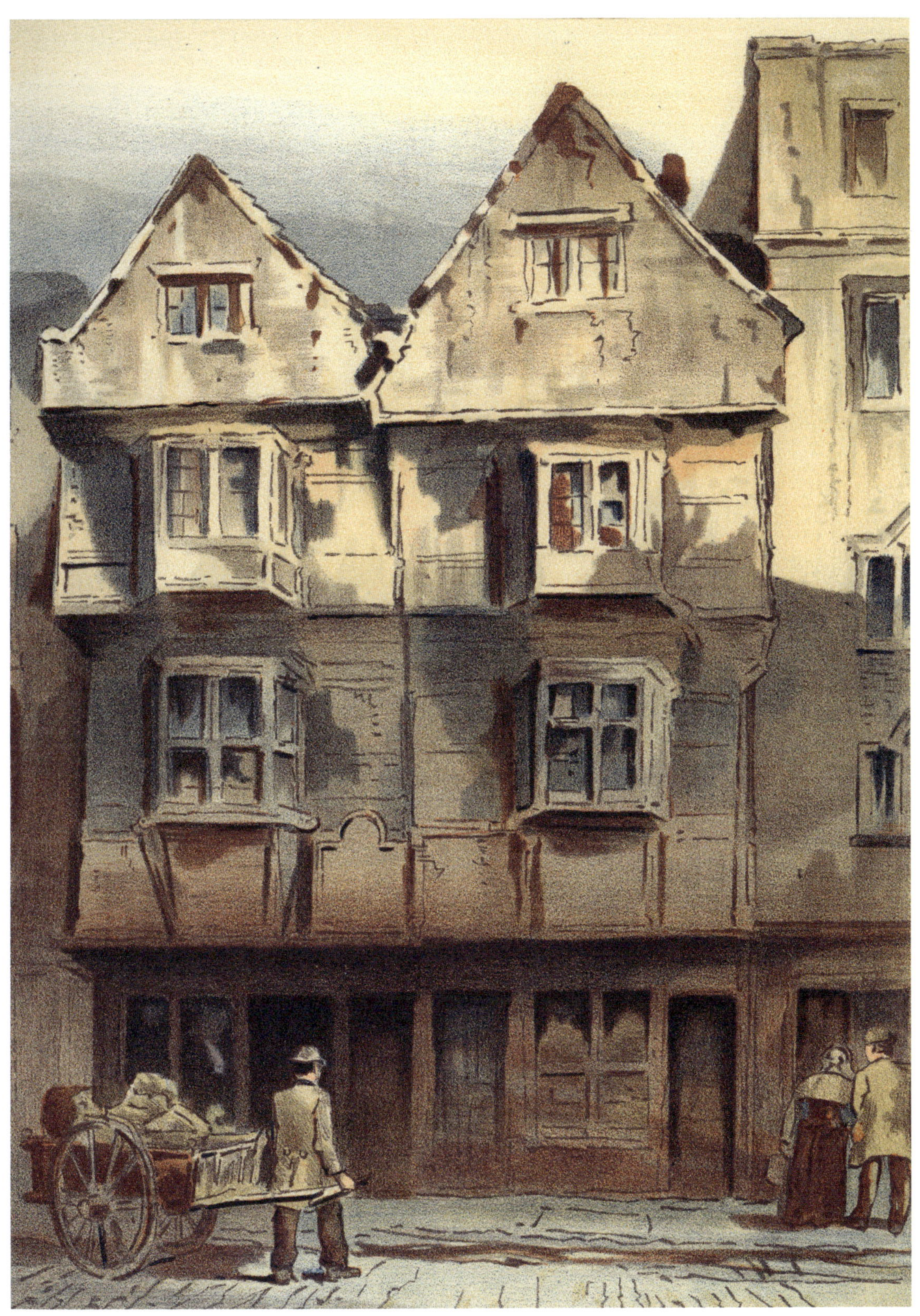

others are part of the same open thoroughfare where pedestrians and vehicles come close together. The adjacent courts and alleys are free of traffic other than the most rudimentary, and the solitary wanderer can saunter at ease and pause to look about at shops, dwellings and people. Drury Lane, for example, leads into the obscurity of Vinegar Yard and Red Lion Court. A court is a dead-end alley crowded with poor dwellings. At night you may hear the measured tread of the policeman with his lantern, but even he will not dare to venture into some of these places without a companion, a cosh and a rattle.

In London walking is a necessary activity, and is known as 'Shank's mare' or 'the Marrowbone stage'. A wanderer in the city may see the streets as a study in contrast and contradiction; rich and poor, luxury and squalor, lie side by side. London may seem to be only the sum of its differences. Turn a corner and another aspect of London appears. Each street reveals a changed world, but to some it may seem that there is nothing to see but streets, streets, streets and nothing to breathe but streets, streets, streets. They are all noisy, busy and crowded.

Yet the principal streets do have a distinct and recognizable character. Drury Lane itself is narrow, for example, with high and slender houses on either side. The lower floors are let out to a range of inferior shops, which may consist of no more than an enclosed space for trade with a room behind it and a cellar below. Most such shops are nameless. Here may be sold coarse eatables, cheap and nasty literature, old clothes and economical cigars; on the two floors above live small tradesmen, mechanics and others of that class, while in the garret are those who cannot afford to live anywhere else. In this, it is typical. London does not readily distinguish between the shop and the house. Some say that the second-hand shop, whatever its wares, is London's secret glory. Drury Lane is, in short, a run-down district which, like others of the same kind, is distinguished by a number of gin palaces resplendent with plate glass and gilt lettering.

Haymarket, on the contrary, is a broad thoroughfare inclining slightly downhill, with a theatre on one side and a colonnaded opera house on the other; the street has a large number of shops providing general merchandise but more important than these are the hotels, the coffee houses, the cigar divans, the restaurants, and the establishments for the sale of lobsters, oysters and pickled salmon. If you walk further south, you will find little streets leading down to the river. On Nightingale Lane, in Wapping, are

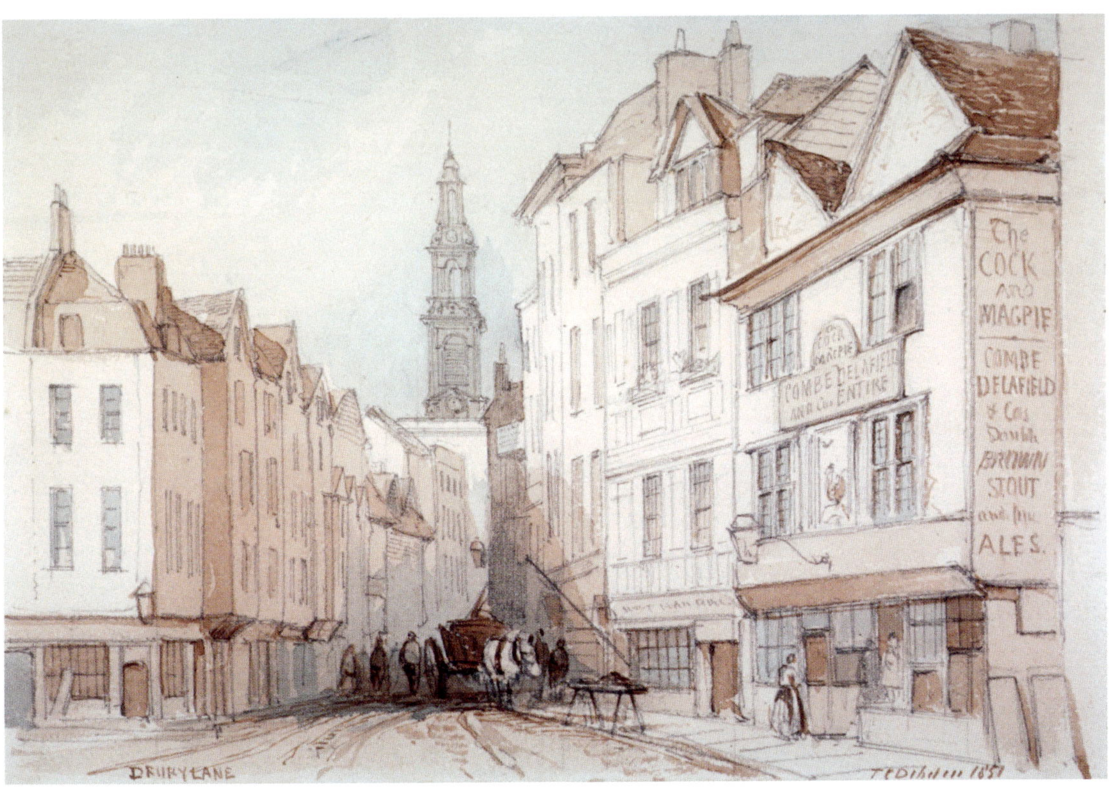

Drury Lane, Westminster, London, 1851 (1851) by Thomas Colman Dibdin.

shops selling ships' stores and nautical instruments with a tavern or a grogshop at every other door; this street is also notable for its bookstalls, with cheap novels and songbooks, and for its cigar shops. Sailors, and children, are everywhere. In the more affluent residential streets, however, silence – or at least relative quietness – prevails. There are no shops and omnibuses are not allowed to pass through; costermongers, ballad singers and other street people rarely venture here. Some parts of these areas display what might be called a fragile elegance; their white, stately houses are nothing if not substantial, but already there are too few families to fill them – at least too few of the wealthy sort. It is just such 'quarters' of London that are most vulnerable to attrition and decay, that so easily disintegrate into shabby tenements. Colville Gardens and Notting Hill, for example, may well face a time of trial in the years to come. Now, at least, they are secure, proud and prim. Lancaster Road would also satisfy even the most particular. Its big grey houses are ranged on each side like city walls.

Holborn is a business street; shops and plate-glass windows are packed close together, with the costermongers and itinerant vendors mixed along the pavement. Busy crowds move up and down both sides, while cabs and omnibuses challenge each other in the centre of the road. The houses are covered with signboards and advertisements, while the sound of footsteps, wheels and horses' hooves complete the scene. On main streets such as these, scavengers are at work shovelling mud into their wooden carts; they are sometimes replaced by new and gaudily painted sweeping machines, pulled by two horses at a slow pace, which sweep and shovel in the same operation. Other workmen are laying down a wooden pavement. The wood surface is replacing granite setts, cobble or macadam. The streets may be 'up' at any time for the installation by roadmen of water, gas and sewer pipes. New streets are also being built week after week as the city expands. For some it adds to a sense of impermanence. Each year, each month, each week, London grows larger. It does not begin and it does not end.

The streets also have their predators, with the street rough, the street thief and the street bully. Children are sometimes snatched and are robbed of their clothes or any valuables they might be carrying. It is known as a 'kinchin lay'. There are fewer riots these days, but men and women can still rally in public places to protest against a parish vestry or a board of guardians

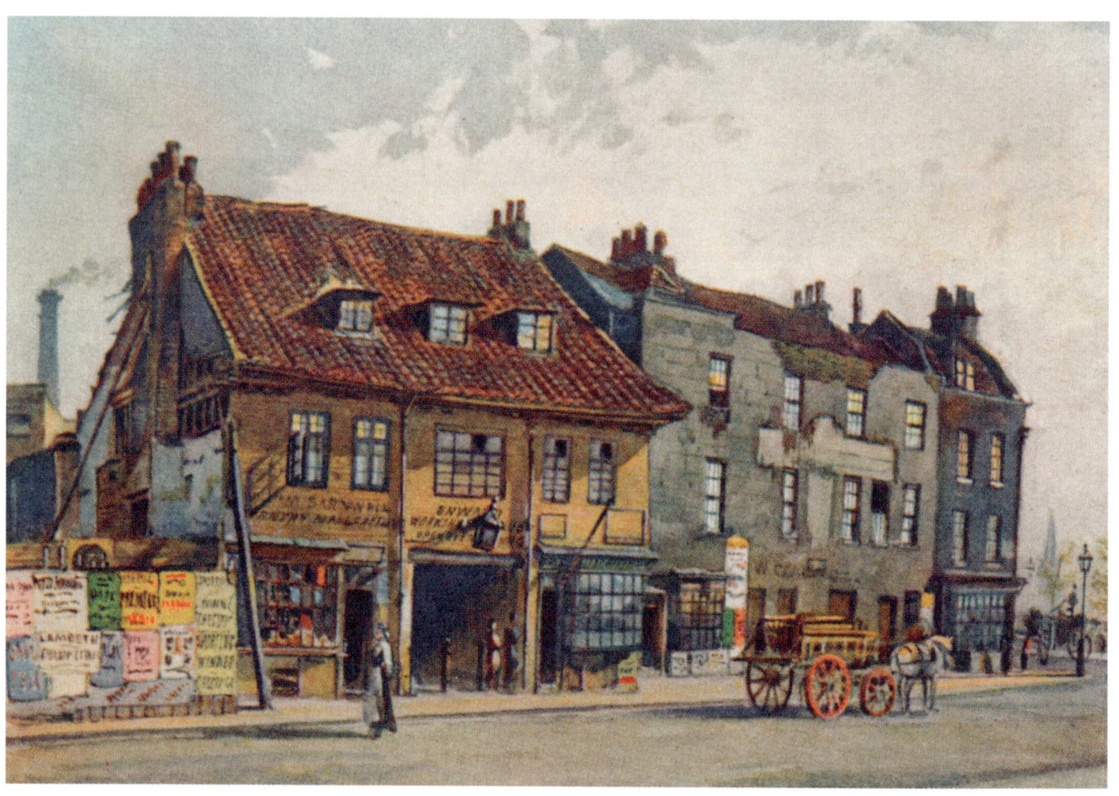

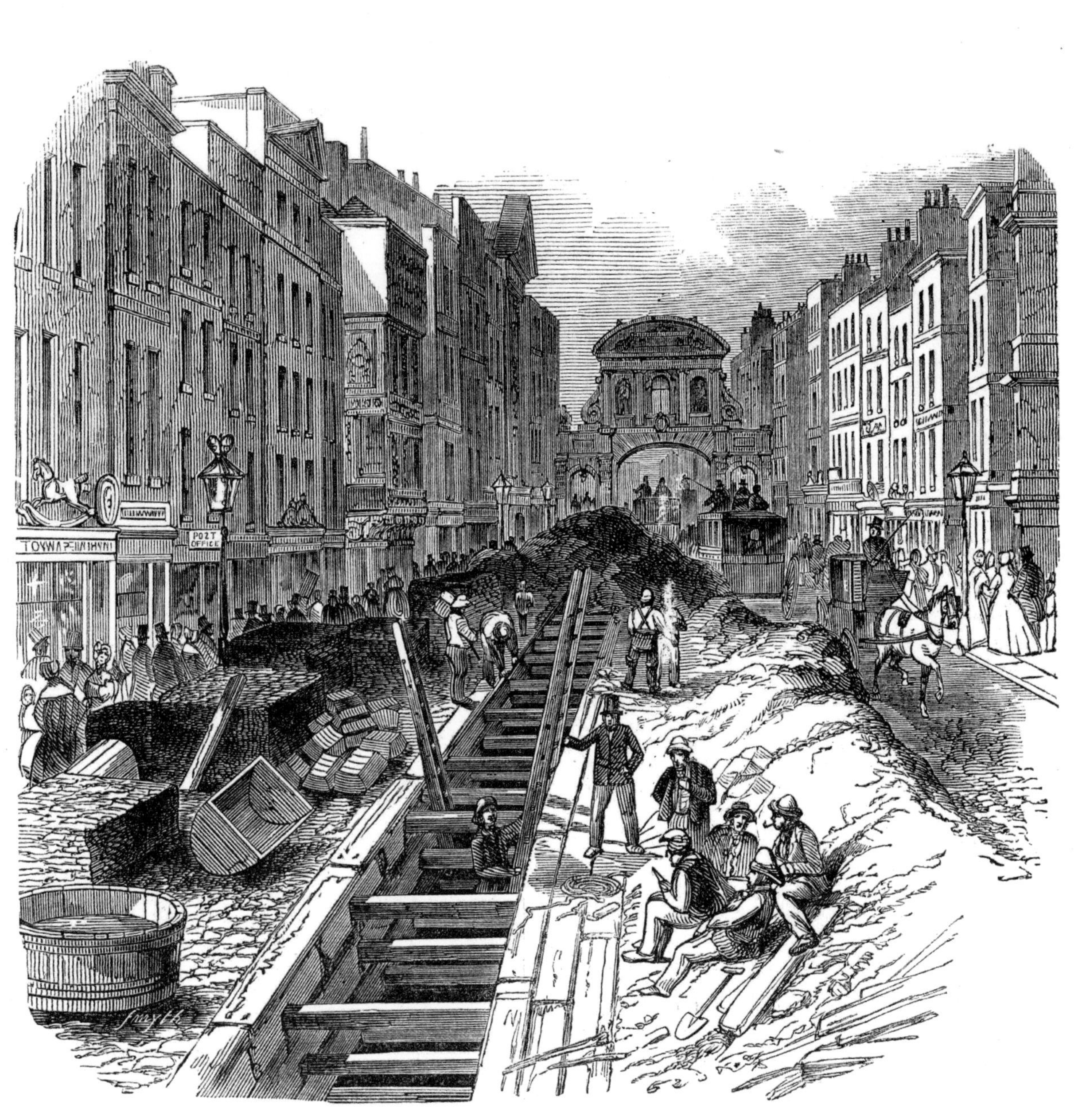

POST
OFFICE

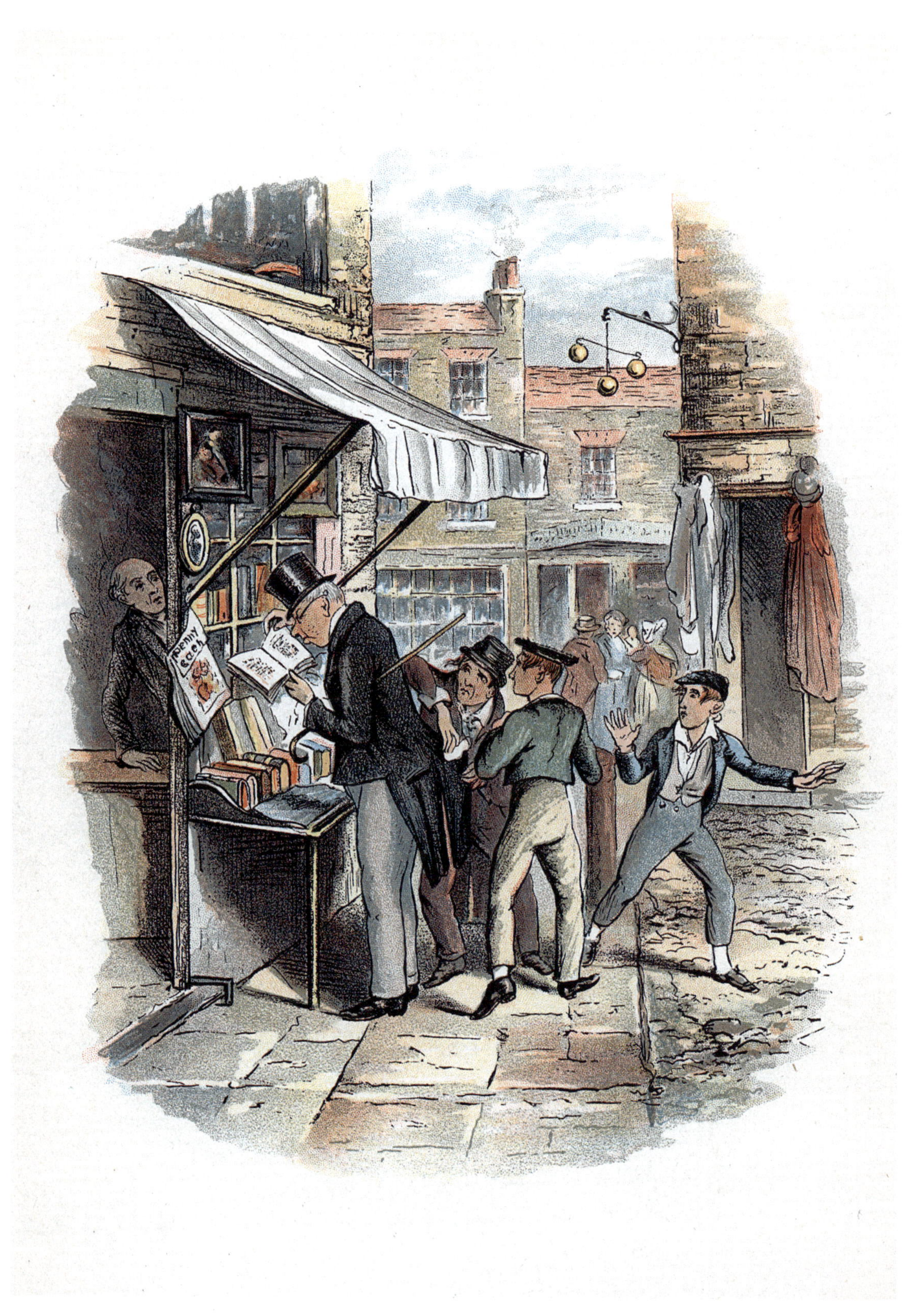

Penny
each

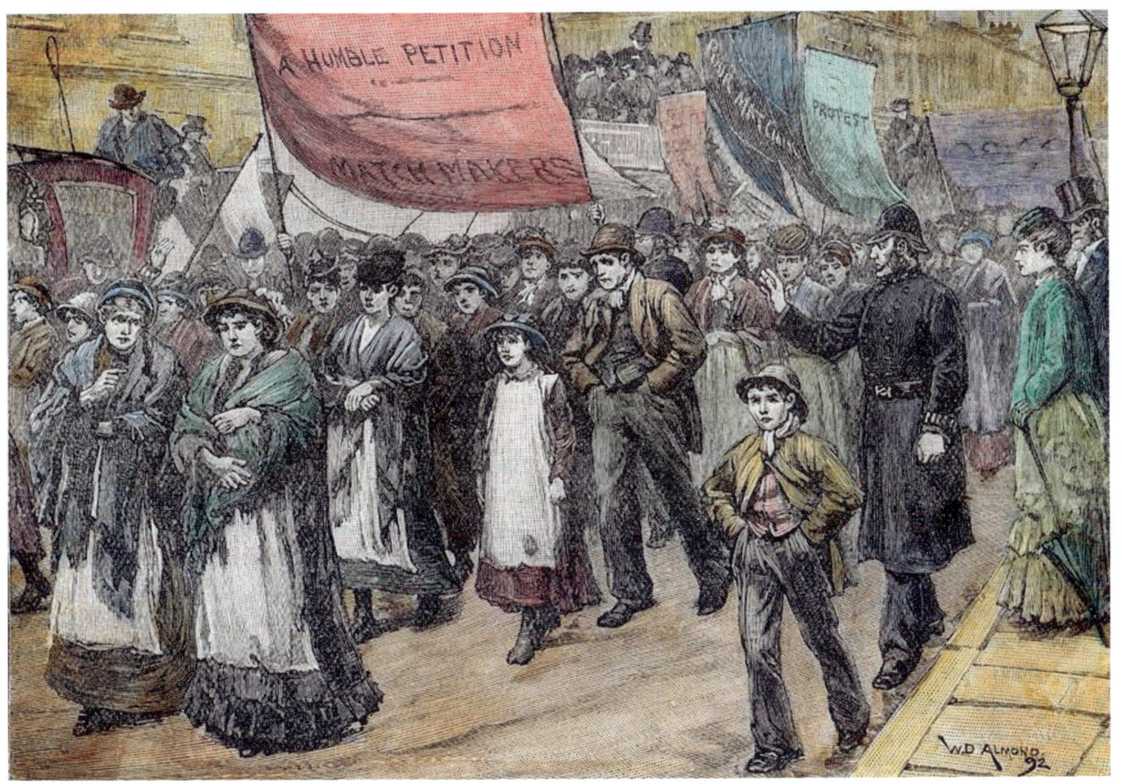

for the local workhouse. The greater political causes, such as those propagated by the Chartists or the newly formed National Union of the Working Classes, seem to have relatively little effect. In a city so large and so various as London, political controversy does not spread from area to area, but if there is a mass protest over, for example, the strict prohibitions on Sunday entertainment, the people from other neighbourhoods will come to watch what is called a 'disturbance'.

Street theft is a perennial problem, since hundreds of men, women and children earn their livelihoods by the lifting of handkerchiefs, purses and watches. It is known that a great many flash houses exist in all parts of the city where stolen goods are received, but certain sharp individuals, working in markets and shops, also carry on the illicit trade. Pickpockets are plentiful at fires, executions and other public events (including dog fights and bear sports) but other petty thieves lift goods from stalls, shops and street vendors. Children are trained for the purpose by other thieves and in low lodging houses. Other more determined villains will use chloroform to incapacitate their victims, and gangs of garrotters are rumoured to wait in the side streets for likely targets. The new police are issued with 4-inch leather collars to ward off these attacks, but some observers believe that the supposed threat is merely an urban panic fostered by the newspapers. Dog theft is also common, and the stolen animals are taken to well-known pubs to be sold. Shoplifting is almost as common as shopping itself, given the poverty of many customers and the closeness of the goods. Linen and other cloths hanging out to dry are another obvious target.

Groups of youths and men can quickly gather to attack a market watch or to mob an unpopular politician. The new Peelers are coming onto the streets, and they are more effective than the Bow Street Runners or the outdated parish beadles, but it is still not unknown for the neighbours of one street to clash with those of another. The boys of one neighbourhood will arm themselves with clubs, iron bars and leather belts with buckles, while another will respond with sticks, stones and kitchen knives. Another violent sport is for the boys to gather in a street and hustle anyone who tries to pass through. It is well-known that certain streets are to be avoided, by day or by night.

In many districts foreigners, strangers and cripples can be met with ridicule. Unusual dress provokes insults and laughter,

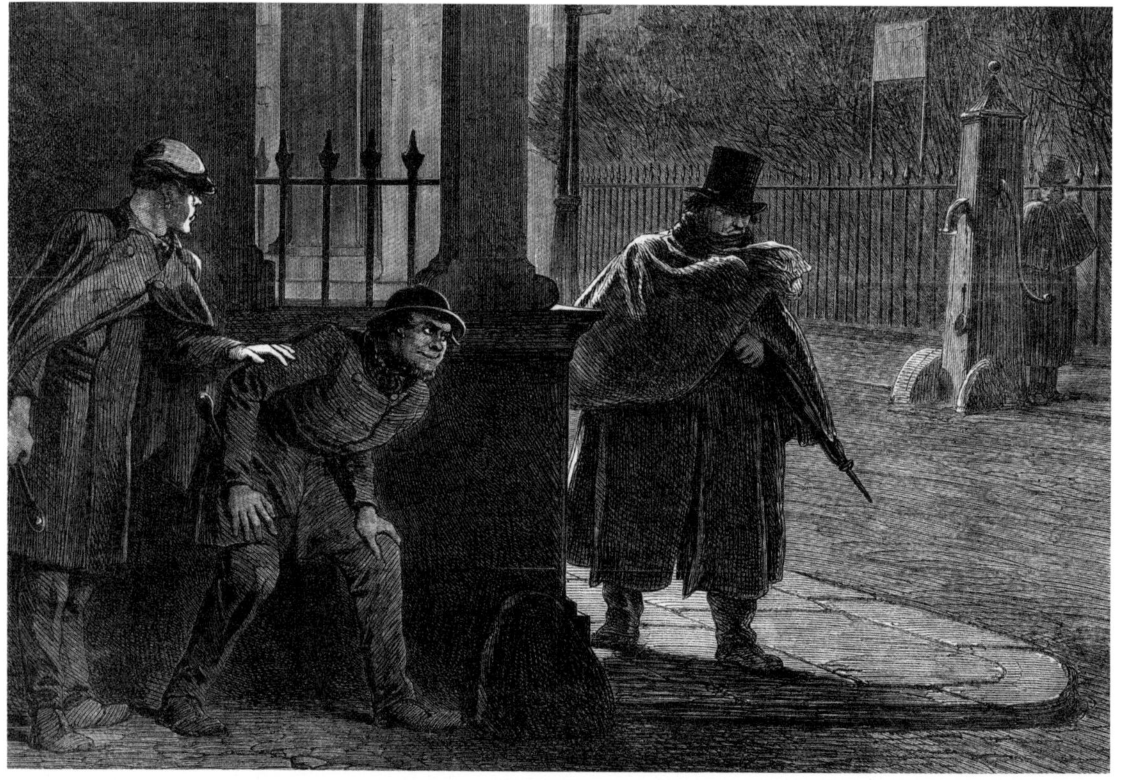

Below Garroters lurking in a London square at the time of the garroting panic, c.1863.

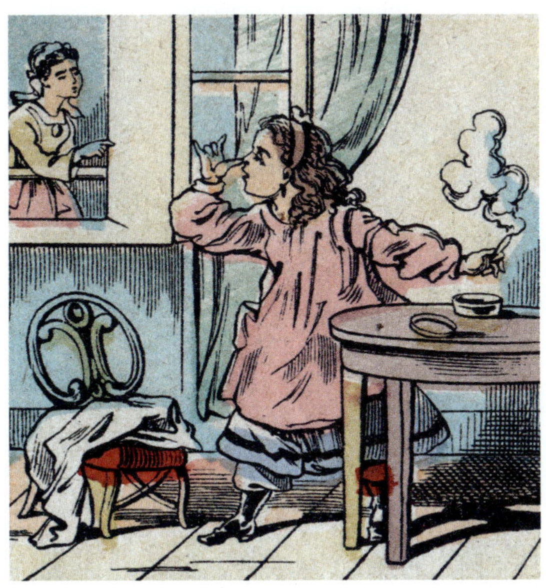

Above A disobedient child, thumbing her nose at a neighbour when reprimanded for playing with matches, nineteenth century.

but these are part of the life of the street. 'What a shockin' bad 'at', 'How are yer off fer soap?', 'Does yer muvver know yer out?', 'Is yer missus quite well?' and 'Has your muvver sold 'er mangle?' are familiar catcalls directed against any stranger who stands out. 'There 'e goes wiv his eye out!' and ''Ows yer poor feet?' join the chorus, along with 'Waal-ker!' which denotes incredulity. If you are accused of being immature or inexperienced, you may retort, 'Do you see any green in my eye?' Another uninterpretable word is 'Quoz!' A mischievous urchin will shout it at passers-by; it is chalked on walls and the street corners are noisy with it. One who is drunk or is angry or has spoken out of turn, is said to have 'flared up'. It is the phrase of the moment, applied to any situation. To put your thumb up to the side of your nose denotes contempt, made even more blatant by wriggling your fingers. So does the phrase, 'Go it!' A ruffian, faced with a rival, may be urged by his friends to 'make game of him' or 'pitch into him'. In the event of a scuffle or confrontation, they will call it 'keeping it up and loving of fun' or perhaps 'done in a friendly way'. A beggar on the street corner might ask for 'the needful' or 'a screw of baccy'.

The language of the London streets is particular, and of course the Cockney dialect is predominant. Its harshness and sharpness have faded over the years, and is no longer the cant vernacular of the past, which was almost incomprehensible to others, but it is still highly distinctive, with 'piper' rather than 'paper', 'Eye O pen' rather than 'High Holborn', 'flahs' for 'flowers', and a thousand of other variants. It is usual for a street seller to cry, 'Here are a lovely pie and here is taters'. A familiar construction is 'And so I goes … and he goes …', along with 'innit? or 'ennit?'. 'Wery' is used rather than 'very', 'vot?' rather than 'what?', 'ax' rather than 'ask'. Another street seller might call out, 'Please to reckleck that at this 'ere stall you gets beets an' happles.' You might be asked, 'Were you never none of them flash coves down the Stren? Yes, my eye, you woz!' or told, 'Please to trouble me no more! You doesn't care nothink for nobody!' This is followed by 'So I says … as I says … and wasn't he a trembling, neither?' You might also be asked, 'Will you please accept of him for to be watchman?' It is agreed that 'Everybody has a more better and more worserer side

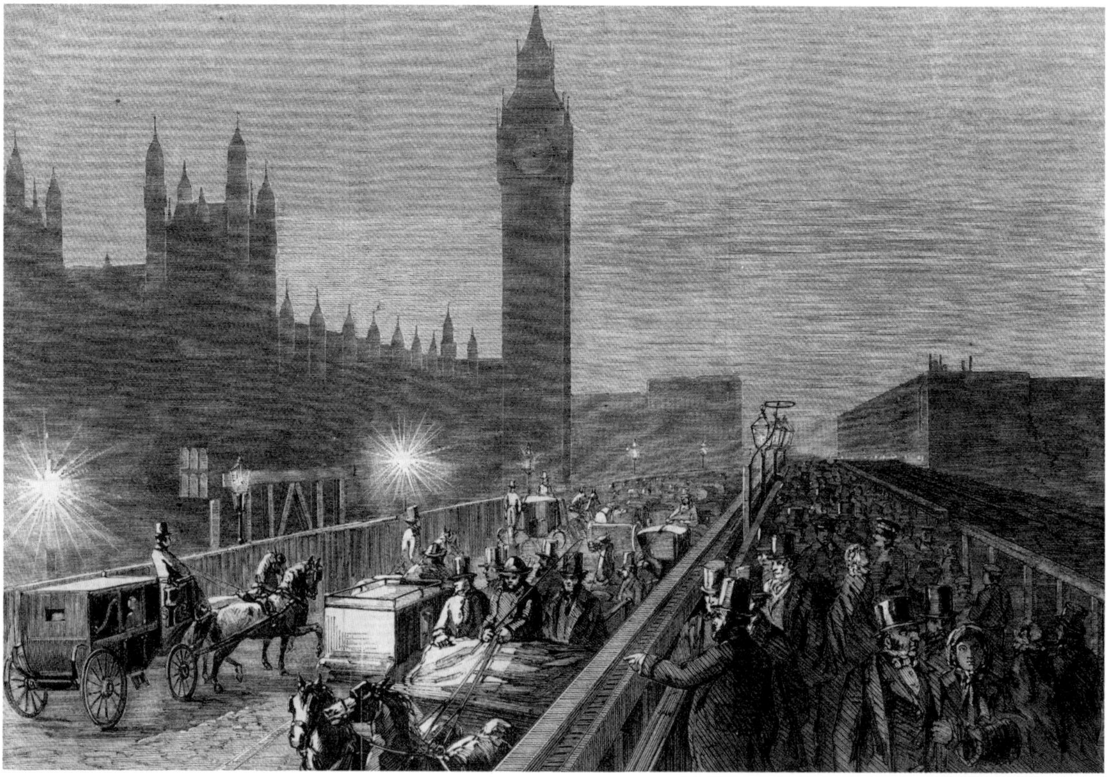

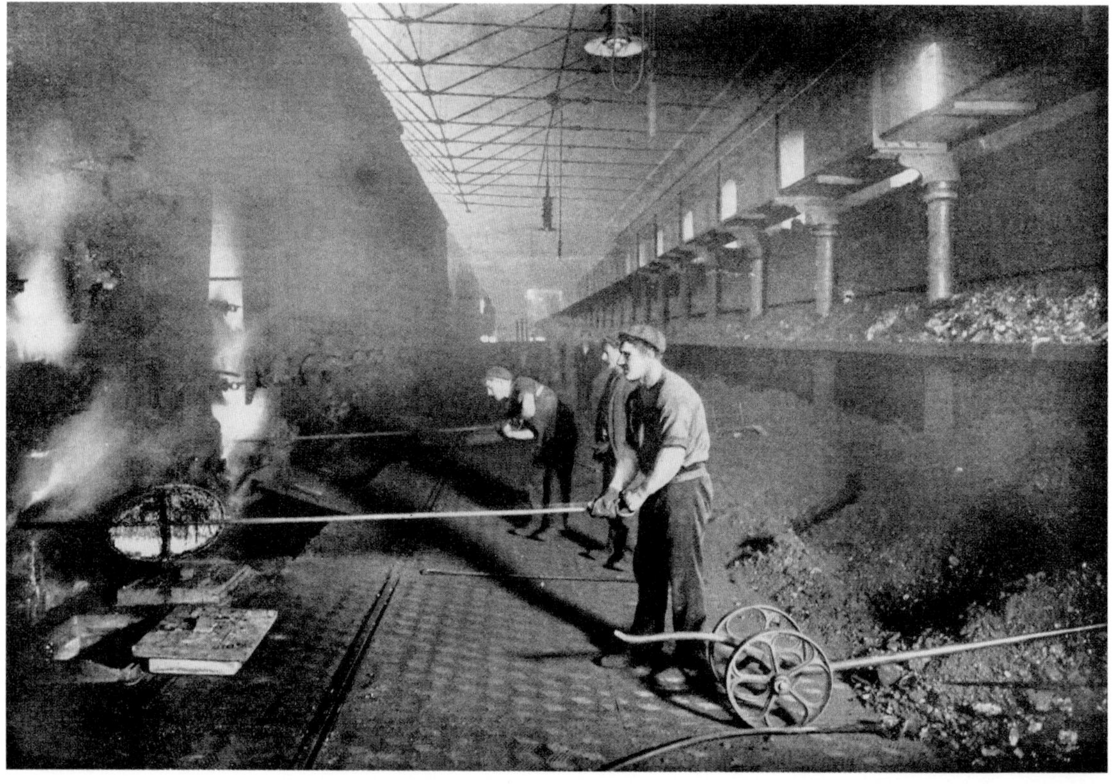

of the face then the other.' Back slang – 'yob' for 'boy' – and rhyming slang – 'trouble and strife' for 'wife' – are taken for granted. 'Nice' is constant, as is 'you know'; 'spoony' suggests someone who is a bit of a weakling and 'bygones' adverts to the past. Very good is 'A1' and bad is 'shoddy' or 'very bad shoddy'. 'In course' is used instead of 'of course' and 'hobble' means trouble. Common words for bravery in confronting the world are 'pluck', 'mettle' and 'bottom'. The exclamations of 'chaff!', 'poltroon!' and 'ta-ta!' are always heard in the streets.

Welcome changes in street lighting have made a certain difference to the levels of local crime. The city is gradually growing brighter and therefore safer. The days of linkmen bearing torches, have long gone. Gaslight has become practical and commonplace in all the major thoroughfares of the capital, so bright that it even illuminates both sides of the street. The suburbs, and the roads to the suburbs, are not so well-served, where oil lamps must still suffice. However, London itself is now a gas-lit city. The bridges and the public buildings seem incandescent. The better houses are alight, although some reserve gas for the corridors and the kitchen, with oil lamps still used in the reception rooms and bedrooms. The shops, the shop windows and the offices are now alight. The Strand, for example, is all brightness and wonder; elsewhere in the city, the shops seemed entirely made of sparkling glass. It is universally agreed that the new light will be good for trade. Some older people find the light too bright and describe it as dazzling or glaring. It is said to fatigue the optic nerve. New instruments, of course, incur new problems. There is always, for example, a danger of gas leaks and of explosions. Householders are advised to keep their rooms ventilated. Candles and oil lamps are still sometimes preferred. Nevertheless, it is agreed that a great change has occurred. Gas reigns.

In much of London, the quality and variety of the shops mark the differences from street to street. New Bond Street at one time had not a single tobacco shop, despite the fact that millions of smoking gentlemen in their time have paraded along it; even today the Strand, with its actresses, chorus girls and hotel population has no shop where a woman can buy a blouse or a reel of cotton. Sackville Street and Savile Row are still exclusively male, while Sloane Street is almost exclusively female. It is the spirit of place, or what we might call the spirit of London. Panton Street, Haymarket, was until very recently the most comprehensively male street in town. It contains a famous repository of chutney, pickles, sharks' fins and elephants' foot jelly, while its chief restaurant, a very old-fashioned place, will not allow a woman within its doors; its finest

shop sells only men's braces, while adjoining shops sell military and
naval prints, guns, sporting boots, tobacco and snuff. However, the
street most charged with town 'quality' is of course St James's Street,
with the old brick palace of the Tudors at the bottom and with Whig
and Tory clubs guarding its approach at the top; the venerable shops
of Lock's the hatters and Berry's the wine merchant ensure that the
air of social pre-eminence has never quite left the street.

Variety prevails elsewhere. In Regent Street there is a row of
variously coloured canvas awnings beneath which may be found
a toy shop with biscuit tins, dolls, tea sets, books and money
boxes displayed behind its bow window; nearby is a pastry cook's
with small cakes hot from the oven, placed on tables covered
with white muslin cloth, a seller of books and a seller of china,
a hosier and haberdasher, their goods decorated with artificial
flowers. There is even a filter shop which sells small machines
for converting foul or muddy water into a crystal stream. In
one window a pair of shoes is floating in a transparent vessel to
demonstrate that they are waterproof. In another a well-dressed
leg, with stocking and buckle, is displayed to show that the legs
made there are excellent. A chemist arranges large glass vases,
filled with coloured waters, as a sign of his trade; at night they are
illuminated by small lamps. A fruit shop arranges pineapples or
apples in little baskets, decorated with flowers and orange leaves.
Around the corner, in Conduit Street, are a confectioner, a draper,
a stationer and a seal-cutter. Two doors down, another shop is
setting out baby frocks as well as boys' caps and tunics.

The shop windows of London form the city's principal attraction
to strangers and visitors, since picture galleries and museums
present no points of interest to compete with them. Oxford Street
is devoted to the fashionable female; for example, with many linen
drapers, silk and satin dressers, several straw hat manufactories,
bonnet shops, woollen drapers, five lace warehouses, three smaller
stores for fancy trimmings and fringes, a warehouse for India
muslin and a button shop. In many of these, large mirrors, set at
an angle from the pavement, illuminate the shopfronts. The stone
façades are then seen to be a smoky or a dirty grey, the shade of that
murky atmosphere which prevails within the city. In Cranbourne
Alley, too, is a range of shops devoted to the sale of bonnets and of
women's stays.

Every type of article has its own centre of business. For
haberdashery it is Leicester Square, and for lace and veils it is
Coventry Street. In May's Buildings, off St Martin's Lane, are the

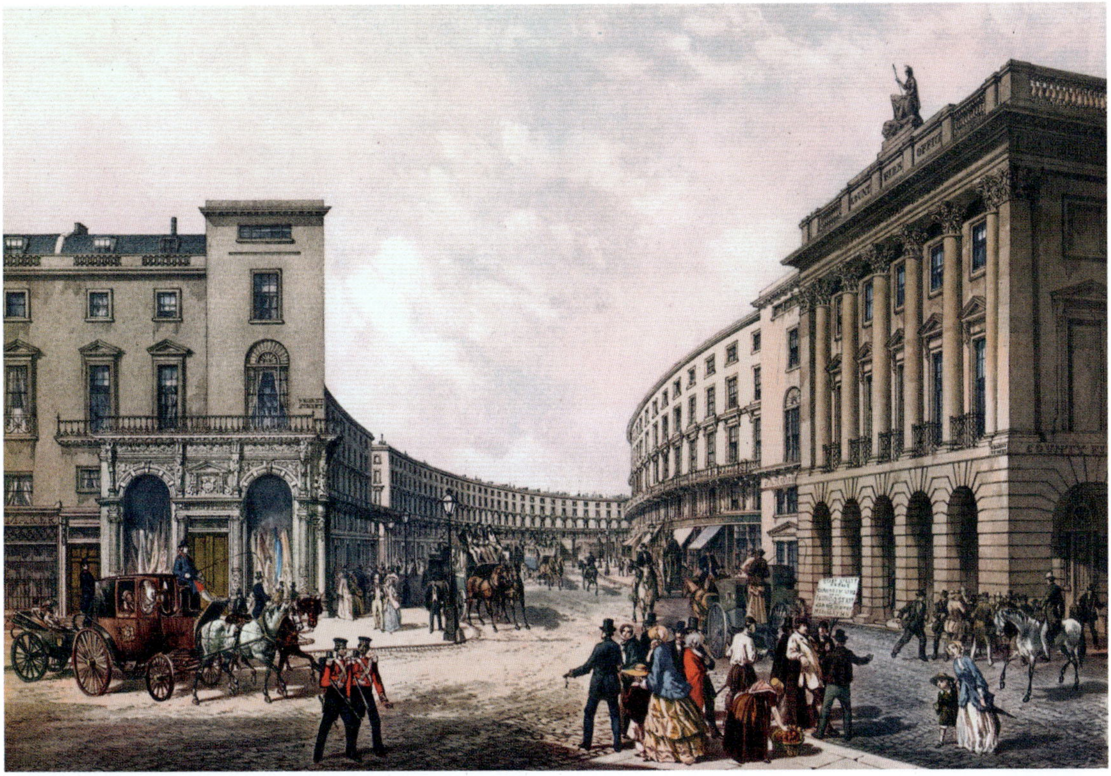

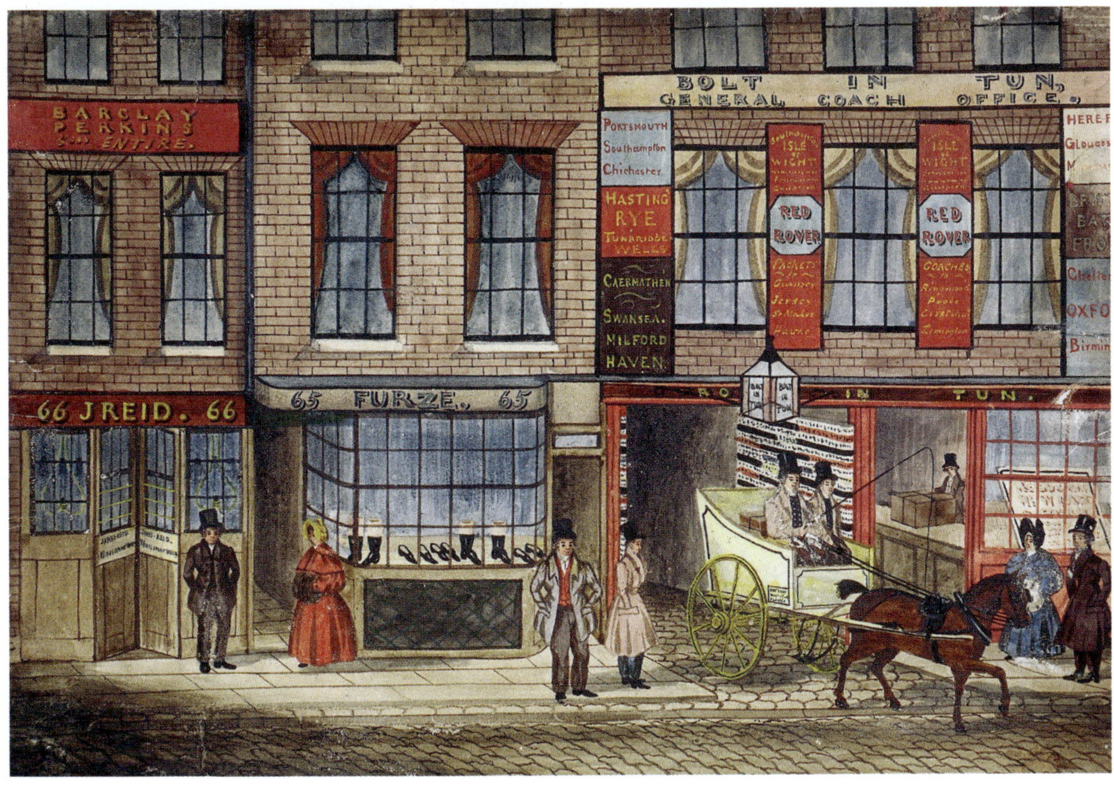

BARCLAY
PERKINS
ENTIRE.
66 J. REID. 66
65 FURZE. 65
BOLT   IN   TUN,
GENERAL   COACH   OFFICE,
PORTSMOUTH
Southampton
Chichester
HASTING
RYE
Tunbridge
WELLS
CAERMATHER
SWANSEA.
MILFORD
HAVEN.
ISLE
of
WIGHT
ISLE
of
WIGHT
RED
ROVER
RED
ROVER
BOLT   IN   TUN.

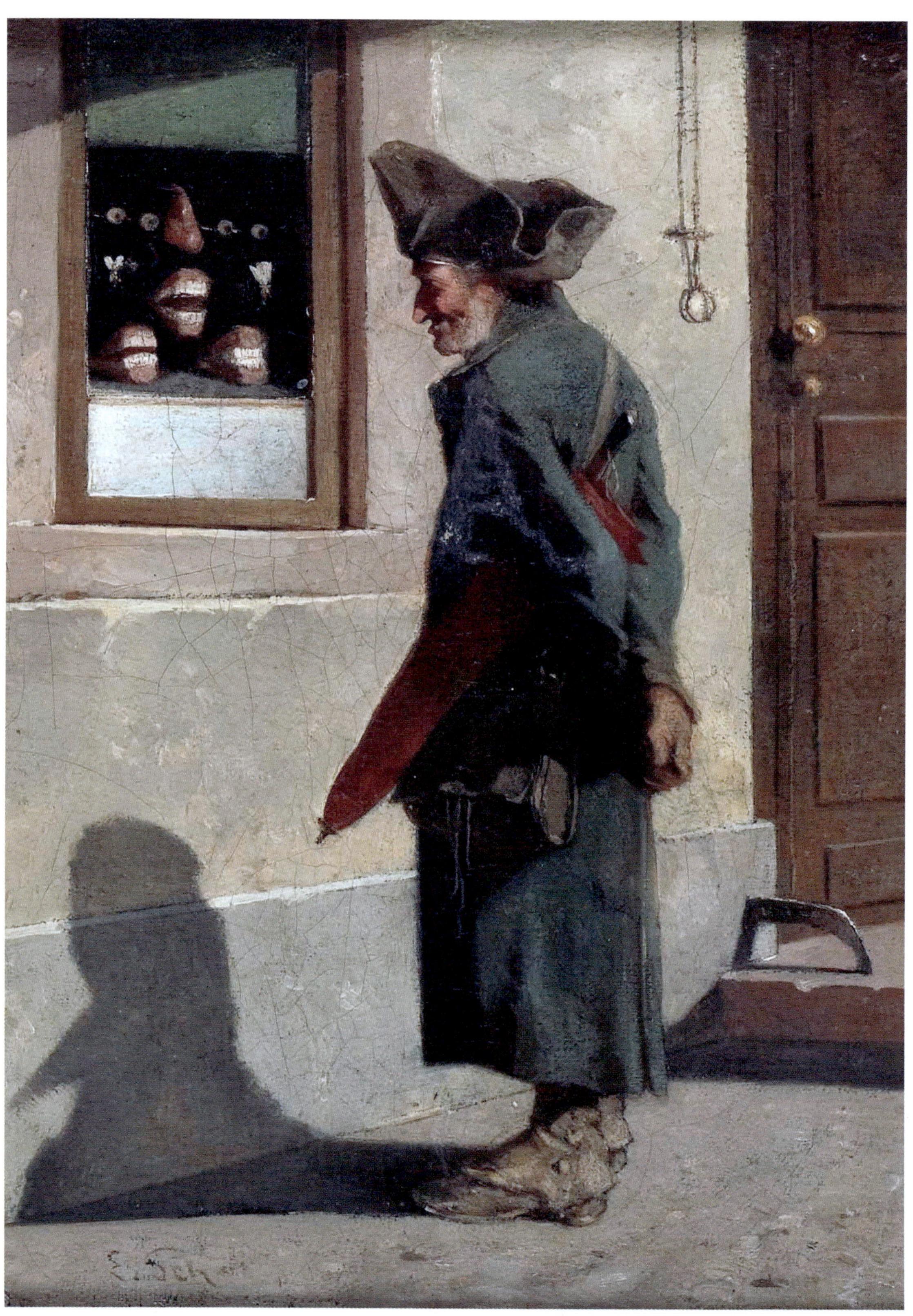

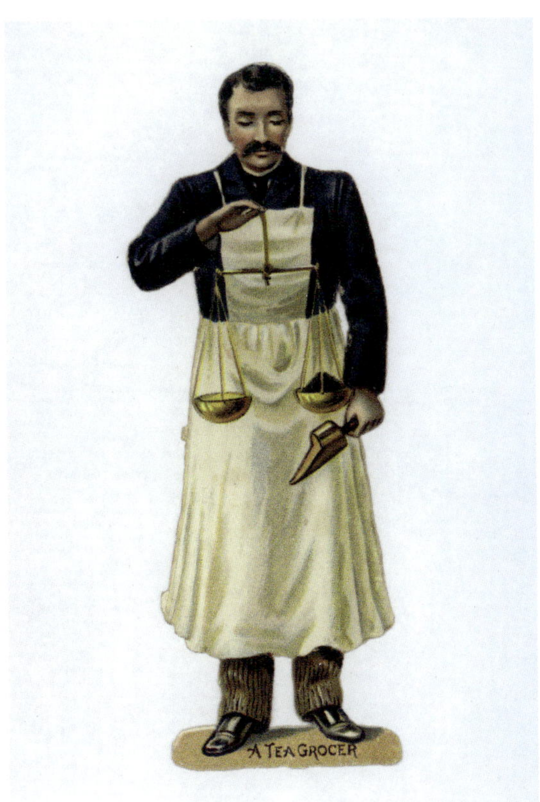

makers of surgical instruments and of artificial teeth. Rosemary Lane, by the Tower, is the place for second-hand boots. Holywell Street, running north of the Strand, is well-known for its sale of obscene prints and bawdy books. The Pantheon Bazaar, the Soho Bazaar and the Belgrave Square Bazaar are converted mansions or small theatres in which stalls and open counters are ranged on both sides of the main aisle, where women sell cutlery, jewellery, children's dresses, sheets of music, porcelain ornaments, alabaster figures and any object of a light ornamental character. The Pantechnicon in Motcomb Street sells carriages and gigs as well as furniture (including pianos and carpets), while the Baker Street Bazaar specializes in horses and riding equipment. St Martin's Lane is the area for print shops, in which are displayed caricatures of royalty, churchmen and statesmen. Passers-by will stop and contemplate these images for a minute or so, sometimes commenting to the others around them.

These are for the more fashionable and affluent customers. In the poorer areas the shops are darker and more confined, with old-iron warehouses, penny-a-bottle ginger beer establishments, marine stores, and the chandler' shops where quarters of sugar and half-ounces of coffee are sold. Tea and coffee are weighed by small pairs of scales. Soap is cut by a wire, in the same manner as cheese. A dilapidated house may, in fact, contain a shop, with the fruit or vegetables set out in the ground-floor front room; other houses have a cellar, to which access is gained by a flight of steps from the street; piles of old boots or shoes, or second-hand furniture or coarse sacks filled with feathers, may be found here. Other cellar shops will provide rabbits, oysters and walnuts. The handkerchiefs for sale in Field Lane are generally known to be stolen. In Percy Street, off Tottenham Court Road, two or three old women, each with a short pipe in her mouth, sit beside baskets of turnips or carrots.

Yet the majority of Londoners find their food in the street markets. Each parish has one, and it seems, sometimes, that every street has one. On either side of the road or pathway runs a line

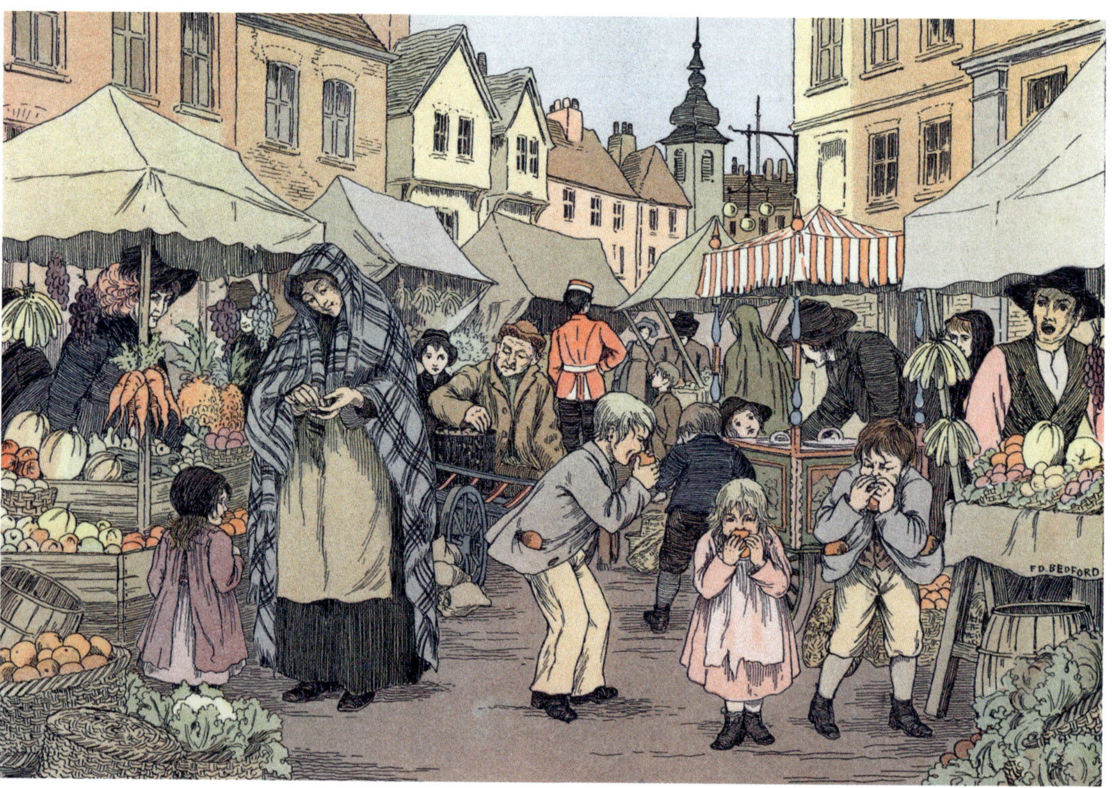

Above Children eating penny oranges from fruit and vegetable stalls in a market in London's East End (c.1899).

Right A woman catching peas in her apron, with a girl ready to catch any stray peas below. From *Cries of London*, (c.1870).

of barrows, baskets, carts, and flat boards on trestles, known as standings or pitches, which carry a variety of meat, fruit and vegetables, together with an assortment of small goods. Between the wagons and barrows of carrots or red herrings are stalls with fried fish and artificial flowers, brooms and brushes, corduroys and fur caps, Bibles and looking-glasses, firewood and walking sticks, cheese and combs and frying pans. A young man, no more than a boy, is selling apples from a donkey cart and calling out, 'Who says the poor aren't looked after?' A blind man on the opposite side is selling bootlaces. An old soldier plays 'God Save the Queen' on a tin whistle. At the other end of the market sits a beggar, wearing around his neck a placard addressed 'To The Charitable Public'. In the winter evening each stall is lit by candles or cheap lamps. If the women cannot afford baskets for their purchases, they carry the produce home in their aprons.

There are large markets which serve the whole of the city. Billingsgate and Smithfield are well-known, if only for their stench. Many Londoners come here towards evening or at the close of business to pick up bargains for the unsold or unwanted merchandise. Damaged meat and fish, close to turning rotten,

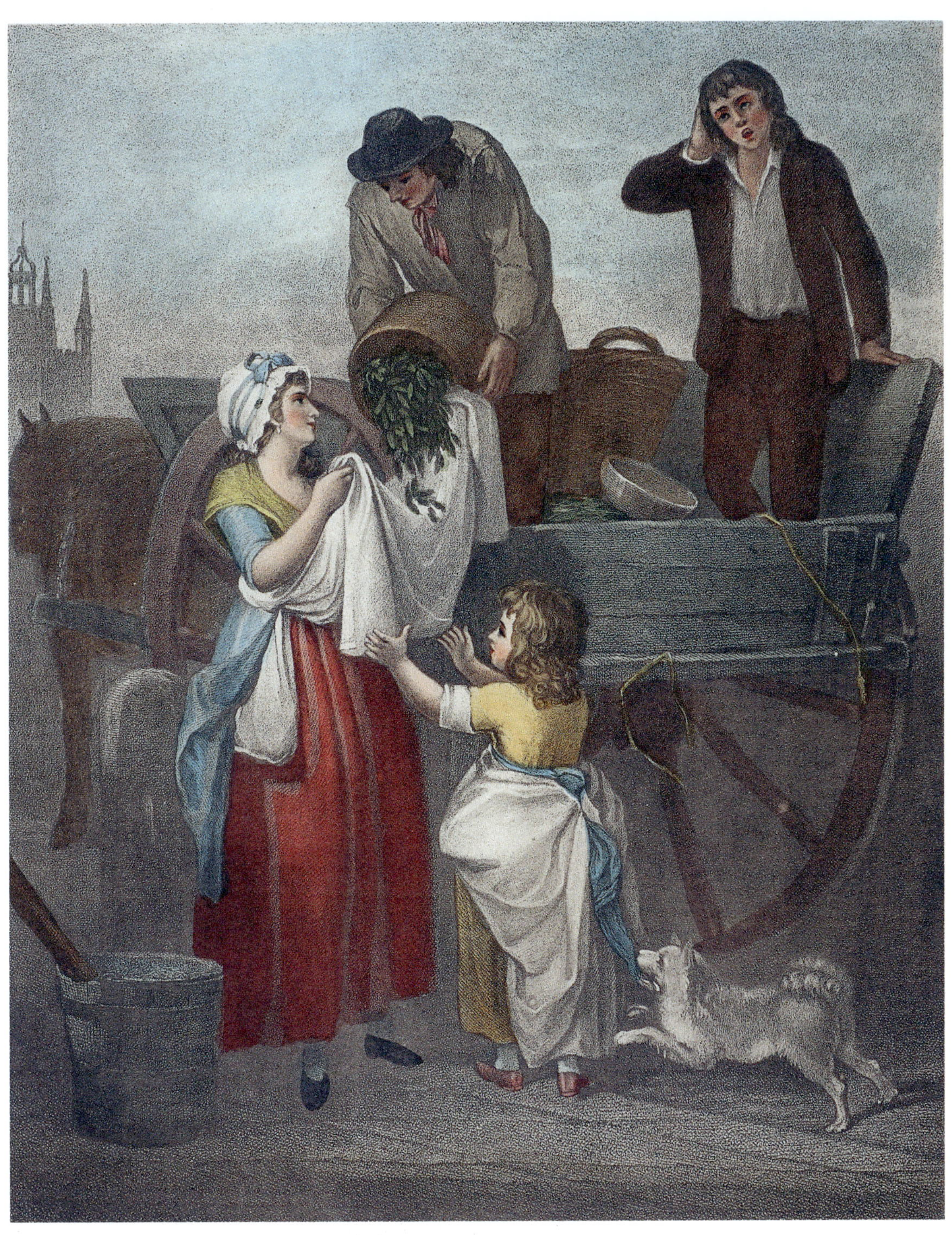

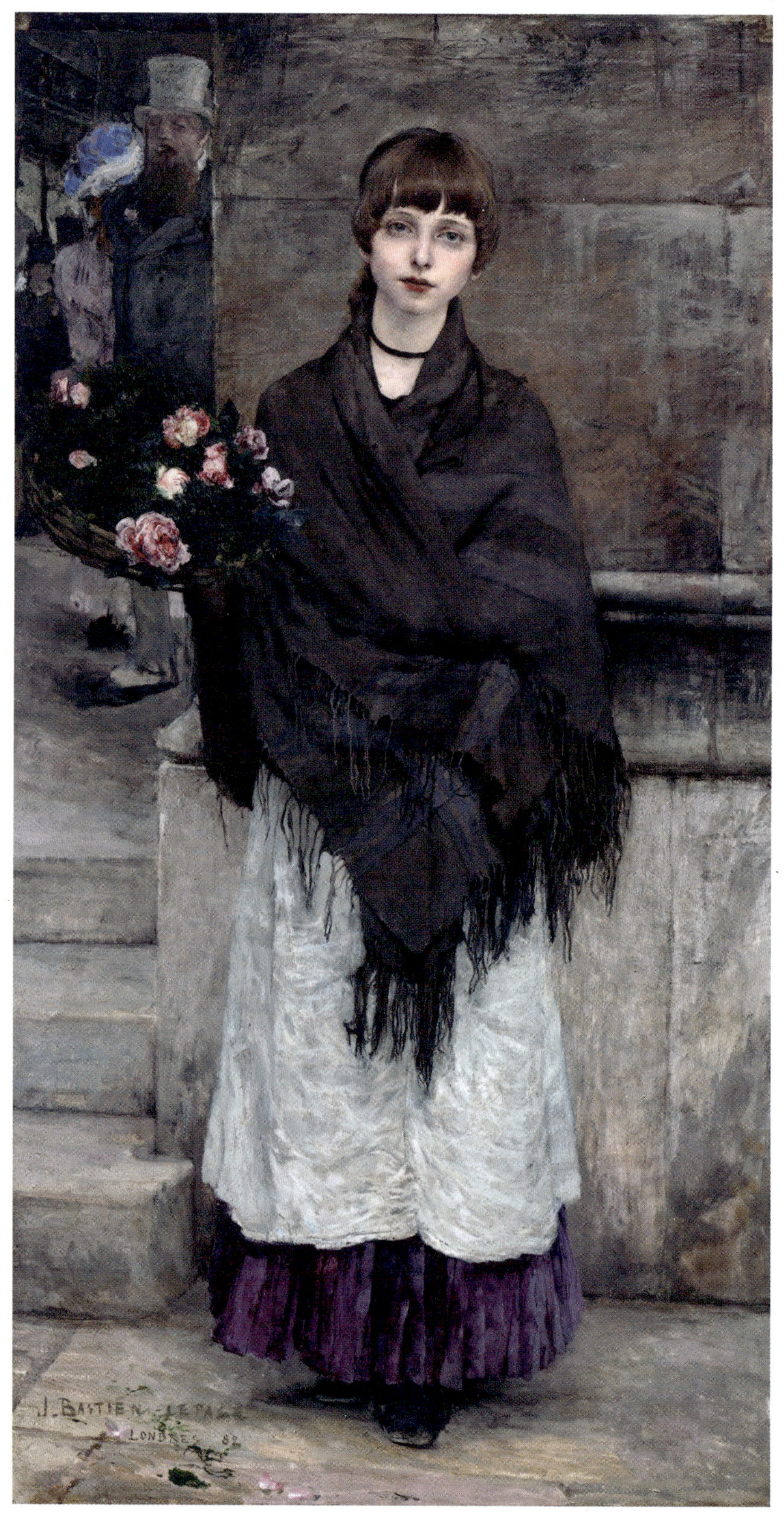

are very cheap but still nourishing, and they fill the stomachs of hungry children. In Covent Garden, at all times of day, are found cabbages from Battersea and onions from Deptford, celery from Chelsea and peas from Charlton, asparagus from Mortlake and turnips from Hammersmith. The shop of J.W. Draper, 'Orange Merchant', has a sign painted in yellow and green, close to the shop of 'Potato Salesman Whitman' painted in red and white, and that of Mr Butler, 'Seller of Herbs and Seeds', with a half-open wooden front decorated in a faded orange. Wheelbarrows are filled with cabbages and turnips, carrots and cocoa nuts, alongside mobile stalls with apples and pears, strawberries and plums. They say that it is easier to buy a pineapple here than in Jamaica. One costermonger's barrow has a red, white and blue flag flying from it, with a sign below saying that four oranges will cost a penny.

It is customary for Londoners to come in the morning and look at the cut flowers laid upon the cobbles, in the northwest corner of the market, and to savour the unfamiliar scents. Young girls may sell daffodils, roses and pinks, as well as their usual street trade in needles or pin-cushions. For such a girl, everything in London may surprise and unsettle. Life, for her, is a series of chores, hastily performed though never quite perfected. We should mark her well, for she belongs to this age and might not flourish in a later one. Yet 'flourish' is too vigorous a term for her; this girl has bones as light as calico and skin as thin as cotton. She might never come to flower.

There are more specialized markets. St George's Market, on the left side at the upper end of Oxford Street, is well-known for meat with its stalls of beef, mutton and veal and its array of loins, ribs, hearts, livers and kidneys gleaming in the open air. The stray dogs run among the legs of the crowd, trying to snatch the food, but they are beaten back by the stallholders with sticks and blows. Hungerford Market is known for its vegetables. In Petticoat Lane, off Spitalfields, are to be found cotton sheets and old clothes. Old bed knobs, rusty keys and lengths of iron piping are sold in Leather Lane. Clare Market, off Lincoln's Inn Fields, is well-known for its rough and comically inclined butchers. Some people walk there simply in order to see and to hear them. Hide and skin are cheap in Bermondsey Market. Fishwives hold their own market along the Tottenham Court Road, and on dark nights they stick paper lanterns upon their baskets. In Brick Lane are sold pigeons, canaries, parrots and guinea pigs.

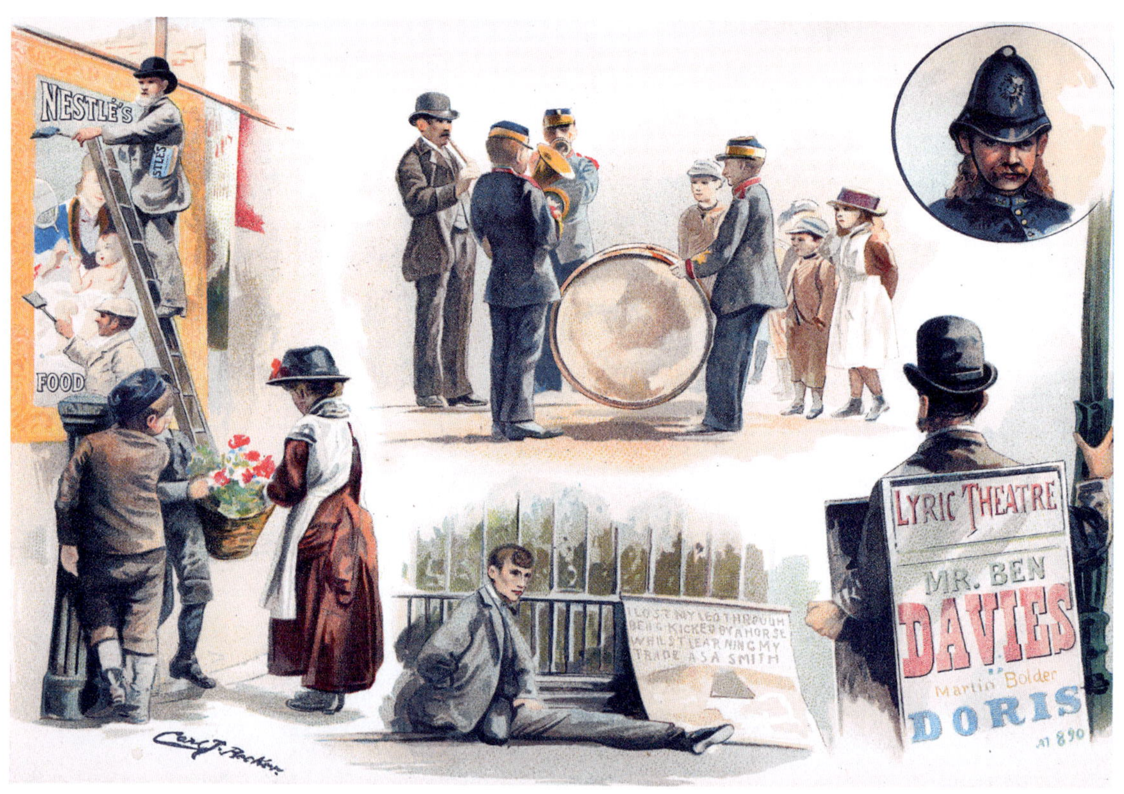

Wherever you go, in the light of daylight or in the lights of night, there are signs and advertisements of trade. It is said that London has grown wondrously pictorial, with a variety of papier-mâché ornaments or simply executed paintings placed in shop windows to denote the trade of the occupant. Many coffee houses have the symbol of a loaf and cheese together with a cup, and some fishmongers will paint the walls of their premises with a group of fish in striking attitudes. Grocers seem to prefer what are called 'conversation pieces', with pictures of London matrons assembled around a singing kettle or close to a simmering urn. Boots, cigars and sealing wax are suspended in gigantic form over the doors of various shops selling the same, while posters, placards and bills are pasted on blank walls, hoardings and the sides of houses. A poster for a new performance of *Otello* is placed over one promoting John Parry in *The Sham Prince*; *Tom & Jerry – The Christening – !!!!* is beneath a narrow strip asking, 'Have You Seen The Industrious Fleas?' A man is shown holding a newly varnished boot in one hand and a basket of blacking balls in the other, with the motto that 'This blacking is so good you may eat it!'

A sign advertising razor strops vies for space with one for soap, one for hair oil and one for mineral water. A colossal hat, mounted on springs like a gig, and with the hatmaker's name prominent upon it, is driven down the street by a fine horse. 'Peripatetic placards' have recently appeared on the street, with old men placed between two pasteboards advertising the latest play or up-to-the-minute novelty. These board-men are often the target of the rough humour of the streets; urchins throw mud at them or tickle their faces with a straw, and omnibus conductors will kick at their boards as they pass by. Imprisoned back and front, they cannot fight back.

*

The houses of London are not, on the whole, very remarkable. There are no apartment buildings, as there are in Paris and other European cities. A family here prefers to live separately, with its own roof over its head. Privacy, and even seclusion, are desirable as alternatives to the discomfort and the noise of the crowd. In these middle-class homes the exterior world seems literally to be kept at bay by a whole artillery of protective forces – screened by thick curtains and by lace or muslin inner curtains, muffled by patterned wallpaper and thick carpets, held off by settees and couches, mocked by wax fruit and artificial flowers, its metaphorical and literal darkness banished by lamps, candles and chandeliers. There is no picture without a frame, no screen or curtain without a tassel, no table without a cover and no maid without her pinny. Calm rather than tumult, quietness rather than noise, are required in the house so that it can become a modern home. It preserves the private life of the woman and child against the menace and forgetfulness of the London streets. Separation, and exclusion, are required. It would be impossible to find a suite of adjoining rooms in London, except in the most expensive hotels, and in fact it is unusual to find two connecting rooms even in the same house. All rooms have a specific purpose and are used, or partitioned, as such.

The better houses of the upper middle classes will perhaps contain four or five storeys, with a dining room and morning room to catch the sun on the ground floor, a drawing room on the first floor, the family bedrooms on the second and third floors and servants' quarters in the attic. The kitchen will be in the basement, together with a scullery. These houses will have an area

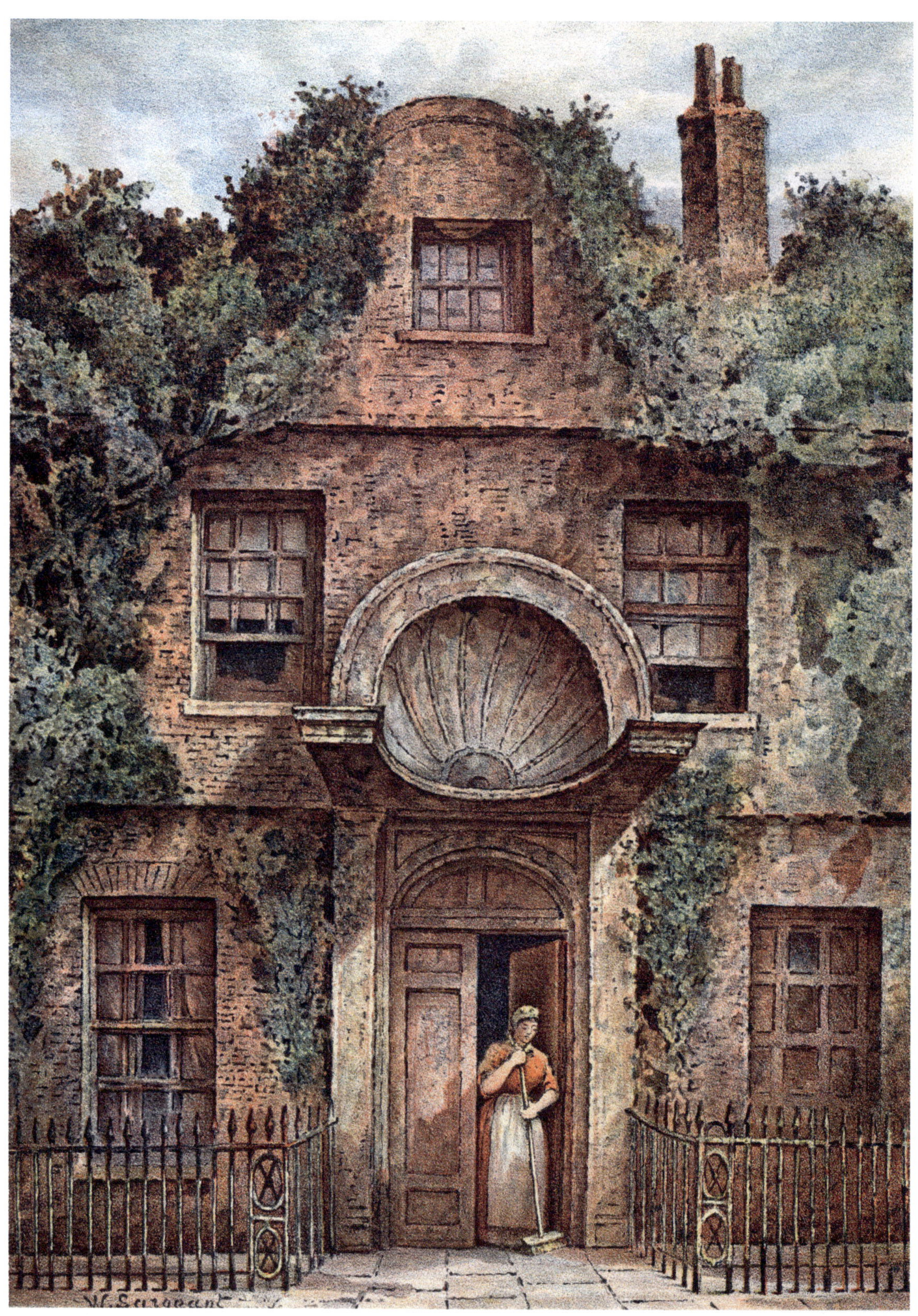

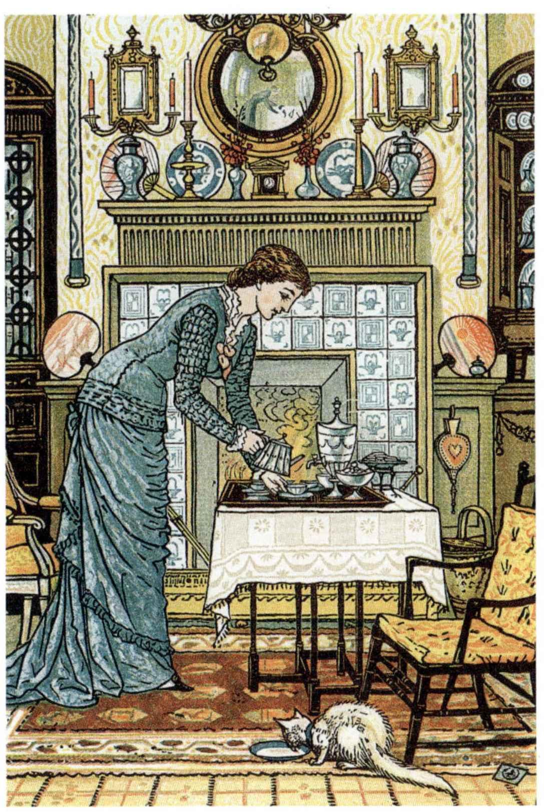

Left The doorway of Fairfax House in Putney, southwest London. An illustration for *Old London* (1900) by Waldo Sargeant.

Above A woman sets tea in a stylishly decorated room. The frontispiece to *The House Beautiful* (1881) by Clarence Cook.

on the basement level, and stone steps leading to the front door. A set of railings will complete the effect. Just as the social classes are graded, so are the floors and rooms of their houses. The 'public' rooms, into which friends and neighbours are invited, will be more luxurious and ornate than the private ones reserved for the immediate family.

The drawing room is primarily for meeting and entertaining. Chairs, both upright and easy, are grouped with small tables and perhaps a writing desk. All may be in mahogany or perhaps, according to fashion, in a lighter wood. Ottomans, sofas and the occasional footstool are expected. An upright piano, or even a grand piano, is generally found here. Everything is placed in a 'conversational' manner. The mantelpiece and fireplace are the centres of ornament, with figurines and flowers, and a clock protected by a glass dome. Dust, the enemy, must be banished. There has been a tendency, in recent years, for more elaborate and heavier furnishings. Flock wallpaper has become popular, and the carpets are becoming more colourful, complete with floral patterns. Turkish antimacassars and Chinese bowls or fans complement one another. The well-dressed drawing room, as with other rooms in the house, will include clocks, lamps, mirrors, vases, watercolours, candlestick, prints, figurines, plants, stuffed animals and etchings. Some regret the passing of the older and plainer style, but most are happy with the new and more colourful interiors.

The dining room is considered to be masculine space, despite the fact that it is administered by the wife and by female servants. It is more sober than the drawing room, perhaps with crimson carpets or curtains, and furniture of a dark mahogany. Dark green is favoured for the painted surfaces. A sideboard, displaying plates and glasses and various table decorations, is essential. In the daytime the room is used for other purposes, such as reading, composing letters or drawing. So there are also chairs, small tables and even a writing desk. In the principal bedroom the large bed may be four-postered, with thick curtains as hangings; other

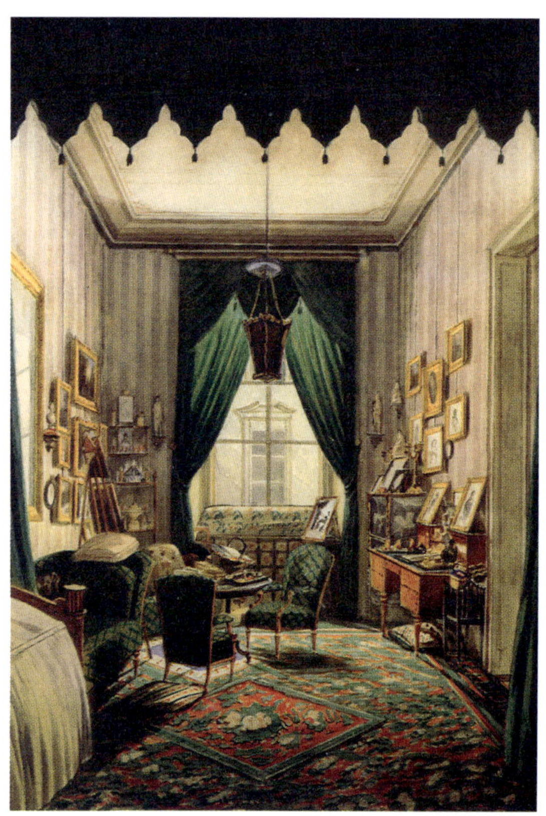

Above An Interior room with a Curtained Bed Alcove (c.1853) artist unknown.

bedrooms may contain an iron bedstead, to repel bugs, or even a folding bed. A wardrobe and washstand are required, together with a mahogany table and chairs, which may once have seen service in the more elegant 'public' rooms. A small cupboard for the chamber pot is also necessary, and a bookcase is always useful. An array of ornaments, flowers and figurines can be expected. It is wise, however, not to clutter the room for fear of nasty stumbles in the dark.

In the standard middle-class houses, two or three storeys may suffice. The small space between the street door and the stairs is called the hall, perhaps furnished with one or two mahogany chairs. The parlour leads off from the hall, and can be considered to be the heart of the house where the family eats, prays and conducts the affairs of the day. Large folding doors separate the front from the back parlour. Plants, flowers and ferns will be found growing in glass cases; even orchids flourish here. On the floor above the parlour are the bedrooms, while the kitchen and the servants' quarters are situated in the basement. Each storey in a typical middle-class home generally has two rooms, one towards the street and the other overlooking a small courtyard. The stairs are narrow, and the rooms themselves are not large. In many such houses, there will be no bathroom and the lavatory will be situated in the courtyard.

The doors are generally high and narrow, and the windows are also narrow with wide spaces between them. Carpets cover the floors of most of the rooms, the stairs and along the hallway to the front door. Muslin curtains replace the heavier curtains in summer. During the day the effect is of brightness, while in the evening the light is dim. Lamps, and even old-fashioned tallow candles, are used; gaslighting makes a room hot and smoky, with an unpleasant smell.

In these various houses the aim is for elegance as well as comfort, for orderliness as well as cleanliness. This can be hard in the London climate and the urban atmosphere, and that is why the external world is warded off. The house is a shelter, to protect its occupants as much as possible from the world of dirt, disease and struggle. The householder who travels to business each day has in effect two selves, the man at home and the man at work, and they will never meet. The street door is kept locked, and you come to recognize a caller by the nature of the knock. The postman gives two loud knocks in succession, for example, while the doctor announces himself with a series of raps. In more modern or recently built houses tradesmen ring rather than knock, employing a bell pull which is connected to the kitchen.

Housework, and all the tasks associated with domestic life, are carefully planned and executed. In this new world of clock time, punctuality and efficiency are essential. Bells are rung for the stages of the day; there is a time for prayer, a time for meals and a time for formal dressing. A servant, before anything else, must be useful and obedient. There are more than enough of them to assist all middle-class households; one in three of young women are in service. They can be selected by recommendation or by advertisement; failing that, they are chosen at the Servants' Hall in Marlborough Street.

The houses are the image of their neighbourhood, richer or poorer. The interminable rows of small dwellings, of red or

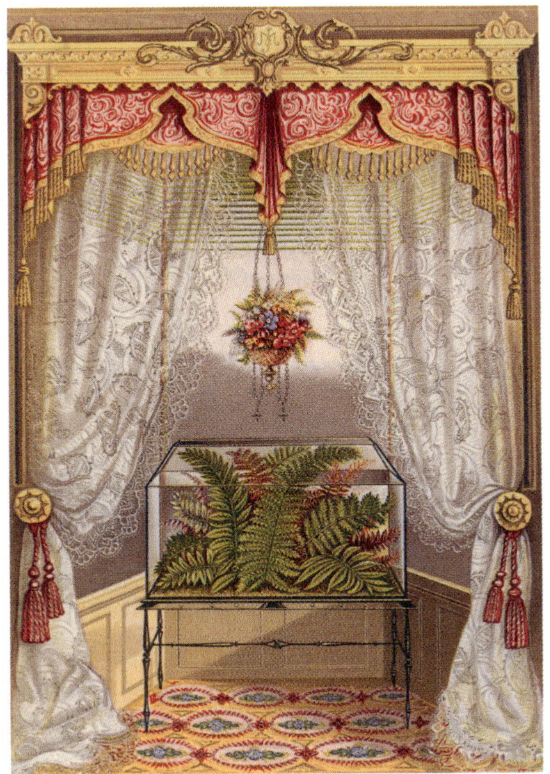

Below left A large wardian case containing ferns, used as a window decoration with hanging muslin curtains, c.1875.

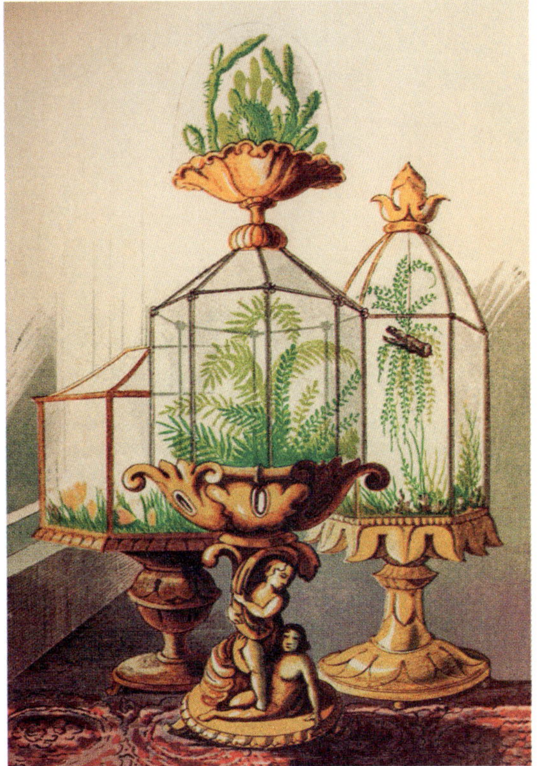

Below right Three wardian cases protecting plants from the air pollution of nineteenth-century London. From *The New Practical Window Gardener* (1877) by J. R. Mollison.

yellow brick, are considered to mark the areas of clerkdom.
If you have no private fortune of your own, as the saying goes,
you cannot have everything. These houses are cramped, but they
are uniform. In the poorer streets, where the men are in steady
work and just beyond the reach of want, the windows are clean
and the steps are well-scrubbed. The whiteness of the doorstep is
a sure mark of respectability. In these streets, two families inhabit
four rooms, and three live in six. In taller houses, the poorest are
usually to be found at the top in rooms on the third or fourth
floors, in garrets or in attic spaces; as you descend, floor by floor,
the position improves.

In most of them the furniture is of the plainest, but it is
sturdy and serviceable, comprising a table, two or three chairs
and a chest of drawers with large glass handles. On top of this is
generally a clock, or a bunch of artificial flowers under a glass
shade. The ornaments, too, are a sign of respectability. On either
side are arrayed the cups and saucers, the plates and drinking
vessels, used by the family. There may also be the bottles of
medicine recently taken by its members. The chest of drawers will
contain the items of clothing which are not already in use, and will
be used a storehouse for the items of daily life. If there is also a
small cupboard, the top shelf will hold little packages of tea, coffee
and sugar, while the lower shelf will hold the family's supply of
coal. On the table at supper time will be placed the teapot, slices
of a loaf and a saucer of margarine.

These represent the familiar and conventional aspects of
city life, but turn a corner or venture down another street
and all is changed. The 'houses' of the poor may consist of one
room, patched and peeling, where three or four people live.
The furniture consists of items barely worth pawning – or,
as it is called, 'going in' – or they would have been pledged.
A makeshift table, with a couple of old stools or backless chairs,
may be the sum. The same room serves for living and for sleeping,
for cooking and for washing (if that activity takes place at all)
for the children of all ages as well as for man and wife. The
window is broken, patched and dirty, covered with brown paper
or stuffed with rags. The space may be clouded in smoke from
the one chimney and the walls are the colour of old leather. The
bedclothes are grimy and ragged, almost rotten, and they are
eked out by the day clothes that have been discarded for the
night and flung onto the bed. There will be, more often than not,
a foul and acrid smell. It is likely that the houses are rotten, with

bad bricks laid in single courses; the woodwork is unseasoned and shrinks, and the stairs are of matchboard. It has been estimated by some contemporary observers that one-third of the urban population live in unwholesome layers, one over the other, in old houses and confined rooms. Some even speculate that a new race is being created, or at least a new phase of human existence is coming to birth.

In the poorest districts some of the dwellings date from the late seventeenth century but the once imposing buildings have badly decayed, their rooms stripped of the woodwork, their doors and fireplaces sold, their windows removed. The men of property buy up these empty shells and fill them with as many tenants as they can find. Every available room is let out to a different family or, in some instances, to two or even three families. The cellars themselves are used as dwellings. The poor, as a result, will be pushed into alleys and courts which are already overcrowded. The atmosphere is typhus and the ventilation is cholera. There will be no drains, only leaking cesspits, no gutters, no street lighting and no water. The roads, unpaved and full of holes, are filthy and strewn with animal and vegetable refuse. Human waste, both solid and liquid, is always plentiful.

A street scene of mothers and children in Victorian slums of Church Lane, Bloomsbury, c.1875.

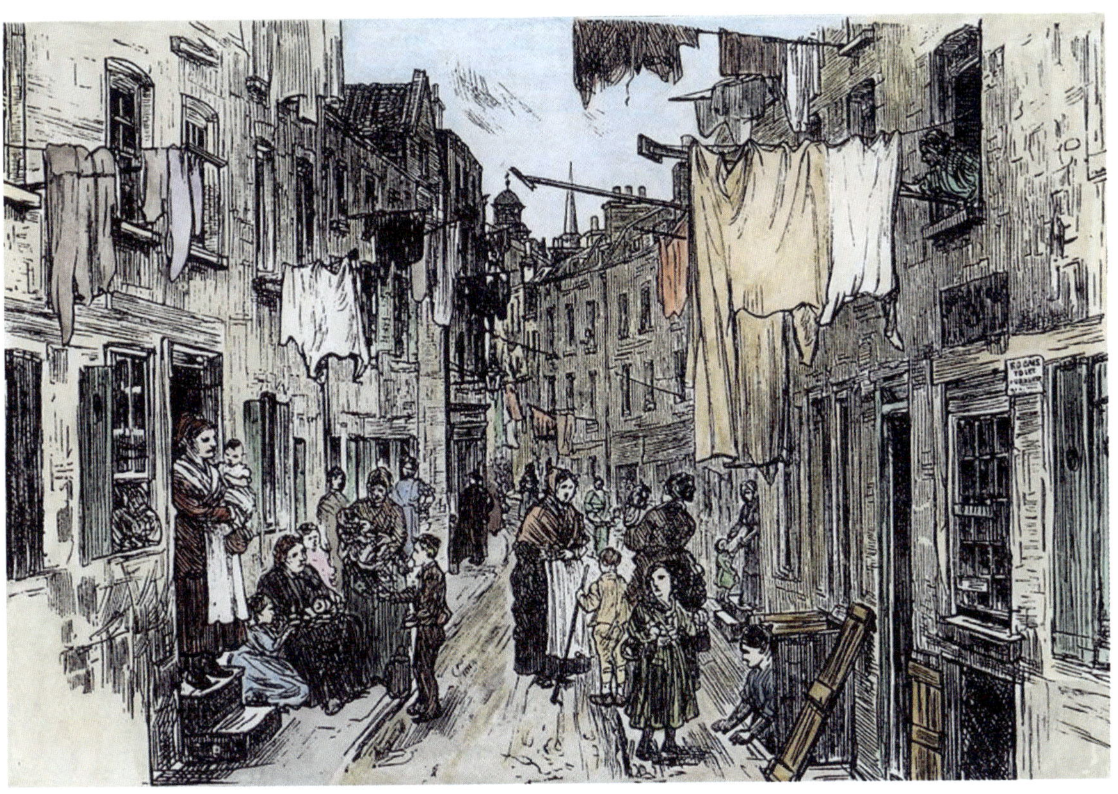

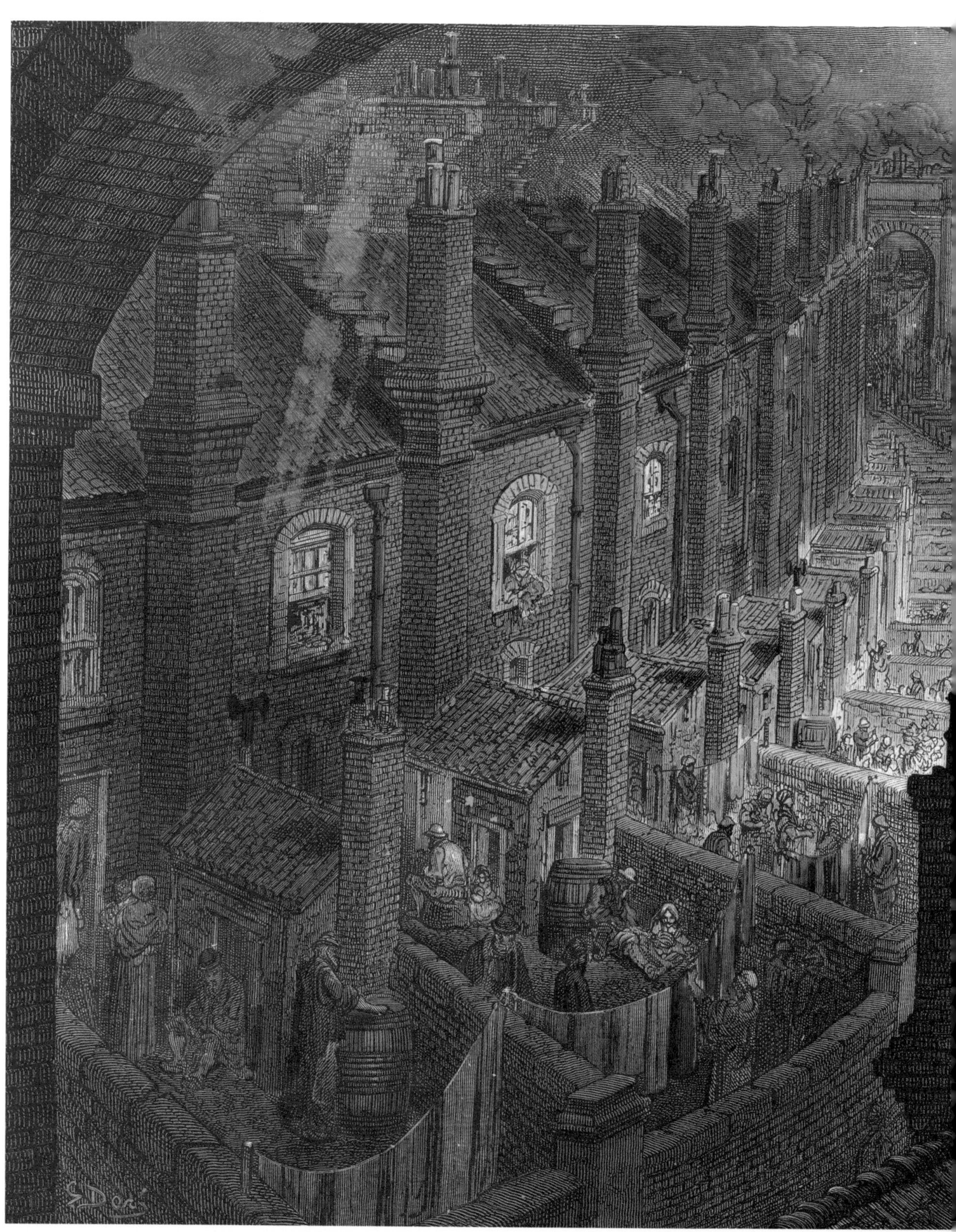

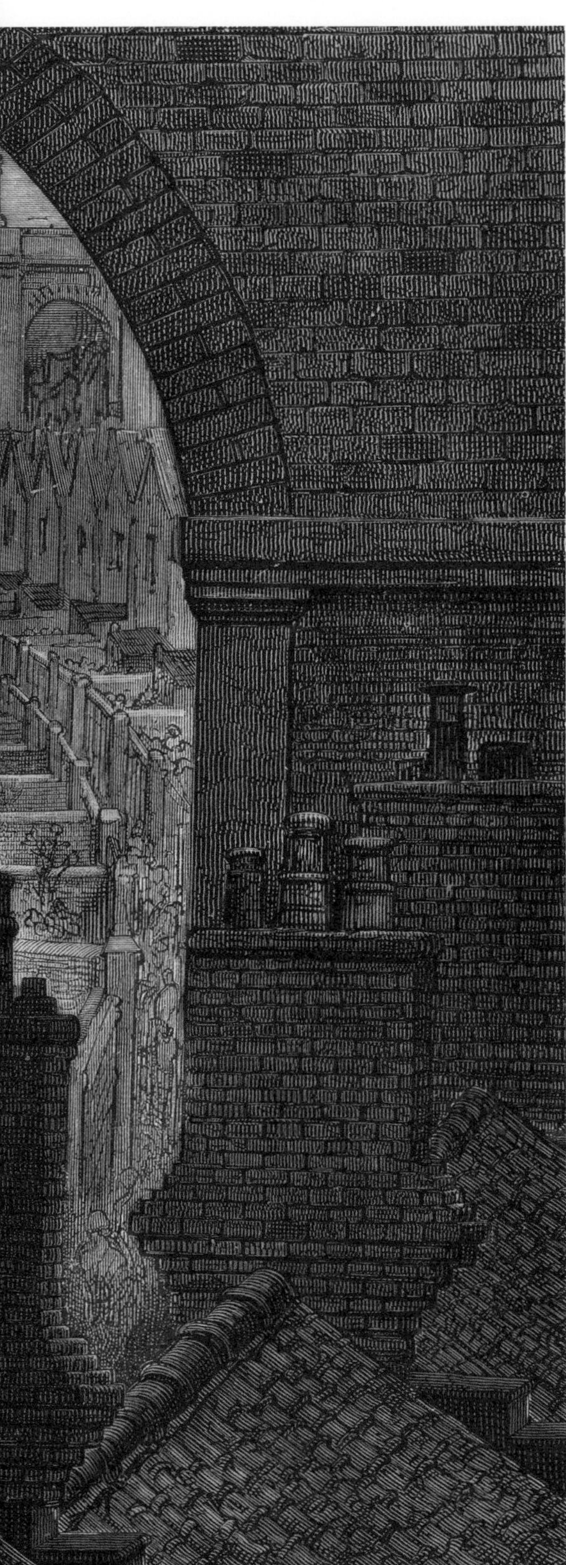

In these neighbourhoods spring up rag-and-bottle warehouses, penny-a-bottle ginger beer establishments, old-iron warehouses and marine stores selling any worn-out or damaged articles. Old women will hang about their doors, soliciting customers for any paltry sale, or will peer out at the dingy street through the patched and papered windows. Food is offered which is much less appetizing than the cat meat of a respectable tripe shop. The rickety children, all of them barefooted, paddle about in the mud and dirt. Some of these areas are known as rookeries, after the crammed and noisy nests of those birds, and an average Londoner will know as little of them as of the wilds of Australia or the islands of the South Seas. A notorious rookery lies in the parish of St Giles-in-the-Fields, in the heart of the city, but it is neither seen nor visited by other Londoners. It might not exist and, for most, it does not exist. It does not matter, either way.

The newspapers have cited a coroner's report on the death of Ann Galway in a court off Bermondsey Street; she lay dead on a heap of feathers by the side of her son, since she possessed neither sheet nor blanket; the feathers had stuck to her side so fast that the doctor could not examine the body until it had been washed. He found it to be emaciated and verminous.

Part of the floor of the room had been torn up, and the hole used as a privy. The improvement commissioners, the medical officers and other reformers, point out that in many quarters the living must eat, drink and sleep beside a decomposing corpse. Yet the houses are still being cobbled together without drainage or ventilation, all of them places of wickedness, want and beggary.

We should add to the multitude of the desperate London poor a floating population of vagrants and homeless drifters, calculated to number between twenty and thirty thousand, who sleep in alleyways or in empty houses. The beggars themselves are filthy beyond description, their clothes so long caked with a layer of dirt that it has become solid. Their faces can scarcely be recognized as human. It is customary to compare this city to a great ocean, and these people are indeed the drowning or the already drowned.

*

The Thames is the ever moving avenue of London. It carries the crowded steamboats and ferries down from Chelsea and Vauxhall and across from Waterloo and Southwark to the Old Shades Pier by London Bridge and to all the other piers in the heart of the City. From there swarm the army of dapper clerks who mingle with the ballast heavers, the labourers, the dock porters and the riverside merchants. The river takes the hay boats with their lateen sails, the passenger boats, the skiffs, the tugs, the penny boats, the cutters, the steamers, the clippers, the coal barges with their heavy load, and the lighters with their cargo of brick and ashes. It passes the wharves, the waterside public houses, the riverside slums, the factories, the mills, the works, the breweries and the sheer blank walls of the warehouses. Some of these warehouses are old and dilapidated, while others are firm and newly built, and in front of them looms a forest of masts, obscurely seen in the perennial atmosphere of mist or fog. On the northern banks lie the large docks built to serve the West Indian trade in sugar and timber; close to them lie the London Docks for such merchandise as wine and wool, coffee and cocoa. It has its own quays and roads and squares, its vaults and its warehouses as grand as palaces. It contains enough sugar to sweeten the Thames and enough rum to make half of London drunk.

It is a far cry from the river at Hammersmith. From its new suspension bridge, all things look vaporous even in fine weather; the light melts into a whitish smoky haze, where the surface of the Thames and the sky blend together to become the pale

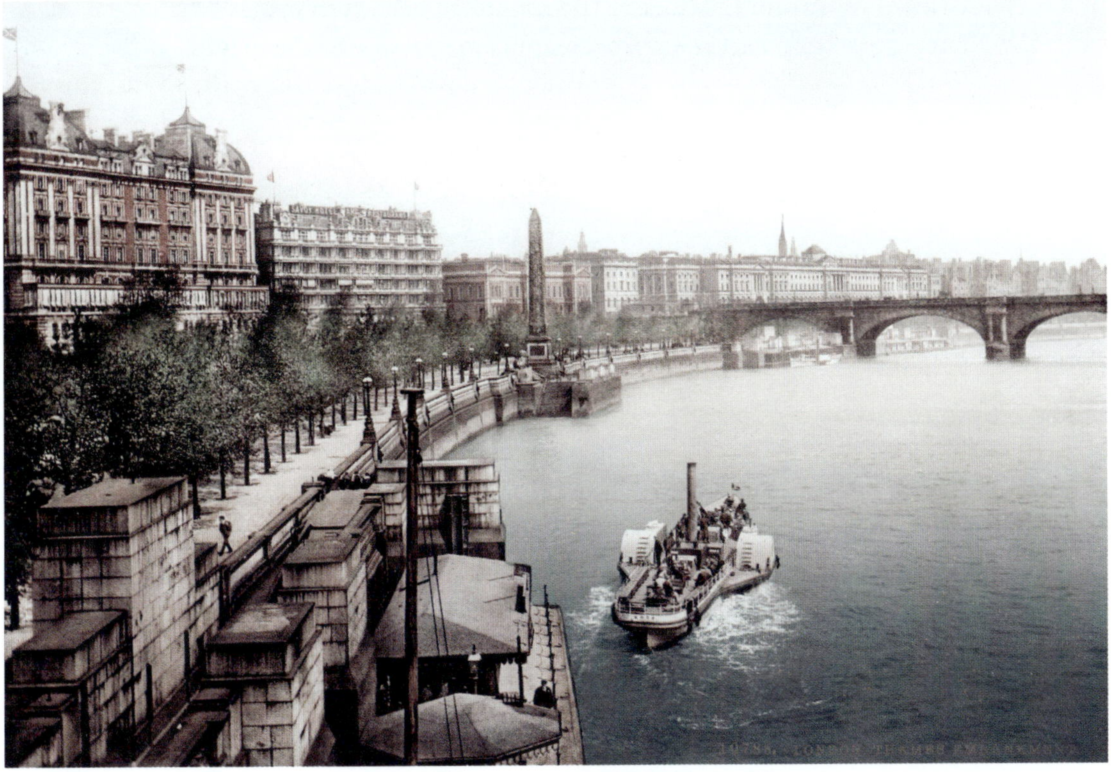

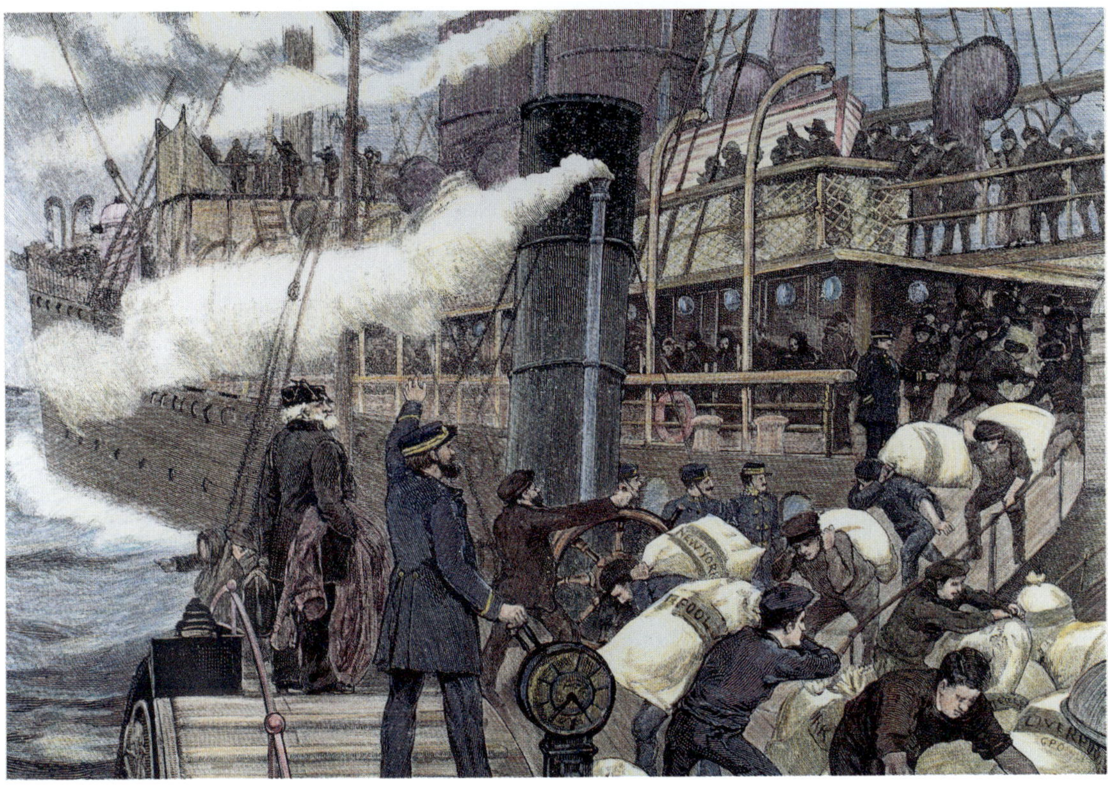

colour of slate or stone. The blocks of new houses on the north bank show a window glimmering here and there, while a group of factory chimneys on the opposite side leaves only an outline. The drowning light, the air irradiated by mists and vapours, the imperceptible and continuous changes in that vast draught of air and water, soften or erase all outlines, shading them with blue, and leave the impression of a vast, vague life, diffuse and melancholy, which is the life of this compliant and yielding territory; it is poised between city and country, brick and field, and it is awaiting its fate.

The Thames is still clear and sparkling here but, as the river approaches London, it changes form and colour. By the time it reaches the city, it has become stained with false colours and smeared with lurid tints. It is black with coal, blue with indigo, grey with tides, white with flour, stained purple with wine or brown with tobacco. It is a dank, dirty river, filled with unaccountable smells and banked by noisome mud, which harbours worms known to riverside children as 'blood worms' because of their colour. On its margins are puddles and ditches, with coarse grass and rank weeds, while the riverside factories belch out smoke and poison the water with their effluent.

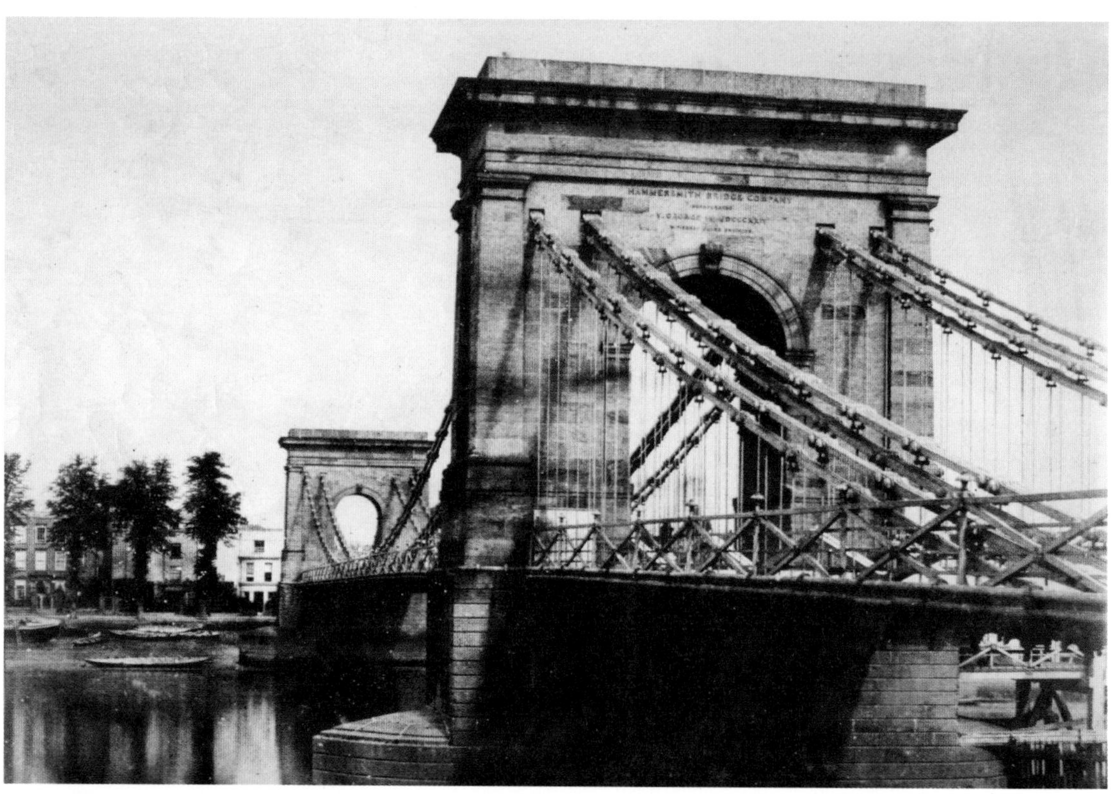

Below Hammersmith Bridge (c.1856) by Peter le Neve Foster.

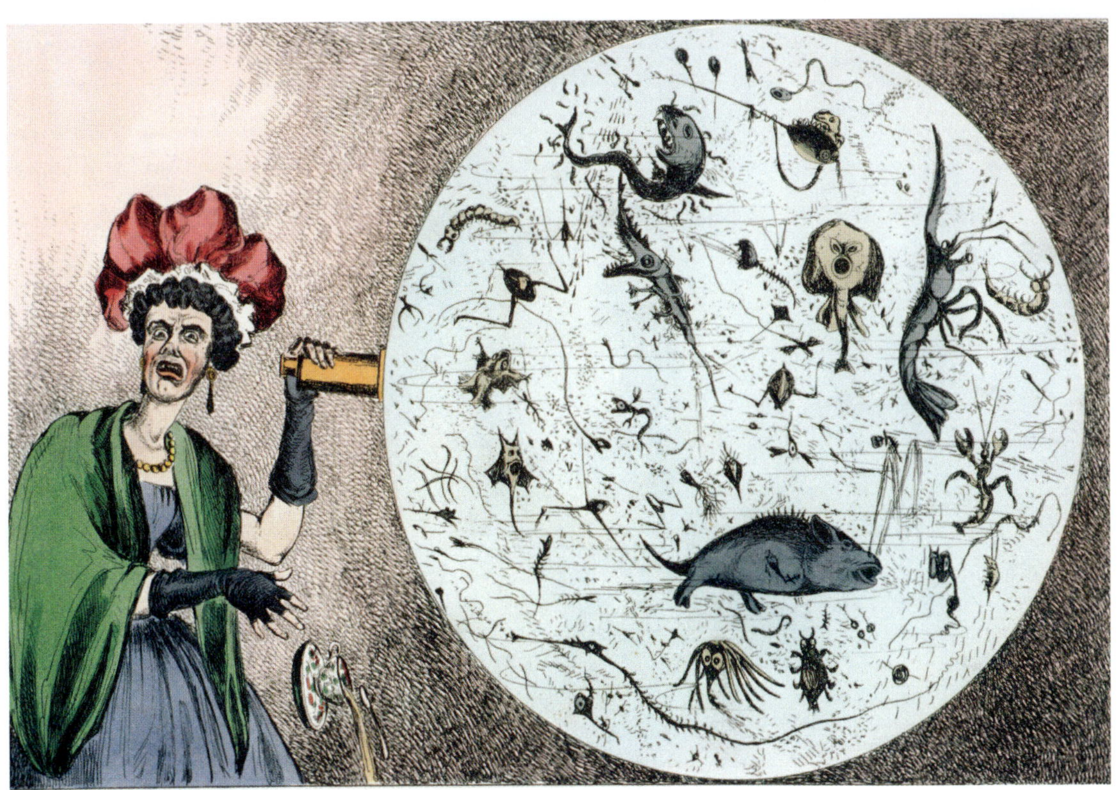

It is no more agreeable under the river. The tunnel beneath the Thames, between Wapping and Rotherhithe, has an air of dankness and dreariness. At five hundred paces long, it was for a time the wonder of the earth, and many people visited it for the novel sensation of walking beneath the river, but its popularity did not endure. You must go a hundred steps down a vertical shaft on each side of the river, and they will take you to the vista of an arched corridor that extends into darkness. The presence of the Thames above the brick arches seems to be an imminent danger and the brick walls of the corridor to be in a cold sweat. The walls run with water, and some say that they can distinctly hear the sound of paddle steamers overhead. Gas jets cast a flickering light, and a thin, tinkling music is heard from the little shops that run along the tunnel. The shopkeepers, principally made up of old women, appear to spend their lives here, scarcely – if ever – seeing the sun, selling fancy goods and other trumpery labelled 'bought in the Thames Tunnel' or 'a present from the Thames Tunnel'.

It is gloomier than any street of upper London, and so who will come to buy? The passage under the water has other visitors, and is supposed to be the haunt of thieves and prostitutes, thus earning

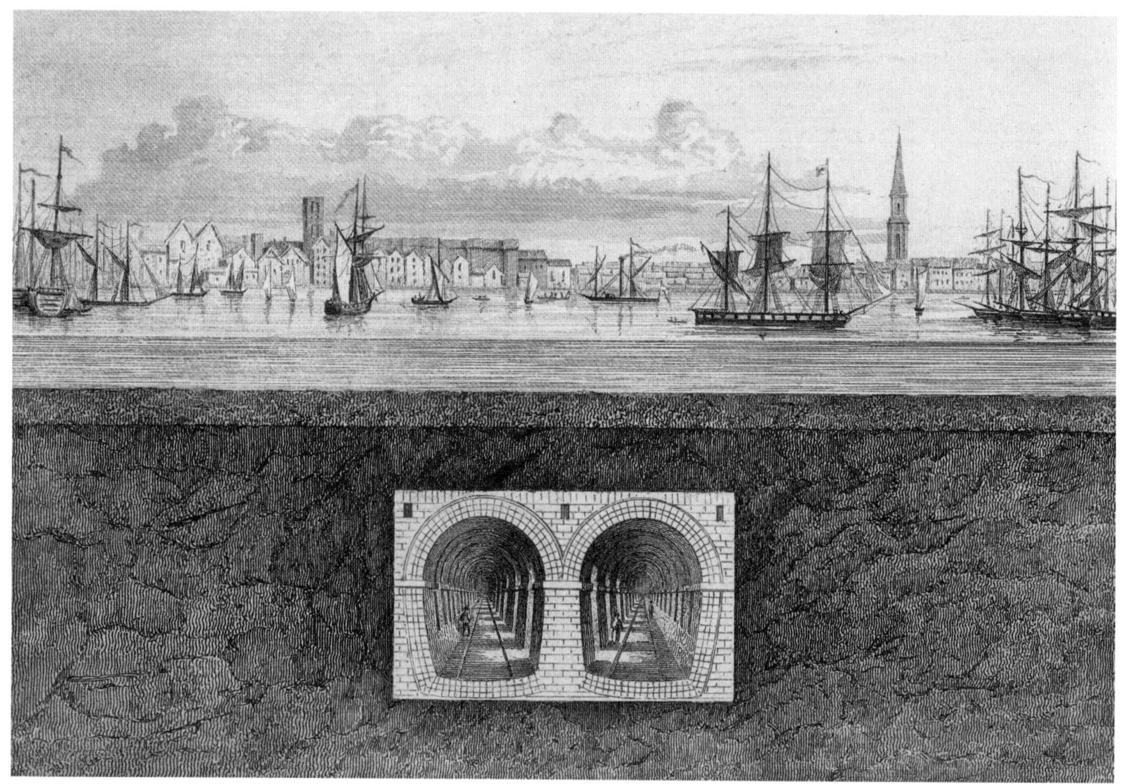

the popular name of 'the Hades Hotel'. The depths of London can truly claim to be the underworld of old myth.

What is to be seen on a return to the surface? By Hungerford Market the dock is raised against the grimy water which slams against its stairs, green with weed and algae. Boats, smeared with tar, are tied up waiting for goods or passengers. On London Bridge itself rows of people, some well-dressed and some in working clothes, line both sides in order to lean over the low walls or along the parapets. Some of them seem to have stopped here while on errands or on their way to business, while others have nowhere to go and are in no particular hurry, but they all gaze earnestly and intently upon the river below, as if they are watching transience itself. They are not country visitors, since these onlookers have the stamp of London upon them. They never tire of the flux and movement below them. They tear themselves away unwillingly, and when one leaves another takes their place.

As the river moves through the city it becomes narrower, with only a slender passage for the multitude of boats. The schooner may be followed by a barge, and then a collier, with a small nutshell of a boat carrying just two passengers in its wake.

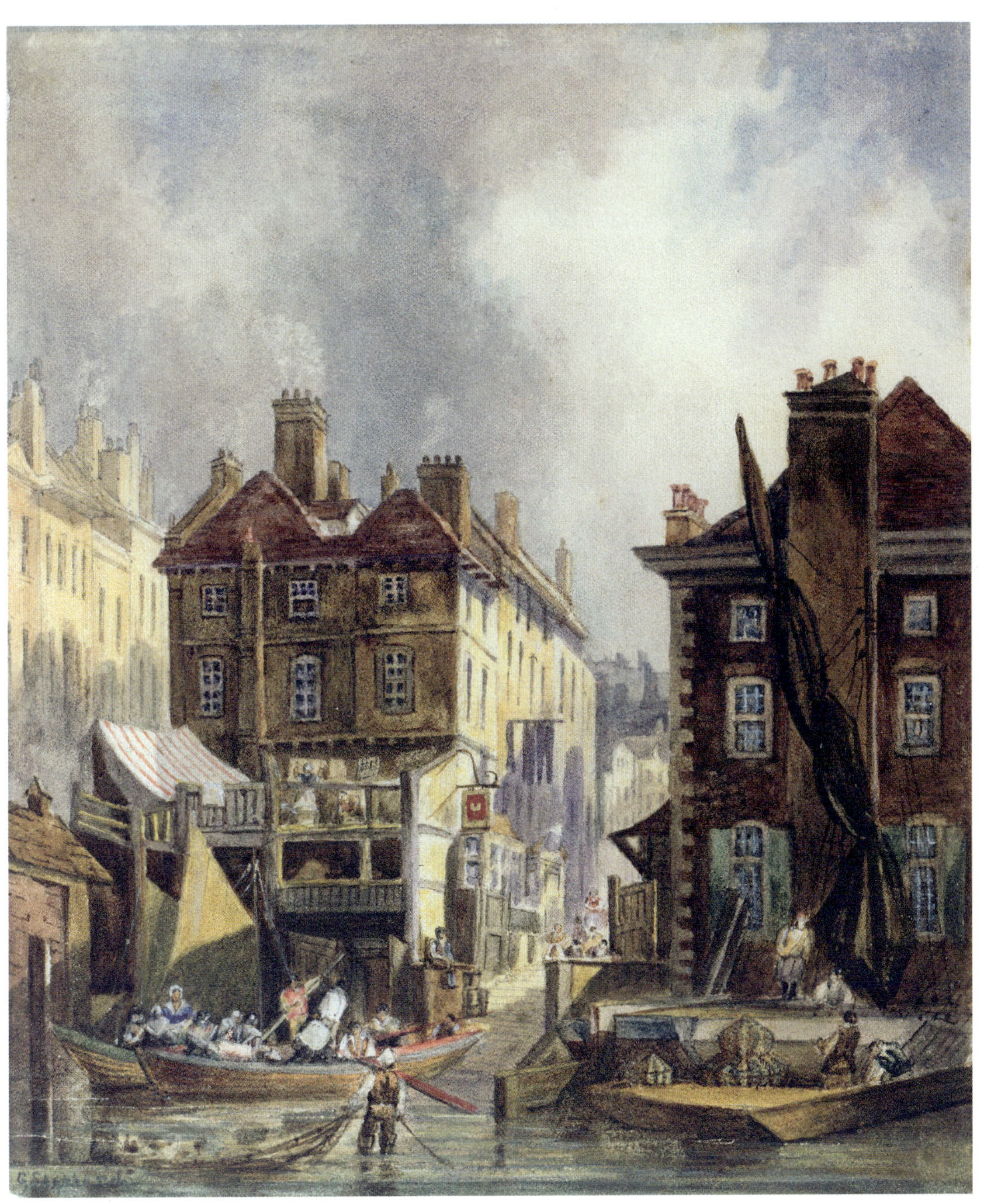

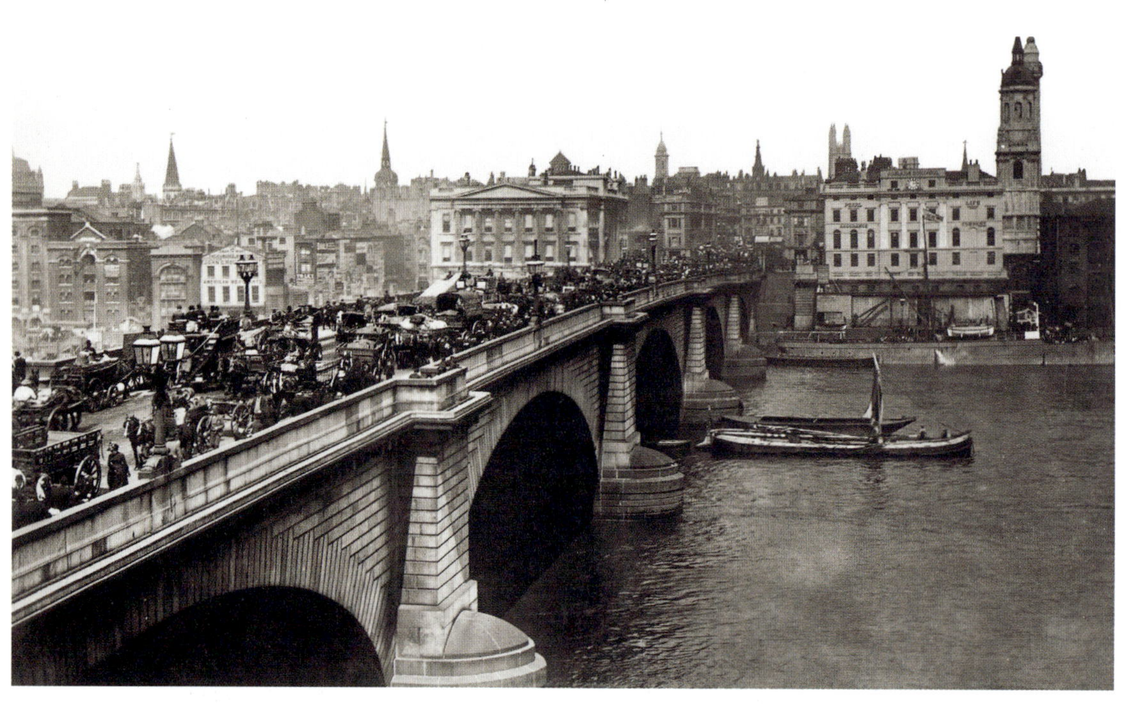

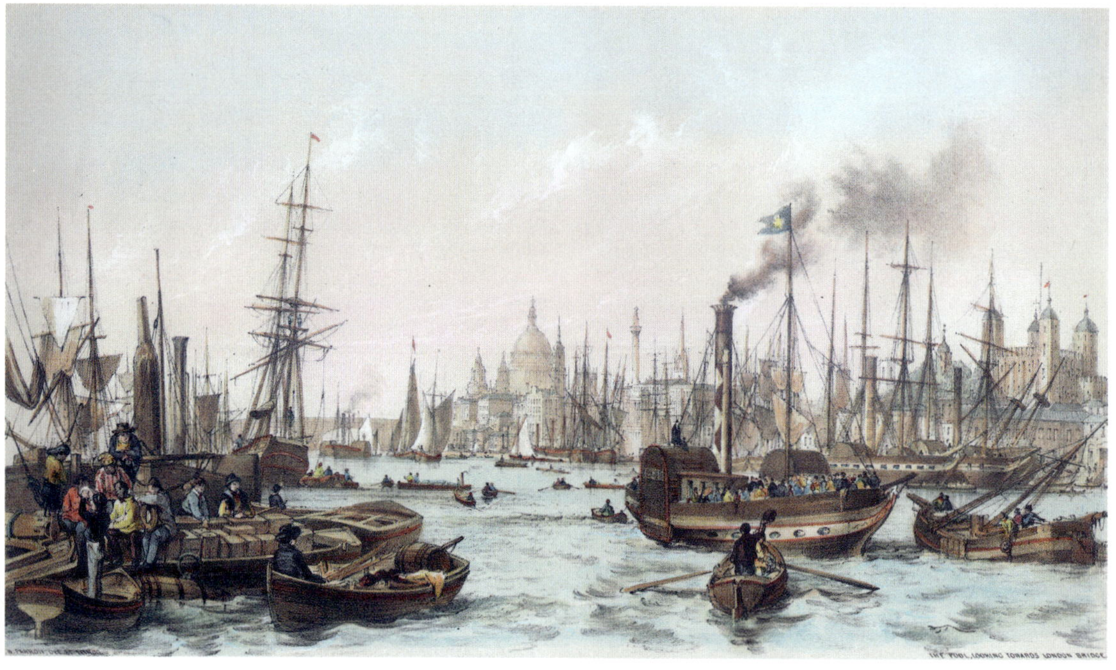
THE POOL, LOOKING TOWARDS LONDON BRIDGE

To the throng of boats can be added American clippers, small skiffs and long wherries. It is said that the steersmen and pilots of the Thames are well-used to preventing collisions and disasters, a necessary skill in the circumstances, but they are not believed to have the 'water-wit' (or the obscenities) credited to their predecessors. Perhaps only the lightermen and bargemen continue that tradition. Rowing matches are still popular, and you can hear loud cries of 'Foul! foul!' and 'Fair! fair!' echoing across the water.

The sea comes closer. The river grows wider and wider as it sustains a monstrous variety of shipping with steamers, clippers and great sailing ships trailing the flags of all the world, as well as a confusion of lighters, of brown-sailed barges, of tugs wallowing in the water. On this journey you pass cranes and spars by the waterfront, wharves and stores and docks and, beyond them, church towers, marshes, dilapidated houses and what look like deserted inns.

*

Londoners live in the crowd, and can hardly be said to know themselves outside it. They are born and they die among other citizens. The average height of a woman is 5 feet and 2 inches, and the men are 3 or 4 inches taller. However, the sizes vary; what looks like a child of five from a distance may turn out to be a woman of fifty. Along Cheapside two uninterrupted streams of people pass one another on either side. No one greets anyone, the eyes meet and then then look away. No one looks up, except for a sign of impending rain or snow. They push and jostle but only occasionally a Londoner, who treads upon a shoe or collides with you, will turn back and beg your pardon. You had better walk with your eyes wide open and never stop on the pavement. Struggle on as best you can and push forward without any false modesty. Some in the crowd will like to touch objects, posts, windows, doors with their hand or with a walking stick, but their movement forward is never interrupted. Hired men or boys stand to one side in order to thrust at passers-by papers advertising pills or potions or boot-blacking, but the people seem to be filled with some driving force, propelling them forward. To 'take the wall' means to take the inside, close against the wall rather than the road. It means to take precedence in the endless bustle, and the line of pedestrians will always give way to those on the right. When a couple are walking, a man will take the superior side over a woman.

It sometimes seems that you cannot get beyond this crowd. In recent years it has become known, in the newspapers and periodicals, as 'the public'. It represents to some observers a new kind of human energy that is even now being created. It may not enter the imaginations of those who hurry and rush forward in the streets, but they are taken to embody the city of mobility, of change, of speed, of clock time; they are said to rival the energy of the steam engine and even of the newly discovered magnetic field. The city itself seems to encourage quickness, apparent in the speed of the cabs and omnibuses; the people walk very fast and often talk very fast, so that touts and bus conductors run a whole sentence into one long word. The clipped language of hurry is heard on all sides: 'So I says … says she … says he … Not a word! … Don't you blame me … now do you see what I mean? … I give you my word on that … I came over all queer.' The members of the crowd, in Fleet Street or the Strand, do not need to enter a pastry shop when they hurry by; they take up the buns or biscuits on display, and throw their pennies in. Those who are not experienced are frightened at street crossings, where the sheer number and speed of the people create the effect of a whirlpool; there is a real fear of being hurled into the road and the fatal onrush of traffic. Nobody will see you. Nobody will hear you. In the less busy streets the crowd can be fragmented. When two men begin to fight, a large group of spectators will form a circle around them with the cry of 'A ring! A ring!'

For some the endless flow of tired or anxious faces can be bewildering, but for others it is a welcome distraction. They join the crowd in order to be free of private thoughts and to be taken up in the vast impersonal life of the city. The presence of ever-moving people may cause anxiety and loneliness, but it may also promote levity and thoughtlessness. Within the immensity of London, the individual citizen is insignificant and unnoticed; this, too, may help to explain the weariness and lassitude to be seen on many faces. It is widely remarked that the crowds are becoming larger; streets, such as those north of Oxford Street, were once relatively quiet but are now filled with people. Perhaps this prompts a vague awareness that the city is growing and expanding in an unconstrained and even unmanageable way. It may also fuel speculation that the character of London is also slowly changing. In the central districts the crowd is also mixed with Americans, Indians, Swedes, Russians, Italians, French and Spanish while, particularly in the streets beside the river, it can be composed of Moors, lascars, Malays, Tartars and Chinese.

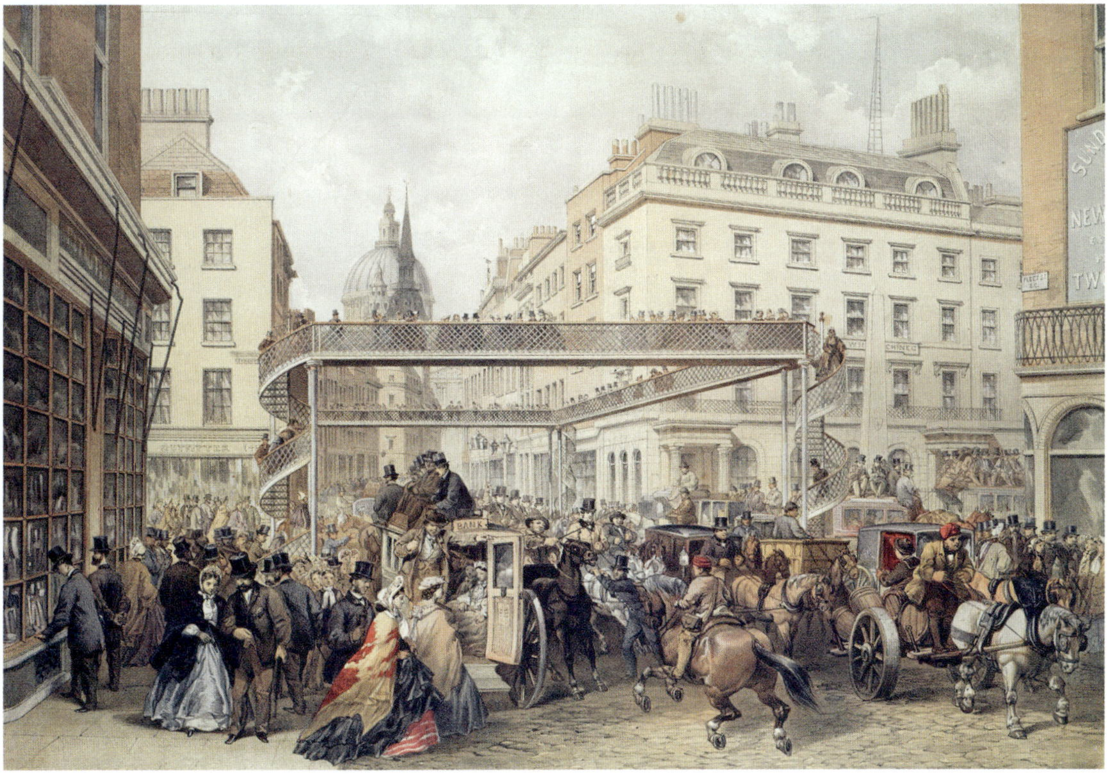

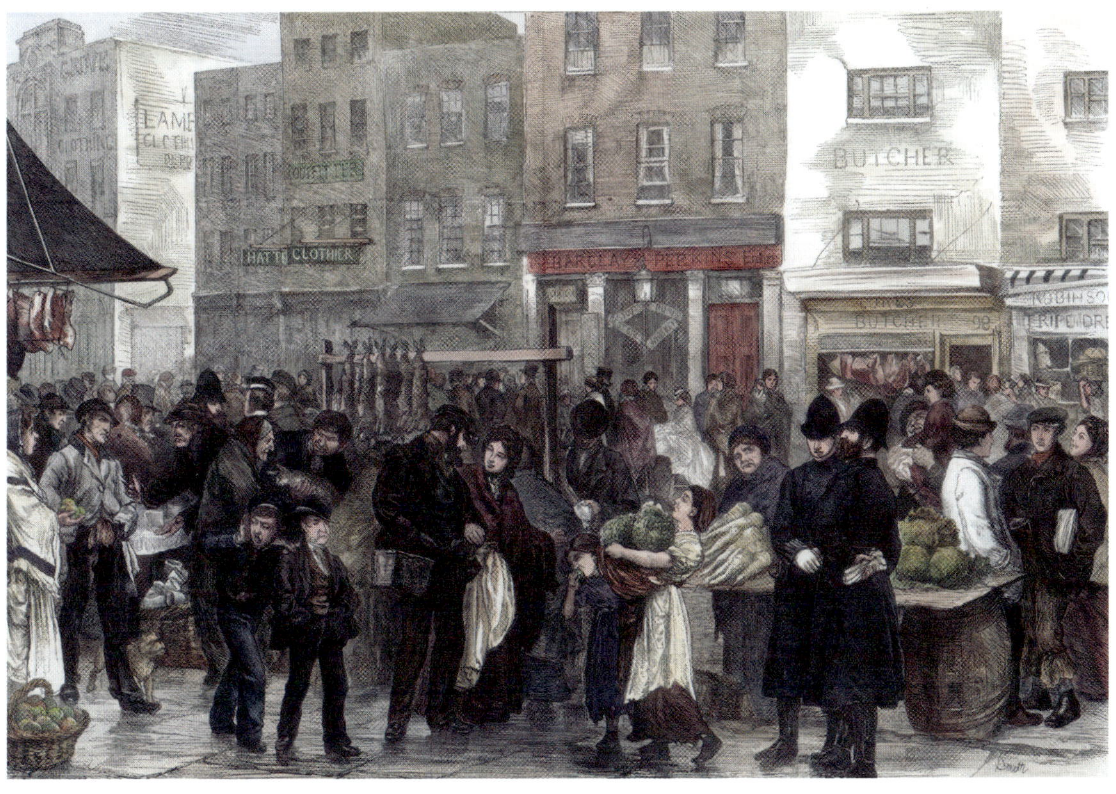

The roads themselves are as crowded and as turbulent as the pavements. Huge draught horses, drawing brewers' carts and coal wagons, are ridden beside dwarf horses, mounted by boys carrying letters or messages. If the horses are forced to come to a halt, and the traffic stops, it is called a lock or block, but nothing can impede for long the stream of hackney coaches, wagons, carts, chariots and cabriolets. An early arrival for city dwellers is the coach known as the short-stage. It takes its passengers to the areas or hamlets just outside the capital, such as Paddington or Camberwell. The cost of a journey from the Bank to Paddington is 6d. Within the city itself, transport is generally left to the hackney coach, a large four-wheeled cab pulled by two horses, with its driver dressed in a bottle-green greatcoat and tall hat often the worse for wear. The fashion of the age is for bright colours in all things, for bright blues and vivid reds, but the hackney is generally of a faded hue, somewhere between green and yellow, with a dingy coat of arms painted on one of its panels. Its great wheels are often of various colours, perhaps in order to match their various sizes. Its small windows may or may not open, and the stuffy air of the interior is compounded by the damp straw laid over the floor. Some Londoners claim that mice, or even rats, take shelter there. Every form of transport seems to be going faster, but the hackney prefers to maintain its steady rate of 4 or 5 miles an hour, complete with sundry starts and jolts. It is never a comfortable journey. The number of passengers is an open question, generally debated between driver and passenger. Two are comfortable, while any more is a squeeze. In case of complaint, about the price or the route, make sure to make a note of the number painted on the metal plates at the side and back.

The hackney is the largest of its species but it is rivalled by smaller, lighter and faster cabs. The cabriolet is a one-horse vehicle with a folding roof, and it has adopted several forms to maintain a brisk passage through the great variety of city streets. In some the cab driver – or cabby – has a seat between the right wheel and the body of the cab, and in others, considered more traditional and therefore somehow safer, the driver is seated behind the horses at the front. The folding roof and open structure of the original cabs are perhaps not suitable in the noise and dirt of the city, and are sometimes replaced by a box-like form which protects the passengers. It is said to resemble a coffin, but it is convenient. The more elegant hansom cab has a relatively comfortable interior, with the driver at an impersonal distance behind the carriage and

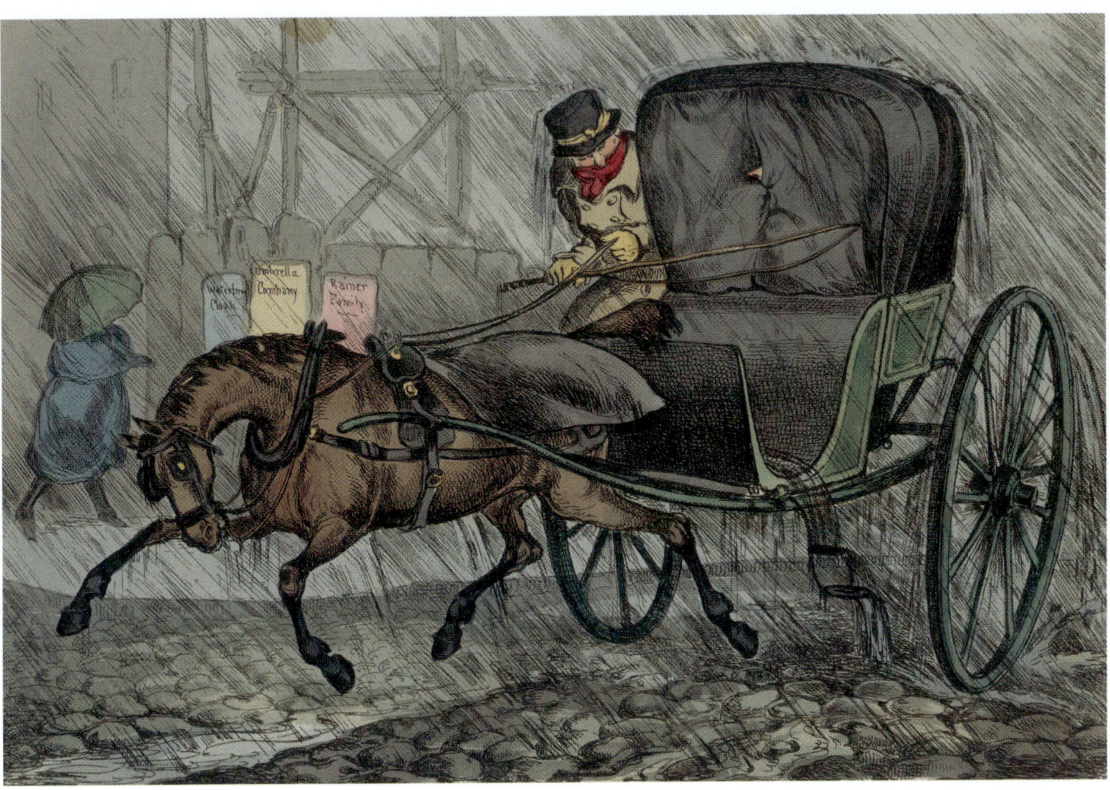

'Cabriolet or Shelter versus Pelter', coloured engraving, nineteenth century.

with the reins stretched forward for the horses. It is becoming ever more popular and, for some, it is now indispensable for any journey within the city.

When you hail a cab, two or three will often come at once, trying to cut one another off. The cab driver is well-known for his 'chaff' or repartee, often for his insolence and sometimes for dishonesty. Once you are confined inside the vehicle, he will sometimes take you on a tortuous route and then, at the destination, argue over the fare. 'What will you give?' is the first question. Since they are also notorious for their drunkenness and general bad manners, it is usually best to pay and have done with them. Then they have coins to spare for their 'dog-noses', a halfpenny worth of ale or a pennyworth of gin.

The new omnibus is, of course, to be found on the London streets. At first it was pulled by three horses and now, with a lighter design, by one or two. The number of its passengers is uncertain. Some say eight and some say 12, but the conductor, known as the 'cad', is more optimistic. When you hail a bus from the pavement or the side of the road, he will tell you that there is 'plenty o'room inside' before hauling you in from his station at the back. He wears a white hat, in contrast to the driver who is

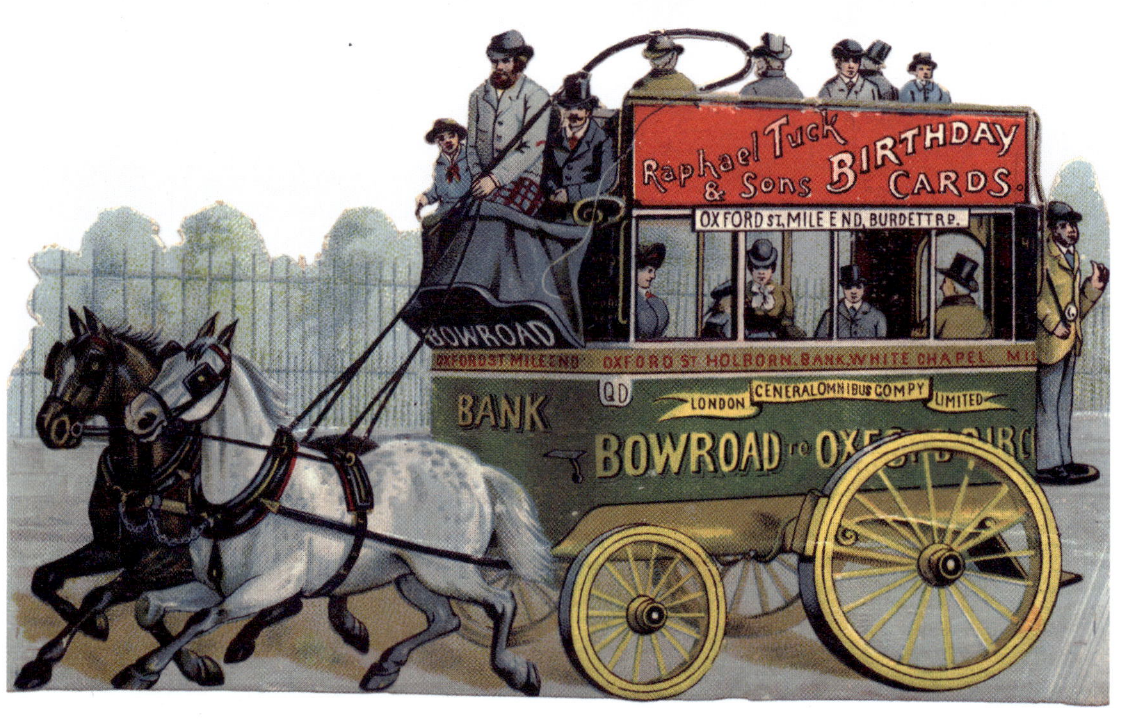

Raphael Tuck & Sons BIRTHDAY CARDS.
OXFORD St. MILE END. BURDETT Rd.
BOWROAD
OXFORD St. MILE END
OXFORD St. HOLBORN. BANK. WHITE CHAPEL. MILE
BANK
QD
LONDON GENERAL OMNIBUS COMPY LIMITED
BOWROAD TO OXFORD CIRC

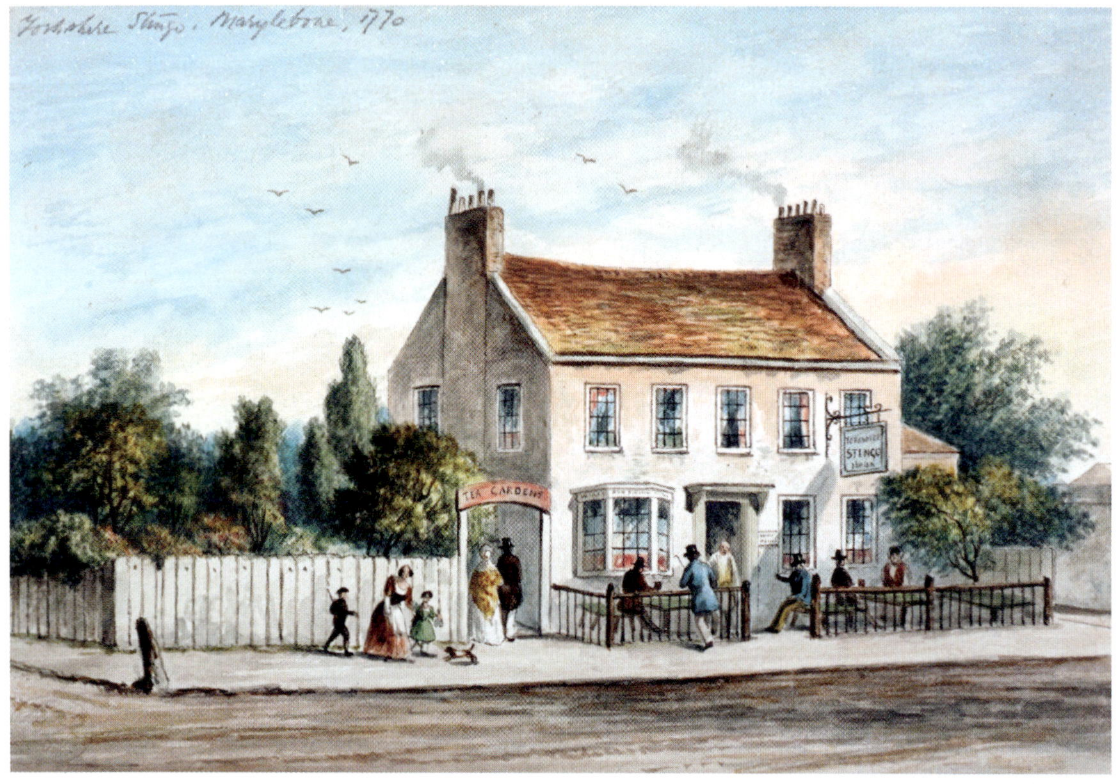

Yorkshire Stingo. Marylebone, 1770
TEA GARDENS
STINGO

crowned in black. You may find 12 or more passengers inside, male and female seated indiscriminately in a confined space, with assorted children, bags and parcels. On rainy days the smell of wet umbrellas is powerful. The long carriage contains some small windows but they do not close. Much of the interior is decorated by posters and advertisements. The bus itself is vividly coloured in bright red, green or blue, with the final destination painted in large black or gold letters on its side, but it can be somewhat dark and dingy within. The billowing coats and crinoline dresses of the women, and the stovepipe hats of the men, serve to obscure the light which, in London, is in any case usually grey. The men take their newspapers with them, but they are as difficult to open as to read.

The cramped conditions have been remedied in the last few years by remodelling the roof so that it becomes a second or 'open top' level, with a narrow bench fastened in the middle to seat four passengers on each side. The customers ascend by climbing a ladder of rungs at the back, sometimes with a little help from the conductor. The space is reserved for men, since it is considered indelicate to have a female seen from below. Rails run around this upper level to contain more people, who generally lean over them in order to contemplate the streets, but you can sometimes take a box place and chat with the driver.

The omnibus is generally considered a smoother ride than the hackney. It follows a familiar route and will stop at the customary places, such as a well-known corner or public house. The Paddington omnibus departs from the Yorkshire Stingo, a public house on the corner of Lisson Grove, and arrives at the Bank of England, passing along the New Road, Somers Town and the City Road. The buses along each route have a particular name, such as 'The Nelson' or 'The Royal Blue', and their own especial colour. Two leather straps run along the interior roof and are fastened to the driver's arms; if you wish to alight on the left, you pull the left strap to alert the driver, and similarly for the right. Over the stones and cobbles of London it can be an uneven and uncomfortable journey, but wood and iron are now used to cover the surfaces. In recent years, too, the roads are being paved with granite. The glutinous mud that still prevails in gaps and holes is known as 'licky'. The border between pavement and road is marked with stone pillars, but in some streets the kerb has been raised a few inches higher than the road. Elsewhere, a kennel or gutter runs down the middle of the road, so that all the remaining space on both sides is used for drivers and pedestrians alike. The driver cries out 'Heigh!' or 'Hi-yi!' to warn anyone in the horse's path. Despite the persistent crowding and confusion, there are few accidents. Everything seems to flow together in one continual movement.

Many different companies own the buses, and the competition between them to find and catch passengers is fierce. The driver will manoeuvre his horses to overtake a rival or to block his departure, and conductors – in equally high spirits – will vie with each other to take up people from the pavement. They call out 'The Habbey', 'The Benk' and 'Con Gardin' in strident terms. They cry 'All right!' and bang on the roof of the carriage as a signal for the driver to move on. There was at first no list of fares, and the conductor was able to charge as little as usual or as much as he dared, but as the bus companies grew larger the prices were fixed. The cost of 6d to 1s is too much for the poorer Londoners, however, and the omnibus is generally used by the more affluent. The first journey of the day is filled with office clerks and the second with their employers, the merchants, the bankers and the higher ranks of the Civil Service; at midday the ladies enter the omnibus for shopping expeditions, together with mothers taking their children 'for a ride'. In the early evening the vehicles are filled with those returning from the city to the suburbs, while in the opposite direction travel those who are 'out for the night' at the theatres or supper clubs. The horse tram or horse-car also takes passengers to and from the suburbs, such as Brixton and Peckham; it runs on steel rails to avoid friction, and as a result it is sometimes derailed. It is driven down the middle of the road and its larger size can be a problem for other traffic. Nevertheless, it is useful, particularly for the early morning worker. At 1d a mile it is cheaper than the omnibus, and it can carry more passengers.

With the roads filled and often congested, the noise of the city seems to be everlasting, but the traffic is only part of its uproar. The continual sound is compared to the tumult of an angry sea, or to the swell of the waves beating upon a pebbled shore. It is compared by some to the torrent of Niagara, and by others to the uproar of a distant crowd. Yet others relate it to the beating of a human heart, and it therefore becomes the sound of life itself, intimate and yet impersonal. It is always present but may not even be perceived by the Londoner, who has become accustomed to it. It is simply something in the air, but it is considered by some to convey the diffusion of human energy and to signal the spread of human power.

There are particular London noises, from the cries of the sweeps in the early morning, to the lament of the barrel organ and barrel piano in the late evening. The din from tinmen's shops, knife grinders, trunk-makers, coopers and cork-cutters, is compounded by the calls from fruit-barrow men and vegetable sellers, as well as by the harsh melodies of street musicians. A poor woman will sing, at evening, beneath house windows in case a copper or two is thrown down to her. Two men with a cart come along the street shouting 'Dustoy-eh!' Popular songs are often sung in a loud voice. Newsboys, eager to get rid of their last batch of papers, cry out, 'Ech-ow! Exteree special! Ech-ow! Steendard!' A brass band lingers over its last notes. Horse-and-cart organists are known for 'ear-stunning' noises. In many areas, too, the digging up of roads, the laying of pipes and the demolition of buildings are a perpetual loud distraction. At night the loud cries of the watchman, calling the hours, mingle with loud brawls and shouts of 'Stop thief!' or 'Fire!' The dark streets are invaded by sudden screams, while the sound of drunkards reeling home is always a nuisance.

One single set of noises is most persistent. The endless rattling of wheels is matched only by the clattering of horses' hooves, and the noise in the streets is sometimes so great that people can scarcely hear each other talk. It is mingled with the sound of carriages, coaches, landaus, wagons, omnibuses, carts and, of course, the endless hurrying footsteps which echo over the stone. Londoners talk louder than anyone else and, sitting by an open widow, you might believe that the city is one long continual shout. In some London churches, the weekday service is inaudible.

If two people in a cab wish to hold a conversation, they ask their driver to turn down a side street. There is a uniform grinding and shaking, but the roar can sometimes be subdued by taking refuge in an alley or courtyard. In the areas of Holborn and Fleet Street, for example, the sound is replaced by the relative silence of the secluded Inns of Court. Only on Sundays, when almost all activity is restrained by custom and tradition, does a

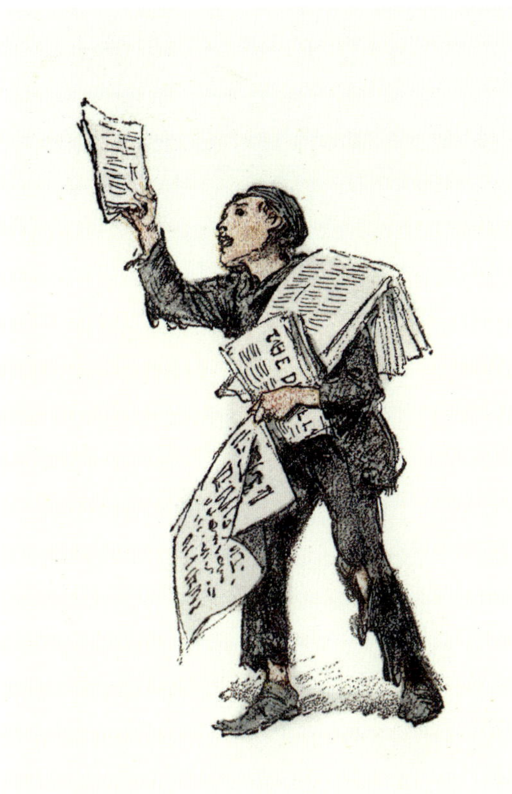

A Victorian newsboy selling newspapers in East London, nineteenth century.

dull quiet return to the city. Parks, zoos and museums are closed.
Concerts are not permitted and street bands are unacceptable.
River excursions are not allowed. The closed shops and the
empty streets give the appearance of a dusty graveyard.

A perpetual haze or 'mugginess', veiled through the rain, is a
familiar companion on any day in these streets. The rain, light or
heavy, leaves its marks in the mud or mire that covers the pavements
and roadways. The pedestrians will congregate in closed passages or
under awnings to look up at the grey sky. Advertisements begin
to peel from wet walls, and the houses themselves seem to be
weeping. In poorer dwellings the rain comes in through cracks
and holes, and is used for drinking water. The taste of London rain is
like the taste of smoke or of old stone. When the wind accompanies
the rain, it blows the refuse of the streets against trees, along iron
railings and upon the windows of shops and houses. The sun glows
like a great copper ball or is wholly obscured, and the houses so
overhang the streets that dawn and dusk are only known for their
darkness. Whatever the season, this is true London weather. Your
clothes are sprinkled with dust and soot, known as smuts and
blacks, when you walk through the streets.

And then there is the fog, particular to the city. It rises
some 250 feet above street level; from a distance the dome of St
Paul's seems to be floating upon a turbulent sea. The fog may be
bottle-green, or as yellow as pease pudding, but as it creeps closer
to the centre of the city it becomes a rich, lurid brown, turning
in patches to orange or dark chocolate. Everyone is aware of the
changes when it is interfused with a haggard streak of daylight or
when the wreaths of one colour mingle with another. It can come
and go rapidly; for a moment or two, the fog melts and reveals
a gin palace, an eating house or a corner shop. It is common
for Londoners to lose their way, feeling their path against once
familiar railings, walls and doors. To take a wrong turning may
be disastrous. Some do not go out into the streets at all. If you are
indoors, you will see from the window only a few blurred lights
beyond, and for the most part nothing at all but a yellowish darkness,
which causes the glass to reflect candlelight and your own blank
face. It often lingers for days, with the sky seen briefly through the
yellow mist; the walls of the buildings are shadows, the lights and
lamps burn less brightly. The gaslights are rimmed with a halo. It
belongs neither to the day nor the night. It can also permeate the
houses, where the kitchen or parlour is obscured by a thin bluish
veil. It may be construed as an image of sickness, too, since all

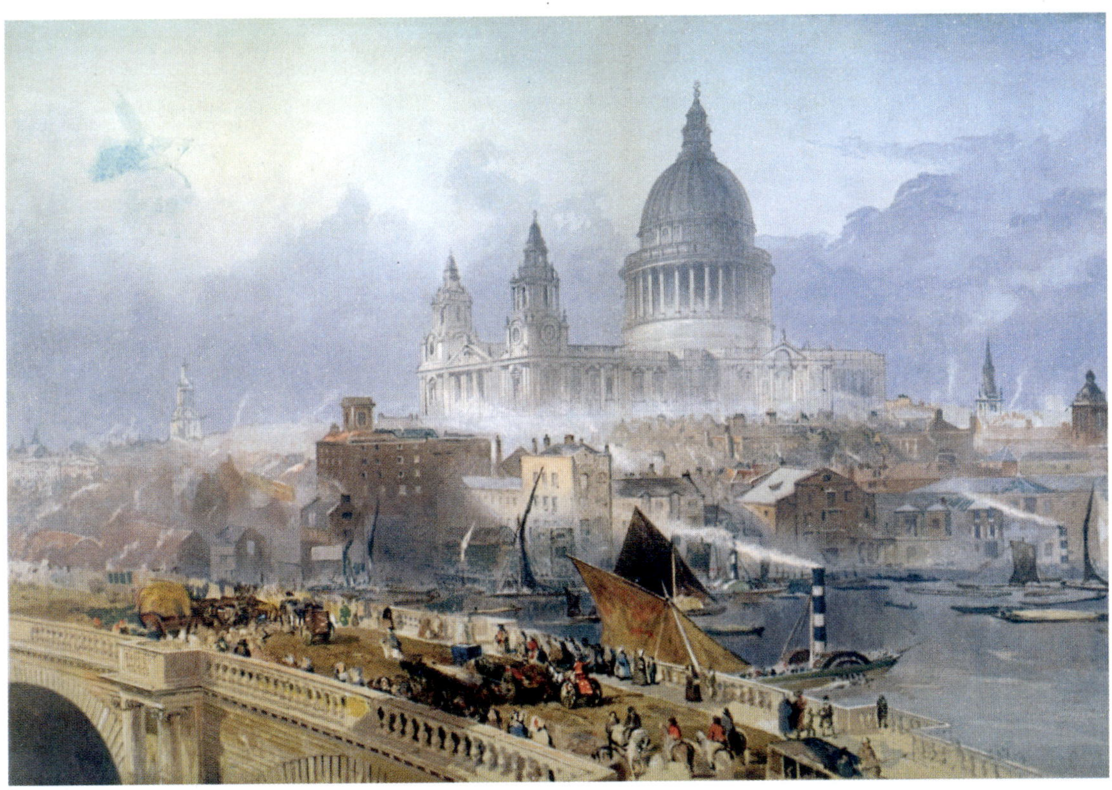

smell is a disease. It does indeed seize upon the lungs of the old and
the infirm.

At the heart of London – shall we say, at St Mary Axe – it
grows very dark, and sometimes seems to be a rusty black or, in
corners and alleyways, as black as fluid ink. It stops all the traffic
and threatens to choke the people still flitting like phantoms
within it. It captures the image of the city as a place of secrets
and of solitude. The sounds of the street are suppressed, and
the tops of buildings are swallowed up. The fog leaves its mark
upon the texture of the city, too, with the bricks of the houses
blackened or turned to a shadowy olive-green. London architects
are now beginning to clothe their buildings in bright red brick
or shining terracotta, so that they might remain visible in the
surrounding gloom.

When the fog lifts, if even for a moment, the winter sun suffuses
the streets with a red and lurid radiance. Along Piccadilly, for
example, its fugitive glow is reflected on the smooth varnished roofs
of the carriages that congregate there, and lights up the faces of those
who pass by. It gleams upon the golden ball and cross of St Paul's, and
the brick-built houses are for a short time red and bright. Yet the fog

of a London winter is still harsh. You wake in the morning to find a thick, grey, chilling shadow cast over the world beyond the window. The gentleman must shave by gaslight and take breakfast with all the candles of the candelabra alight. His carriage will be preceded by a torch. However, the poor man has no carriage and no light. The poorest of all will huddle closely with others beneath the arches, their breath mingling with the misty air, their heads hanging, their bodies shaking with damp and cold.

*

Londoners – women, men and children alike – know only the areas where they work and the districts in which they live. They also know the quickest or cheapest way to travel between the two, but the rest of London is unknown and unconsidered. Wherever they happen to be, that spot marks the centre of their urban world. It is impossible to imagine the city as a whole, and nobody contemplates anything but the neighbouring streets or the stores and markets closest to hand. The West End does not know the East End, and would no more travel there than to the Arctic regions.

Palace of Westminster (1878) by Giuseppe De Nittis.

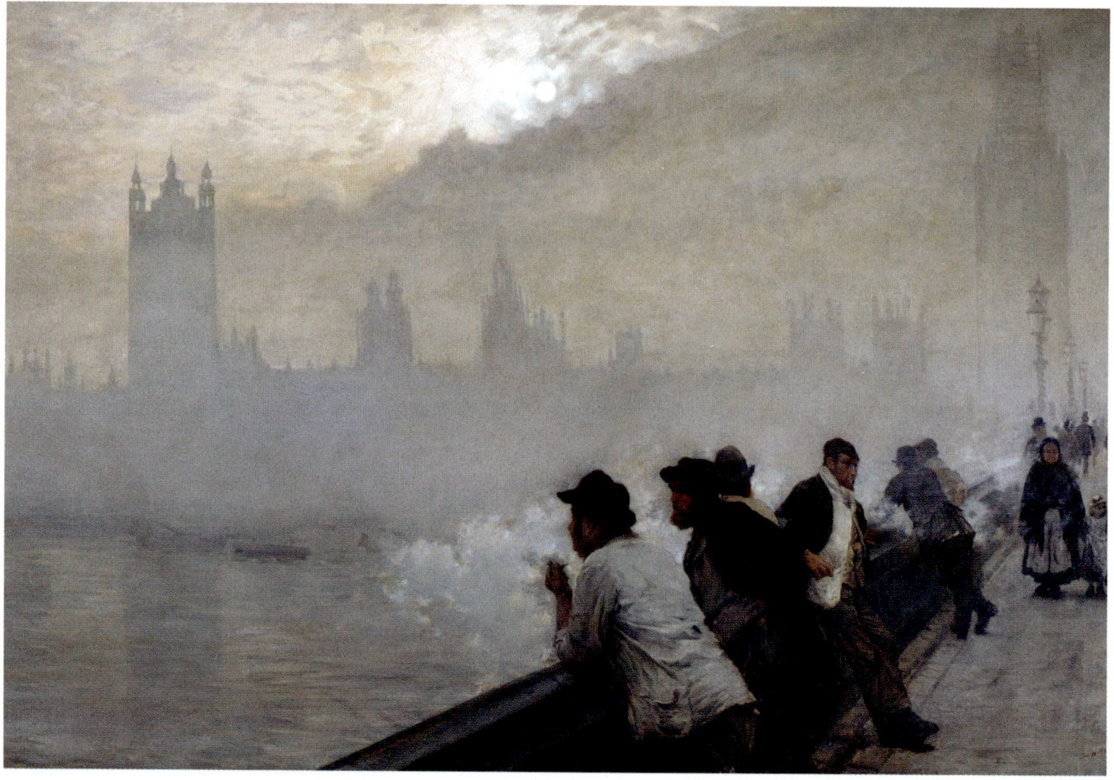

Stepney is only a word and Hackney is a mystery to those in
Kensington or in Acton.

For ordinary Londoners, east and west, their own streets are
their territory. The costermonger comes by, with his donkey cart
piled high with fruit or vegetables; sometimes his son goes from
door to door with a tray around his neck or a basket on his head,
but will also stop by the side of the road to attract passing custom
with the call of 'All ripe! All ripe!' The coster wears a cap or a
battered hat, with a red scarf tied around his neck. The salt man,
with donkey and barrow, is also welcome; he will cut as much salt
as you need from one large block. The knife grinders, the chair
menders, and the tinkers who mend pots and kettles, all make
their rounds at their customary time of day. More irregular hours
are kept by the young girls who sell lavender or watercress. The
fancy-ware merchants set up long and narrow tables with bracelets,
brooches, ear-drops and scarf-rings; these are always known as
'swag-boards' from which the traders make their profit or 'bunce'.
For the thirsty, sellers of ginger beer and sherbet abound.

In any mile of road you will find a dozen stalls set up for the
sale of fish, meat, linen, ornaments, pans, bowls, herbs, all cheaper
than those sold in the neighbouring shops. A woman stands by
a set of railings with a basket of flowers. A whiskered man in a
bowler hat carries a pole of skinned rabbits over his shoulder.
The geranium merchant is selling three pots for a penny. An
elderly man calls out 'Old clo!' with his hand barrow full of shirts,
jackets and trousers. Another in the same trade carries a variety
of stovepipe hats in both hands. The potboy carries a long stick
with jugs of stout and porter hanging from it. The muffin man,
with a tray of muffins and crumpets on his head, announces his
arrival by ringing a handbell. A young trader has set up a barrel of
shrimps on a pavement, and the sellers of shellfish find much of
their trade in the poorer quarters. They transact business in the
vicinity of a music hall or a theatre, and a whelk stall is invariably
found near a public house. Eels and herrings are also very popular.
Some ingenuity is needed to find the right 'pitch' or location. Of
the two sides of a street, for example, one is always better than the
other. This is a matter of intuition as well as experience. Your stall
should, if possible, be close to a cabstand or an omnibus yard, or
of course to a street market.

Other street people add to the business of the day. The long-
song seller carries song sheets or songbooks crying out, 'Beautiful
songs! Newest songs!' or, if the song is printed on a narrow sheet

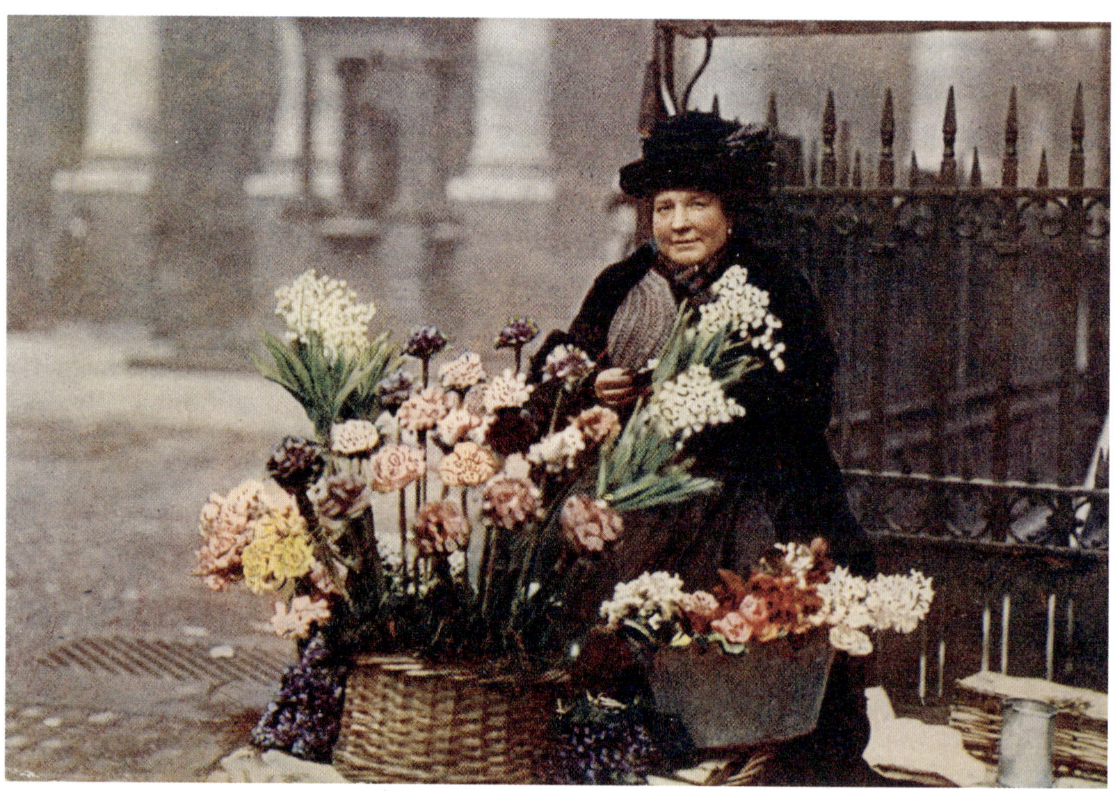

of paper, 'Three yards a penny!' The running patterer, with a
sheaf of papers under his arms, calls out, 'Murder!', 'Horrible!' and
'Barbarous!' They convey the latest news for a penny or halfpenny
a sheet. The baked-potato man and the penny-pie man are also
advertising their wares. On a summer morning you will pass a boy,
his face darkened with soot and dirt as tokens of his calling, crying
out, 'Weep! Weep!' On some streets you will see the Italian with
his ice-cream cart, then another Italian with his pedestal organ
and monkey, and then the Turk with a bundle of slippers under his
arm. The lamplighter goes by with his long ladder. In the public
house, on the corners of the street, the traders in boiled shrimps,
sheep trotters or pickled whelks make their appointed rounds.
The world is one continual market, with the cry of 'Buy! Buy! Buy!'

There are other calls. The dustmen shout, 'Dust-ho!' They wear
leather caps with an extra flap to cover the neck, and they ring
a bell to warn householders to close all windows and doors. The
morning milkmaids sing out 'Mee-yul-koo', 'Milk-ho!' or simply
'Mi-o!' They carry pails suspended on the two ends of a yoke that is
carefully shaped to fit their shoulders. They may also carry small
tin cans of cream. They wear white smocks and straw bonnets.

Every trade has its characteristic dress to attract customers. The
cat meat man has a black waistcoat and corduroy trousers, with a
spotted black and white handkerchief around his neck. The baker's
boy always wears white; the butcher's boy wears a blue smock and
a dark blue apron. They knock on every door and, in more affluent
areas, ring its bell with frequent pulls. Trade can also be a form
of exchange. A housewife might barter a sugar bowl for a shirt,
or a pair of old boots for a brush and broom. Everybody is busy.
Everybody has business to transact.

The street, or court, or alley, is itself an object of intense
interest. If a shoe-black is robbed of his brushes, or a cart
is overturned, people will stop and stare. If a pickpocket is
discovered, a crowd will gather to haul him to the nearest
watchhouse. A street 'row', especially between two housewives,
always draws onlookers who will join the catcalls of abuse or
sympathy. The arrival of a carriage in a poor neighbourhood will
often attract a group of boys, intent on seeing the passenger. If
you hail a cab in any part of London, adults and boys alike will
stop to watch you step in.

In this changing and growing city, anything can be of interest.
People gather in front of a house where a murder has been
committed or a burglary has just occurred. They gaze at the closed
shutters of a house in which someone has recently died. Passers-
by surround a fallen horse and encourage it to get up. If a horse
refuses to move in a thoroughfare, people will advise the driver
on the best way of spurring it on. Any fire naturally attracts a huge
number of spectators, for whom it is the best kind of theatre. The
appearance of a fire engine creates great interest, therefore, and a
crowd of people follow it.

Street entertainment itself takes many forms. Dancing dogs,
under the watchful eye of their master, perform on the side of
the road. Stilt dancers appear in the streets. A bear is led by a
rope and cavorts to the amusement of the bystanders. A donkey
carries monkeys, wearing red jackets, on its back. The strolling
minstrel and the wandering ballad singer are so familiar as to be
an intrinsic part of any neighbourhood. The same might be said for
the Italian organ-grinder. The ballads themselves fill the London
air, sung or whistled by apprentices and workmen. Some eight
hundred yards of wall on the south side of Oxford Street were,
until recently, used to display the song sheets; they have now been
replaced by new shops. However, 'Wilkins and His Dinah', 'Billy
Barlow' and 'The Rat Catcher's Daughter' still remain favourites

with London crowds. An impoverished couple, usually husband and wife, may stand on a street corner and wail, 'Will you meet me at the Fountain?' or 'Oh where is my boy tonight?'

Street conjurors and street jugglers, complete with pipes and drum, are also part of city life. An acrobat rolls out a narrow carpet by the kerbstone. On Tower Hill mechanical figures are set working, with the sign 'Please to Encourage the Inventor', and in Parliament Street a donkey pulls along a peep show entitled 'The Battle of Waterloo'. Children stand in line to peer through a 'Kelidascope'. 'German bands', not German at all but simply brass bands, are frequenters of the streets where their loud and harsh sound annoys many residents, especially when it is compounded at other times by Indian drummers and blacked-up 'Abyssinians' who play violin, guitar, tambourine and castanets. A blind musician who plays the violoncello with his feet, and a crippled trumpeter who drives around in a dog cart, are well-known in different parts of the city. A male performer, wearing a tall hat with tiny bells around its rim, plays simultaneously a drum, a pair of cymbals, a tin whistle, a concertina and a triangle.

The puppet shows are a travelling favourite, both among adults and among children. Punch and his Judy, accompanied by the Doctor and Jack Ketch the Hangman, always draw a crowd.

Public hangings of a more realistic kind are also part of city entertainment when many thousands flock outside Newgate and Horsemonger Lane gaols to see the latest malefactor despatched into eternity. It is treated as a holiday, when much food and even more drink is consumed. The top rooms of houses adjacent to the site are hired well in advance, and families and their children, walk to the execution from all parts of the city. It is considered to be a 'day out'. The large crowds are always in good spirits, with hoots and whistles and catcalls. The appearance of the gallows is greeted by cheers and applause. There may be silence for a second or two when the condemned are turned quivering into the air but, as they sway under the rope, there is a resurgence of yells and laughter. Violent delights are acceptable in a violent city. In the poorer areas dog fights are still arranged in basement rooms, in lofts or on waste ground; trained dogs also compete for killing rats.

Street entertainment can be theatrical. The lowest and dirtiest is to be found in the 'penny-gaff'. All it requires is a stage and a piano, and a penny for entrance. It is often a converted shop, with a back parlour that has been knocked through to accommodate a few wooden boards, which make up the stage. The customers

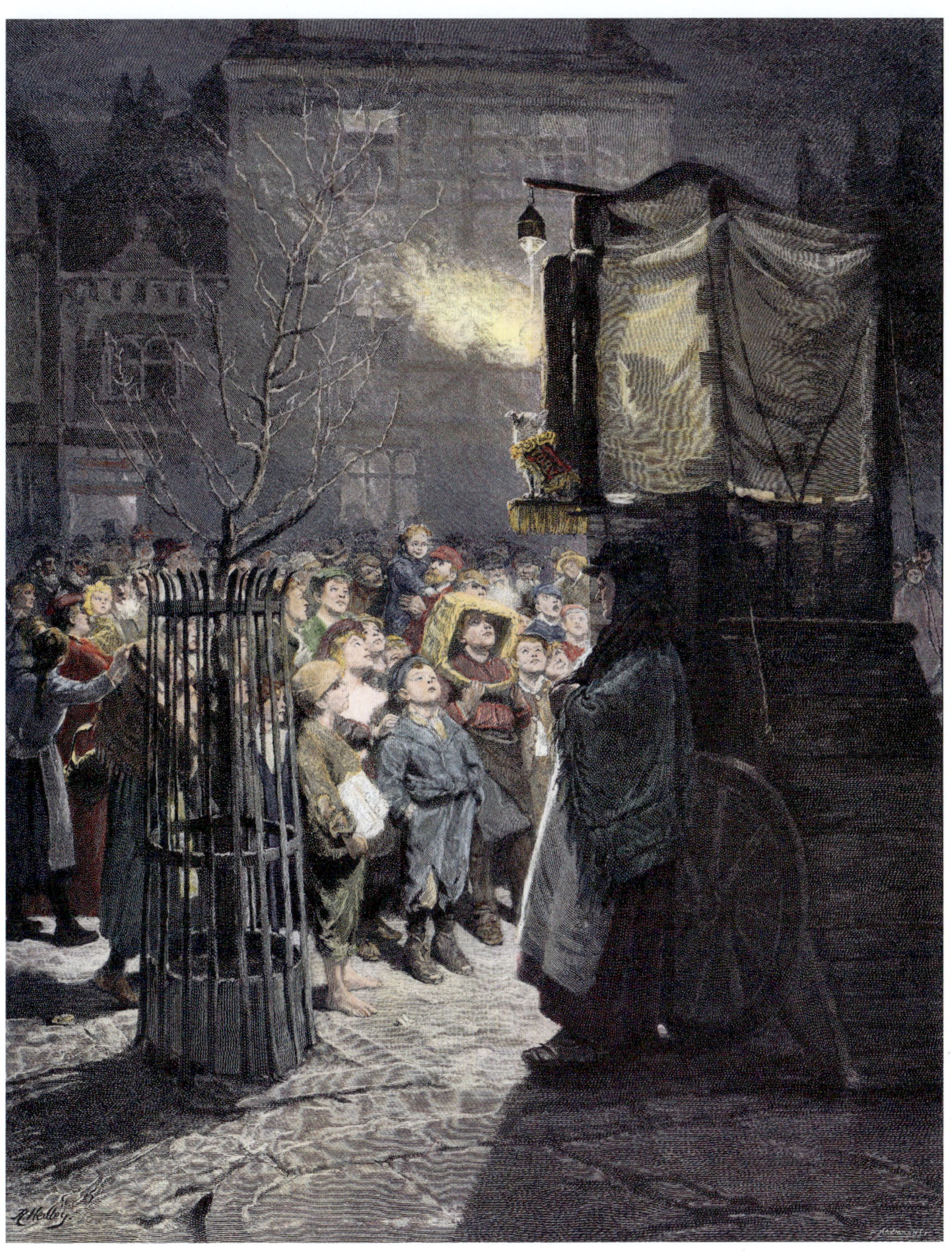

are costers, minor copying clerks, shop assistants, street children and ruffians of the neighbourhood with their women, who have come to see the story of the latest Newgate villain, the last days of a notorious poisoner, a battle scene distantly derived from Shakespeare or a ghost tale taken from an old tragedy. In the smaller gaffs, most customers have standing room only, but for popular shows a bench or two will be placed on the stage itself. The performers are introduced by the manager, who also collects the proceeds and tries to maintain a modicum of order. A better-sized hall can accommodate some two hundred spectators, many of them young and many of them female. The atmosphere in any venue is fetid, and most Londoners cannot endure it. The parts in the larger premises are taken by semi-professional actors who have perhaps once worked in the circus or are the remnants of a travelling company fallen on hard times. Two or three performances are given each evening, accompanied, or interrupted, by filthy songs and clumsy dancing. The comedy is broad enough, and the action melodramatic enough, to entertain what is by any account a rough audience. Once well-furnished with pints of ale or half-pints of gin, it is happy to spend hours watching these garish dramas, with titles such as *Seven Steps to Tyburn* and *Murder in the Red Barn*.

The private theatres, known also as small theatres or minor theatres, are much in demand. In some of them, members of the

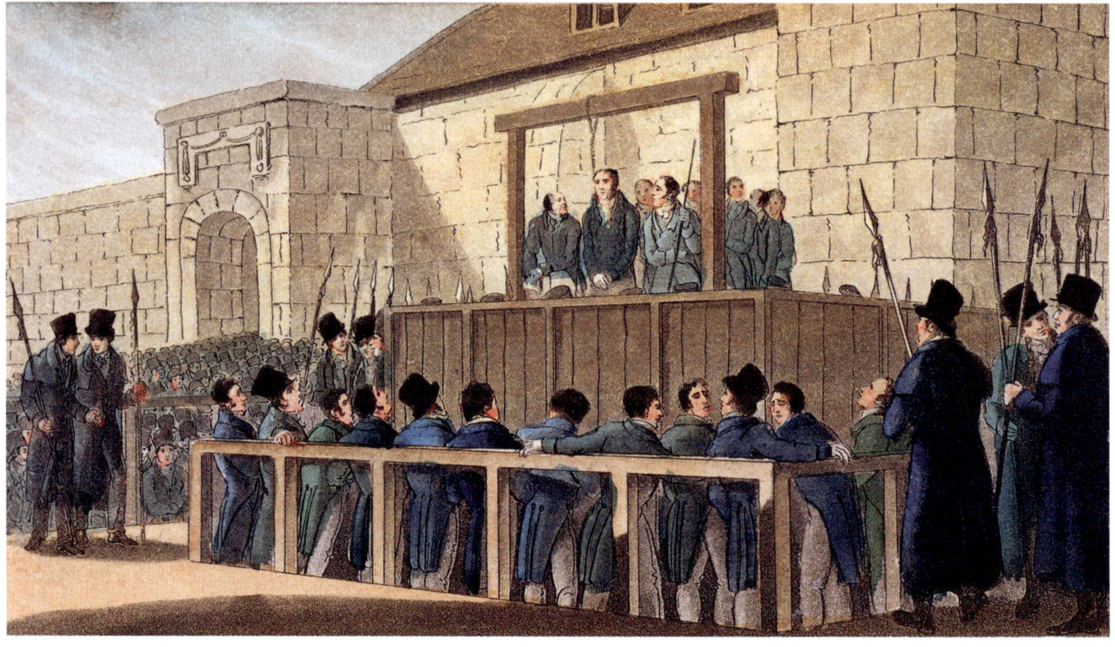

Below The public execution of John Thurtell in 1824.

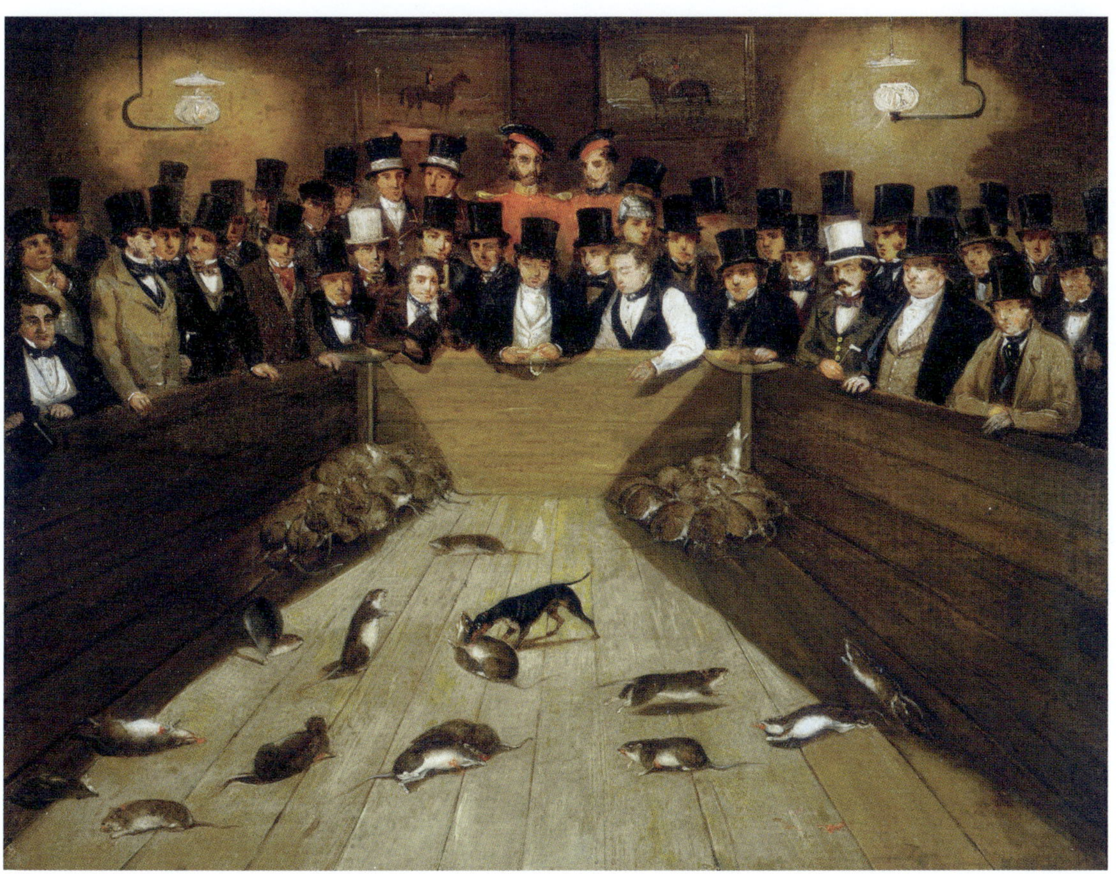

public pay a fee in order to take on roles in certain famous dramas. We may see Lady Macbeth played by a seamstress, or Hamlet by a butcher's apprentice. The passion for drama today is intense. Many observers see London itself as a grand theatre, and in small theatres, such as the Albert Saloon in Shepherdess Walk or the Britannia in Hoxton, the people are ready to assume any heroic or villainous character. This enthusiasm is also apparent in the more respectable amateur theatricals which are so much a part of middle class and even noble households. A theatre is created in a drawing room or a ballroom, with scenes expertly painted and the parts taken by family or by friends of the family. The action is rehearsed and the lines memorized just as rigorously as in a public theatre; invitations are sent out to a select few and the performance is generally followed by a dinner party for the assorted guests. The drama is more of a social than an artistic event. It may also contribute to the belief, held by some, that all life is play-acting.

In the various popular theatres of London, Gothic melodrama, sentimental comedy, domestic farce and romantic fable are interspersed with Spanish dancers or Italian opera singers; sentimentality is combined with grotesquerie, and pathos with sensationalism. Waiters from the neighbouring saloons will offer lemonade and ginger beer, as well as more intoxicating liquors. Among the audience will be the usual London concourse of mechanics, dock labourers, petty tradesmen, stay-makers, shoe-binders and other poor workers, dressed in fustian, corduroy and caps. Their wives or 'doxies' wear bonnets, shawls, muslin gowns and jackets. They revel in the adventures of Ali Baba. They love the horror of *The Castle Spectre* and the action in *The Siege of Gibraltar*. Burlettas, such as *The Jovial Cobbler* and *The Secret Avenger*, abound. Acrobats tumble during the comic sketches, and the figures of Revenge and Misery stalk through the melodramas. At Sadler's Wells, for example, you will see giants, dwarves, clowns, conjurors, posture masters and harlequins. Astley's Amphitheatre, on Westminster Bridge Road, excels in equestrian spectacle, where the horses perform as actors in a series of dramatic pieces; they mount the boards of a stage covered with

A performance in Astley's Amphitheatre located in Lambeth, considered the first modern circus ring. Etching (c.1800s) by Thomas Rowlandson.

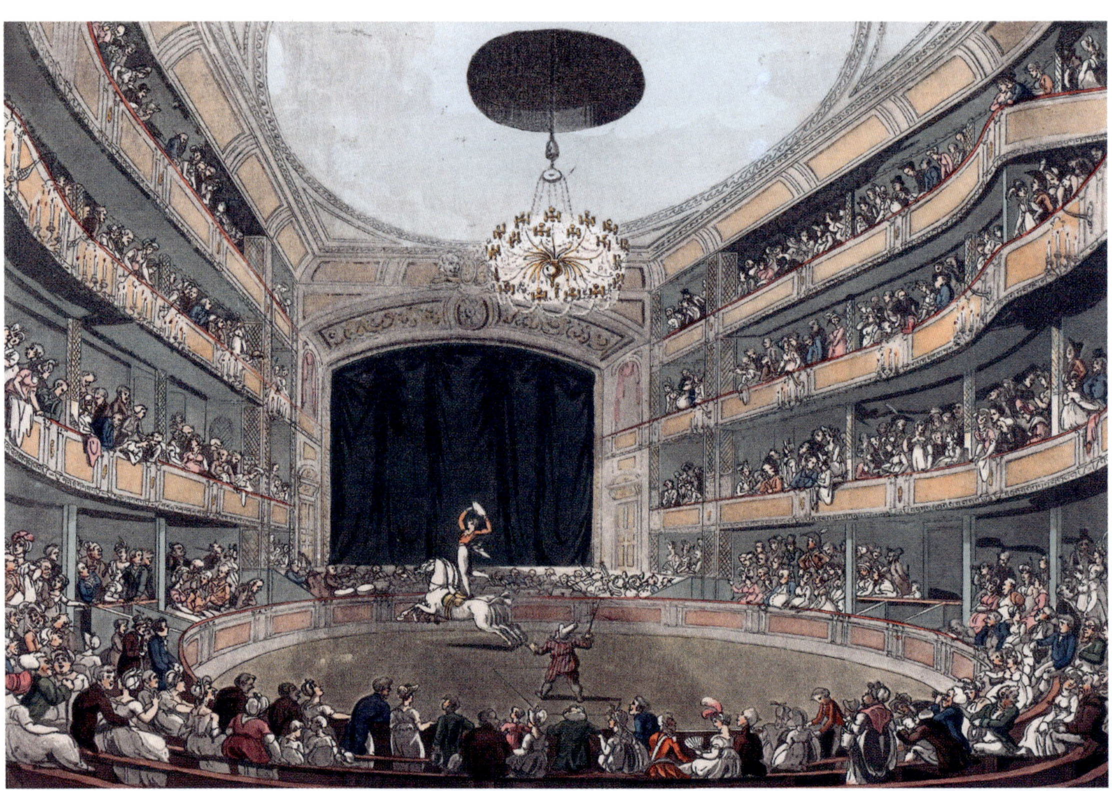

earth; they rear and they prance, they storm walls and ramparts
to the loud delight of the spectators, who in other circumstances
will be grave and demure citizens. The appetite for such productions
is immense, and a single performance may continue long after its
formal closing time.

Those in search of more informal pleasures will make their
way to harmonic meetings, song and supper rooms, or free-and-
easies, where musical and communal harmony are maintained. If
the life of London is harsh and impersonal, these venues offer the
prospect of relief and release. In the harmonic meetings communal
singing and individual performances are loudly applauded; three
men sitting at the top table will stand up to perform a catch, at the
conclusion of which a waiter will call out, 'Pray give your orders,
gentlemen, pray give your orders'; he is answered by demands for
'goes' of gin or 'goes' of brandy, together with all kinds of stout and
ales. The gathering will then attempt a glee, to general approval
and congratulation. These exercises in solo or group singing are
sometimes accompanied by conjuring, juggling and mock trials
under the general title of 'Judge and Jury Shows'.

These musical evenings are complemented by the appetite for
tavern concerts in such settings as the Coal Hole in Fountain Court,
the Strand, and the Cider Cellars in Maiden Lane, although their
fame is now being eclipsed by Evans's Song and Supper Rooms off
Covent Garden; from that venue has emerged such songs as 'I'd
Choose to be a Daisy if I Could be a Flower' and 'Look Always on
the Sunny Side'. The suppers are said to be equal to the songs, with
such favoured dishes as poached eggs on steak and devilled kidneys
seasoned with red pepper, or perhaps with anchovies.

Despite this competition, musical and gastronomical, the serious
theatres still prosper. The two largest are the winter theatres of
Drury Lane and Covent Garden, with the smaller summer theatre
at the Haymarket. These are the principal venues, with the prices
proportionately higher than the halls of variety and spectacle. Seats in
the boxes, arranged in a semi-circle around the theatre, are 6s, while
to enter the pit, which stretches from the orchestra to the back of
the house, costs half as much. The seats in the two galleries above
the boxes are 1s or 2s. These prices are still too high for the ordinary
Londoner, and the theatre is generally patronized by the upper
and middling classes. The boxes contain several spectators, seated in
rows one above the other, and they are as brightly lit as if it were
daylight. If the ladies wish to appear in the front rows of the boxes,
they must be in full dress, with gentlemen also in formal attire.

The ladies must not wear large hats. No lady will ever enter the theatre without a male escort.

Since the price of the tickets is so high, the spectators demand as much entertainment as possible, and the performances may continue from six-thirty in the evening to midnight or even later. A finale at one o'clock in the morning is not unusual. Two pieces are generally staged, the first in five acts and the second in two or three. The longer play may be from Shakespeare – *Much Ado About Nothing* is a favourite – or from a modern author such as the celebrated Dion Boucicault. After the third act, spectators are admitted at half-price. The final piece of the evening might be a grand pantomime, which elicits perhaps more enthusiasm than Shakespeare. The figures of Harlequin, Columbine and Pierrot appear with their familiar spirit of gaiety and are always welcomed by the public.

The old pleasure gardens are still to be found in Vauxhall, now a little the worse for wear and less fashionable than previously, but Cremorne Gardens has opened across the river in Chelsea. Cremorne has many attractions, including a theatre, a banqueting hall, an orchestra with a dance floor, several restaurants and a bowling saloon in the American style. It has its dark walks for those in pursuit of amorous adventure, as well as its decorative walks with many hundreds of bright lamps hanging among the trees. Tableaux are arranged with all the effects of sound and light; a large pond contains a figure of Neptune together with eight seahorses. Cremorne is also the site of the new rage for balloon ascents. Rival teams, suspended in the basket beneath the balloons, might compete on the speed they can travel or the height they might reach. A common enquiry before the start of any event is, 'What time does the balloon go up?' Vauxhall Gardens, on the south side of the river, still has its familiar temples and saloons, its theatre and its fountains, its supper room and its firework ground. Entry is 1s. It has also retained its rotunda for ballets and vaudevilles; the first acts of vocal or instrumental concerts are performed here, with the rest conducted in the open air. A 'celebrated siffleur from Altona', Julian Van Joel, has been hired for feats of ventriloquism and bird imitation; he wanders freely through the gardens so that he can jump out on visitors in unexpected places. He is very much like a Merry-Andrew and might ask, 'How are you tomorrow?' He is not to be confused with another performer here, Joel il Diavolo, who is advertised as 'sliding on a rope from a tower above to a bosquet beneath'. Slack-wire dancing, double juggling and Chinese postures are also

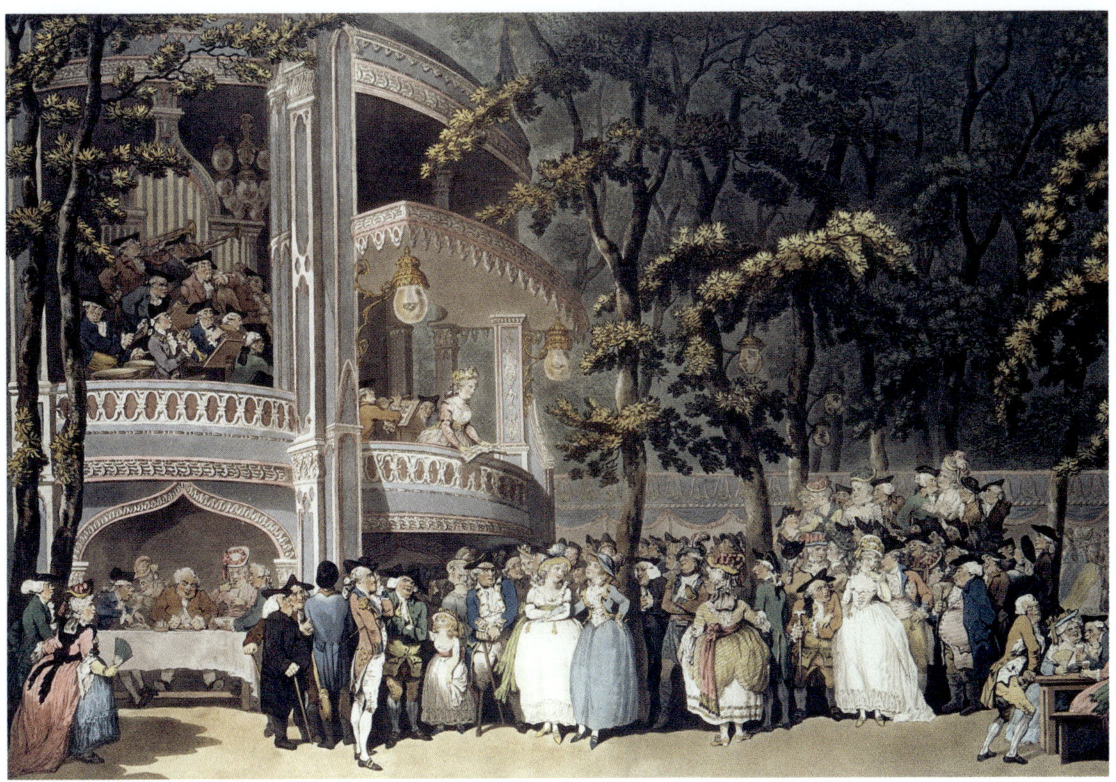

Vauxhall Gardens in Microcosm of London (1809) by Rudolph Ackermann.

provided at Vauxhall. Elsewhere, the diorama beside Regent's Park presents large translucent images of Canterbury Cathedral, Mount Etna in 'evening, sunrise and an eruption', as well as several rivers, cities and mountain ranges; the spectators sit in a darkened room as the images revolve around them. It also provides 'optical effects and laughable mirrors'. Entry is 2s. In other galleries of invention, you might see the gas chandelier, the self-acting piano and the clockwork waterfall.

The citizens also make their own entertainment. On a Sunday morning in winter, a family might take a trip to Waterloo Bridge with bread to feed the gulls. Winter also offers ice-skating on the Serpentine, in St James's Park and on Hampstead Ponds; summer allows outdoor bathing in the same localities. Spontaneous dancing takes place in the streets, between children and between adults; two young women, or perhaps two young men, will sometimes improvise a jig.

The parks are also a place of rest and recreation. The children ply their boats on the Round Pond, and nursery maids patrol the Serpentine with their prams. Apprentices, on their way to work in the early morning, try to catch carp or roach in this London lake, while many hundreds of the poorer people bathe in it. From a different vantage, Hyde Park may seem to be one vast meadow and give the illusion of being somewhere beyond London. The ground rises in gentle hills, with groups of trees on the summits and in the valleys; it extends far to the west and to the south, until it finds its boundary in bricks and mortar. The grass is fresh and green, despite the fact that everyone walks upon it. Even if there is no rain for many weeks, the mild and moist atmosphere nourishes it and fosters the growth of moss and ivy upon the bark of old trees. A slight blue mist hovers in the distance, through which can be seen church spires and towers. The London world does intrude upon this pastoral scene in another sense, however, with a throng of horses and carriages moving along the banks of the Serpentine into the more formal paths of Kensington Gardens. Between five and seven in the evening, the members of London society congregate here, partly to take the air and partly to be seen, if not necessarily admired.

What are known as the middling people – the clerks, the shopkeepers and their wives – generally frequent Hyde Park. Families picnic under the trees or form a queue at the refreshment stalls. There are occasions when a preacher will park his cart on a

The Serpentine at Hyde Park, c.1851.

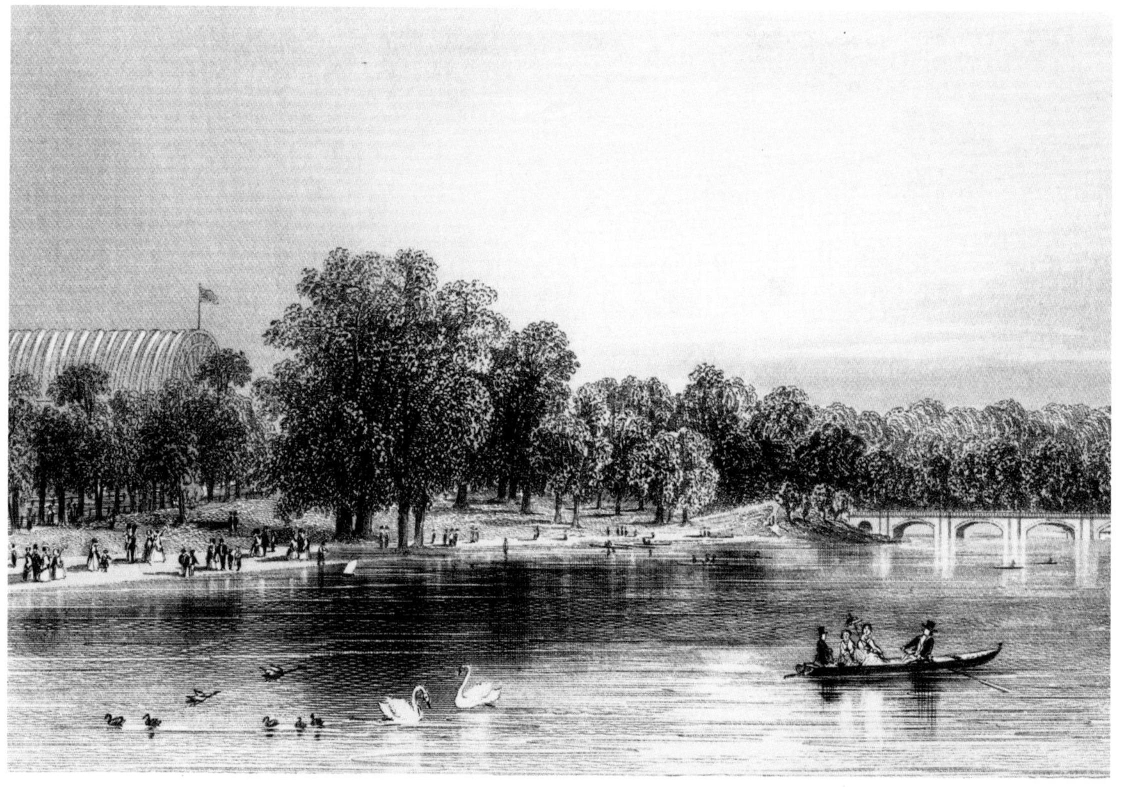

path and deliver his sermon to a few bystanders. Herds of sheep, cattle and goats are also to be found here; they keep the grass down and provide good manure. Cows are tethered in several stalls, from which are sold cans of fresh milk. St James's Park, however, has an ancient reputation for robbery and for indecency among the bushes. It is also used by vagrant men and women who have no other place to sleep. In recent days a notice has been fixed to the gates stating: 'It is hoped that the public will abstain from damaging what is cultivated for the public pleasure.' On another entrance will be found the announcement: 'The park keepers have orders to refuse admittance to the park to all beggars, any persons in rags, or whose clothes are very dirty, or who are not of decent appearance and bearing.'

*

The clothes of Londoners may be of the finest, or the most ragged. Many prefer a brighter or more colourful dress, which is believed to be legacy from the last century. It is not uncommon for a man-about-town to wear a sky-blue jacket, yellow waistcoat and olive-green trousers. Light yellow gloves are also acceptable. A young man might in contrast wear a frock coat of dark blue cloth, with trousers to match, or a dress coat complete with high hat. For an evening event he prefers a swallow-tail coat with a velvet collar; this is complemented by a voluminous satin stock and crimson velvet waistcoat. When attending a dinner, a guest might wear a blue dress coat, faced with silk and adorned with prominent brass buttons, together with a waistcoat of black satin and an embroidered shirt. If the clothes are considered too gaudy, they are called 'loud'. Other items of appearance are regulated. No respectable man will be seen with a beard or moustache. All gloves and items of linen must be fresh and clean. Plaid trousers have recently become fashionable, together with tartan waistcoats, and are called 'Scotch dress'. Trousers are also known as 'inexpressibles' because of their sometimes close fit. Sartorial rules also apply to the lower classes. Working men will be seen in their fustian or heavy cloth jackets together with Blucher boots of open lacing and great yellow waistcoats. Some will still wear breeches, stopping just below the knee, but many have turned to loose-fitting corduroy trousers.

Since the atmosphere of London is full of dirt and dust, clothes have to be changed and replaced very frequently. Every newspaper

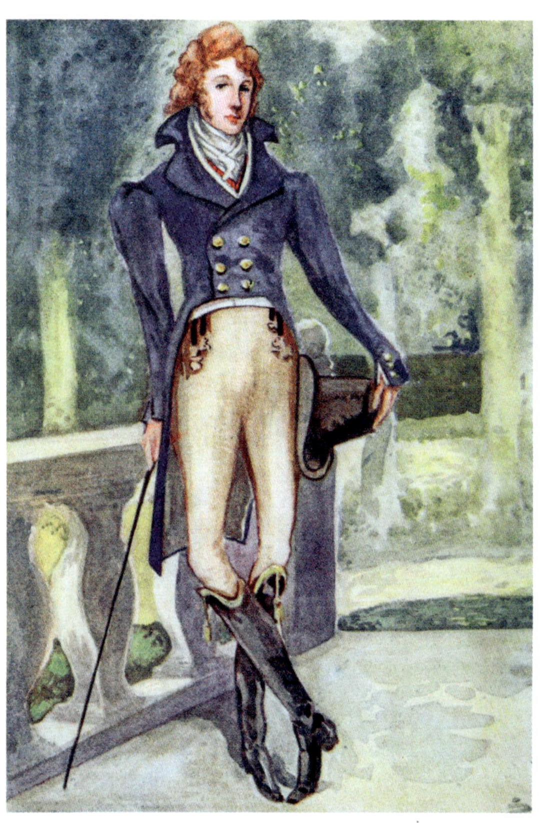

A Man of the Time of
George IV (1820–1830)
by Dion Clayton Calthrop.

carries the advertisements of dealers who will come to your house and buy your part-worn clothes. Immaculate appearance is obligatory for a gentleman. His suits, once past their best, go to a man of inferior rank and eventually end up in rags on the back of a pauper. Hence, one's clothes are a badge of social rank.

In nothing is the distance between classes so clearly indicated as in a man's appearance. Imagine the fate of a dandy's evening suit that has been discarded. You will see it next on a servant performing his duties and then on a junior clerk hastening to work in the City; as it proceeds downwards, it will fit a coster wheeling his barrow before being passed to a poor wretch huddled on some steps leading to the Thames. Finally, it will be taken up by a rag or rubbish picker who may find it useful for any purpose.

Hats are essential for all classes. A peaked cap, or a flat cap, is common among the working people. It is a token of respectability among street traders. Hats are worn even by small children and workmen will sometimes wear caps made out of paper. There are felt hats and straw hats, 'castor' or beaver hats, and pot hats. A bowler is also known as a billycock. A black silk hat is required for many occupations and, in recent years, a black dress coat with black hat and white cravat has become standard wear; a white cravat can be seen on barbers, waiters and even omnibus drivers. Costermongers, and other street people, will sport a silk 'kingsman' neckerchief, brightly coloured, tied around their necks. It is as much part of the street life as the tall hat or 'topper'.

A young woman of the working class will wear a dark-coloured gown (green is a favourite colour) with a Paisley shawl and a straw bonnet trimmed with red or blue velvet. Some will add to it real or artificial flowers. A cotton dress is usual and even essential; it is pinned up, to avoid the mud of the streets, and is covered by an apron. A maid might also put on a mob hat, a useful soft hat covering all of the hair, which may be decorated with frills.

Women of the upper class wear brimmed hats, riding hats and small bowler hats. For the middle-class woman, the circular crinoline is needed beneath the dress. It is important that people cannot glimpse the female body. At night a modest woman might wear thick woollen combinations with stockings of the same material; others prefer cotton drawers and a white flannel petticoat. The ornate and fanciful dresses of the day conceal a camisole, a corset and a petticoat. The corset is believed to be evidence of a well-disciplined mind and well-regulated feelings. However, there is always a demand for cuffs and collars, ribbons and bows. The modern woman dresses according to rank and status, of course, but also according to the location and to the time of day. The costume for a carriage ride, for example, is not the same as that designed for a promenade in the more genteel streets. A morning gown is quite different from an evening gown, and as many as four or five different changes of clothing can be prepared for the course of one day. It is not a question of dress being comfortable, but of being appropriate. To be appropriate is to be proper. Women can now come and go in the street without an escort, for example, a practice that had once been inadvisable. However, they rarely venture out in wet weather. The mud clings to the lower fringes of their garments, and an umbrella rarely covers the more voluminous outfits.

There is a want of taste in much modern fashion. The 'dome' or 'bell'-shaped skirts are sometimes outrageously crude with gold lacing, shocking green or flower-patterned materials, and upper garments are often bedecked with a multitude of ribbons and scarves, as well as floating gauze. The whole of this scaffolding can be badly matched, striped, fussed, overdone, with loud and excessively numerous colours each screaming at the others. If you tell a young lady that her clothes are more 'showy' than those in France, she will probably tell you that they come all the way from Paris! But all is change and variety. Female fashion changes much faster than for the male.

In general terms the female is commonly regarded as the weaker sex, prone to emotion rather than reason, weak and therefore subservient. Despite the fact that a quarter of women have to work in order to survive, the destiny of middle-class women is still considered to be that of wife and mother devoted to the peace and happiness of the home. They are supposed to engage only in 'fancy work', such as decoration and embroidery, to maintain the elegance of the house and to please the husband. They will be

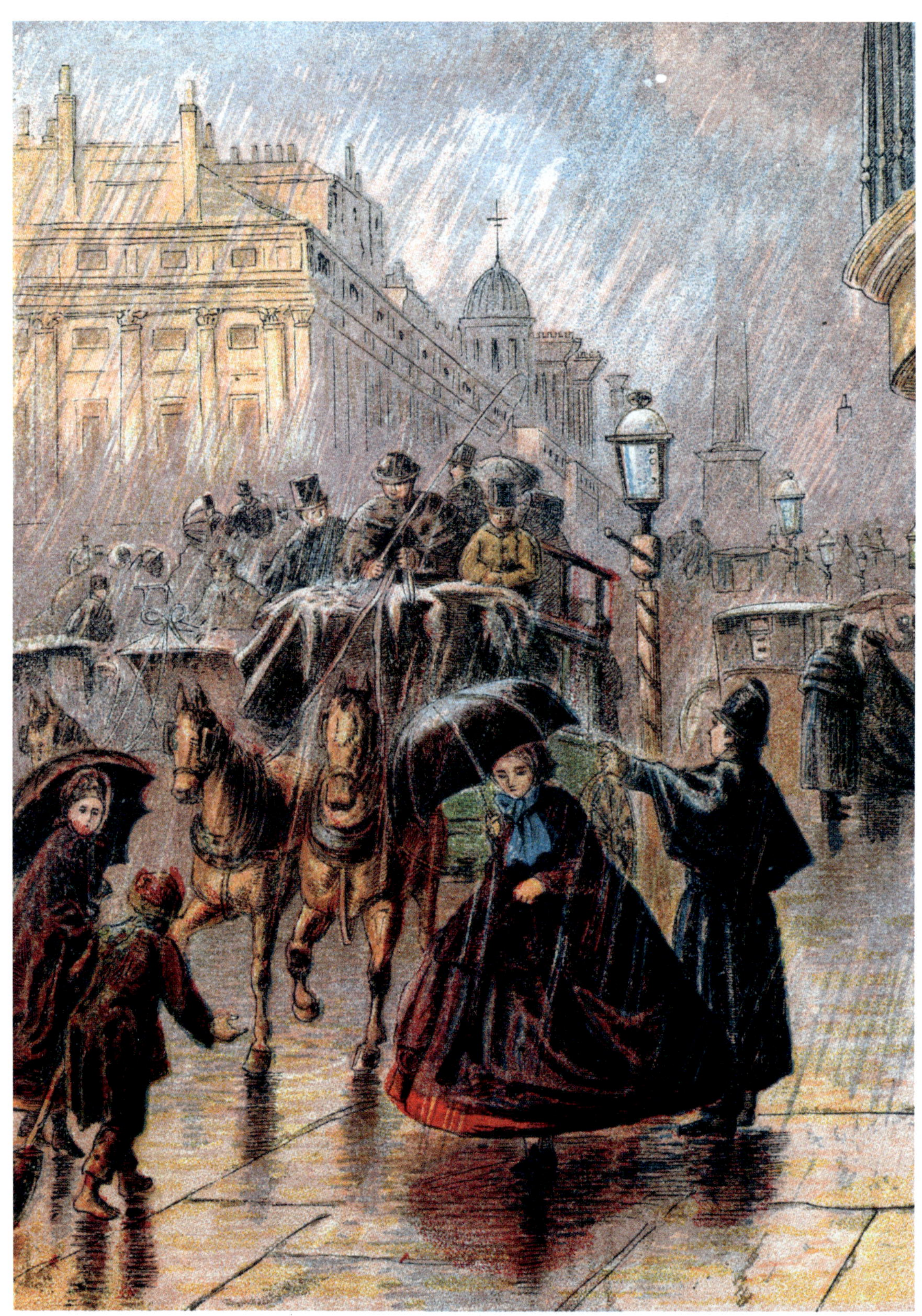

wary of expressing an opinion or manifesting their feelings. Silence is a sovereign salve. It is better to be gentle than severe, to appear ignorant rather than knowledgeable. Married women can have little recourse to the law. A woman has no right to control her property after her marriage, since in the marital state, as one judge has put it, 'the very being or legal existence of a woman is suspended'. The law does not allow a married woman to call anything her own. Her husband might sell her clothes if he wanted, and she cannot object. She cannot draft a will or dispose of her property without his consent. Despite these conditions, to remain in an unmarried state is still considered to be a dead failure.

If her role, however, is sometimes compared to that of 'a bird in a gilded cage', the reality is generally very different. The good wife, for example, is also a good manager. She must supervise the servants and of course also govern the children. In practice she will do more than administer the household. She will lend a hand in cooking and cleaning, taking up tasks which the servants neglect. If she wants a particular job to be done, in the kitchen or in the parlour, she will often do it herself. She will learn to argue with tradesmen and bargain with shopkeepers. As the mistress of the house, she must be calm but firm. Women are also often required to perform the duties of a sick-nurse for husband, children and various relations; quietness, cleanliness and love of order are believed to come naturally to her. She can of course make calls and receive visitors. Such occasions will last for approximately 15 to 30 minutes. She will be 'at home', perhaps on one day a week between three and five in the afternoon, when she greets and entertains guests.

The women of the lower class can have no such daily regimen. They must work in any conditions. They will be seen in the markets, selling fruit and vegetables or selling 'knick-knacks' to others of her own sex. There are female porters and female crossing sweeps, female vendors of old clothes and of old iron. The women undertake as many jobs as the men out of sheer necessity. On street corners and on busy thoroughfares, they offer flowers or combs or watercress or practically anything else, but perhaps the majority of women go into domestic service in the various roles of chambermaid, cook, scullery maid, lady's maid and general household servant. Many are washerwomen who take care of the household laundry. Others will go charring. A char is a woman of all work who will generally perform the hardest household chores, such as scrubbing, polishing and cleaning.

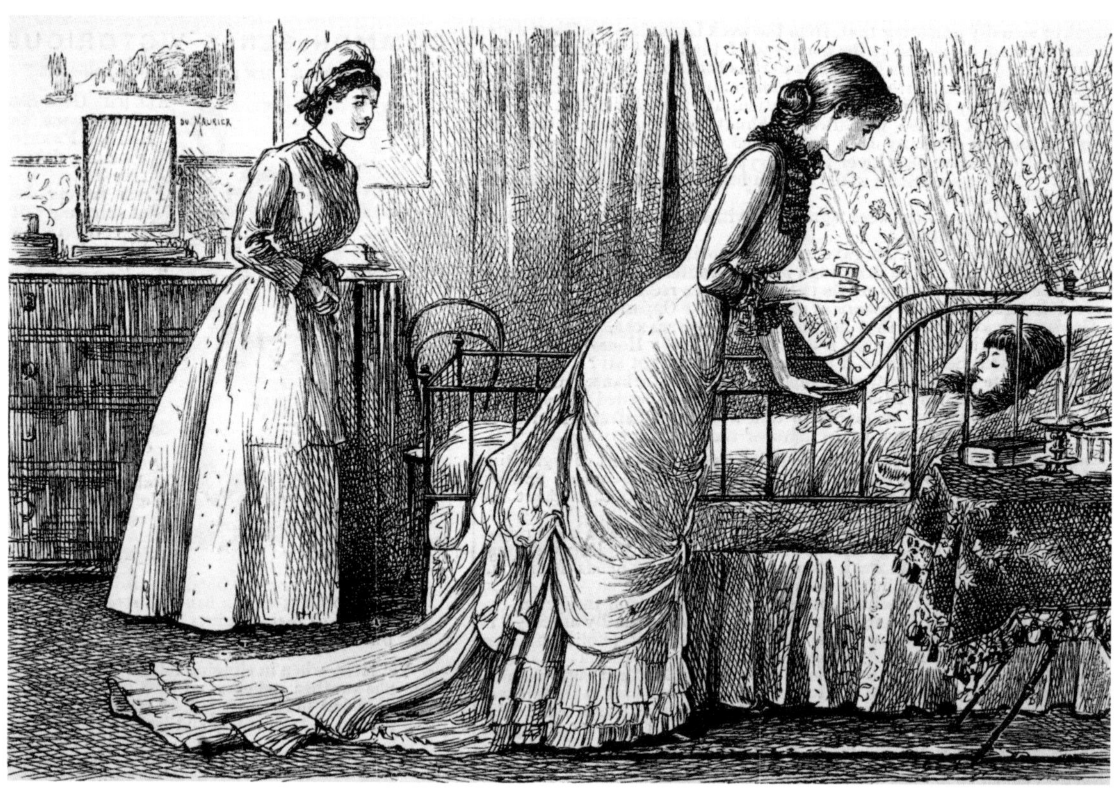

A mother and nursery maid checking in on a sick child (c.1800s) by George du Maurier.

*

The children of a respectable household are trained and disciplined to be obedient, quiet and polite. The doctrine of original sin, by which every child is born with the primal stain of sinfulness, is generally accepted by Christian families. So there is no need to spare the rod, and every reason to use it. Children must be good, or be punished. Stubbornness and anger are not tolerated; laziness and obstinacy are inexcusable. It is important that the imperious infant will is well-broken, so that it may be conformable to society in later years. You ignore the crying of a baby to teach it self-restraint. You feed your children only at fixed times to impress on them the virtues of orderliness and punctuality. This is to be firm rather than to be harsh, but as a result the relationship between parents and children can often by guided by convention and formality. In some families the children are separated from their parents by a phalanx of servants who will feed, wash and generally supervise them. Husband and wife may naturally prefer each other's company, and do not want to be unduly troubled by their offspring. Father is first, and then mother; the rest are subordinate. Some families are now more informal, however, and rely upon companionship rather than discipline. As a result, the children are treated with more indulgence than was once the case. There was a time when it seemed that the parents' only duty to their offspring was to marry them well.

A child's food is nourishing rather than enjoyable; at breakfast time, toast with a meagre portion of butter is acceptable. The top of a parent's boiled egg is considered a luxury. The largest portion of the general diet consists of meat rather than vegetables or raw fruit, which are considered suspect for the infant stomach. Beyond the provisions of the table, the mother is obliged to instruct her children well before they reach the age of any formal schooling. Both sexes will take the first stages in reading and perhaps of writing while still at home; the beginnings of numeracy are also to be encouraged. The boys will be despatched to school at the age of seven or eight, while the girls will often remain to be trained in sewing and crocheting. The girls may also take up piano lessons and will learn enough about figures to understand a shopping bill. Schools, in general, are often considered to be bad for hygiene and dubious for morals.

In these more indulgent days, adults and children will play games in the parlour, such as all-fours and old maid, or more exuberant games such hide-and-seek, squeak-piggy-squeak, Tom-come-tickle-me and blind-man's-buff. Toy theatres entertain middle-class children as well as adults, with miniature versions of the plays taken from the contemporary stage, such as 'The Miller and His Men' and 'The Castle of Otranto'. The scenery and characters are made out of pasteboard, penny plain or twopence coloured. Girls have wooden hoops and boys sport with iron ones. Spinning tops are also seen in the street, together with skipping rope, marbles and hopscotch. Street games, such as 'Jennie is a-weeping' and 'Here comes the duke a-riding' are favourites. Wooden toys, clockwork toys and ingenious mechanical toys can be found on the floors and in the corners of the children's bedrooms.

In contrast, the children of the poor will be left to their own devices or in the charge of an older sibling; they will run and play in the streets without restraint, with toys of wood or bone or oyster shells. This period of licence does not last for very long, however, since poor households consider their children to be a major source of income. That is why many adult couples want to have as many offspring as possible. It is a form of insurance. They can stay at home and assist their mothers in sewing or making small articles for sale.

They can beg and they can steal; cases are known of infants of barely six charged in the courts with crimes, but the majority will engage in casual labour. They can pick up pieces of wood or metal in the street, or collect vegetables from the sweepings of the market. Some find employment as apprentice sweeps or sweepers at the crossings. Others will become messengers or errand boys. They will hold horses for those who wish to make a purchase; they carry trunks for the omnibus passengers; they stand at the doors of the theatres ready to call a cab, especially if it has turned out wet; they help porters and cab men who are befuddled with drink. Young boys and girls, known as 'anybody's children', are hired by costermongers or market traders to 'cry the goods' and sell the stock upon a small commission or 'the bunse'. Another occupation for the children of London is to provide light entertainment for the citizens; they will, for example, turn cartwheels in the street or keep pace with carriages by walking on their hands with their feet in the air. Both sexes will normally start full employment at the age of 10, but can begin at four or five if required. The poor family cannot allow any of its members to be idle.

In fact, children are everywhere, and it is estimated that they make up the larger proportion of Londoners. It is a very young city.

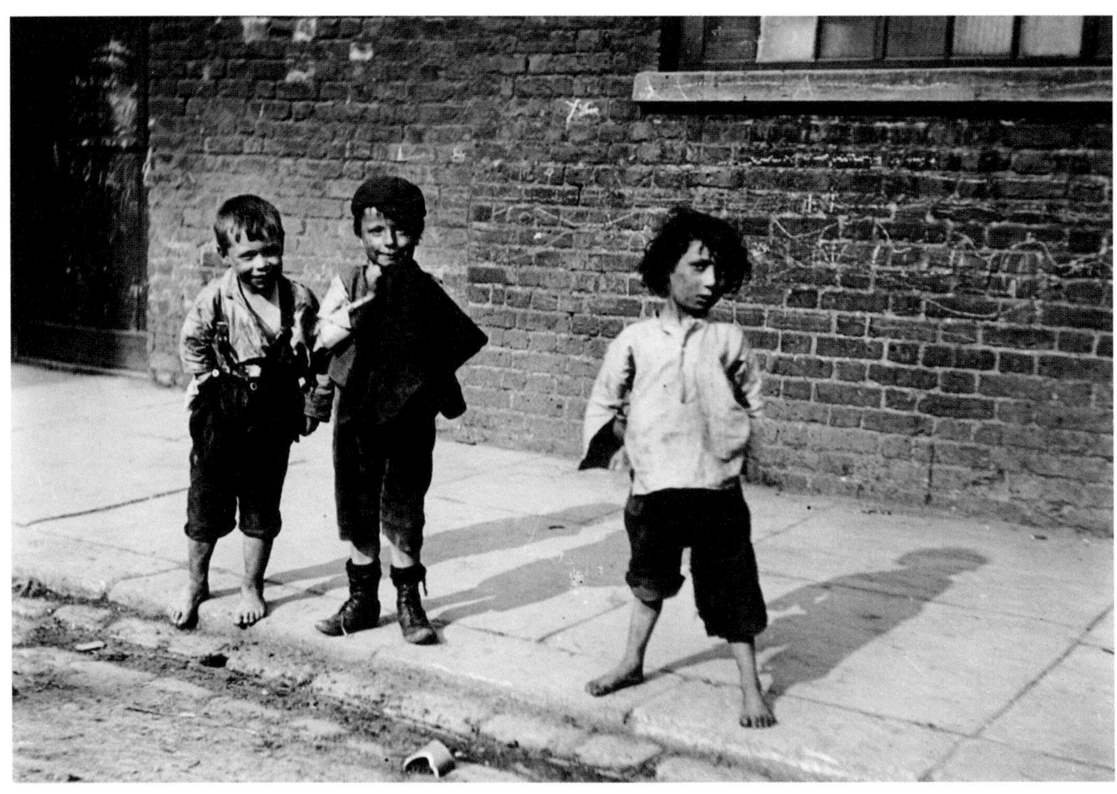

Below Children playing in Lambeth, c.1850.

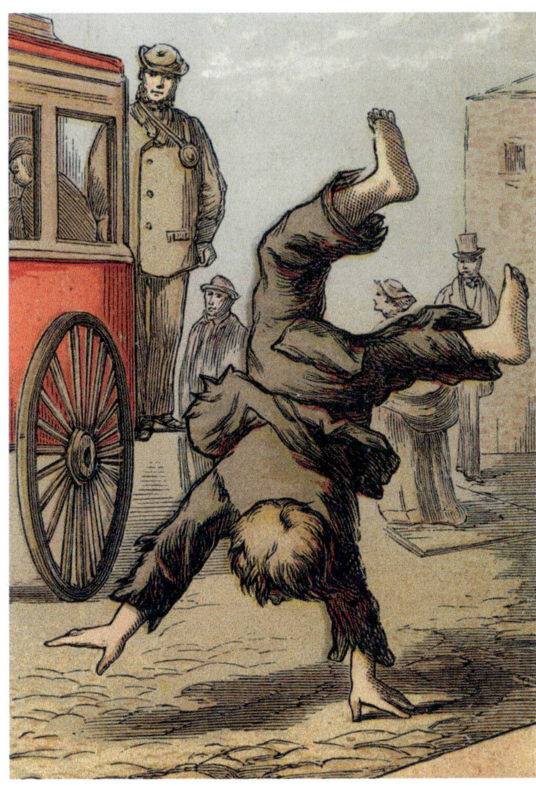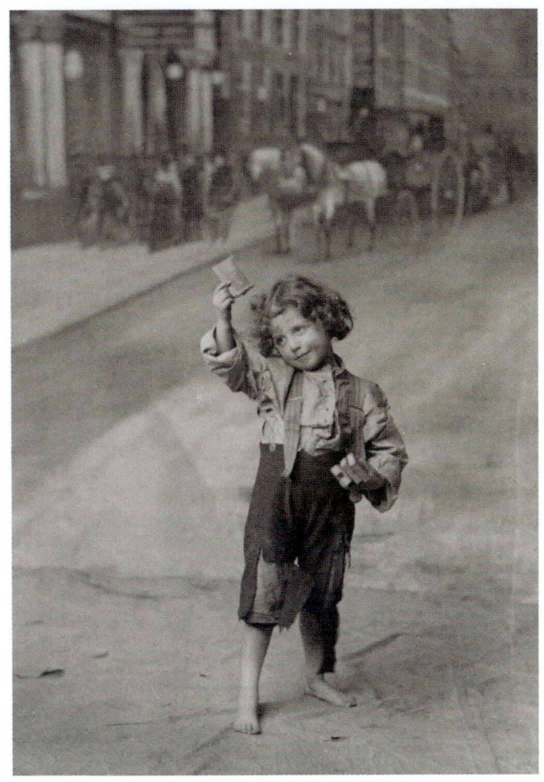

The number of those under 15 is 10 times greater than of those over 65, and it is inevitable that some of them will become part of the restless population of the street. The 'street Arab' is one of their number, by which is meant a destitute boy or girl in bare feet and with a few rags to cover them. You may see them wearing the ragged clothing of an adult, with a tattered greatcoat and pitifully torn breeches; the hat and shoes are often much too large, and a tin bowl is carried both for drinking and for cooking. These destitute children, of both sexes, may easily turn to prostitution – although this is rarely, if ever, discussed. It is said that no lad of spirit needs to starve in London, but it is also known that there are ways of living in the city of which most people do not wish to have any idea.

*

Prostitution is of course the profession of many females, young and not so young. It is seen by some as an alternative to domestic service. Working women, such as seamstresses and servants, are regular sources of supply. They may take to it as easy and profitable

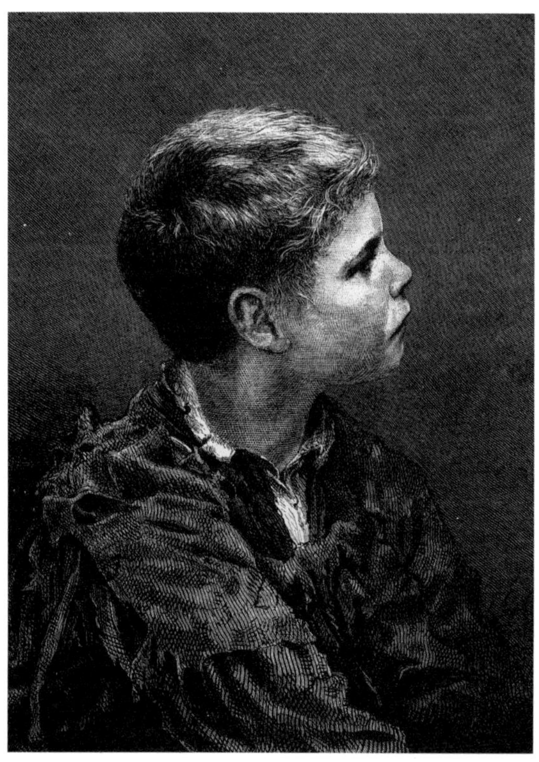

A side-on portrait of a 'street Arab'.

employment. The most successful are 'kept' by men of wealth or rank; they can be seen, dressed in silk or satin, on the more fashionable streets. Everybody recognizes them as courtesans, even the children, but nobody scorns them or insults them. Many will, in fact, admire them for their social success, even if they could not occupy a place in respectable households. They are sometimes known as 'Cyprians', although the term is also used for male inverts (those inclined to traditionally female pursuits and dress).

In the second rank are those young women who may have been educated to a modest level and are even genteel; certainly some of them pose as such. They are well-dressed and well- spoken. They can be found in assembly rooms and concert halls, or they are lodged in fine apartments where they entertain gentlemen in equally fine style. They may have started work as milliners or dressmakers, and thus acquired a taste for luxury. Others have been servants in houses or waiting maids in hotels, who have been seduced and the abandoned by the men for whom they worked.

They will have rivals in the young and pretty girls who come up from the country to advertise their charms. On first arrival these girls may find a welcome in certain houses of assignation, while others will make their way to the well-known streets where they can ply their trade. 'Are you good natured, sir?' is the opening remark of many. The most favoured spot is the corner of Haymarket with Piccadilly, and this area has become an open market or, it is said, a flesh market to rival Smithfield. It is no more than a highway of sin and shame. It is always an offensive place to pass, even in daytime, but at night it is hideous with its sparring snobs and flashing satins, its sporting gents and its staggering 'drunkies', its painted cheeks and its brandy-sparkling eyes, its bad tobacco and loud indecency. The conglomeration of foul elements will form a barricade before a gin shop or a low tavern, so dense that nothing can disturb it except the tawdry bacchantes blundering about the pavement. You cannot witness anywhere else such open ruffianism and wretched profligacy as besmirch those Piccadilly flagstones any time after the gas is lit.

Waterloo Road, at the end of Waterloo Bridge, is also infamous for the number of prostitutes with their masters or keepers who are sometimes known as their 'fancy-men'. Langham Place and Tichborne Street are always busy, and in fact many of the principal thoroughfares are useful for this shameful trade. The sisters of the street may dress as brightly as they can, to catch attention rather than to provoke comment, but some prefer black silk cloaks or light grey mantles as a sign of their calling. Their silk bonnets may be trimmed with ribbons or flowers. It is not difficult, in any case, for prospective clients to pick them out. These females might attend public venues like the Argyll Rooms off Regent Street and the Alhambra Music Hall on the east side of Leicester Square, or they might prefer the quiet corner of a local wine vault or coffee room. They take their clients to temporary lodgings in the area or to certain coffee shops which often display a card stating, 'Beds are to be had within'. It has been calculated that there are some eighty thousand prostitutes in London, but this may be an exaggeration. Who can know the exact number?

Some of them will be very young. There are reports of poor mothers bringing their children for sale to Haymarket and elsewhere; other children will come on their own to the usual haunts. The older prostitutes – and in this setting 'old' may mean 30 years of age – are often ravaged by disease as well as by time. The hospitals do not as a rule admit them, the dispensaries cannot cure them and even the soup kitchens for the sick will not help to feed them. They may plaster their faces to disguise sores or to mimic youthfulness, but they generally rely upon drunkards to make use of their services at very low cost.

Walk a little further into St James's parish and Leicester Square, and you will come upon the quarter where a number of gambling houses are established. The handsome gas lamp and the green or red baize door at the end of the passage mark these 'hells', as they are known, where the stakes vary from a £5 note to a humble half-crown. Although they have now been abolished, at least on paper, something of the kind is still going on in the same neighbourhoods. That is the story of London. Although the police force knows, or pretends to know, nothing about them, the gambling fraternity still come together under the lamplight amidst an admiring audience of pickpockets, flower-sellers and country folk who think that they are 'seeing life'. However, all the life they see is of low sporting ruffians with their strong-flavoured cigars and highly coloured brandies, their gaudy coat-links and

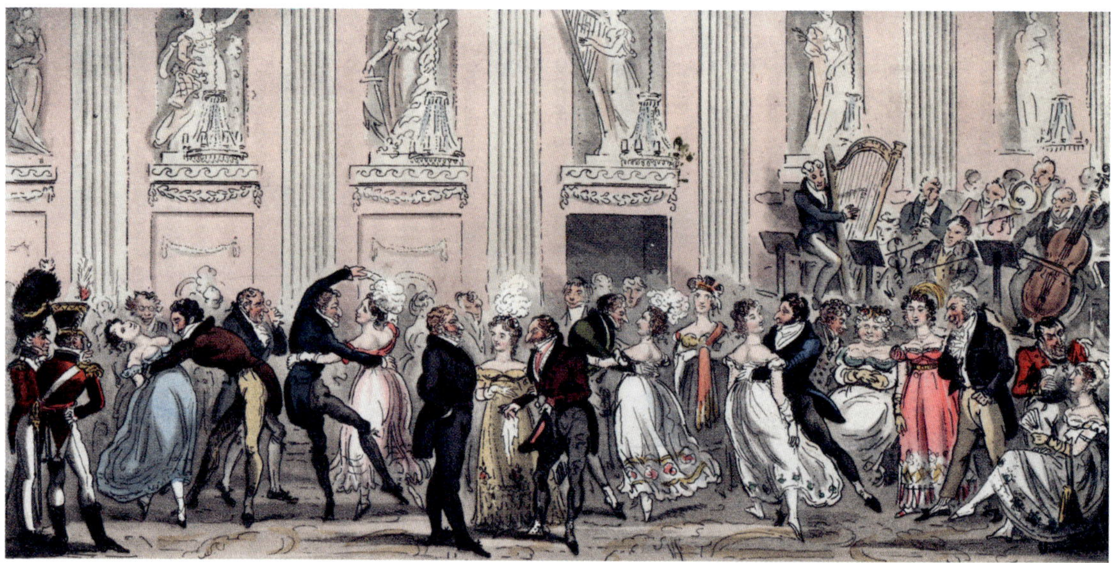

large breastpins, their ostentatious handkerchiefs and coloured hatbands. All modest ears and eyes are shocked by this scene of profligacy in some of the city's greatest thoroughfares.

When you walk through the streets your clothes are sprinkled with dust and soot; the compound of grit and powdered stone attaches itself to the skin and clings to the nostrils, so that you can never feel wholly clean. In some quarters of the city, the tables of the poor are covered with swarms of flies, while outside on the street, at the level of the hip, a broad, dirty mark is visible where the young men are in the constant habit of standing. In more affluent areas, small pieces of fabric are placed in front of the keyholes and muslin is nailed across the windows to curtail the dust. However, in dry weather it cannot be resisted, and in wet weather the feet of visitors bring in the mud that soon dries. It is described as 'dinginess'. It is everywhere.

In wet weather, too, Londoners are used to the soft and stinking mud which accumulates in the gutters, in the cracks within the pavement and between the cobbles. In the Strand there will be puddles of filth, while the surface of other streets will resemble a stagnant lake. The smoke from thousands of coal fires hovers in the air, and mixes with the effluent from factory chimneys. The conspiration of oil, gas and candle add to the effect. Some citizens seem to love the smell of it, and profess to be at a loss without it. However, in the tortuous lanes and alleys, where there is little passage of air, a residue of soot and grease will stick to the houses and walls. The brick and stone become filthy.

The 'flying dustmen', their carts pulled by a single horse, take away the dross and refuse from rateable houses in every parish. The fine dust is used for making stock London bricks, and the coarse dust or 'breeze' is also employed for mixing with mortar. The contents of dust carts will include rags, bones, fragments of metal, old boots and other assorted articles. They form the dust mounds and dust heaps all over London; these large piles of waste are the object of female scavengers known as 'bunters', who stand up to their thighs in the accumulated rubbish and breathe the corrupted air, but they are also a very profitable source of business for the contractors who sell on the scrap and waste. Everything has a price. Oyster shells can be used a form of insulation for houses, for example, and old shoes can be boiled for dye.

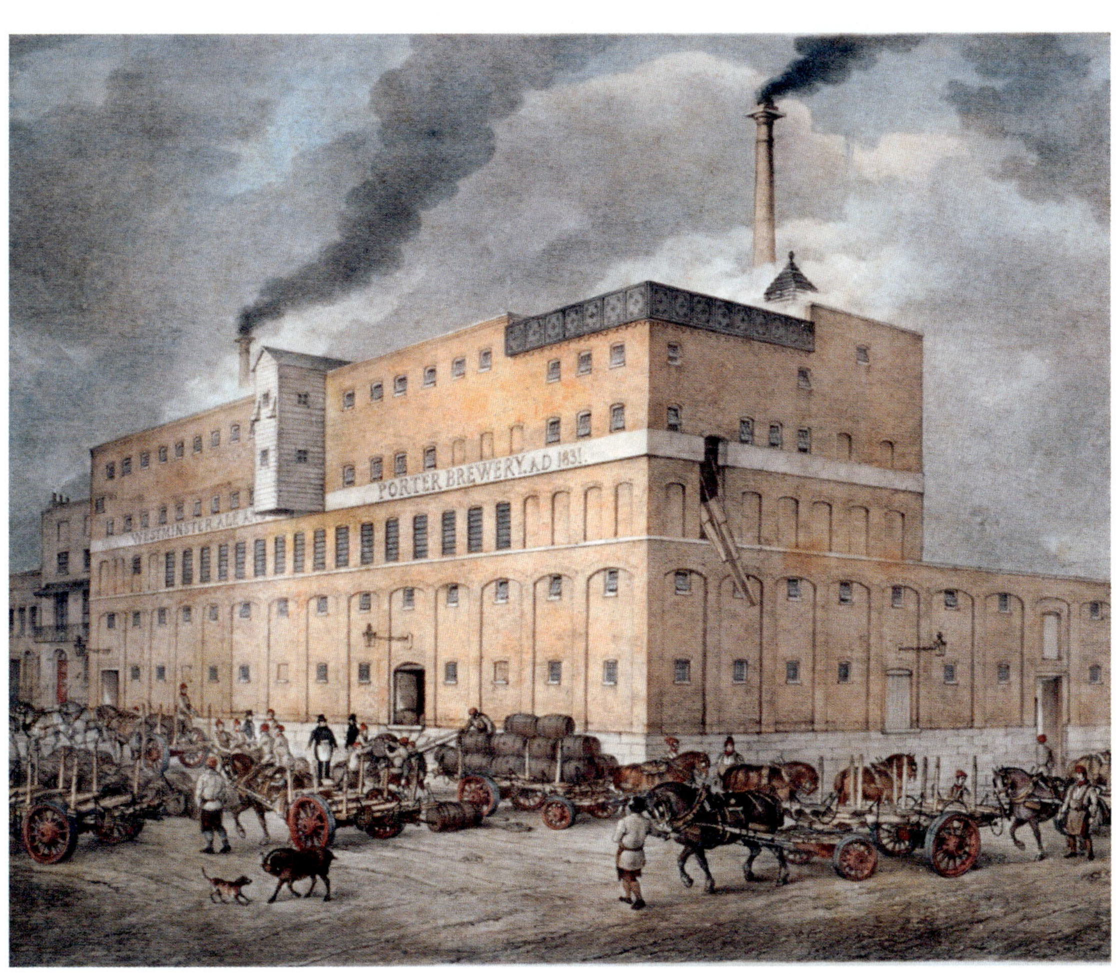

Below Westminster Ale and Porter Brewery on Horseferry Road, London (c.1840) by C. Warren.

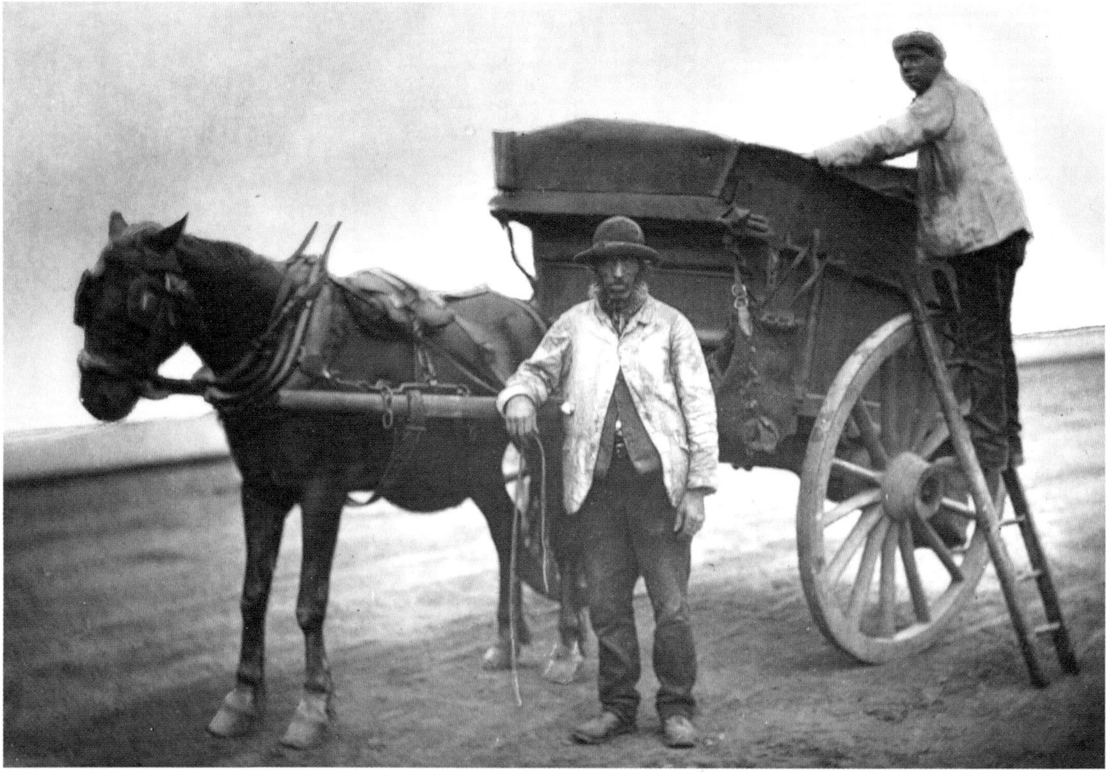

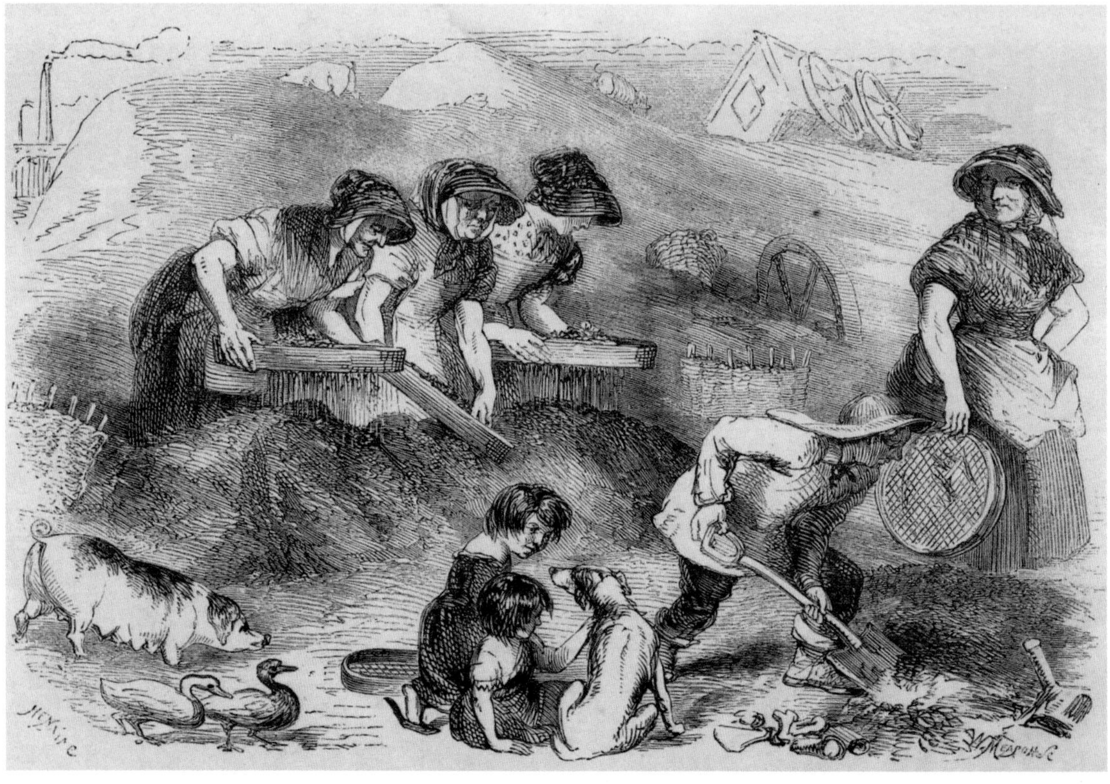

*

In London, no one is ever wholly well. That is why it is known
as the Great Wen, the Oven, the Fever Patch and the Smoke. The
mortality rates are a direct reflection of your social rank and of the
district in which you live. The average age of death for a middle-
class man in Bethnal Green is 45, that of a tradesman is 26 and
that of a labourer is 16; in Kensington, the equivalent ages are 44,
29 and 26. It is unusual for any male Londoner to live above 50.
The death of children, under the age of five, varies from a third to
a quarter of all new births. The large number of deaths, of both
young and old, is of course a bonus to the medical profession;
the bodies of those who die in the workhouses are available for
dissection in the medical schools.

In the closely packed streets and houses, where one family
may inhabit a room and where the available water may smell or
have a brownish tint, some of the greatest dangers concern typhoid,
dysentery and influenza. Asiatic cholera has recently become a city
killer, with the early symptoms of violent vomiting and continual
diarrhoea leading to total dehydration and an agonizing death. It
is not certainly known how it starts or how it is transmitted. It is
widely known that all disease is spread by smell, but some argue
that it can be conveyed by breath or touch. Others speculate that
the noxious taste of the water, coming from the local pumps and
the standpipes, might be related to the spread of what has become
known as 'the blue death'. One other point can be made. It is
common enough to catch fleas from a journey in cab or omnibus,
and that connection should not be ruled out. Public disinfectors,
dragging a sealed handcart behind them, are now observed in
the major thoroughfares; they wear long white blouses and white
leggings in order to protect themselves from any contagion.

Many neighbourhoods have also been invaded by bouts of
smallpox and scarlet fever. It is common enough to see Londoners
with scarred and pitted faces, and some can become blind from
either condition. A large number also suffer from one physical
debility or another, such as a curved spine or an amputated limb.
The death of children is often put down to convulsions, although
it is not clear what causes them. Children in the poorer areas of the
city are, in general, pale and sickly. It hardly needs to be mentioned
that everyone, without exception, suffers from coughs, blocked
noses, headaches and a score of other ailments. Those affected are

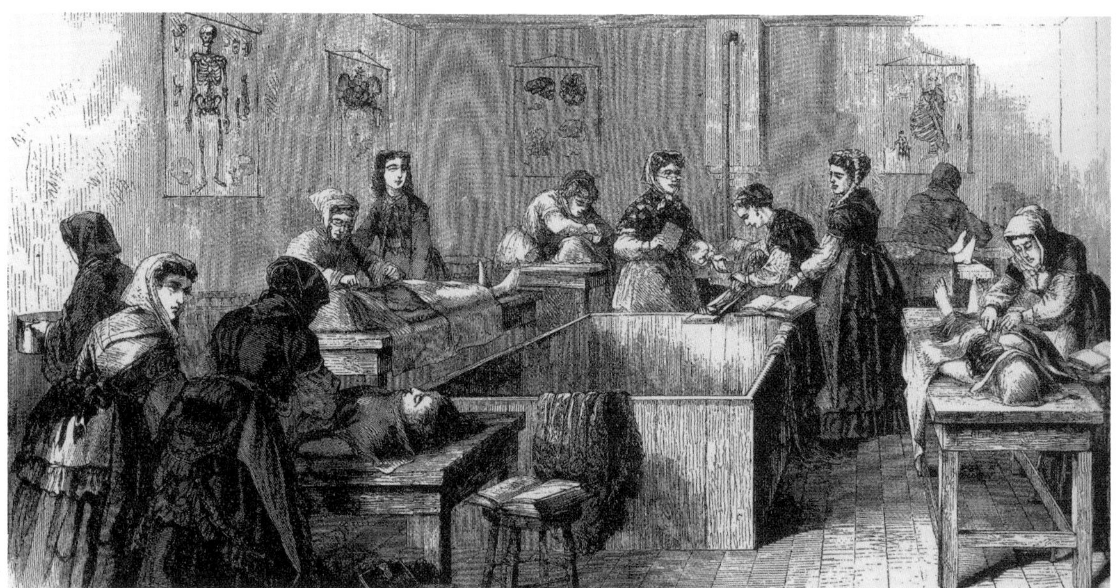

Above   An anatomy class
dissection with female
medical students.

Right   A photograph of
public disinfectors dressed
in white, c.1877.

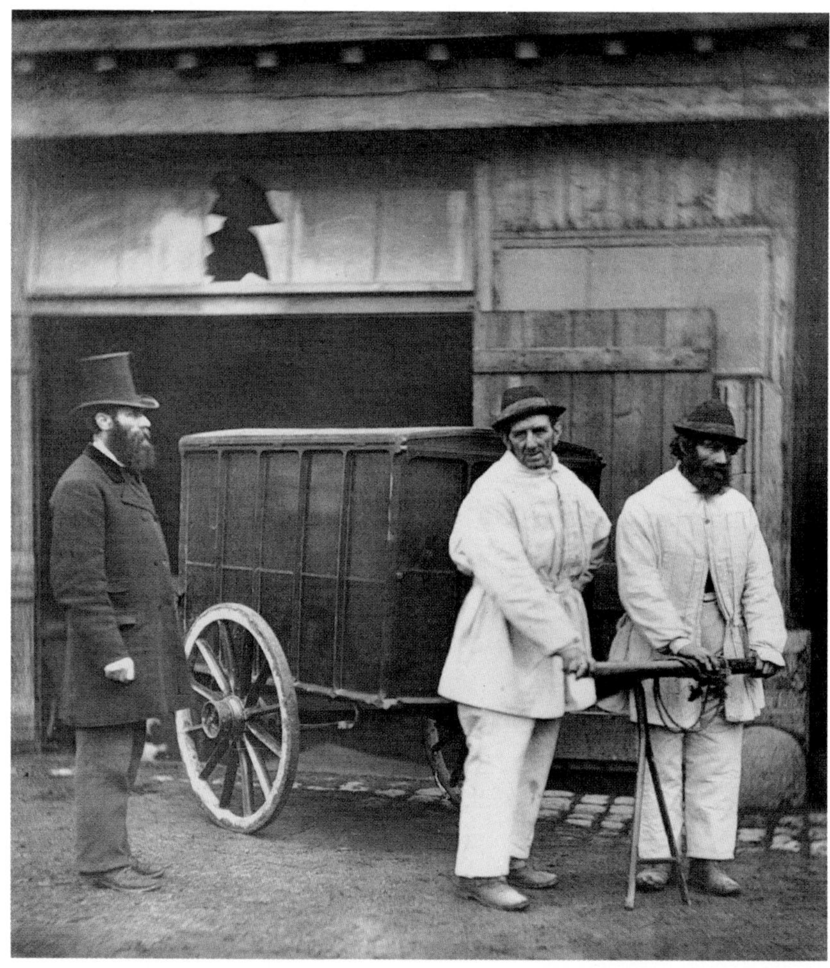

said to be 'feeling queer'. Severe cramps and aches are familiar to all except the young. One popular remedy is a slice of toast, covered in boiling water, placed on the affected area. There are specific London conditions known as the 'catch-cold' and 'foul-air fever'. Clean rooms, from which all furniture is removed, are believed to be beneficial. A decrepit room or a house is, in contrast, considered to be 'full of fever'. Perhaps that is why the periodicals describe city life as 'feverish', and its restless inhabitants often portrayed as being 'in a fever'.

The simplest and most natural foods can be suspect. In Camden Town, on the edge of the city, the profuse beds of watercress are grown in an old brick-field and are watered by the Fleet Ditch notorious for its detritus of dead dogs and other remnants. Some even believe that the health problems are down to 'drains', a term which can apply to the cesspools under the houses, to the rackety pipes of the water system or to the raw sewage floating in the gutters and being flushed into the Thames. They are described, in the language of melodrama, as the thousand gates to death. It is true that half of the people rely on water that is piped directly from the river, which looks like and smells like an open sewer, but a direct connection has yet to be proved.

Doctors are too expensive for the poor and even for some of the middling classes. If you visit the doctor it costs 1 guinea but, if the doctor visits you, it costs 2 guineas. There are a few 'sixpenny doctors' in needy neighbourhoods, but they can do little to halt or prevent disease. Laudanum and morphia are in any case available at druggists. Street sellers offer a choice of herbal remedies, bottled or wrapped in paper, while chemists can dispense Morison's Vegetable Pills, Godfrey's Cordial, Solomon's Cordial Balm of Gilead and other sovereign remedies for a variety of ailments from consumption to constipation. There is also much demand for street doctors who go from door to door with their boxes of cough lozenges, healing ointments and other remedies. The Arabian Family Ointment, for example, soothes chapped hands, lips, inflamed eyes, cuts, scalds and sores. It is sold to the poor for a penny a box. The medicated lozenges are halfpenny a packet.

A relatively new complaint of 'nerves' has appeared, and is described as nervous exhaustion or as nervous depression. It is believed to manifest itself in fits and seizures which can occur with alarming frequency. People suddenly collapse in the street or fall to the floor. Nerves may also be responsible for conditions such as 'suppressed gout', faintness and nausea. They may be alleviated by Mother Bailey's Quieting Syrup or a dose of wormwood. The

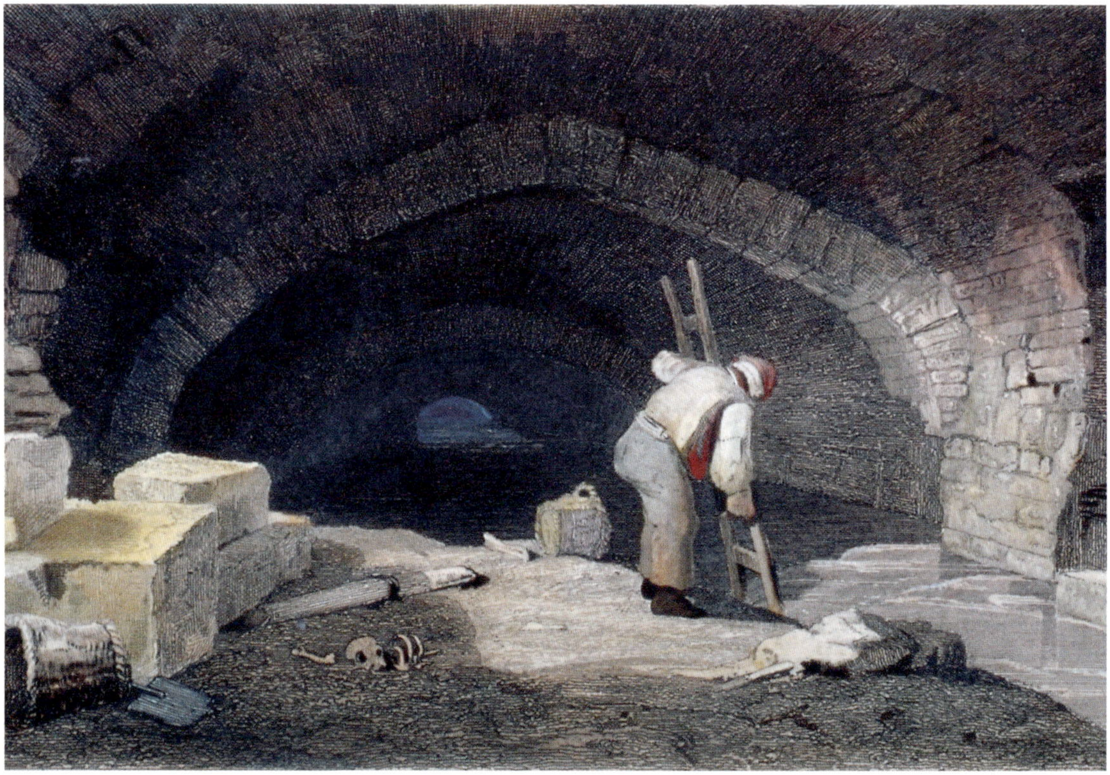

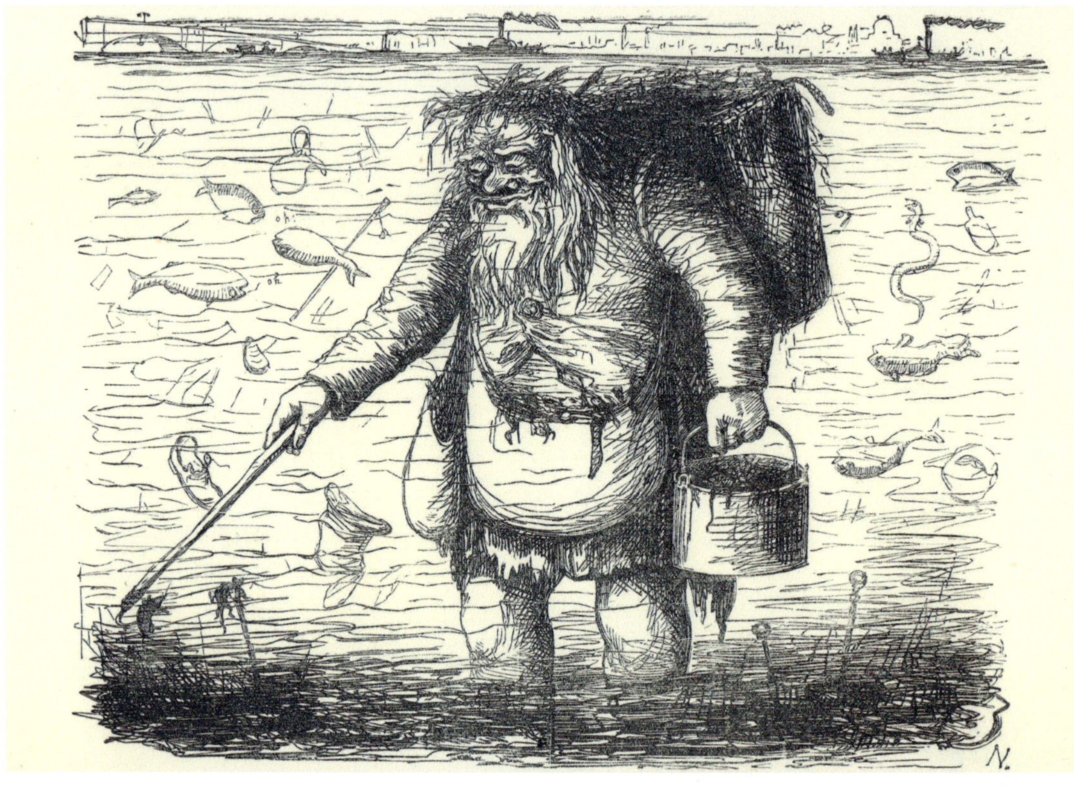

more affluent sufferers can visit Dr Caplin's Electro-Chemical
Bath off Portman Square or travel to the celebrated spas of Europe
where the medicinal water of the hot springs may bring out the
'suppressed' condition.

Many, both the poor and the wealthy, take refuge from their
problems in drink. The poorer sort are of course most visible in public
places. In the lowest and most disreputable inns, they sit on stools or
chairs with dirty tables in front of them. A quick sketch, along the
lines of 'Phiz', may set the scene. Customers are lying or lounging
on a bench against a wall. One tilts his head back, as a friend pours
liquor down his throat. A large woman sits in a corner with a pipe
in one hand and a jug of ale in the other. A fiddler is beside the door,
and to the scrape of his bow a chimney sweep and a Black woman
are dancing or 'jigging' with extravagant gestures. One man leers at
what may be female vagrants. Amorous excitement is in the air. Bowls
of gin toddy are passed from hand to hand. One cordial is known
as 'heavy wet', otherwise called malt liquor, and another is 'flash of
lightning', which is pure spirit. The happy medium is 'purl', a mixture
of hot beer and gin. A customer can always order 'half and half',
which is a mug of mixed beer, half-dark and half-light.

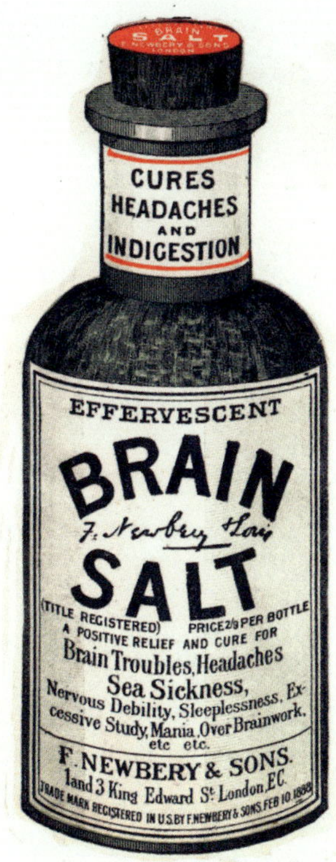

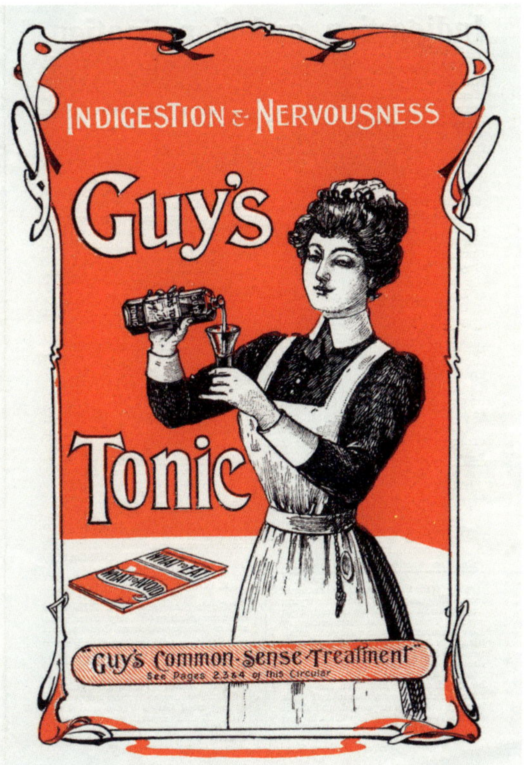

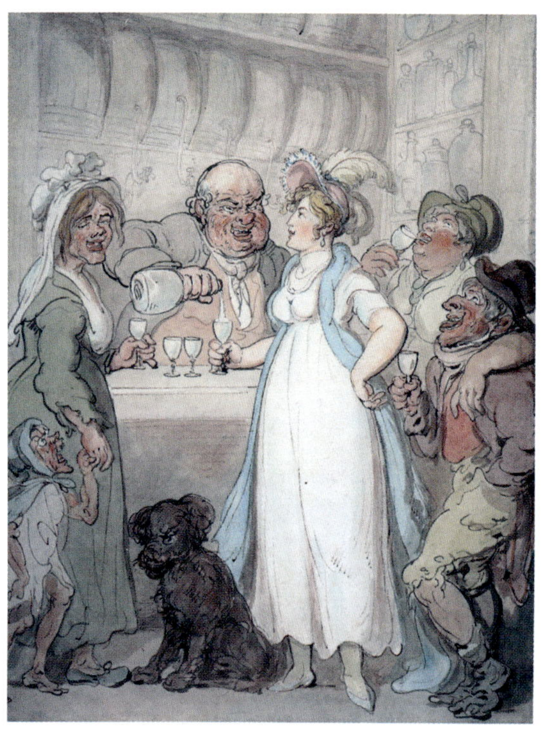

Above A Gin Shop
(c.1808–1809), watercolour
by Thomas Rowlandson.

In the gin shops, mechanics, costermongers, street sellers and their customers congregate with a complement of short pipes, thick sticks and mildewed umbrellas. The smell is not at all pleasing. It is often a lofty room, but the space between customer and bar is generally narrow; large men in white aprons, used to the constant clamour of brawling and shouting, take the place of barmaids. Upon the sanded floor are large barrels of gin, marked with the number of gallons they contain; in the western districts of London the stuff is called 'short' or 'blue ruin', but in the eastern areas it is known as 'tape', 'max', 'duke' or 'jacky'. An old barrel flung in a corner may serve as a seat. In the gin shops around Drury Lane and Seven Dials, a different atmosphere prevails. The customer throws down his three halfpence on the counter, and drinks with a slow, measured draining of the glass; then he smacks his lips and passes his hand over his mouth in a gesture of contentment before making a quick exit. This is the regular dram drinker, always alone and generally silent, who takes his 'drain' and is off, even if he is back again within a short time.

The gin shops are slowly being replaced by gin palaces, glittering with burnished columns, large mirrors, handsome clocks and ormolu candelabras. What were once secluded corner premises have now been torn down or transformed with stuccoed fronts and gold lettering. Gaslight and plate glass, Turkish carpets and rosewood fittings are now the latest fashion in these places of public entertainment and private ruin. Posters, displays on frosted windows and inscriptions fixed to the wall proclaim 'Wine, Rum and Brandy Vaults', 'Old Tom, Rum and Compounds', with signs for Cream Gin, Honey Gin and 'The Famous Cordial Medicated Gin Which is so Strongly Recommended by the Faculty'. The fine lettering announces compounds such as The Out-and-Out, The No Mistake and The Real Knock-me-down. A card in the window states that you can obtain 'A go of brandy for sixpence and a go of gin for fourpence'. A glass of port wine and a bit of sugar, or a glass of gin and peppermint, is always available.

The public house is also popular and is accepted as the genuine chip off the same block as the tavern and alehouse. It caters for the neighbours in its street or adjacent streets who collect there regularly in the evening to drink stout and porter, to smoke pipes short and long, or to play cards and bagatelle. If a stranger is brave enough to ask directions in the street, he is likely to be told to go 'Straight on till you come to the Three Turks, then to turn to the right and cross over at the Dog and Duck, and go on again till you come to the Bear and Bottle, then to turn the corner at the Jolly Old Cocks, and after passing the Veteran, the Guy Fawkes, the Iron Duke, take the first turn to the right which will bring you to it.'

Some of these venues are known as 'finishes', where men and women go to complete the night. Clerks and tradesmen drink ale, smoke cheap tobacco and get drunk with their female companions. They take part in 'sing-song', smoke cheap cigars and crack nuts. In the larger public houses more fashionable or more respectable clients – and, perhaps, cleaner ones – drink cognac, punch and wines from France and the Rhine; they also order sherry and port, and purchase Havana cigars. They, too, have female company, most if not all of whom are prostitutes. It is obvious enough how

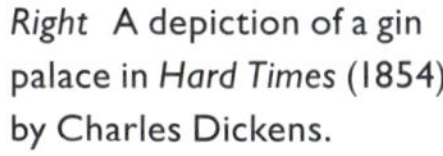

Right A depiction of a gin palace in *Hard Times* (1854) by Charles Dickens.

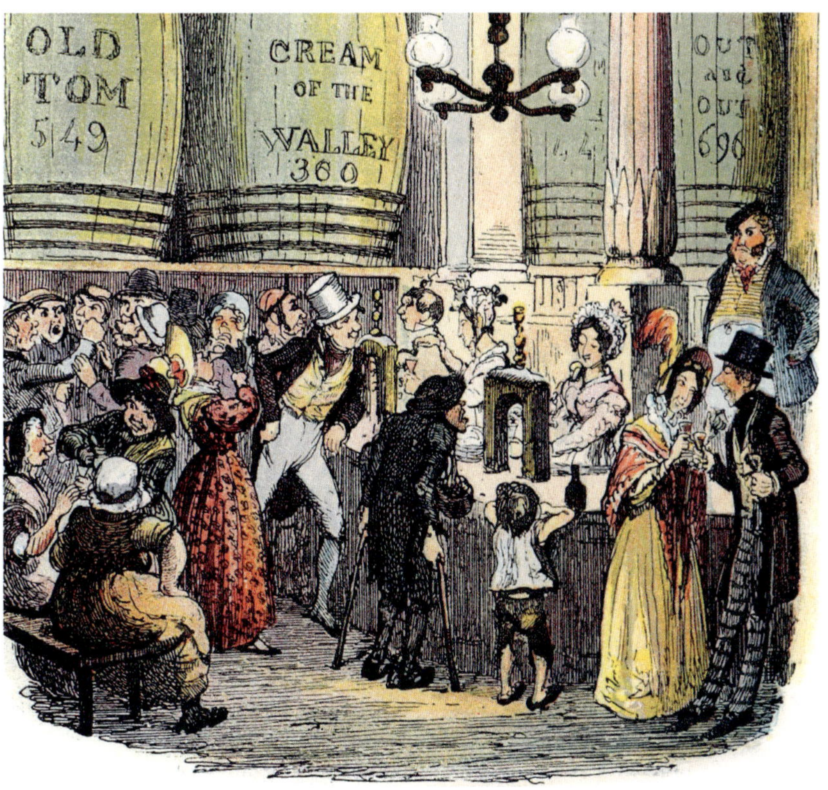

in certain quarters these nights will end. The customers, having debauched themselves, leave at seven or eight in the morning; they gather up their clothes as the waiters run into the street to fetch cabs. Those who still cannot stand are left lying on straw in a small back room known as the 'drunkard's hole'.

Drunkenness is, in fact, a familiar feature of the city, and is known by a variety of names. To be 'cut' is a favourite. To drink hard is to 'lush'. Many have been brought low, and even made destitute, from lushing. A drunkard is also known as a sweater. The addiction to drink used to be called dissipation, but the newly fashionable medical term is dipsomania. Affluent men drink as deeply and as freely as the poor, and it is easy to spot in the streets those with bottle noses and pimpled faces. The spectacle of children drinking in the streets and in alehouses is also common. There is no age limit for drinking in the public houses and, until very recently, no licensing hours. The girls are fonder of gin than the boys, since they say that it keeps out the cold. The boys prefer beer. Monday is washday, a laborious day for adults, and is the one day of the week when the women enjoy 'a little fuddle'. Others come in for a 'nip' or a 'dram', a 'drain' or a glass of 'rum-shrub' at any time; they may also visit the jug-and-bottle alcove of a public house to fill the vessels they bring with them. It is common enough for labourers and workmen to be paid at the end of a week in a local tavern, and no doubt some of their earnings are spent in the establishment. Many Londoners seem ready to drink themselves into insensibility, and can be seen sprawled outside a public house or staggering, groaning and cursing, inside. This may be described sarcastically as 'very genteel' or, more critically, as 'shocking vulgar' and 'rotten bad'.

The thirst for drink is equalled by the appetite for food. At all times of day, in eating houses, cook shops and coffee shops, can be found eggs fried or boiled, chickens poached or roasted, rashers fat or streaky, haddocks or Yarmouth bloaters, pots of anchovy paste or preserved tongue, chops or kidneys, accompanied by piles of salt and quartern loaves. Breakfast in oyster bars might include toast and a 'relish', egg or bacon, but some customers will manage with slices of bread and butter washed down with a cup of coffee; a pint of pale ale or porter is also welcome.

Breakfasts in the more affluent households will include eggs, prepared in a variety of ways, together with bacon or kidneys, or grilled fish, or cold meats, or some combination of these. Some families favour porridge or kedgeree. Dinner was once at midday,

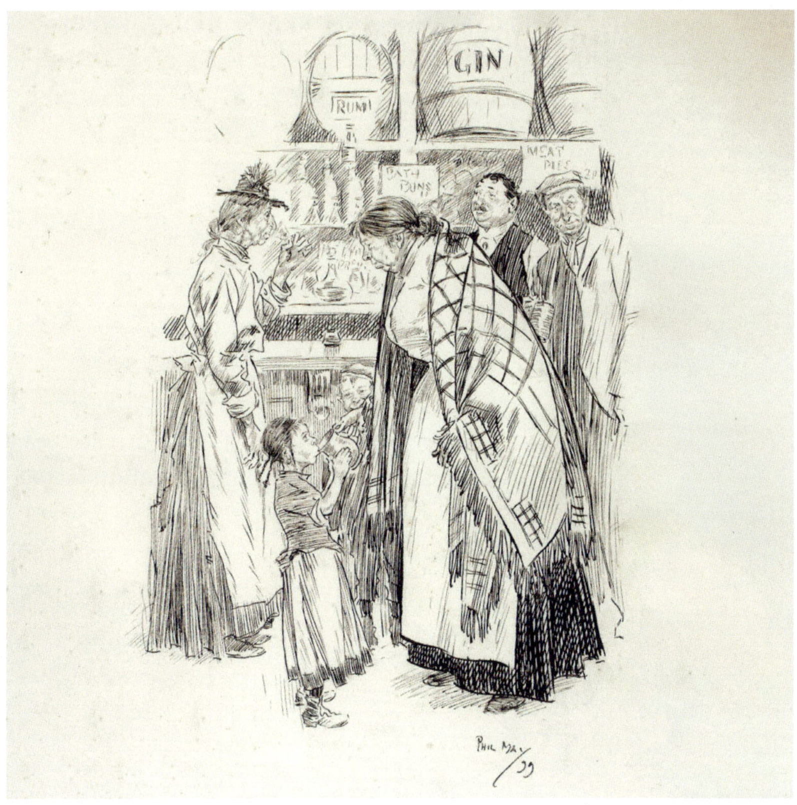

but the hour is slowly getting later. At this meal you might enjoy
cold fowl or slices of ham, beef and tongue; the meat will be
accompanied by bottles of ale or by a half-pint decanter of sherry.
You could of course be provided with roast goose and a bottle of
stout, or a plate of boiled beef followed by plum pudding. Cold
mutton and potatoes is also a popular dish. Supper, in the evening,
does not materially differ from dinner. Fruit and vegetables are
not always considered to be wholesome unless they are thoroughly
boiled or stewed.

Elsewhere, for poorer families, the bakehouses cook the
food you have already prepared. This is perhaps the easiest and
cheapest way of providing hot dishes. The pastry cooks sell cakes
and tarts, but they can also offer a variety of dishes, including
roast chicken, boiled beef and sundry vegetables. The cook shops
sell hot meats, vegetables and puddings to customers who sit
on shared benches and tables or in in separate compartments.
The food here is of the simplest kind with pease pudding, baked
potatoes and pies; pie crust is sold for halfpence a plate. A 'ha'porth
and ha'porth' is a meal of fish and potatoes. A familiar order is
'Tea, please, an' 'n egg.'

Dining rooms, in contrast, cater for the business trade in the City and its environs. A waiter will come to your table and read out the bill of fare, which mainly consists of a chop or a dish of meat and vegetables. The coffee shop has a more informal air. It may be small, little more than a room, or large enough to spread over two floors with several rooms offering different bills of fare. Breakfast costs around threepence. Some may be respectably furnished, while others contain no more than wooden tables, stools or benches; on dark days, candles provide the only light.

Coffee houses, rather than coffee shops, are preferred in the banking and mercantile quarters. Newspapers, such as *The Times* and *The Morning Chronicle*, are provided in some of them. Others have books and periodicals. The customers can play draughts and dominoes. The Jerusalem Coffee House in Cornhill is linked to foreign trade, and John's Coffee House by Gray's Inn is naturally patronized by lawyers. Some can even be classed as small London hotels, with rooms and staff, where strangers stay in order to see London. Beef houses and soup houses cater for junior clerks, with bread and meat or bread and broth at threepence a plate. Beyond the space assigned to the public, there

A group of men playing a game of dominoes, c.1883.

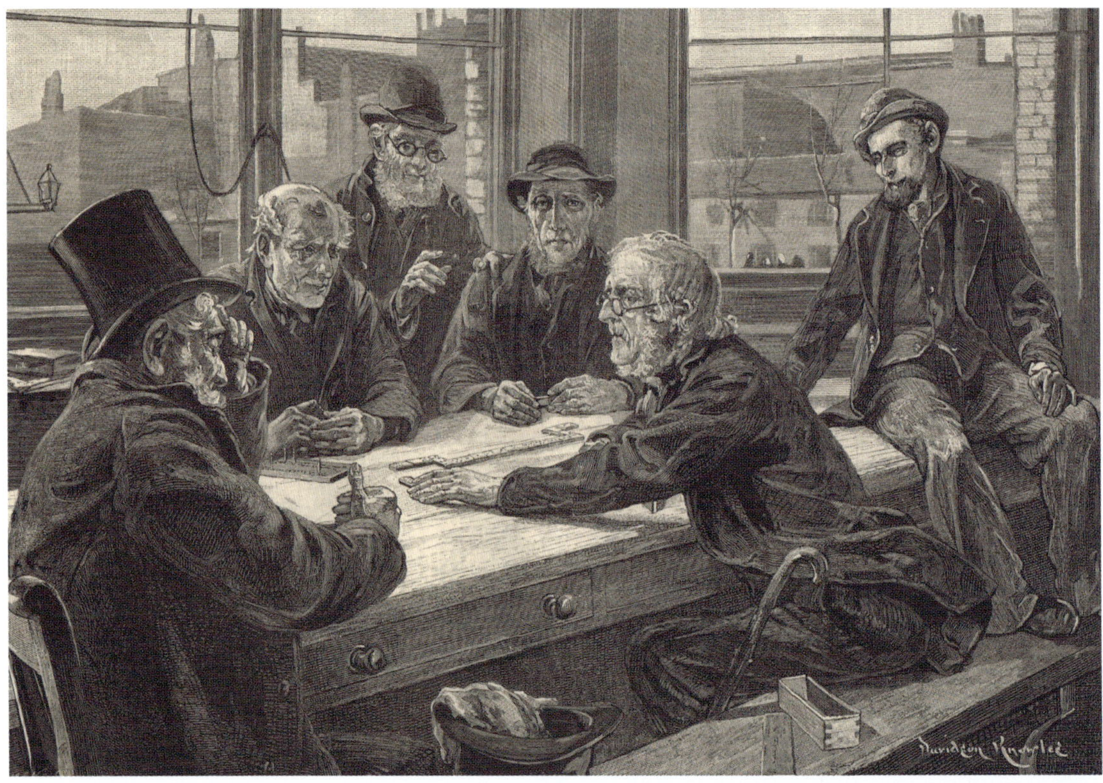

is often a partition of wood, 4 or 5 feet high, with a door in the middle; this conceals the kitchen, from which come clouds of steam, the sound of frying and odours manifold. Chop houses serve hot joints, chops and steaks with side dishes of cheese, pickle and salad; these, too, have to be served quickly, since the hard-pressed employees are given half-an-hour or less to fortify themselves for the long hours ahead. These venues are often called 'slap-bangs' for their speed in serving and eating. Some customers stand at the counter while others have their favourite boxes. A few chop houses in the City are well-known. Dolly's is prized for its mutton chops and beefsteaks, the Cock for its oxtail soup and the Ship for turtle soup. Turtle soup is, in fact, one of the more popular London dishes.

The more luxurious eating houses are called restaurants, after the French example, where the waiters in swallow-tailed coats patrol the tables. Clean linen is used for tablecloths and napkins, together with plated forks and spoons; the dishes are also of a superior quality, with sole and salmon dressed in melted butter and lobster sauce, shoulder of mutton and onion sauce, or jugged hare and peas. One restaurant has a printed statement that 'nothing but the finest margarine is spread on bread in this establishment'. The meal may be completed with small glasses of brandy and a bunch of pipes is laid on the table, but you need not go out in order to eat. Some restaurants, or lunching rooms, advertise the fact that 'all goods delivered free of charge within 10 miles'.

Many Londoners, however, rely upon street food. Stewed eels are sold for halfpenny a cup and four oysters for a penny; mussels and whelks, all vinegared and peppered, are sold from stalls and open shop windows, while periwinkles are advertised by the cry of 'Winketty-winketty-wink-wink-wink'. You can also buy small pots of hot green peas or fried fish with a slice of bread. The hot-potato man is a familiar figure, with his portable tin box and a charcoal fire beneath it. Down the same streets come the muffin man with basket and bell, and the pieman with the tray of pies balanced on his head. Pie shops will also sell ham sandwiches, German sausage sandwiches and rump steak pudding with watercress. In other shops joints of meat are steaming, with a pile of boiled beef pegged onto a board with a metal skewer. In some establishments, puddings and pies are kept hot by steam rising through perforated metal. Gravy is always provided. Sixpence is more than enough for a couple of meals. For the poorer customers, a penny can buy a ha'porth of bread and a ha'porth of cheese. Early breakfast stalls

are set up on street corners or on main thoroughfares; they purvey
halfpenny slices of bread and butter, together with large urns of
coffee or tea heated over charcoal fires. These are complemented
by coffee stalls, resembling something between a gypsy tent
and a watchman's box, which are in use day and night. They are
generally painted red and run on wheels; they are hauled by a
horse to such familiar locations as Charing Cross, the foot of Savoy
Street, Westminster Bridge, Hyde Park Corner and the gates of the
West India Dock. These stalls sell everything from saveloys to hard-
boiled eggs as well as coffee and penny rolls. For a penny you can
have 'two thin', comprising two slices of bread and butter together
with a hot drink. They cater for the denizens of the night.

Below The muffin man crying
'Muffins and crumpets!' with
a bell in hand and goods atop
his head, nineteenth century.

Right A busy London coffee
stall, c.1850s.

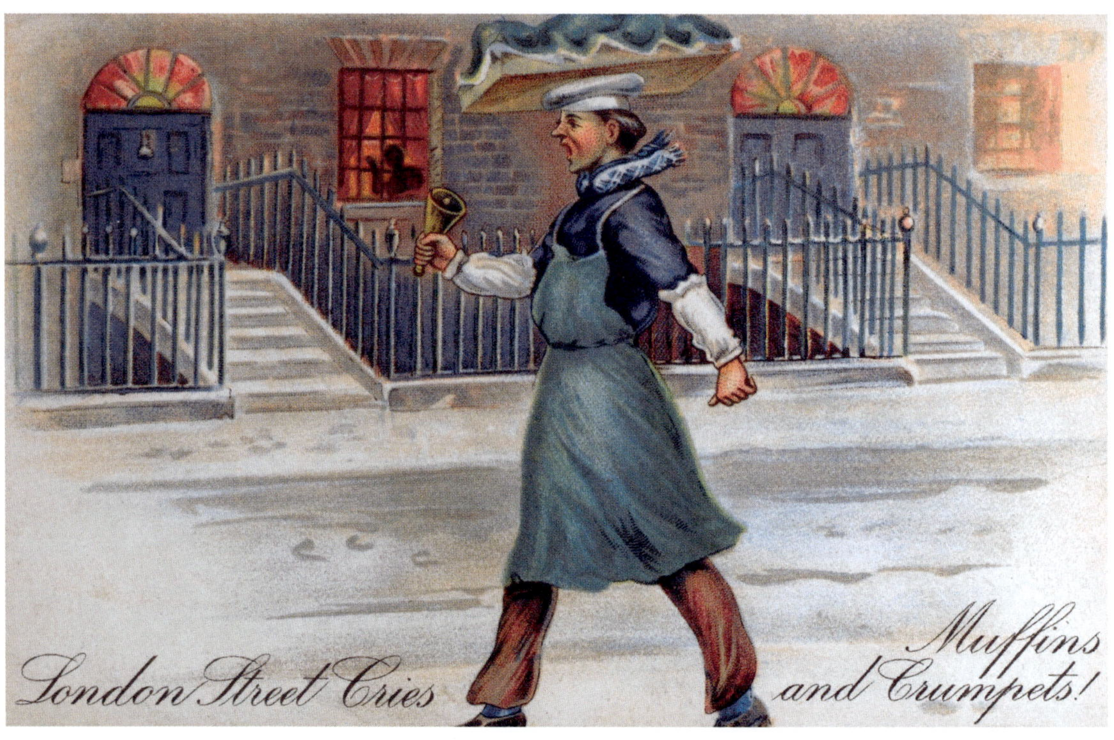

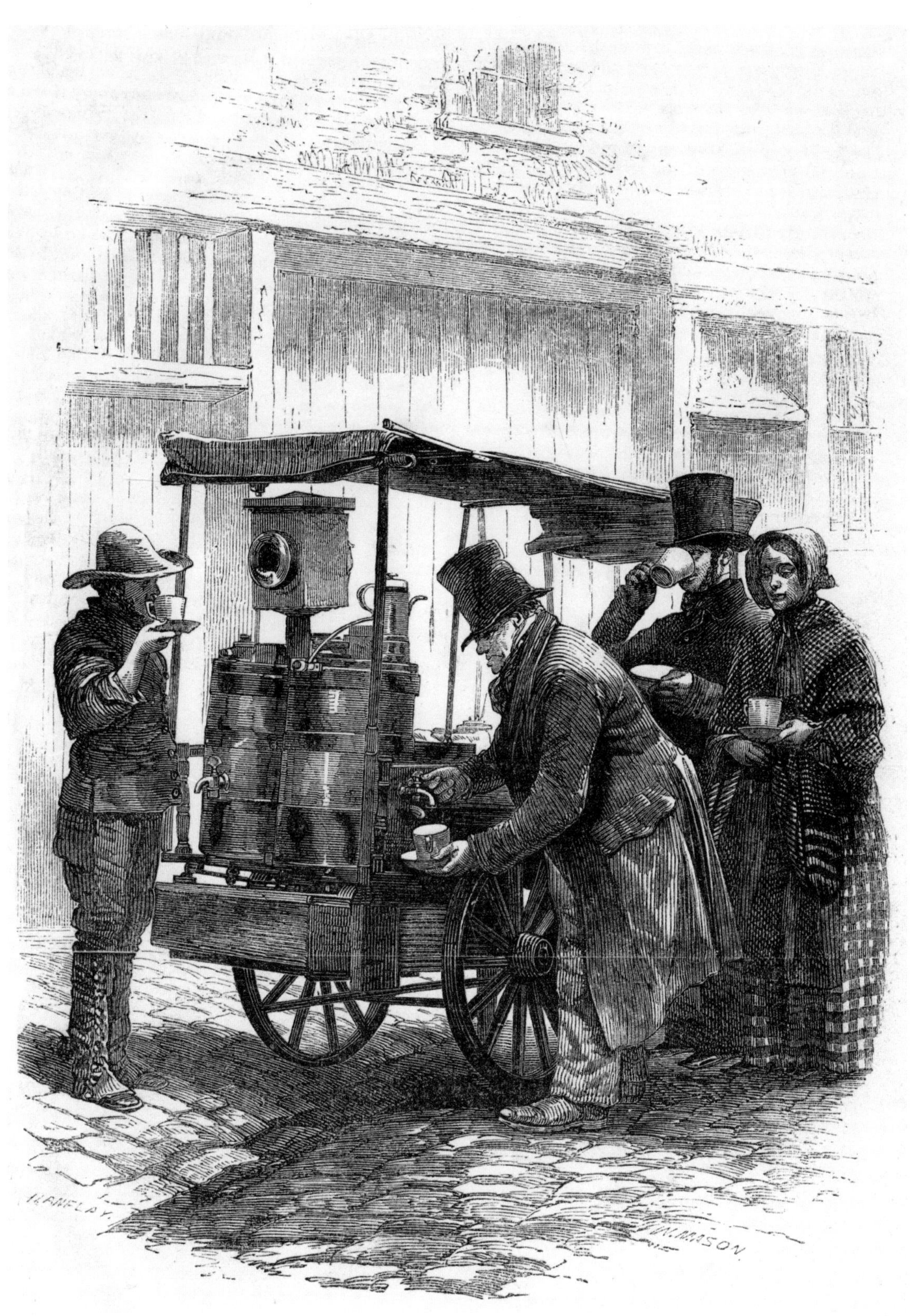

99   1837–1850 SMOKE, FILTH AND FOG

'It is called the city of dreadful night,
the modern Babylon, the nether world,
the abyss.'

1851–1900
LONDON ON THE MOVE

London is changing at a faster pace than at any other time in its history. It is turning into a modern city. New streets are being created everywhere, and in the process the old city is being erased. The railways have already been established and, just as importantly, a new system of underground trains has been introduced. It is the first one in the world. London has truly become the city of empire; the public spaces, the vast railway termini, the grand hotels, the wide thoroughfares, the great docks set up by the Thames, the rebuilt markets, are all the visible expressions of a city of unrivalled strength and immensity. It has become the centre of international finance and the engine of imperial power; it is vibrant with life and expectancy. But it comes at a cost. Some of its gracefulness and variety has now gone, since its Georgian compactness and familiarity have also disappeared. It is a larger and more anonymous city. It is of course a more public and powerful London, but also a less human one.

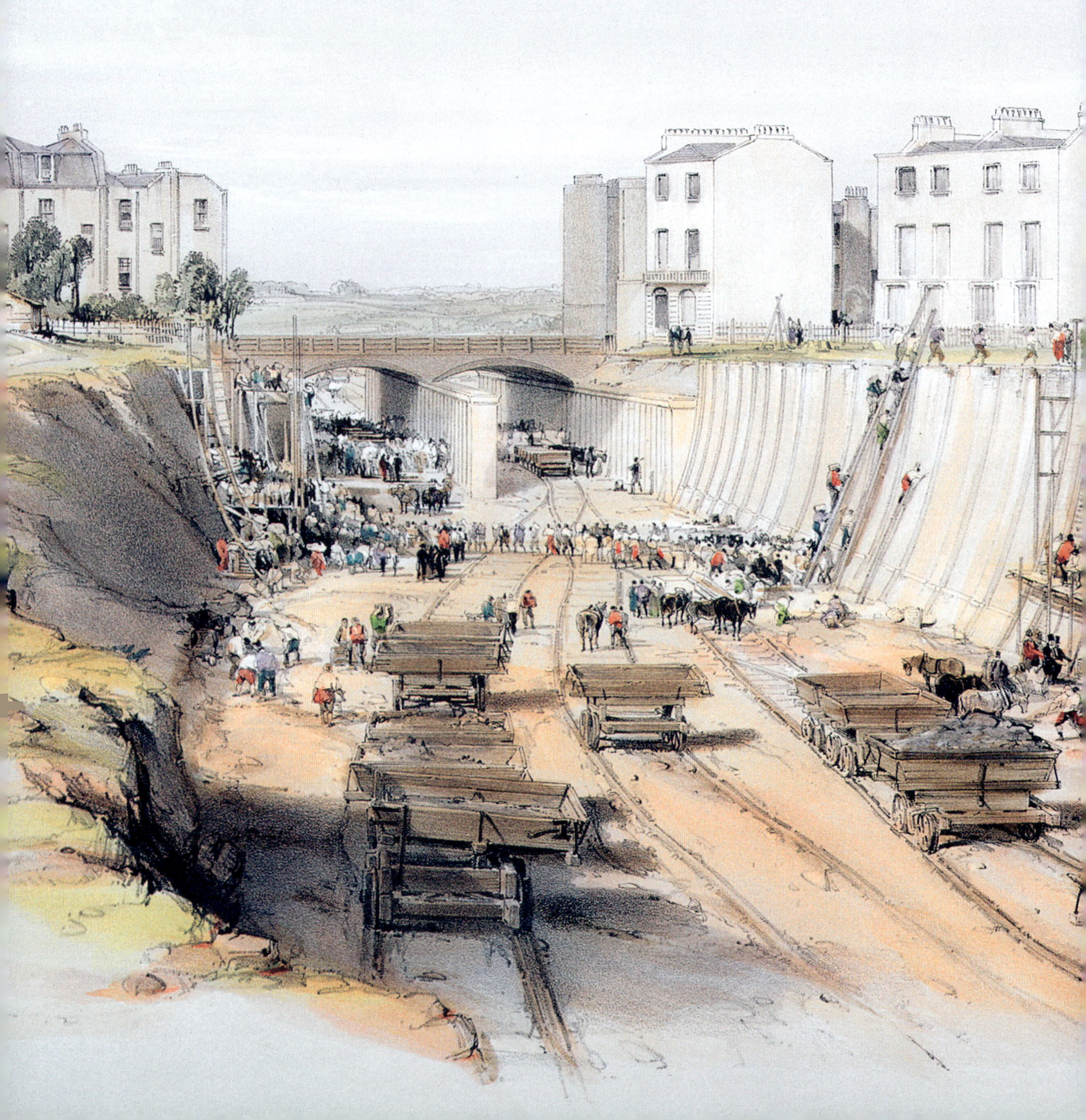

There has been a rage for building. London is being altered beyond recognition by street improvements; it has already been cut up and excavated by the arrival of the railways, and is now being refashioned by the commercial development of the City. New streets are being created in every direction. Cannon Street has been extended. Farringdon Street and Garrick Street, New Oxford Street and Clerkenwell Road have been built on the 'open cut' or 'cut-and-cover' method, which has turned parts of London into vast building sites of dust, noise and wooden scaffolding. The narrow streets have given way to wide and ever wider thoroughfares lined by new dwellings, great hotels, office buildings and mansion blocks in brilliant limestone or in burnished brick or terracotta. Shaftesbury Avenue, Northumberland Avenue, Queen Victoria Street and Charing Cross Road are all being driven through the capital. Westminster Bridge and Blackfriars Bridge have been rebuilt. The Hungerford Suspension Bridge and Hungerford Market have been demolished.

It is instructive to note the quality of stone in the capital. The smoke, and the contrary directions of the winds that pass through the confined and irregular streets, ensure that the weathering of stone is affected by hundreds of chance effects. A rain-bearing wind cleans every surface on which it has free play and Portland Stone, in particular, is whitened by every shower. It has been said that it is the only stone which washes itself. Holborn has a shade of green in its white. The new stone of Northumberland Avenue has a lemon tinge – still with the nature in it, as masons say – while the buildings of Farringdon Street seem already to have 'greyed down'. Everyone must notice that the general tendency of London buildings is to whiten towards the southwest, growing darker on the far sides, with the chief darkness at the east and northeast. St Paul's is an example.

Many of the old streets have been demolished or uprooted, buried beneath new streets and new buildings. It is true that many of them were uncomfortably narrow and inconvenient, that some of them were unsightly and others unsavoury, but all of them possessed the atmosphere of the city as many still remember it. The streets around Drury Lane, about to be destroyed, are an example. Other changes are just as important. Trafalgar Square has been in existence for some years, and is already taken for granted. It is part of the same desire in London for the erection of great monuments and for the creation of museums, law courts and other grand public buildings.

The Holborn Viaduct has been built to span the valley of the Fleet; the great enterprise of the Victoria Embankment has transformed the northern bank of the Thames and has been extended into the heart of the city by Queen Victoria Street, while Victoria Street itself further west has improved all of Westminster. The great arterial sewers north and south of the river are in operation. The railway has also changed the face of London. The building of Euston was followed by the great termini of Waterloo, King's Cross, Paddington, Victoria, Charing Cross, St Pancras and Liverpool Street. It is testimony to the energy and efficiency of the city that all of these principal stations have been completed within a space of 30 years. This process seems akin to the recent, if controversial, theories on the 'evolution' of species.

For much of the present century the city has been caught up in the celebration of speed and motion and now, with the advent of the electric telegraph as well as the railway, it has become the great centre of communication. All lines of commerce and of transport lead directly to it. The old London, the London of our youth, seems close to being obscured and even destroyed by another city which is rising up through it. This is a new London in regard to its life

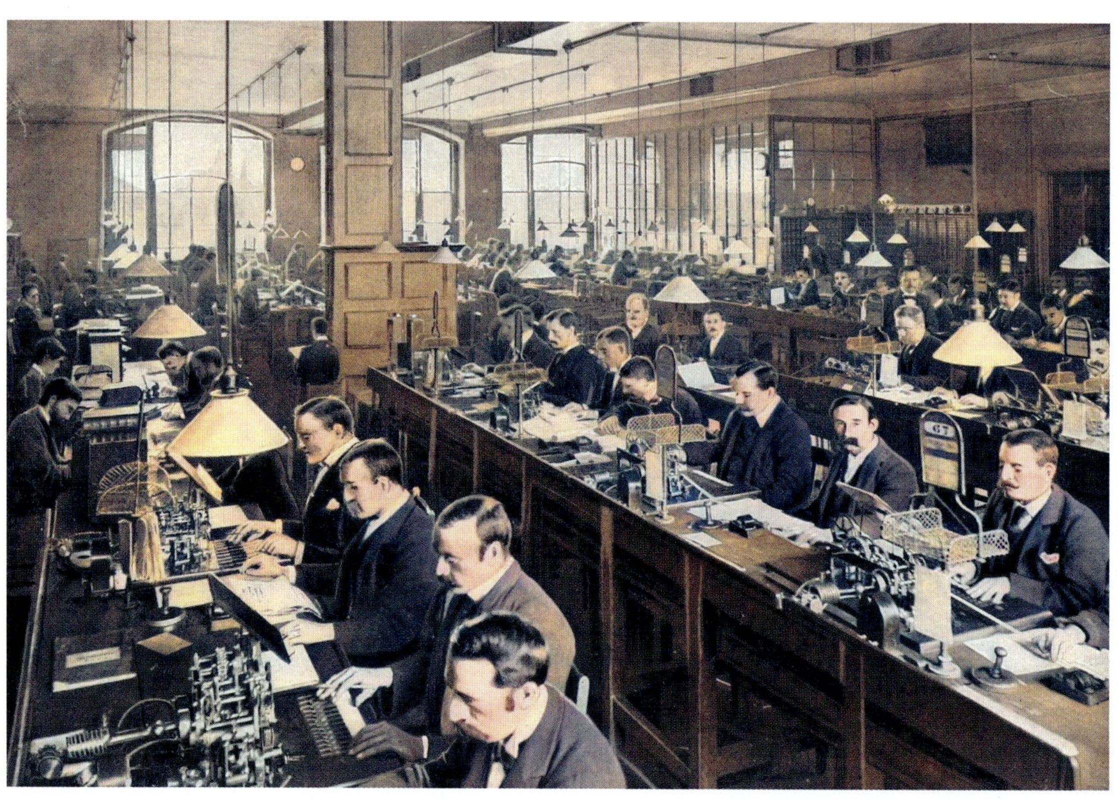

Below Around a hundred telegraph clerks at the Central Telegraph Office, St Martin's Le Grand, c.1900.

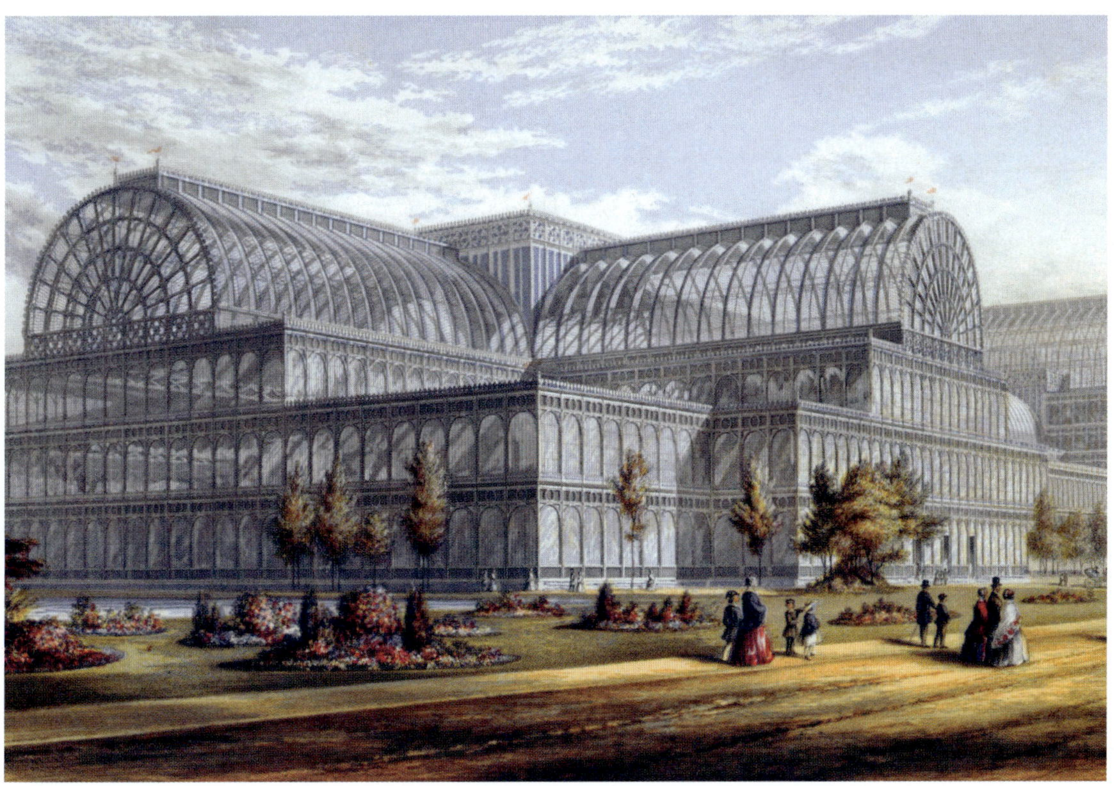

and size, but it is also new in regard to the daily existence of the millions who now dwell in it. Surveys and statistical reports, which have multiplied in recent years, emphasize the fact that the manners, habits, occupations and even amusements of the people have undergone as great a change in the past half-century as the city itself. However, opinions on its nature vary. Where some see only poverty and deprivation, other see the improvements in health and education; where some recognize only shabbiness and ugliness, others note the blessings of trade and commerce, but all are sensible of great change. London is larger and cleaner than before, but it is also more anonymous. It is a more public city, the seat of empire and of commerce, but perhaps a less humane one.

The vast transition is symbolized, and celebrated, by the Great Exhibition of 1851. It is accommodated within the Crystal Palace (as the satirical magazine, *Punch*, named it) built in the southern part of Hyde Park. Glass has never been employed on so large a scale, stretching over 560 acres from the Serpentine lake to Knightsbridge. It is three times the size of St Paul's Cathedral and encompasses 200 cast iron girders, 4,000 tons of iron and 900,000 square feet of glass. The Exhibition itself is an equal marvel, and is still vividly remembered.

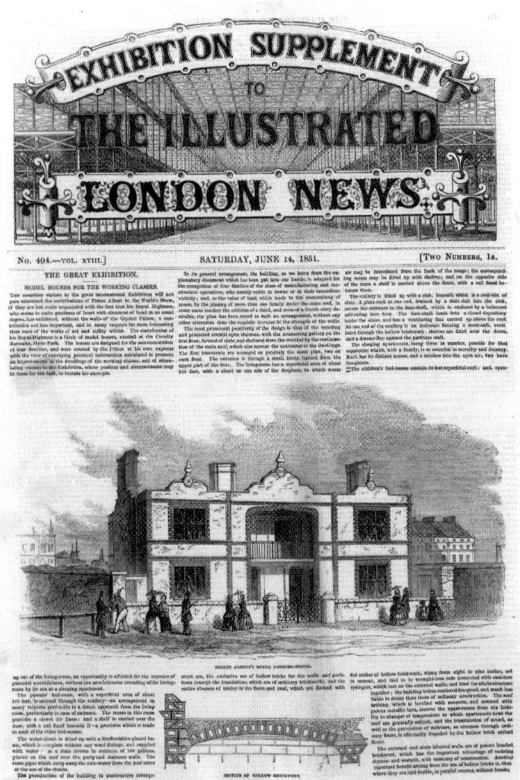

Above The exhibition supplement page of *The Illustrated London News*, 14 June 1851.

Right top The Indian Court (1854) by Joseph Nash. A lithograph of the India exhibit inside the Great Exhibition.

Right bottom De La Rue's stationery stand and envelope machine. Entrance to the machinery stands (1851), an illustration by C. T. Dolby for *Recollections of the Great Exhibition*.

The entrance fee is at first 5s, but 'shilling days' are soon introduced for the poorer members of the public. It is expensive enough, but considered to be worth the money. The newspapers report that one hundred thousand exhibits and marvels from all over the world are displayed. Entire parishes, led by their clergymen, arrive in London; colonels come with their soldiers, admirals with their sailors, schools come with their pupils, and enlightened manufacturers with their workers. Estimates put visitor numbers at as many as six million. Different sections are created, comprising raw materials, machinery and mechanical inventions, manufactures, sculpture and the plastic arts. There are classic, Oriental and medieval courts, with other sections such as the Indian and the Egyptian, the Arabic and the Byzantine.

On show are steam locomotives and gas microscopes, air pumps and cameras. Just outside the hall is placed a block of coal weighing 24 tons, as a symbol of England's material wealth. A copy of 'The Dying Gladiator', in Roman marble, stands beside James Nasmyth's steam hammer, and a penknife is displayed next to a graphic telescope. There's a cigarette machine producing 80 cigarettes a minute, and an electric printing telegraph creating copies of documents at the other end of 'the line'. An envelope-making machine can be used to fold and gum 60 envelopes per minute. The 'silent alarm bed' pitches the sleeper onto the floor at any given time. *The Morning Chronicle* hails it as a cathedral of the modern world. One of the great imperatives of this age is innovation, and the whole world came to see it.

*

The most spectacular change in London itself has been the underground railway system. This great feat of engineering was at first ridiculed. It was considered to be no better than schemes for flying machines or for tunnels under the Channel, and it was regarded with some dismay as a possible haven for Fenians or

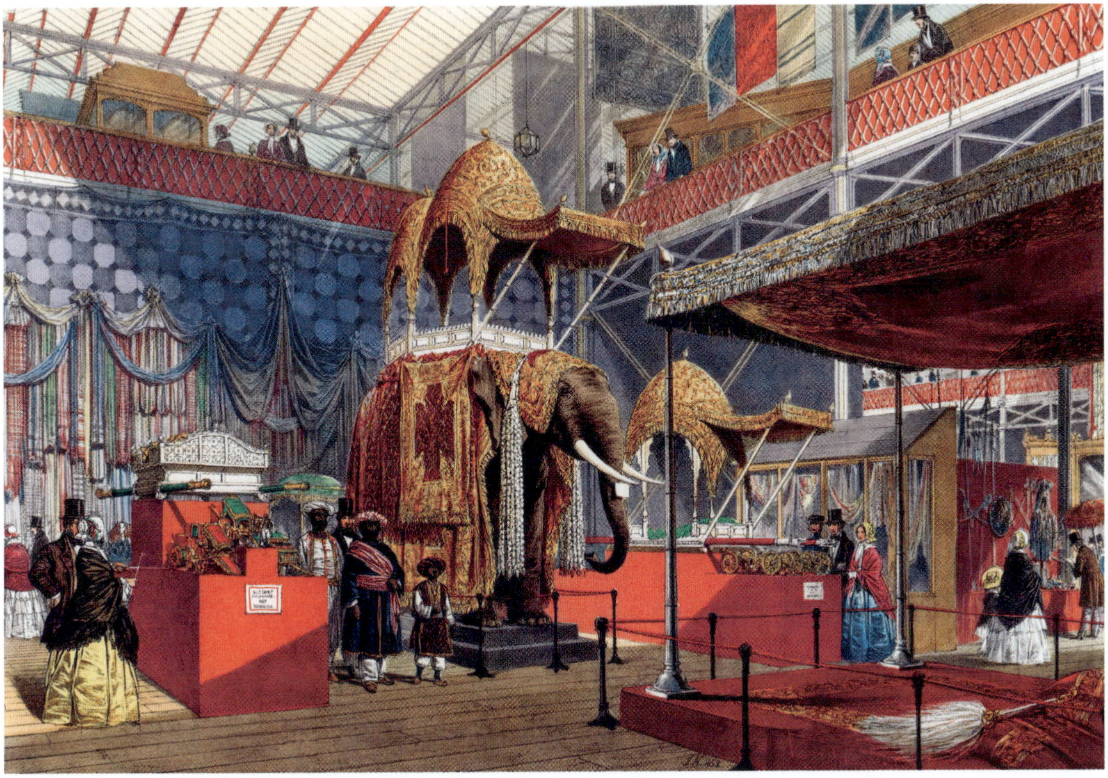

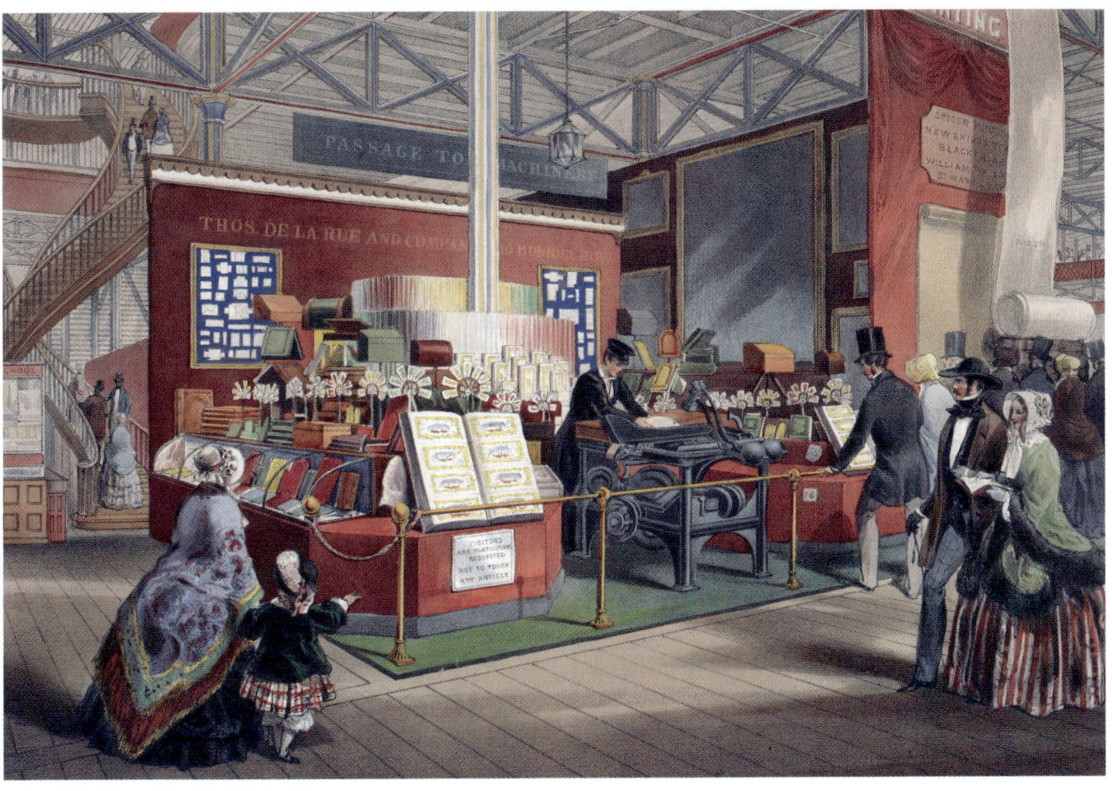

PASSAGE TO THE MACHINERY
THOS. DE LA RUE AND COMPANY
VISITORS
ARE PARTICULARLY
REQUESTED
NOT TO TOUCH
ANY ARTICLE

Dynamiters who could destroy parts of the city. Some clergymen even believed that it would awake the devil. The doubts were either ignored or resolved, and the first shafts for this journey under the surface of the earth were dug at Euston Square and Paddington. The subsequent turmoil was repeated all over London. In most areas, a few hundred yards of road were closed and the traffic diverted. The noise and confusion were immense. The omnibuses were directed down alleys and back streets, and many outside passengers can still remember how they had to dodge street signs and barbers' poles. Then the navvies arrived with their steam cranes and horses. The sound of pickaxes, spades and hammers, the puffing of steam, the shouts and jokes of the workmen did not cease either by day or by night.

Within two years the line from Paddington to Euston Square was complete. When it was opened to the public, the crowd was compared to the crush at the doors of a theatre on the first night of a pantomime. It was, and for some still is, a wonder and a spectacle to rival anything on the stage. The trains are driven by steam engines, more compact than those on the railway lines above, and accommodate three classes of passenger. The first class

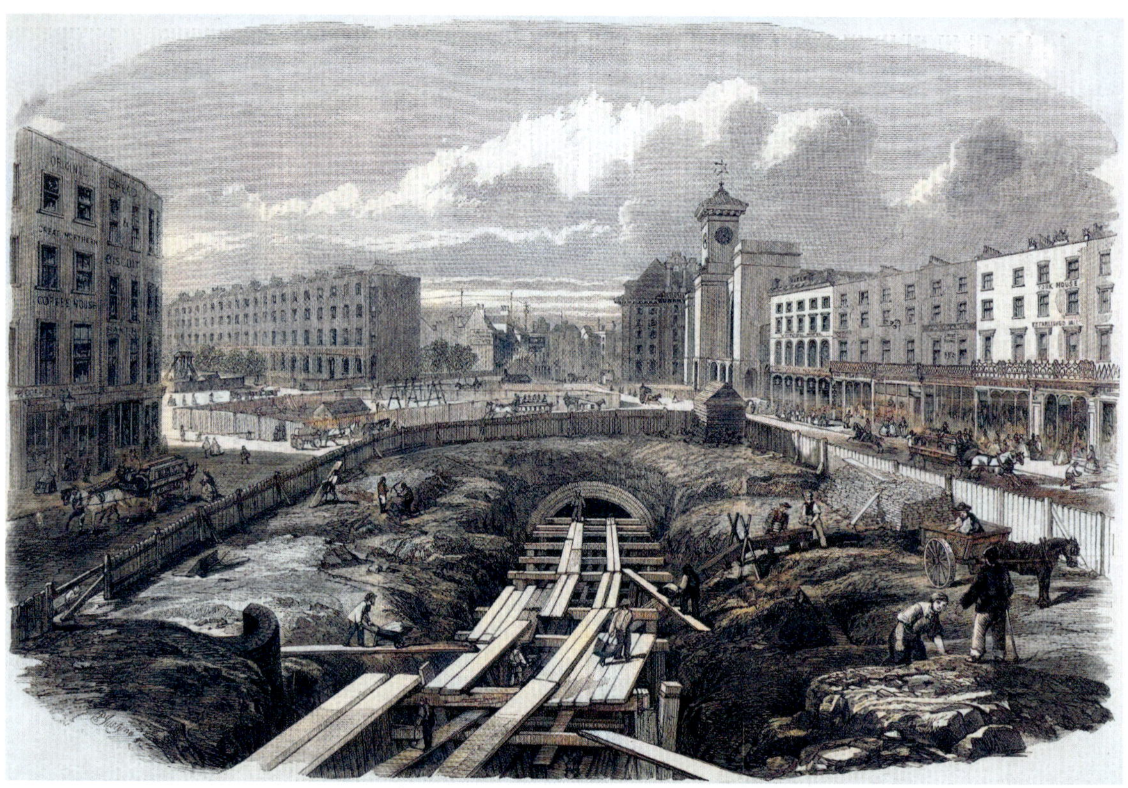

Below Construction work in progress on the world's first underground railway near King's Cross, in *The Illustrated London News*, 1861.

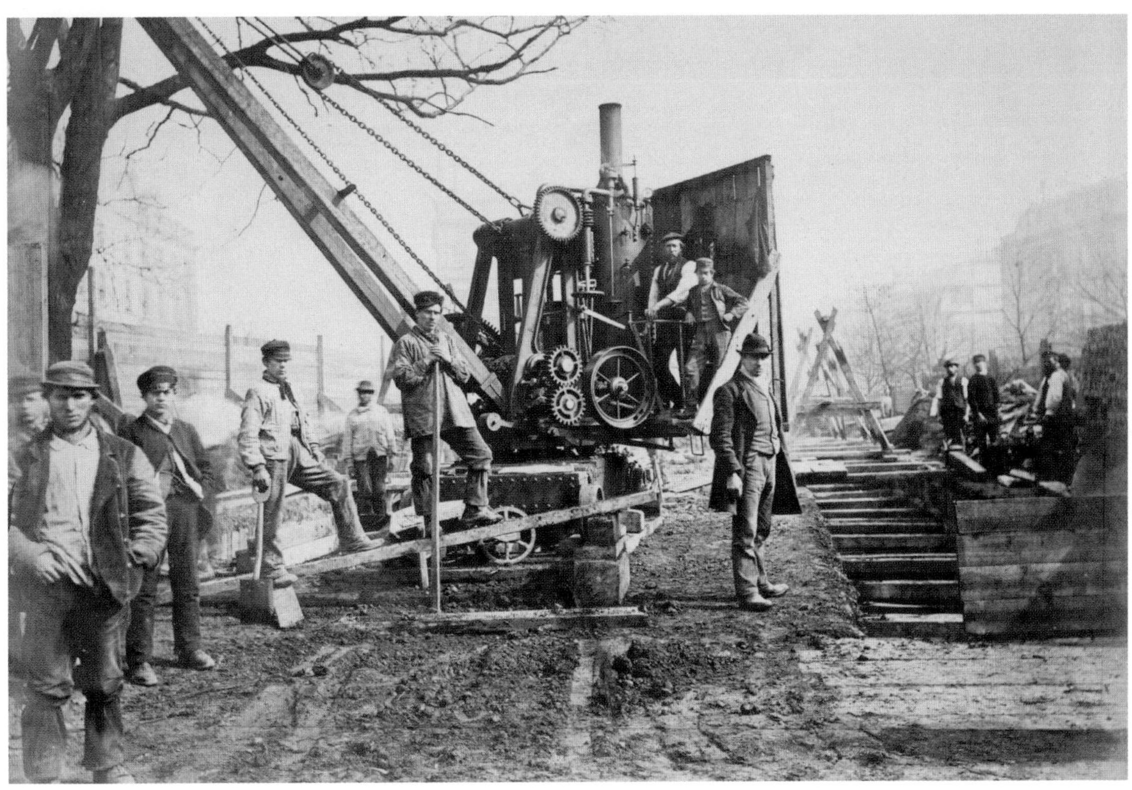

carriages, for example, contain mirrors and carpets to make the journey more agreeable. Gas burners above the seats enable the passengers to read. Foot warmers can also be hired. It is considered safe enough for unaccompanied women, and even for children, to travel in them. The second-class passengers have minimal facilities, and the third class sit or stand in open wagons. The system was so popular that soon enough the trains were lengthened, and the pause at the various stations lasted for 20 seconds. The full journey on most lines costs from 1d to 3d, according to the time of day.

Complaints are of course made about the noise and the smell, but the fumes are believed to be beneficial for those afflicted with asthma and other bronchial complaints. Great Portland Street is said to be better than a sanatorium. The smoke and sulphur do fill the tunnels, but it is seldom thick enough to obscure the view of the driver. Since the journey is entirely underground, on some lines the need for windows is deemed to be minimal, and tiny slits are placed high on the sides, as it is feared that some passengers might panic at the sight of the walls of the tunnel rushing past them. Many of the seats are quilted. The carriages are known by

London humourists as 'padded cells'. A guard stands at the end of each carriage and announces the names of the stations on the route. He also calls out warnings, such as 'Beware of card sharks on this train!' and 'It is forbidden to ride on the roof!' In a recent development, the underground trains on the Stockwell line are powered by electricity rather than steam. On this line there are no classes of passengers. All tickets are charged at the same rate, and all carriages are identical. This has caused outrage in some quarters, with the suggestion that lords and ladies will now be travelling with Billingsgate fishwives and Smithfield porters.

Other forms of transport in London have changed beyond recognition. All kinds of vehicle now flood the streets. The omnibuses and the hansoms, the carts and trams, the growlers and the landaus, the broughams and the victorias, the four-wheelers and carriages all somehow manage to manoeuvre along the crowded roads, while the pedestrians run and dart between them. A cart, a carriage, a dray and an omnibus will follow each other in slow procession, while the quicker cabs go between them, but the major element is still the horse. There are said to be upward of forty thousand horses on the road, pulling all manner of vehicles at uncertain speed. A wagon may break down and bring a long line of carriages to a halt. A policeman or two, in bright blue coats and wearing white gloves, will appear as if by magic to unravel the knot, assist the horse and direct the traffic. They raise an arm to stop the coachman or driver, and lower it as a sign to move on. The boys in red tops run among the vehicles to clear up horse dung, while the braver or younger pedestrians make sorties into the road.

The bicycle may also now count as a hazard. The braver spirits can ride on the 'high-wheeler', with the front wheel 4 or 5 feet in diameter, and otherwise known as a 'penny- farthing', 'velocipede' or 'bone-shaker'. The styles may change, but the design is much the same. In recent years, however, many have turned to the smaller and cheaper 'safety bicycles'. Since Hyde Park is now closed to bicyclists, hundreds migrate to Battersea Park or to Richmond Park where they race about at a pace like lightning, looking neither to the left nor to the right. It is said that some of them are roughs or, perhaps, members of a bicycle club. Those who ride their vehicles too fast are known as 'scorchers'. The newspapers now spread fears about this new cyclemania. It is reported that enthusiastic riders might develop 'bicycle hump' by leaning too long over the handlebars; acute cases of 'bicycle

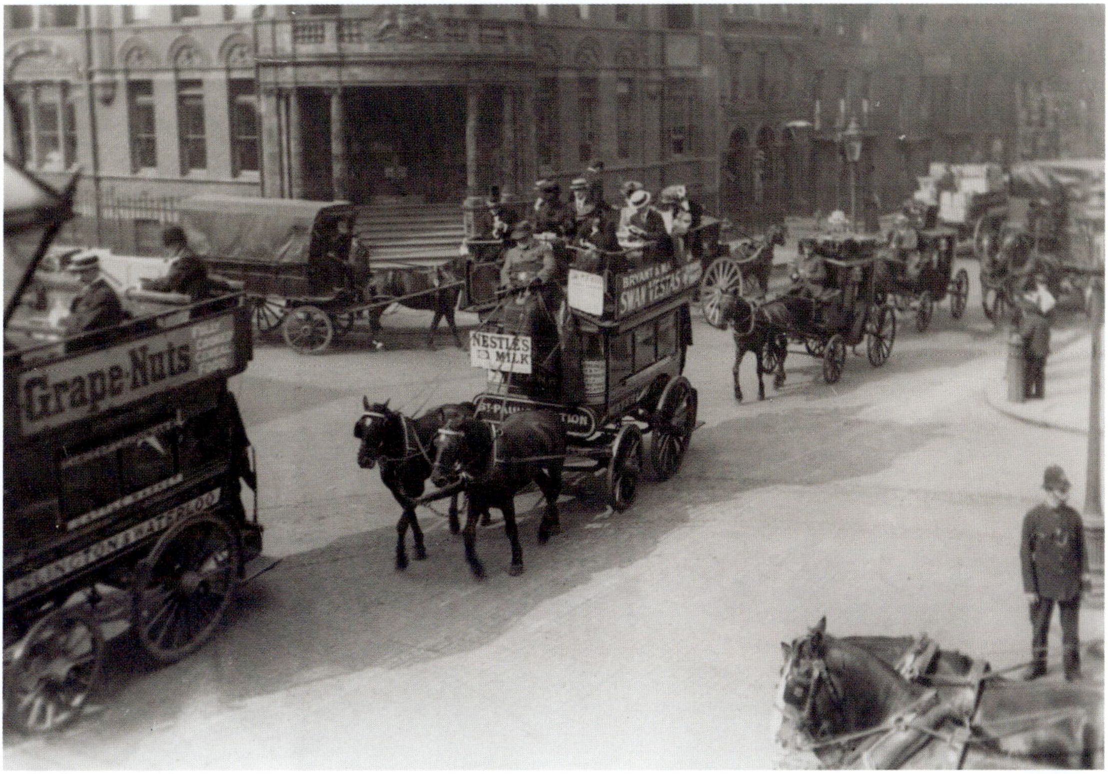

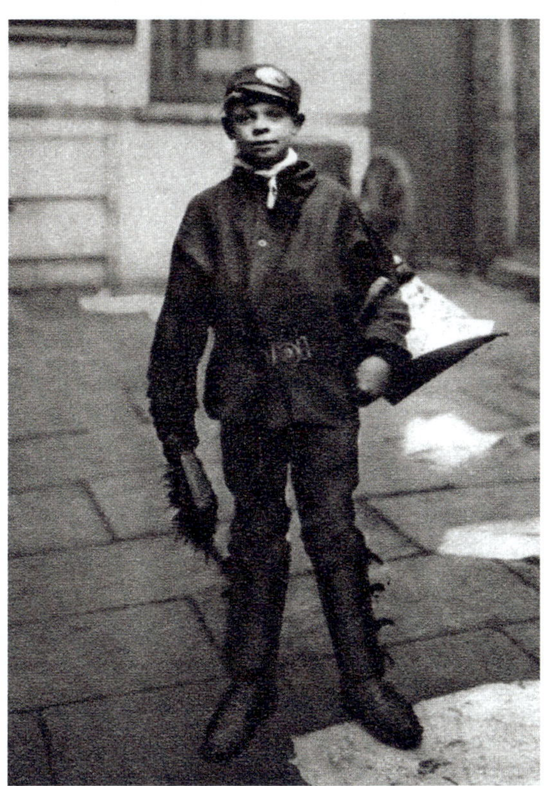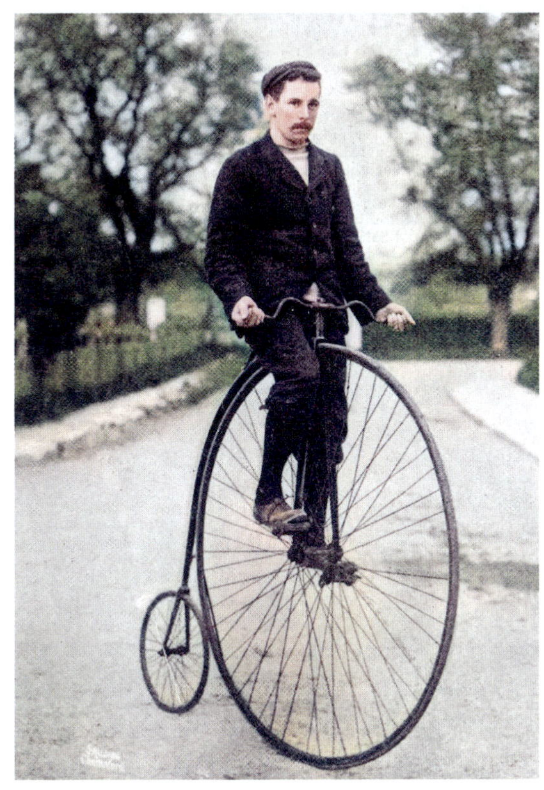

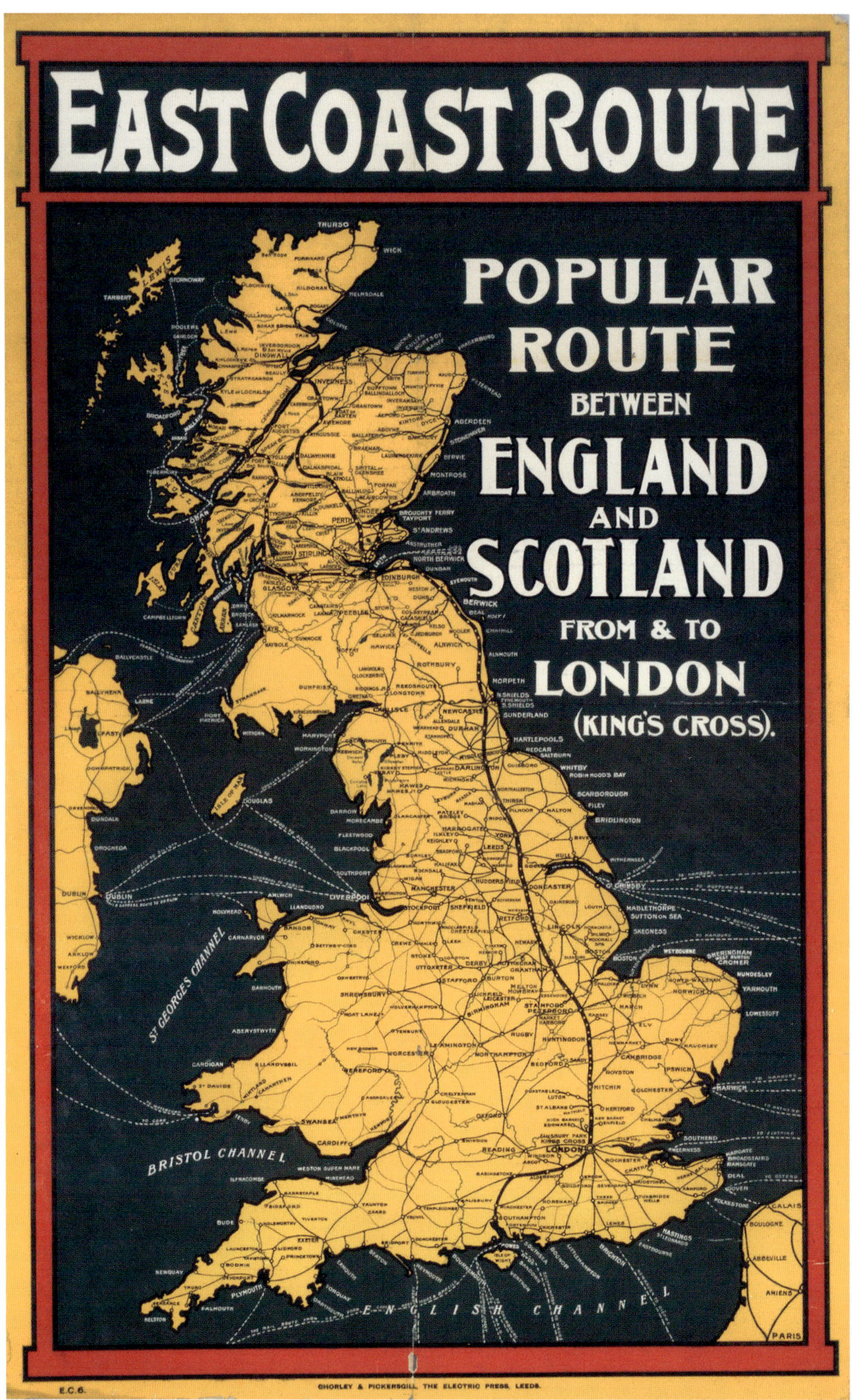

EAST COAST ROUTE
POPULAR ROUTE BETWEEN ENGLAND AND SCOTLAND FROM & TO LONDON (KING'S CROSS).
E.C.6.
CHORLEY & PICKERSGILL, THE ELECTRIC PRESS, LEEDS.

foot' and 'bicycle face' have also been discussed. However, the vehicles have now become standard equipment for delivery boys, postmen and messengers. Even policemen, known colloquially as 'bobbies', use them in the course of their duties.

*

Building sites, for excavation and for construction, are now commonplace in all parts of London; there is hardly a parish or district untouched by improvements. These areas are guarded by wooden boards and fences, by great hoardings plastered with advertisements and placards. On a vacant space, on an empty building, on scaffolding, on shopfronts and in shop windows, on pillars and posts, printed bills are placed. When you walk through the loud and busy streets, you may notice nothing but signs and images. The advertisement is now set to become the street theatre of the city.

The hoarding and the poster are, in fact, the great innovations of our century. The gaudy colours and great images can be seen lining the streets and the new railway stations, displaying everything from Pear's Soap to the *Police Gazette*. There are certain popular sites, among them the north end of Waterloo Bridge and the dead wall beside the English Opera House in Wellington Street, but no one can escape the pictures of pens as gigantic as the Monument, or of spectacles fit for a Brobdingnagian. Underneath the arches of the bridges, bills cover the walls promoting the steamers to Dover, Margate and elsewhere. Posters are plastered everywhere, in any available space or corner, with appeals to buy Bovril, Bird's Custard, Idris Lemonade and Nestlé's Fruit Pastilles; they will be placed next to a picture of Irishmen dancing under the influence of Guinness's Dublin Stout or of children relishing the steam from a plum pudding. There are bright advertisements for Singer sewing machines and Dewar's Whisky, for Batey's Ginger Beer and Batey's Kola. A sign will say 'You'll Feel Better When You've Had a Guinness', 'Drink Perrier Water' or 'Smoke Player's Navy Cut'. The search for novelty is in these days always intense, and Vinolia Soap has been spelled out in illuminated letters above Trafalgar Square. It is well attested that people stop and star at the sign, as if observing a new constellation in the night sky.

We are learning from social scientists that all things work together for a common purpose, and some suppose that the great extent of advertisement is in some way connected to the changes in trading. The working people now have more money

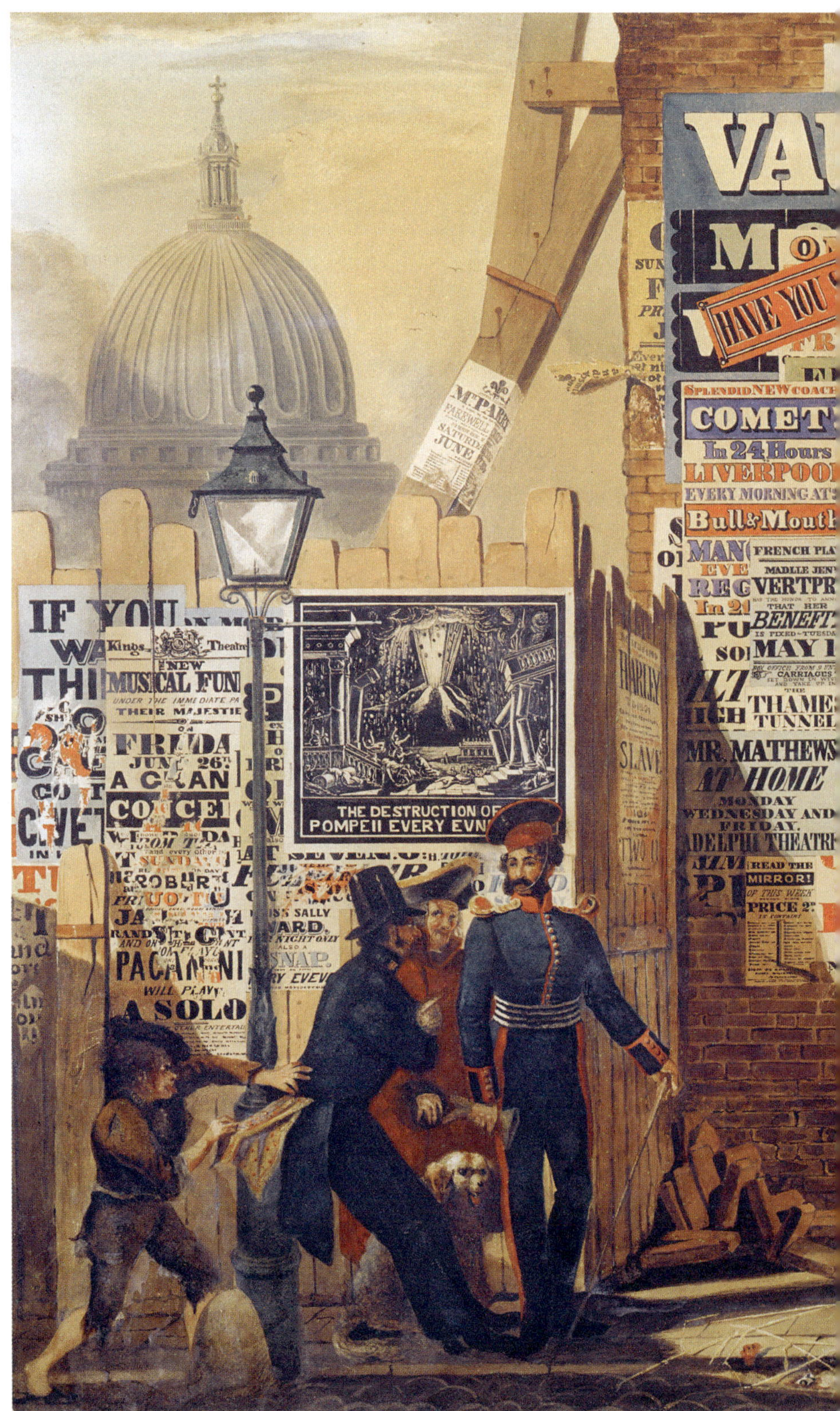

A *London Street Scene* (1835),
watercolour by
John Orlando Parry.

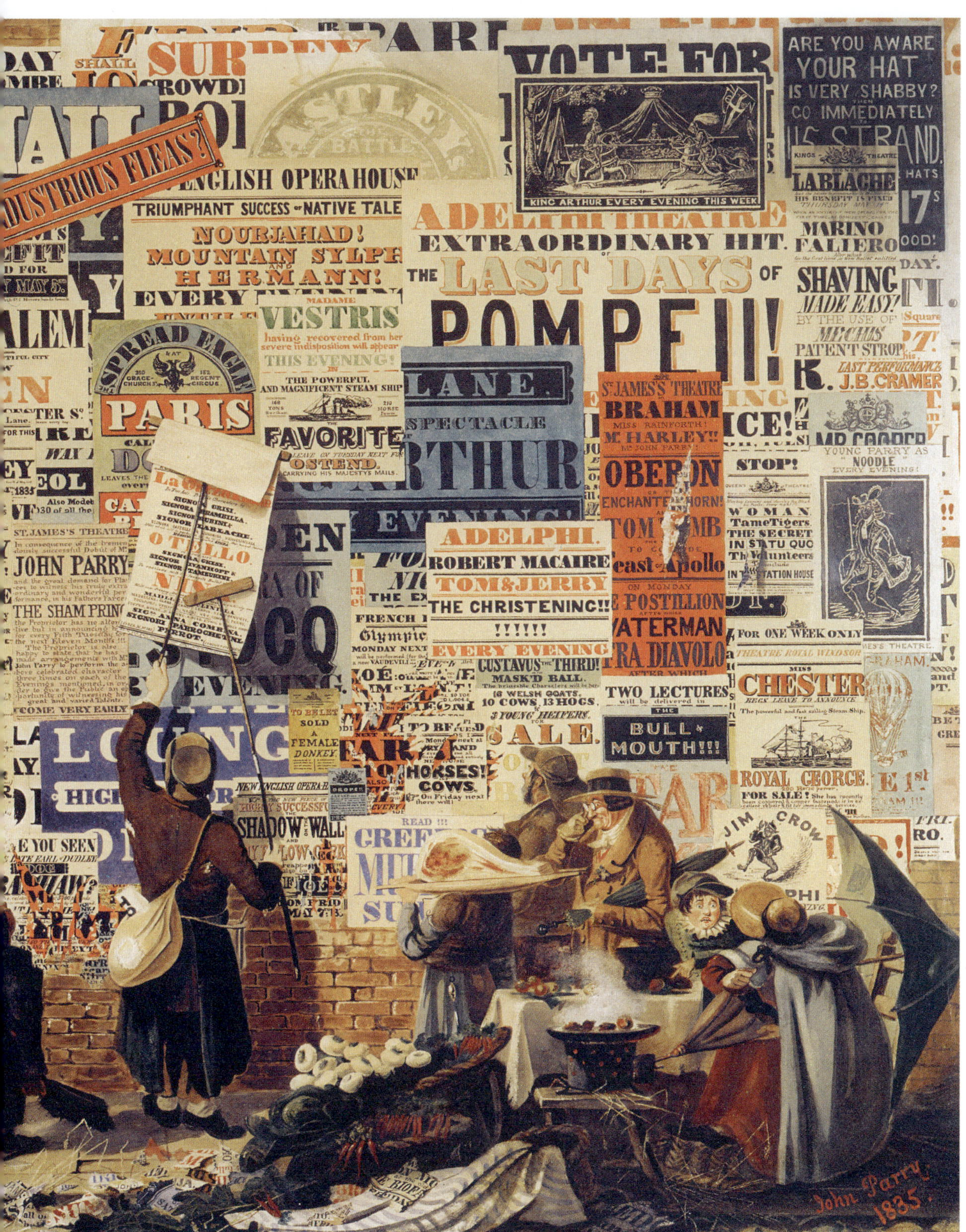

INDUSTRIOUS FLEAS?
SURREY
CROWD
ENGLISH OPERA HOUSE
TRIUMPHANT SUCCESS of NATIVE TALE
NOURJAHAD!
MOUNTAIN SYLPH
AND
HERMANN!
EVERY
MADAME
VESTRIS
having recovered from her
severe indisposition will appear
THIS EVENING!
AND THE POWERFUL
AND MAGNIFICENT STEAM SHIP
THE
FAVORITE
LEAVES ON TUESDAY NEXT FOR
OSTEND
Carrying His Majestys Mails.
SPREAD EAGLE
AT
GRACE-
CHURCH ST
REGENT
CIRCUS
PARIS
DOG
LANE.
SPECTACLE
ARTHUR
EVENING
VOTE FOR
KING ARTHUR EVERY EVENING THIS WEEK
ARE YOU AWARE
YOUR HAT
IS VERY SHABBY?
GO IMMEDIATELY
STRAND,
HATS
LABLACHE
MARINO
FALIERO
17s
SHAVING
MADE EASY!
BY THE USE OF
MECHIS
PATENT STROP.
LAST PERFORMANCE
J. B. CRAMER
ADELPHI THEATRE
EXTRAORDINARY HIT.
THE LAST DAYS of
POMPEII!!
St JAMES'S THEATRE
BRAHAM
MISS RAINFORTH!
Mr HARLEY!!
Mr JOHN PARRY
OBERON
OR THE
ENCHANTED HORN!
TOM THUMB
east Apollo
ON MONDAY
THE POSTILLION
WATERMAN
FRA DIAVOLO
AFTER WHICH
TWO LECTURES
will be delivered in
THE
BULL &
MOUTH!!!
STOP!
WOMAN
TameTigers
THE SECRET
IN STATU QUO
The Volunteers
at
STATION HOUSE
FOR ONE WEEK ONLY
THEATRE ROYAL WINDSOR
MISS
CHESTER
BEGS LEAVE TO ANNOUNCE
The powerful and fast sailing Steam Ship.
ROYAL GEORGE.
FOR SALE!
JIM CROW
JOHN PARRY
THE SHAM PRINCE
ADELPHI.
ROBERT MACAIRE
TOM & JERRY
THE CHRISTENING!!!
!!!!!!
EVERY EVENING
GUSTAVUS the THIRD!
MASK'D BALL
18 WELSH GOATS,
10 COWS, 13 HOGS
3 YOUNG HEIFERS
SALE.
OTHELLO
YOUNG PARRY AS
"NOODLE"
EVERY EVENING!
TO BE LET
SOLD
A
FEMALE
DONKEY
HORSES!!
COWS.
TO BRED
FRENCH
Olympic
MONDAY NEXT
NEW ENGLISH OPERA H
HIGHLY SUCCESSFU
SHADOW on the WALL
LOUNG
HIGH
GREF
READ !!!
E 1st
FRI-
RO.
John Parry
1835.

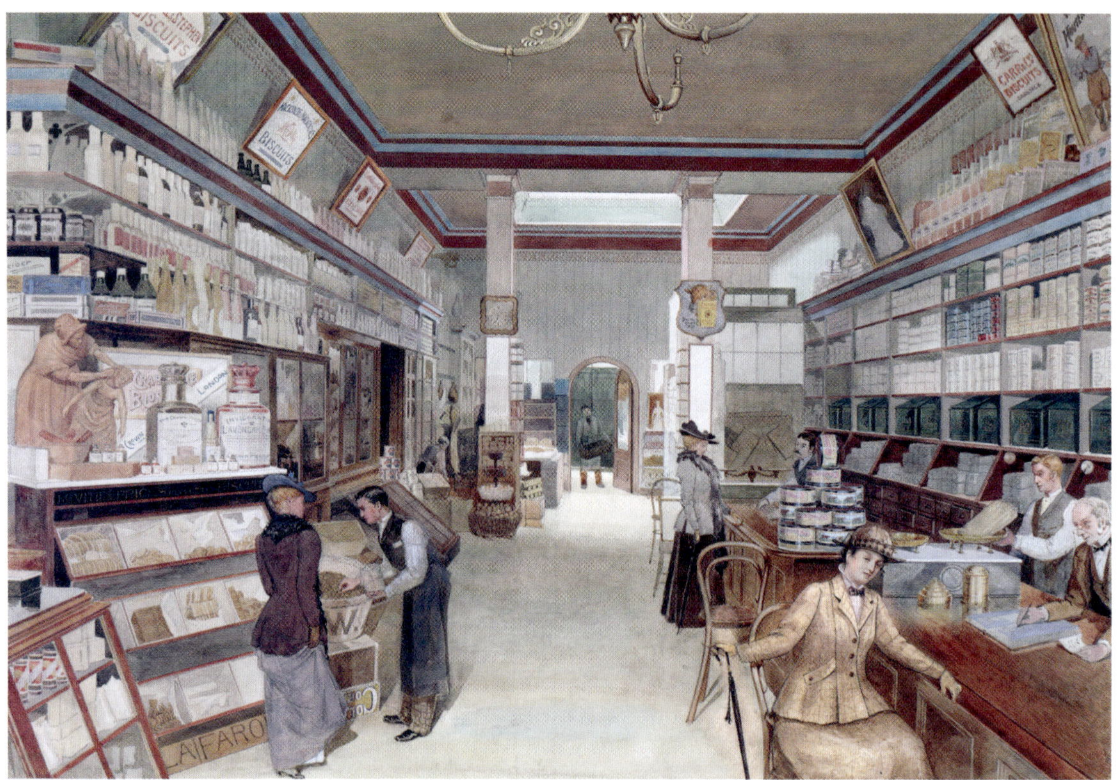

Above Interior of a London Shop (late nineteenth century), watercolour by the British School.

in their pockets and, as a result, the single shop selling a range of different items is being challenged by many stores which sell a particular category of goods, such as groceries or clothing. Certain manufacturers have flourished in the process. You can buy the same bread or the same tobacco in a number of different neighbourhoods. In addition, a large shop may contain several departments. It has become known, quite naturally, as the 'department store'. In these establishments the dresses and the shoes, the linens and the silks, are sold at fixed prices. The staff are treated as domestic servants who live, eat and sleep in rooms above the main store. It is considered to be a mutually satisfactory arrangement, combining the blessings of an alternative family with the benefits of trade.

*

All of these developments are fuelled by the common appetite for the 'new'. The present age has, in fact, often been satirized as the 'period of the new', when new fashions and new habits – even sometimes new people – sweep across the city. You will see a 'new woman', for example, wearing bloomers and riding a bicycle. It emphasizes the fact that this has also become the epoch of 'the woman question'. Some believe that it was inaugurated by the strike of the young women in the Bryant & May match factory, but this is likely to be a symptom rather than a cause. It has not gone unobserved that the new trade unions, particularly those of the shopkeeper and box-makers, contain a large number of females. The 'new woman' is, in general, the representative of advanced and adventurous ideas that have been developing for some time. In modern drama, and in contemporary fiction, there has been a vogue for independent and strong-minded women who rise above their traditional roles. The emancipated woman, which she is also called, has challenged our conventional ideas of marriage and social respectability as well as our acceptance of legal and educational inequality. As such she is the object of much comment. In a recent article in *The Fortnightly Review*, for example, a high-spirited young woman is reported as receiving visits in her bed-sitting room from a young man whose acquaintance she has made on the Underground railway. This would once have seemed offensive on all levels. Cartoons in the satirical press are filled

Below left A woman riding a bicycle wearing bloomers, early twentieth century.

Below right Match girls at the Bryant & May factory in Bow, 1888.

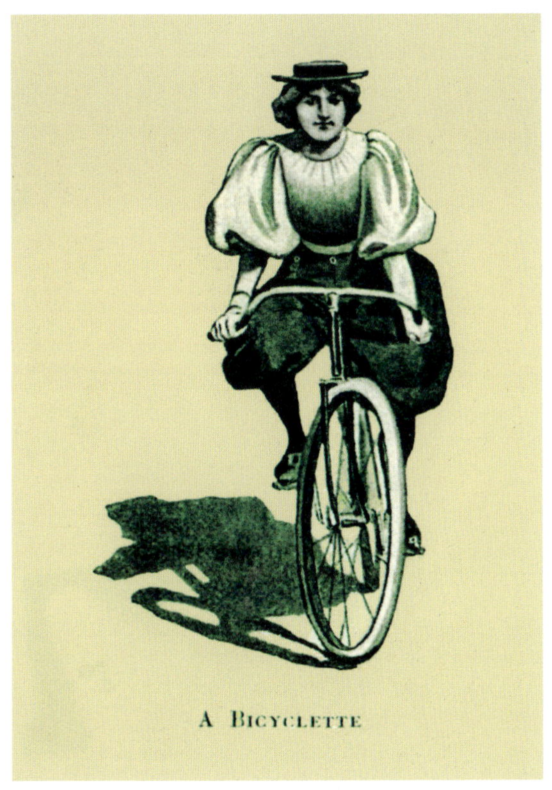

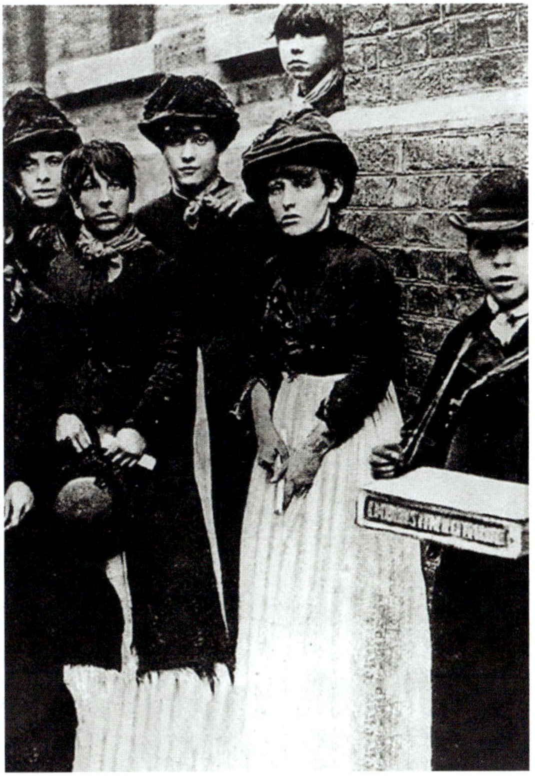

with images of females riding bicycles or sporting wire-framed spectacles. Bicycles are, in particular, a sign of independence. In any case, no one now expects a woman to step through the streets of London with a chaperone, a maid or a footman. Instead she is depicted as striding out, unaccompanied, in her trilby hat, her bloomers or divided skirts, her tweed jacket and collar.

These 'new women' are often derided as mannish, and as part of 'the shrieking sisterhood' who clamour for recognition and who demand in strident tones 'deeds, not words'. However, such females are also leading the way to votes for women and for entrance to all the professions reserved for men. They demand education for the female on the same level and of the same calibre as that of the male, and for the freedom to pursue a career. In the more domestic sphere, they are determined to travel, to visit friends and to ride in a public vehicle unaccompanied by a relative or by a domestic servant.

Their less bold or determined sisters are still subject to a number of constraints. In *The Girl's Own Paper*, it is recommended that in the morning young women should use pure water for a preparatory wash, after which they must avoid any gusts of passion that might affect their

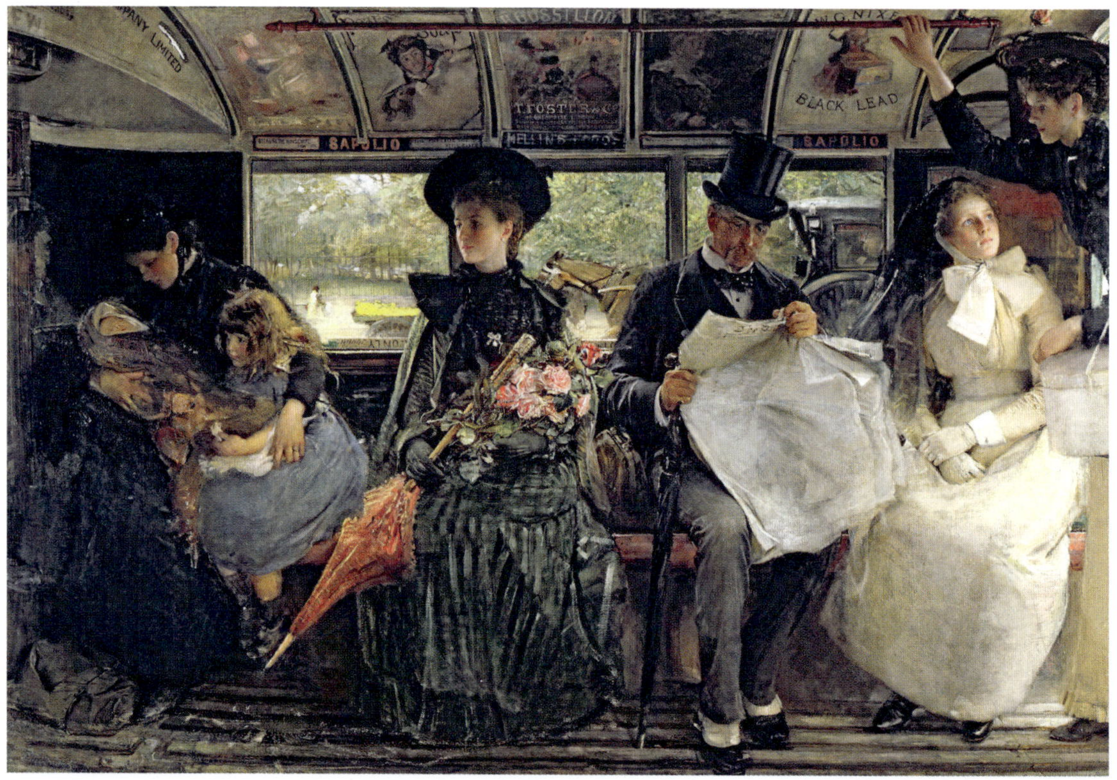

Below The Bayswater Omnibus (1895) by George William Joy.

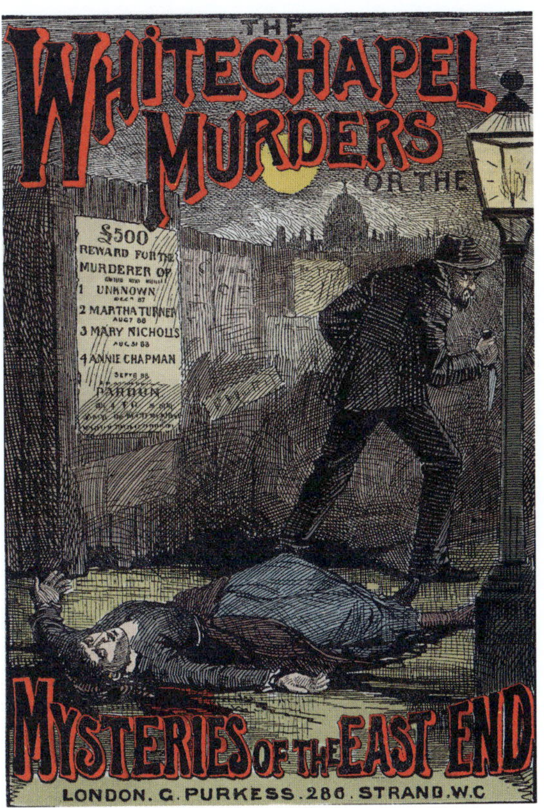

Above The front cover of a penny dreadful, published at the same time as the Jack the Ripper case, in the late 1800s.

complexion; envy, for example, gives the skin a sallow paleness. The young woman must not stay up late, play cards or read novels by candlelight. The exercise of callisthenics is strongly approved, even if only means waving your arms in all directions.

The belief that men represent the stronger sex prevails. Some men are described as nervously sensitive, which renders them melancholy and passive, but this is in direct contrast to the cult of masculinity which is gaining favour in certain circles; it comprises, in various degrees, horse-racing, athletic sports, pipes, beer, betting and billiards. It is complemented by the notion of Muscular Christianity, now becoming fashionable, which encourages manly duty, self-discipline and athleticism. The regimen of public school and university, namely cold baths and organized games, is assiduously cultivated by some in later life.

However, novelty and diversity are apparent in all aspect of modern life. The newspapers are filled with innovation and sensation, whether it be the inauguration of the London County Council or the recent Whitechapel murders. The papers themselves are in the process of change with the evening *Star*, for example, addressed to a less educated public than that which enjoys *The Times* or *The Daily News*. Weekly newspapers, such as *The London Journal* and the *Family Herald*, are also popular with a large audience. They include serial fiction, letters and advice columns on all matters social and domestic. Some of them seem to breach the principles of decorum, such as the notice that 'married women who have committed little frailties, please consult the editor'. These calls for advice throw an interesting light on the perils and problems of our moving age. You should not shake hands with a lady on your first introduction to her. You can sell ointment without a patent. A reader wants a recipe for gingerbread, while others want cures for grey hairs, warts, nervousness and intestinal worms. Another reader wishes to know what an esquire is, and another asks for the correct pronunciation of 'picturesque' and 'acquiescence'. Yet another enquires for the right hour of the day to visit a newly married couple. Is there any inconsistency in being a dancing mistress as well as a teacher at a Sunday School? Can I sell lemonade without a licence? I have been in love with a woman for four years, and have not yet mentioned it to her. Please advise as soon as possible.

The number of more independent women may be a cause for the rise of the tea shop as a London institution where they may sit alone. It is something like an old-fashioned pastry cook's shop, but it is more domestic in atmosphere and has been blessed with that new-found adjective of 'Victorian'. It suits the time. Sometimes known as the milk-and-bun shop, it is part of that new atmosphere of democracy and civility which surrounds us.

The Aerated Bread Company launched a similar service a few years ago with plain fare as well as no-nonsense efficiency and cheapness, and within a few years it has played a large part in the Londoner's life. ABC shops are now being challenged by the firm of Joe Lyons.

These larger establishments are no longer reserved for females, however, but cater for all walks of life from peers and writers to barbers and policemen. They fill, as the comedians say, a long-felt want. A tea shop of Whitechapel will cater to furriers, one in Fleet Street to barristers and one in Bloomsbury to students. The old coffee shops are still the best stop for carmen and others, but the tea shop, like many other venues of London life, has obliterated all outward distinctions. You may once have only seen the postman when he rapped on the door in his scarlet uniform, but now he may be sitting at the table next to you.

*

No one can now claim to have walked down every London street. That feat may have been possible 50 or 60 years ago, but now the city is too elaborate and too immense. If you wander at will or whim, however, you may still be intrigued by signs and activities that illustrate the new city. A horse-drawn van, bearing the sign of the 'Electric Power Bakery', will draw up in the road beside you, with a number of boys standing in the back. They are wearing caps and are dressed in starched white collars and short jackets. On the street behind them is a poster advertising the Shoreditch Empire and promising Kate Carney, the Terry Twins and the Ten Loonies. On the frontage of a dusty shop is painted 'Why Suffer From Rheumatism, Sciatica & Cold Feet? Try Edwards' Electric Heel Pads Within. 1d per pair'. Further down the street a large pointing

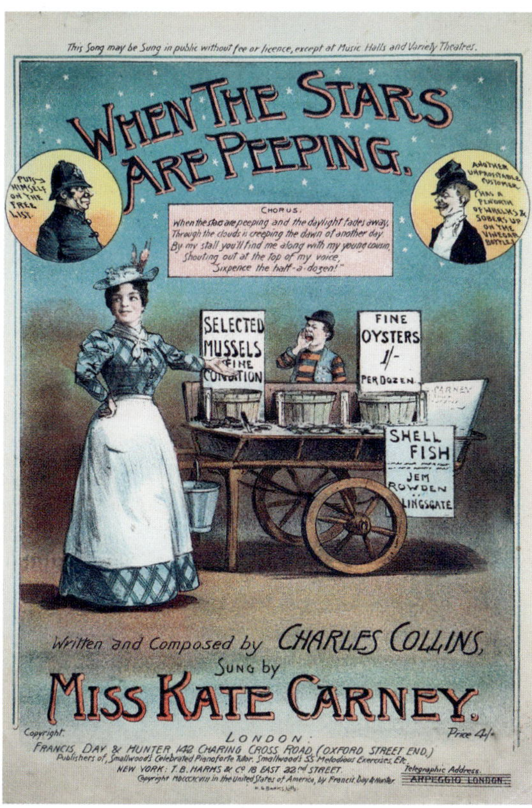

The cover of the sheet music for 'When the Stars are Peeping' sung by Miss Kate Carney, lithograph (1898).

hand directs you to the 'Middlesex Music Hall with Monster Variety Entertainment at 7pm'. A man, who may be young or old, is slouched in a doorway, head down, with a coat torn and dirty. He may be part of a new race bred in the new city, who have no home but dens and lairs into which they creep. On the corner of one thoroughfare are signs and posters for hot and cold baths, hosiery, shaving, new gloves, white shirts and handkerchiefs. London Bridge, if you walk that way, is filled with horse-drawn omnibuses plastered with advertisements for Pears Soap, Reckitt's Blue, Cadbury's Cocoa and Nestlé's Milk. A horse-drawn cart has stopped at the side of the road bearing piles of wooden crates. Another cart has on its side a placard for 'J. Lyons & Co. Ltd. Universal Caterers'. Pedestrians dodge between cabs, vans and wagons. Men in straw hats or bowlers, small girls in white pinafores and ladies in wide hats and long skirts crowd the pavements. If you walk along Cheapside you will pass a shop selling telescopes and opera glasses beside one that deals in rocking horses and perambulators; further along is an establishment for the repair of clocks, watches and chronometers. On the floors above are a dentist, an optician, a firm of sanitary and heating engineers, and the premises of an Orphan Working School. On a bright day the awnings, striped or many coloured, are all pulled down to subdue the glare of the street.

The streets of any neighbourhood may harbour taverns or stout and ale merchants, family hotels or temperance hotels, dining and refreshment rooms, coffee shops and coffee rooms. Hair-cutting saloons are to be found everywhere. However, contrasts also abound in London. In Chequer Yard, off Dowgate Hill, the City Bicycle School can be found beside a Rags, Bone and Fat merchant. On Great Queen Street, Ye Old Candy Stores is next to a cheap lodging house for 'respectable men only'. Ranged beside them are a carpet warehouse, a diamond merchant and a fishing tackle shop. Ackermann's on Regent Street is proclaiming the Diaphone, ''Tis the Voice Itself', while still selling sporting prints. On Fleet Street can be found the *Daily News*, the *News of the World*,

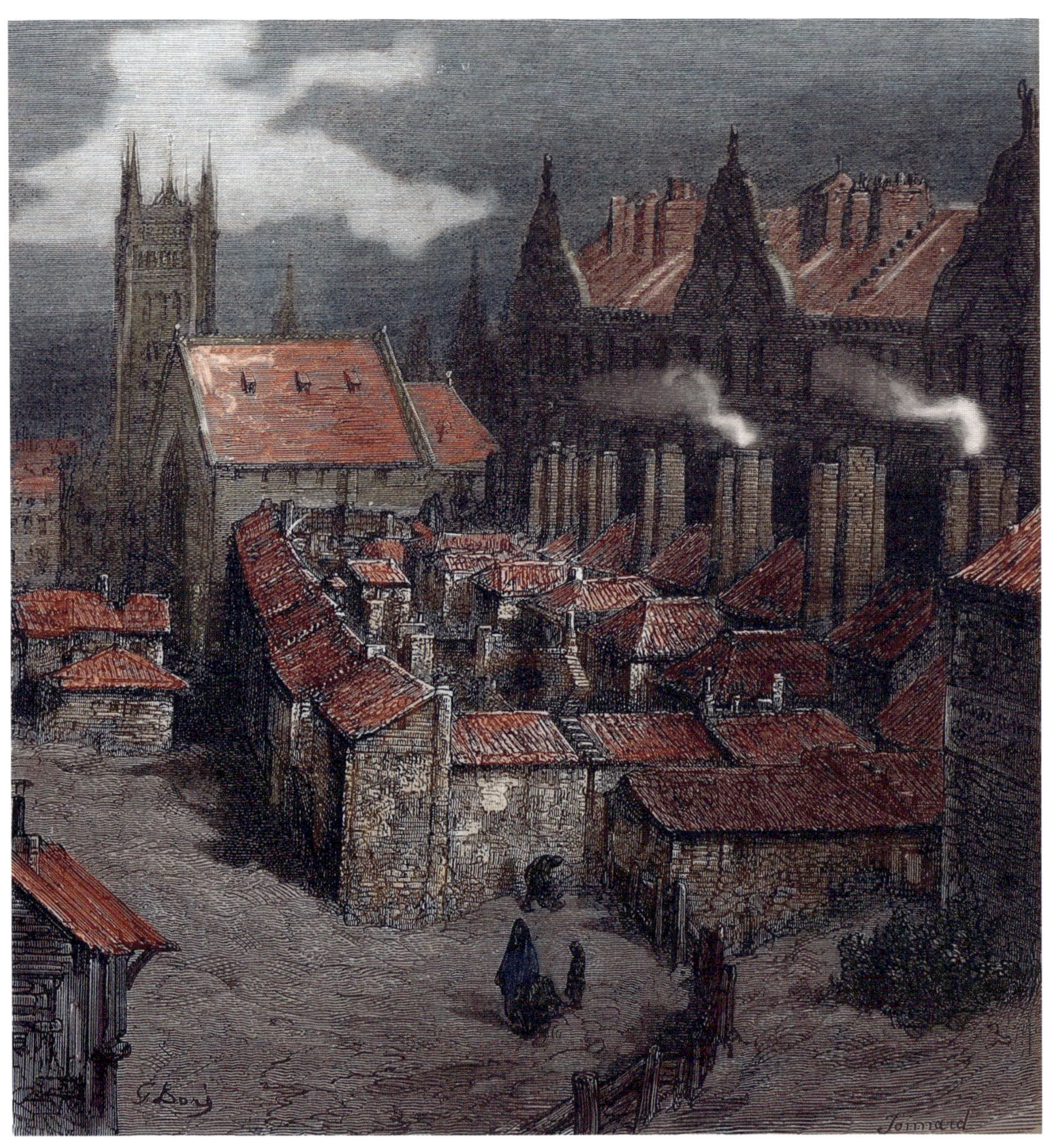

The People's Friend, *The Dundee Advertiser* and other newspapers of the day. Attached to some railings on the same street are two postal boxes, guaranteeing eight to ten collections a day. You may also note, in your wanderings, the weather-boarded houses, the pots of plants and the bird cages placed on the window sills, the drinking fountains, the dogs running wild, the litter of paper and peel in the streets, and the plethora of children.

*

The outer limits of London extend further each day. South London, for example, has grown immeasurably over the last few years and has the appearance of another city, darker and more dangerous. The slums of the south part are worse than anywhere else in London, perhaps with the exception of the 'Devil's Acre' in Westminster. By the docks and factories, on the southern bank of the river, there is desperate poverty. It is compounded by the menace of the Thames itself. The low-lying and densely populated area of Lambeth, for example, can be invaded by floods. The high tides leave a trail of misery in their wake, with thousands of tenements suffused with a damp, noxious and fever-breeding atmosphere. Rheumatism, bronchitis and congestion of the lungs have become common complaints. The distress is not confined to one particular class but the majority of sufferers are the poor families of labourers who are engaged about the wharves and warehouses set in those dark canyons of dirty brick which run down to the water. The inhabitants are forced to live in an area where destitution as well as crime flourish, and they will occupy one or two rooms for a few shillings a week. On the shout of 'The tide! The tide!' from beneath the window, they rescue whatever poor possessions they can carry from the invading Thames.

These calamities are reported in the newspapers, but the south still remains relatively unknown to other Londoners. Some citizens will venture as far south as Westminster Bridge Road, with its flower shops, restaurants and music halls, but few will travel any further. Southwark is perhaps the most familiar district, but it is relatively undeveloped and little regarded. It has remained an enclosed and self-sufficient neighbourhood for many years. Its parish vestry collects the rates and distributes poor relief, and its local courts supervise all aspects of trade. It has its own shops for the local people, as well as its workshops, its mean lodging houses and its small factories. Like other parts of south London, too, its

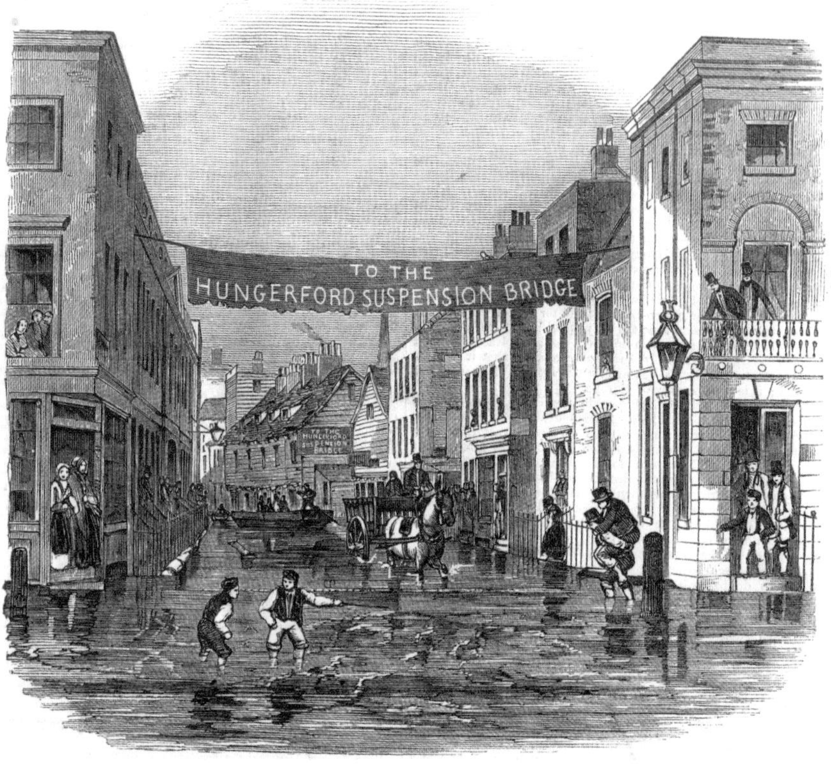

inhabitants live in the same houses and intermarry in the same neighbourhood. A stable population has therefore fostered its own communal atmosphere.

Close by, on either side of the high street in Borough, the houses and tenements are bursting with people, and so the women and children spend much of their time in the streets close to their dwellings. The women sit outside on their chairs or lean from their window sills and, as a result, the neighbourhood itself rather than the individual household is the true family. Wives look out for each other and the children play together. However, in other circumstances it may seem less of a family and more of a jungle tribe. The wretched remains of rickety structures are connected to the main street by entrances that are no more than tunnels. One narrow alley is no more than a row of stables, with its front yards as a dumping ground filled with house refuse and horse manure, with broken bread and orange peel, peanut shells, bones, banana skins, apple cores, bits of rag and the heels of shoes. Yet there are local differences. The present neighbourhood of Rotherhithe, for example, is quite distinct from that of Brixton or of Camberwell. In these districts, too, the people will rarely move

from one area to another. In this respect the character of a street,
or even a parish, may be maintained over many generations. It a
mark of London itself.

The south, or 'London-over-the-Water' as it is sometimes called,
is in any case a source of disquiet for other Londoners and is still
regarded as a boundary zone to which the rest of the city can
consign its dirt and its rubbish. This is where some of the 'stink
industries', like the tanneries of Bermondsey or the pickle-makers
of Kennington, are located. It is the site of other noisome trades,
such as hat-making and leather-tanning. The manufacturers of dye,
and the suppliers of tallow, of biscuits and of jam, are also to be
found here. Glue factories stand adjacent to timber warehouses
and close to slaughter houses. The predominant smells are those
of vinegar and of dog dung, of hops and leather, of smoke and beer,
all of them compounded of course by the stink of poverty.

South London is frowsy; it is shabby; its shops are small and
generally dirty. It has none of the power or the energy of the
city on the other side of the Thames. It moves at a slower pace,
and is considered by most Londoners to be a distinct and alien
place. It is in that sense cut off from the general life of the greater
city, and this may account for the sense of exhaustion or torpor
which strikes the visitor. Some even believe it to be airless, by
which they may mean lack of energy. You cannot live here and
harbour any ambition.

It is well-known that a preponderance of prisons, of institutions
for the insane and of asylums for the poor are also to be found
south of the river. It might be considered a matter of chance,
except that there is no such thing as chance in London. The city is
guided by powers which we are only just beginning to understand.
The south has also acquired a reputation for dubious taverns and
doubtful pleasure gardens. Yet it has grown and grown. The three
great toll bridges erected earlier in this century – at Southwark,
Waterloo and Vauxhall – have opened it up to an increasing
population, and the whole area is being covered in roads and
houses as far as Peckham and Camberwell, Clapham and Brixton.
Nevertheless, the great swathe of the river will always isolate
the south.

That cannot be said of the other great district that has
grown up in later years. The area to the east of Aldgate Pump
has become known only recently as the East End, but it was once
the centre of shipping and of industry, and thus the home of the
working poor. It is now covered with houses and is so densely

populated that once suburban villages such as Hackney, Clapton, Stoke Newington and Stepney have become small cities within a larger whole. What were once the hamlets of West Ham and East Ham are now unrecognizable. What Chaucer knew as 'Stratford atte Bowe' is no more. The people of the original east end have now overflowed and crossed the Lea, spreading themselves over the marshes and meadows beyond. This industrial population represents a migration over the last 20 years. As a result, the poverty and the industry have steadily intensified until it has all the appearance of a bricken wilderness of factories and tenements, a noxious part of the city in which more poor people are crammed than in any other. There is no fashionable quarter, and so no private carriages. There are no bookshops and no free libraries. Can anyone read? There are no hotels and no visitors. The east seems to have no history and so, unlike the rest of London, it harbours no sense of the past.

Soon enough it has become known in the sensational press as a most dangerous quarter of thieves and ruffians and now, with the murders in Whitechapel, it is a byword for savagery and immorality. There is no need to ask, the East End of what? The term has been taken up by the halfpenny press, in the music hall and in the pulpit. It is depicted, by novelists and reporters, as the shadow which London itself casts. Everyone knows of it, but few know about it. So it is an urban Proteus, capable of assuming many forms. For some it has become a microcosm of London's own dark life, a pest-stricken region swarming with a nameless populace. For others it is a haven and a sanctuary, as for the thousands of Jews who are coming from Eastern Europe. For many it is marked as the site of Christian endeavour, with many missions and settlements established for social and religious purposes. Yet, for still more, it is the home of revolution, promoted by Marxian socialists and French anarchists; their capital is in Whitechapel, and in particular Jubilee Street, Fieldgate Street and Whitechapel High Street.

In general, however, the East End is a quiet and dreary place, not at first sight a neighbourhood of radicals and freethinkers. You may find a few people milling outside a shopfront which contains vases, watches, old clothes and silver; the large sign above proclaims 'Money Lent'. Another establishment will declare 'Loans of £2 Upwards on Note of Hand. Forms Within. No Enquiry Fees'. The sign of the pawnbroker is not unusual. That shop has been the resort of Londoners for years uncounted.

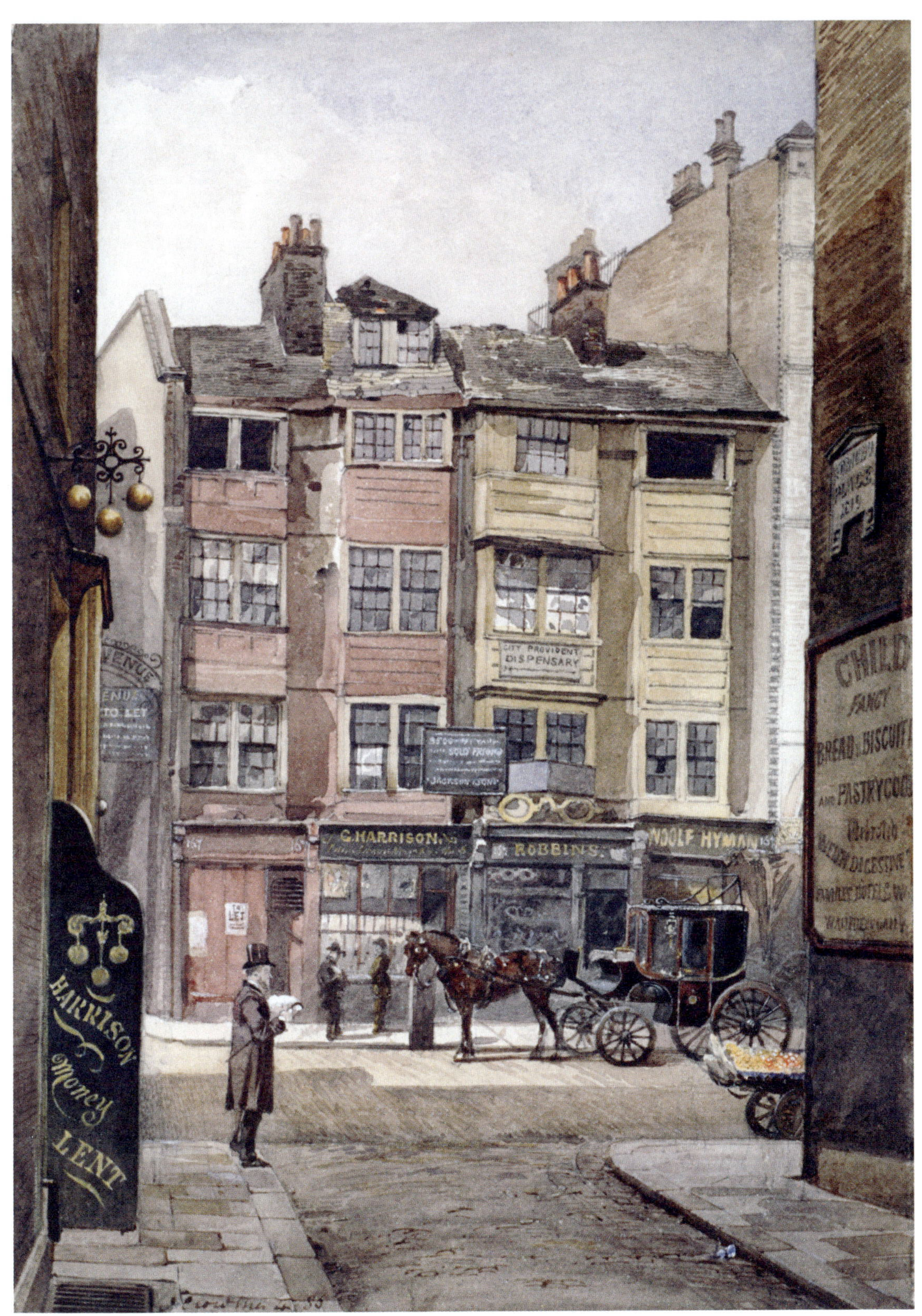

AVENUE
TO LET
HARRISON
Money
LENT
CITY PROVIDENT
DISPENSARY
SOLD FRIEND
JACKSON
C. HARRISON
ROBBINS.
WOOLF HYMAN
CHILD
FANCY
BREAD & BISCUIT
AND
PASTRYCOOK
TO LET

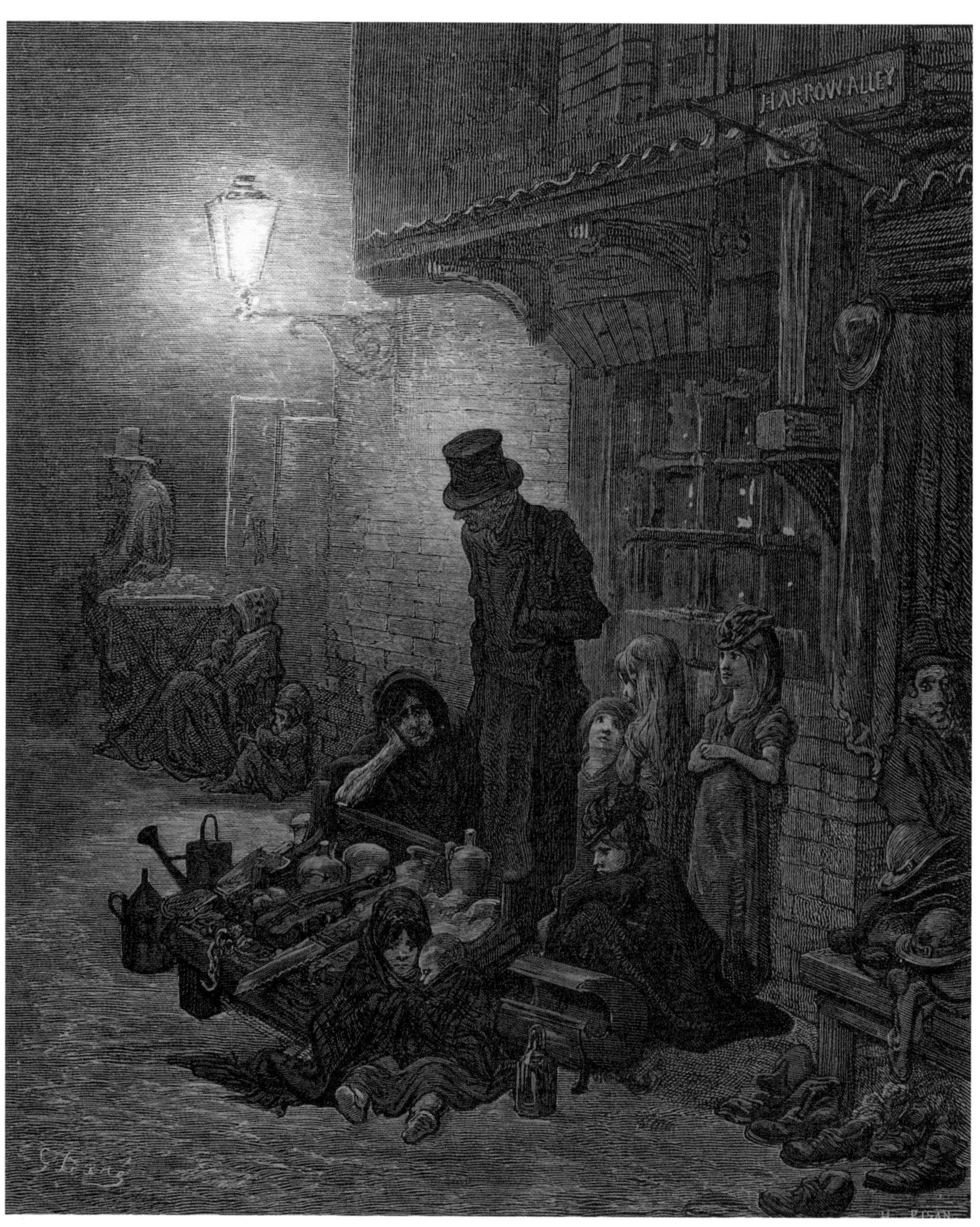

HARROW ALLEY

The three spheres that swing above the door may be seen in all but the grandest districts, indicating that you may pledge your goods there and receive in turn what you will be sullenly assured is their true value. Should you ever be unfortunate enough to enter such a place, you will find a side doorway, and, through an inner door, you pass into one of a series of compartments constructed before the pawnbroker's counter. Two or three gas jets light the interior, but the boxes are in shadow. It is hard, even impossible, to ignore the atmosphere of indigence. There is the strong musty odour, the gloom, the narrow compartments and the low tones of conversation. For the heap of shillings you had hoped for, you are offered a handful of pennies. There is no bartering in a pawnbroker's: you must accept what you are given. Naturally enough, he casts a garland of roses over his trade; he is performing a public service, an act of neighbourly charity. However, as every Londoner knows, poverty is a token of vice and this institution, like the workhouse itself, scolds and sneers at the indigent. The sour, flat accents of the man behind the counter, his cold disregard of courtesy, rather give the lie to the claims made on this great institution's behalf.

In truth, the East End is the domain of the working man, of the labourer and the artisan, who earns a weekly or even daily wage. It contains about 500 miles of streets, perhaps more, but they are all turned out on the same pattern as if they are built by machinery. Most of them are narrow, dirty, poverty laden and stall-lined thoroughfares made up of long lines of low houses, comprising one or two storeys with a basement, of the same yellowish brick, all begrimed by the same smoke, every door-knocker of the same pattern, and every window blind hung in the same way. They are to be found beside a similar array of marts, emporiums and warehouses. The same corner 'public' lies on every corner, open from early morning until half past midnight. Some local women will visit it at seven in the morning, and stay until three in the afternoon.

The doorsteps and roadways, and pavements where they exist, are swarming with children. The street is their only playground, from the barefooted and bareheaded boy to the girl of six bearing in her arms her much younger sister. To have no shoes is a sign of desperate poverty. It has been calculated that, out of a hundred infants born in these neighbourhoods, more than fifty will die before the age of five. Many children go down to the river at low tide; they run out upon the mud in their bare feet and pick up

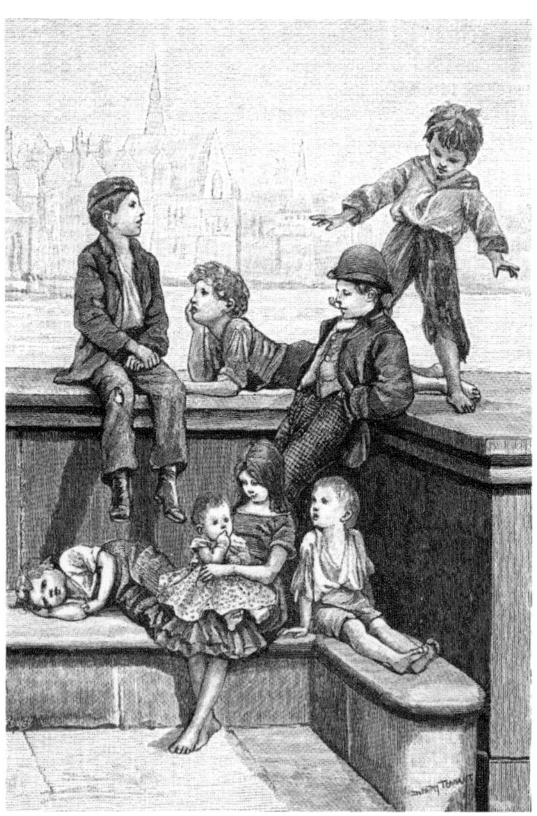

Above 'Street Arabs' at play by the Thames, with one young girl holding an infant.

handfuls of coal to carry home. Many of their fathers and older brothers are to be seen lounging or slouching, or as they say, 'hanging around' the dock gates or against the dock walls, waiting for a call to work on the ships. If they are chosen, they fetch and carry, load and unload, pack and unpack, but the work is sporadic and uncertain. The colour of life is grey. The people themselves are dirty, and any attempt at cleanliness is a thing impossible and an object of mockery. Some vagrant odours come drifting along the noisome wind, and the rain, when it falls, is more like grease than water. The cobbles themselves are scummed with it. In some respects, the area resembles a geological formation made up of soot, dust and sweat.

In other neighbourhoods, such as Poplar, little shops of various shapes and sizes are mixed with rows of one-storeyed houses, standing a few feet back from the pavement behind iron railings. Whitechapel itself is occupied by a network of courts and alleys, none of which have serviceable or even recognizable roads. Some of the courts are, in fact, made up of low, wooden and dilapidated dwellings. The horse omnibus and the stream train have now linked some parts of the East End to the City and, as a result, builders in areas such as Hackney and Shoreditch have erected houses for the workers where there once had been ditches, dirt and dust mountains, but the 'improvements' really improve nothing at all.

The poor quarters are still being destroyed, but the unhoused have nowhere else to go. They stream further east, according to reports, and join the vast army of dockers, artisans and seamen in search of dwelling space. The demand for jerry-built cottages is increasing daily, but supply is slow and limited. That is why the East End has become known for the cheap lodging houses and doss houses in which the living conditions are poor or altogether wretched. Rents are going up all the time, of course, and so there may be notices of 'Part of a room to let' in a house which already contains many families. The only solution then becomes the

Salvation Army hostel, where you sleep side by side in wooden boxes or, more likely, the workhouse, which is known to poor Londoners as the 'Bastille' or 'the House'. All of them fear the prospect of going there, where you may have to break stones in order to be served a rudimentary meal.

The pictures in the popular press, such as *The Graphic* and *Reynold's News*, engrave in the readers' minds the images of violence and assault in these East End streets, of cock fights and dog fights, of ratting and of gambling, of a woman being savagely beaten by her husband and of a child lying hungry and neglected in a passage. The readers are informed that if the men work at all, it is as casual dock labourers, but that most of them do not exert themselves to any degree. They spend their time in stealing or in receiving stolen goods, in hawking, gambling, betting and cadging. They also read that the women are vicious and drunken, generally hostile to outsiders or strangers. It is recommended that any visitor should take a companion and always walk down the middle of the street. It is called the city of dreadful night, the modern Babylon, the nether world, the abyss.

This may be the rankest melodrama to serve as sauce to the general public, and the accounts of poverty and deprivation,

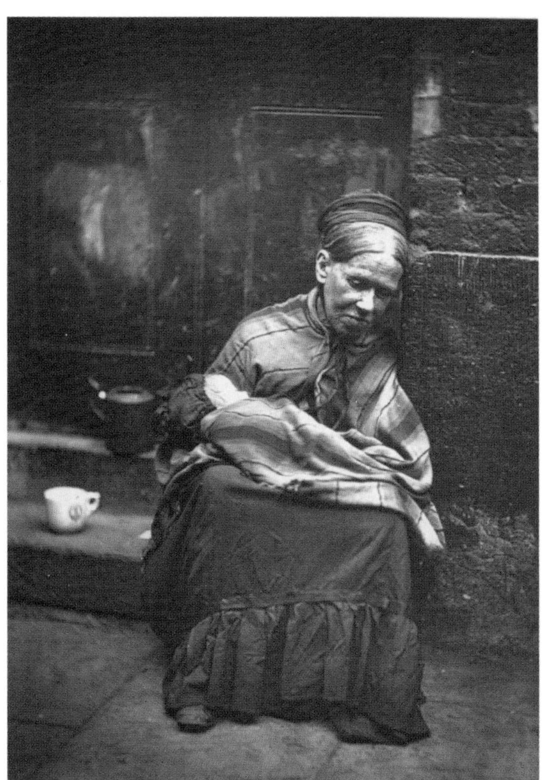

Below left A poor woman and child on a doorstep, c.1881.

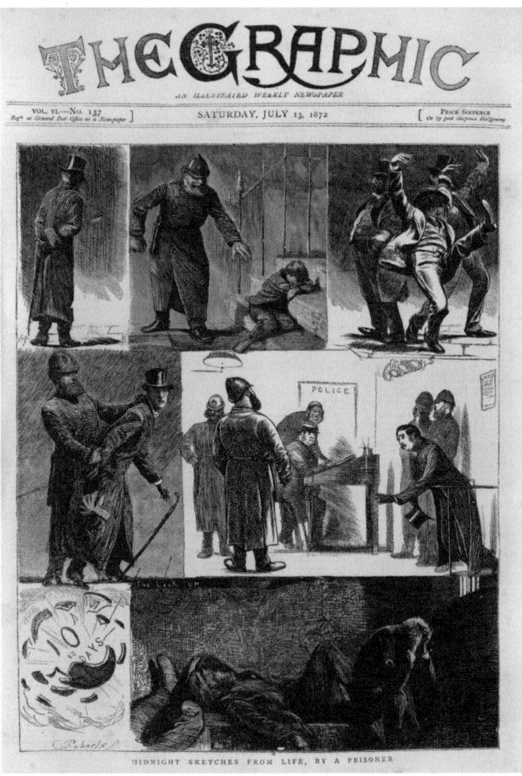

Below right The front page of *The Graphic* newspaper, 1872.

of sickness and hardship, must be balanced by observation of
the East Enders themselves. Everyone who has ventured into
their neighbourhoods remarks upon the cheerfulness of the
inhabitants in the local shops and markets, eating houses and
public houses. The real East Ender moves like an eel through the
press of people, hardly touching as he goes, always giving way
yet always going on with an impersonal but interested eye. He
knows where the crowds are, and knows how to avoid them, and
he never asks questions except mocking ones. He knows that he
knows as much as anyone else. That is his attitude towards life.
The whining vowels and ruined consonants of his speech are
often linked with a ready laugh and with an indomitable strength
of character in which humour and bravado are easily mingled.
That is what many now mean by 'Cockney' character. His life
is not always monotonous. The charitable missions run outings
which allow families to escape their 'out-of-the-way' streets and
to visit Epping Forest or other rusticated areas; the pubs, churches
and street clubs of Bow or Stepney make expeditions into the
country, often by charabanc, while sports clubs arrange events
for their members. The London, Tilbury & Southend Line takes
East Enders down to the sea. On Wanstead Flats stalls and shies,
shows and swings are all packed closer together than those on
Hampstead Heath.

From the East End, also, has emerged the music hall, which
has now become the major form of public diversion in the
capital. Four halls thrive in Bethnal Green alone – the Rodney,
the Lord Nelson, the Eastern and the Apollo – but now they have
appeared all over London to the number of almost four hundred.
Tower Hamlets harbours a large proportion of them. No form of
entertainment has ever been so popular. Low music halls, like the
Raglan in Southwark and the Pavilion on the Whitechapel Road,
do a good trade among the locals as well as the toffs and swells
who like the 'sozzled' atmosphere, but they are outshone by the
grand palaces of variety, such as the Canterbury in Lambeth, the
Old Mo in Drury Lane, the Royal in Holborn and the Oxford off
the Tottenham Court Road. London is the city of music halls. They
have become more ornate in recent years, with gilt and plaster,
balconies and stage boxes, lights and mirrors. Some of them are
beautifully decorated with frescoes, in the modern style, and
the promenade bars are dressed with flowers and coloured glass,
stocked with brass-bound barrels and fancy bottles. They are all
furnished for eating as well as drinking, with chops and steaks

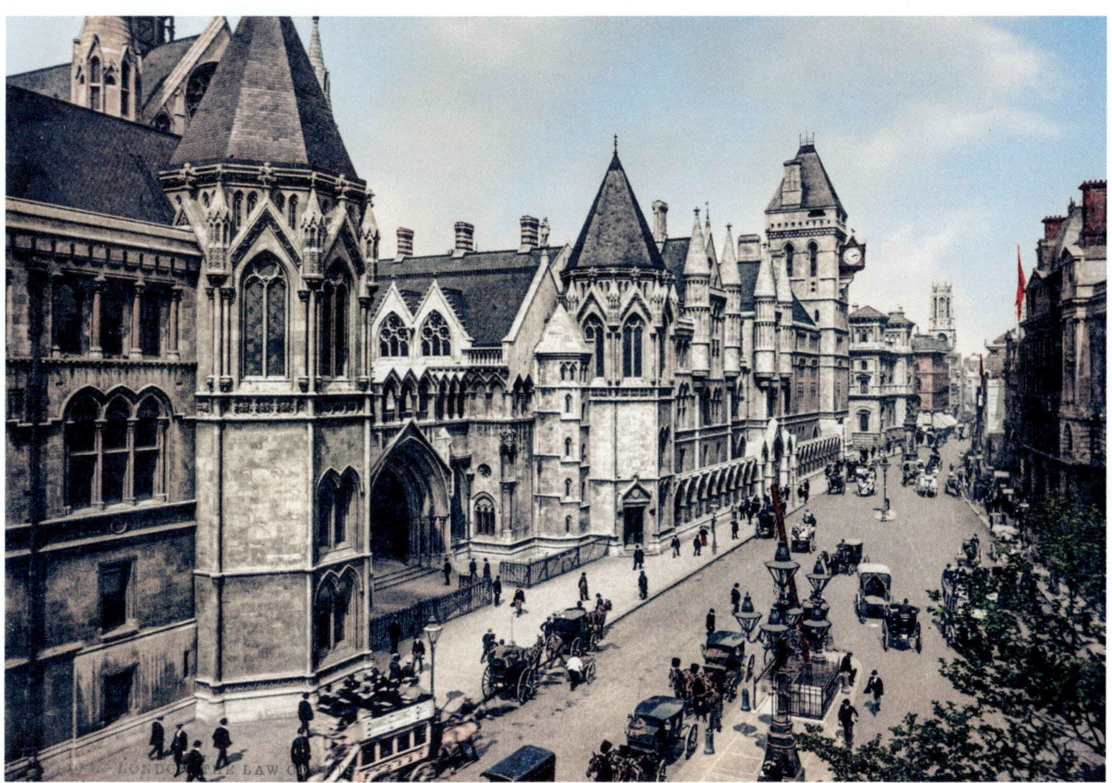

The Royal Courts of Justice in Holborn, with horse-drawn bus and carriages, c.1890s.

served at the various tables. In this respect they differ markedly from the theatres which are their principal rivals.

The halls are visited by all classes, except the very poor, who come to see the most celebrated singers and performers of the day. The people are united in their jollity, their jokes and in their patriotism. It is no accident that the new all-variety theatres are often called 'Empires'. Various comic artistes will come onto the stage as dustmen or as vagabonds, as drunks or as policemen, burlesquing the various features of street life which their audience know so well. Familiar roles, such as the waiter, the shop-walker and the muffin man are always a success. Females who specialize in serio-comic parts will take on the role of chambermaid or washerwoman with a conviction sometimes born out of experience, breaking into songs which may be melodramatic or farcical. For those who listen, or sing along, it represents the only world they recognize. It is lower class London in its essence, with its fried fish shops, its public houses, its pawnbrokers, its shellfish stalls, its old clothes shops and its markets. Of course the performances come from the tradition of the tavern concerts and the harmonic meetings, from the song-

and-supper rooms and the night cellars, but they are now pitched at a higher level to fill a hall and to entertain a varied crowd.

Many of the performers are already well-known. Whether it be Vesta Tilley or Dan Leno, they summon up the heart and soul of London. They celebrate the spirit of the people in comic songs and in burlesque. Leno himself impersonates the characters of ordinary life with a ribald humour and an attention to dress and manner which go beyond caricature. He is small, but full of grievance. He is frail, but he is determined. As a critic has said, he is incarnate of the will to live in a world not at all worth living in. He does not amuse or astonish the audience. He *is* the audience.

The other acts are also much anticipated. Any single performance lasts for a short time, between five and fifteen minutes, in front of an often raucous audience. The halls have an odour of oranges and beer, of unwashed bodies and tobacco. They are loud and rowdy places, where the audience may engage in impromptu dances or in violent squabbles. The women of the town wander at the back of the gallery. When ushered onto the stage the sand dancers, the acrobats, the ventriloquists, the Black serenaders and the magicians will be greeted with enthusiasm.

Below left Vesta Tilley, a popular music hall male impersonator, early twentieth century.

Below right Vesta Tilley in the uniform of a British army officer during the First World War. She was known as 'England's greatest recruiting sergeant' due to her frequently encouraging men to join up during her act.

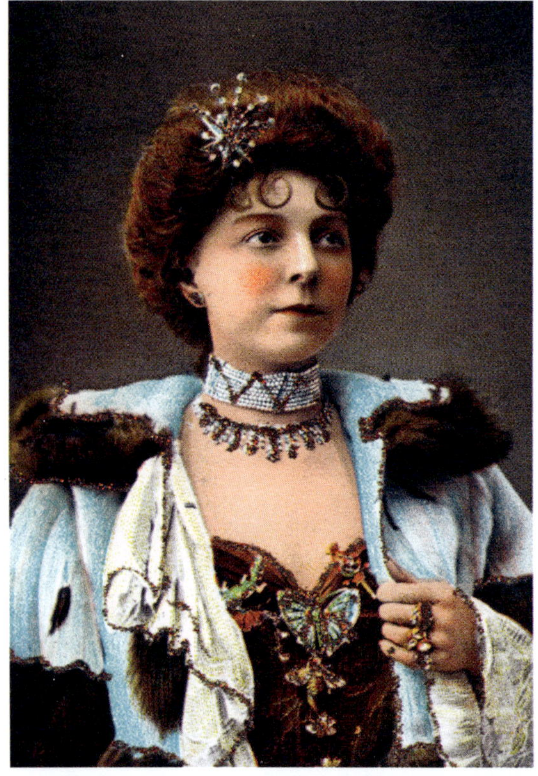

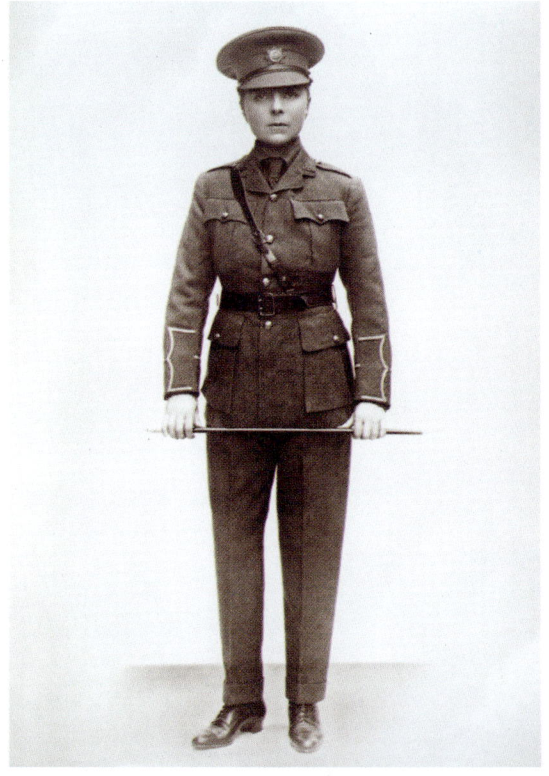

The people sing along with the familiar ditties, and call out the catchphrases of a favourite comedian, but they can turn ferocious when acts are whistled off to the accompaniment of jeers, nuts and orange peel.

Much attention is also paid to the chairman of the proceedings. He is in his own way a lion comique, to use the professional term, with his playful puns, purple passages and endless alliterations. He introduces many acts, makes many jokes and generally encourages the members of the audience to drink up and enjoy the fun. They hardly need encouragement, of course, and have already paid 'wet money', which is the price of admission including 'a glass of something'. The performers are often no more sober than the audience, and many are known to have died of the drink. The life of the music hall is always tough and demanding, with the constant echo of the cry that that 'I must hurry along to my next hall!'

The artistes generally favour coster songs and those written in the 'flash' or Cockney dialect. These ditties, more often coarse than clean, are devoted to the woes of the working people, to the little details of social and domestic life, and to the perils of living on the edge of downright poverty. All of us recall the famous 'Sam Hall', with its refrain of 'damn your eyes!' sung in cellar rooms and shouted out in the street by men and boys. Its notoriety is now being challenged by bawdy 'character songs' such as 'Did You Ever Hear a Girl Say No?' and 'Off She Goes Again!' The characters include tramps, cab drivers, waiters or the 'shabby genteel', as gentlemen down on their luck are known. Some comedians dress oddly or walk in a peculiar manner, complete with umbrella or walking stick. The sketches include boxers, drunks and bicycle thieves. It is cruel, crude and boisterous. It is the East End of the present moment.

'Once the city reeked of power
and wealth, but now it has become
slick and snappy.'

1900–1914 SPLENDOUR AND UNREST

It is as if the city has gained a fresh access of strength and vitality with the new century. One of the most striking and permanent characteristics of London is its ability to rejuvenate itself. It has the ability to dance on its own ashes, and it is now notable for its *thé dansants*, its tangos and waltzes and Blue Hungarian bands. There are 12 music-halls and 23 theatres in central London alone, with another 47 in the outer areas. This is the first age of the cinema, too, with the advent of the Moving Picture Theatre and the Kinema as the first of the 'picture palaces'. In a similar spirit of innovation, the new underground system has abandoned its steam-engines and the whole network has been electrified. Gas has already given way to this new source of power. The city can be compared to some organism which sloughs off its old skin in order to live again. With the appearance of the electric tram and the motor-omnibus, not to mention the emergence of the petrol-driven motorcar, London is gathering momentum. The shops and restaurants have grown in size while the presence of soda-fountains, cafés and nightclubs has created the atmosphere of a 'fast city'.

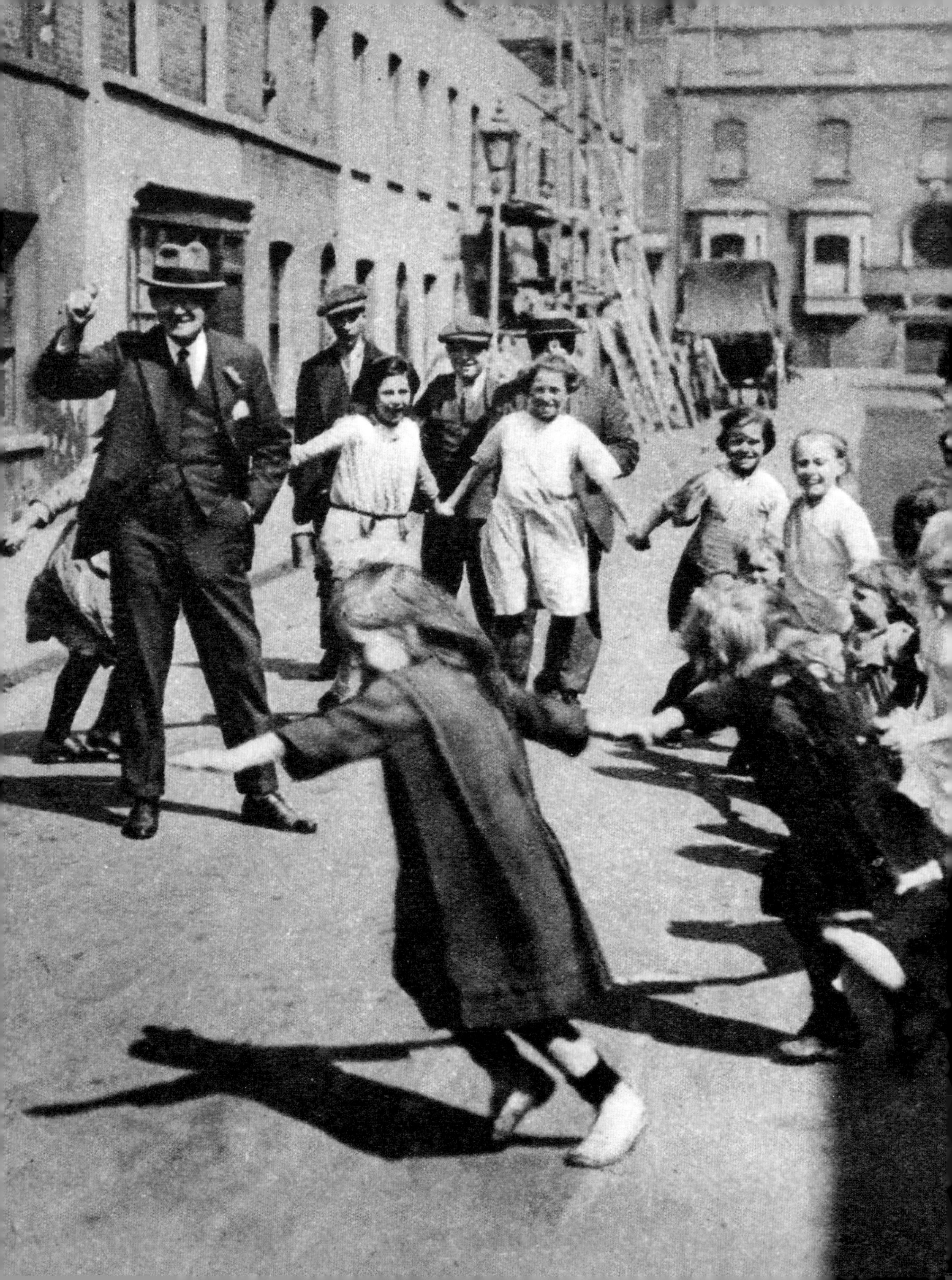

The new century has been greeted with more doubts and anxieties than celebrations. On the death of the queen the church bells of London tolled, the theatrical performances were abandoned and the people poured on to the streets to find comfort in the crowds. They may not have felt much sorrow, as the newspapers claimed, but rather bewilderment. London somehow no longer feels the same. It is no longer the abiding city. New ideas are flying about. Some are in favour of votes for women, and others of socialistic reform. Many people are against vivisection, and even more against vaccination. Some believe that the city has fallen to the Irish and others blame the Jews. There are so many large causes and movements that it is hard to know what to believe.

The population has increased by so much that London is extended in all directions. In what were once the outer limits of the city, new houses have been creeping over the green fields of Sydenham and Streatham, Wimbledon and Wandsworth, Hampstead and Highgate. These are detached or semi-detached dwellings, predominantly of red brick, with slate roofs and bow windows, timber frames and small front gardens. An earlier map, will show green spaces around Willesden, Lee, Mitcham, Wanstead and Finchley. You will not see them now. Main roads, which were once lined with hedges and ran through open country, are now built up with shops and residences. Open fields are pitted and pocked all over with factories, warehouses, 'works' and new building operations. You must travel at least 25 miles before you can shake off the fact and rumour of London.

Behind the hedges that protect the privacy of these new homes, carefully arranged window displays are glimpsed beyond the lace curtains. In their tidiness, cleanliness and air of modest comfort, these houses and their surroundings are in striking contrast to the conditions of the rest of London. They are being occupied by families who wish to escape the noise and smells of the city and who are lured by the prospect of cleaner air and safer streets. The exodus is now reaching giant proportions, and it is estimated that within ten years more than a million people will have migrated to the 'suburbs'. Their departure has been hastened by the Metropolitan Railway, and a season ticket can now take the clerk or businessman into the heart of the City.

The suburbs are intended for the middling classes, but they differ one from another. The 'inner suburbs', as they are known, of Islington and of Holloway, of Leyton and of Clapham, are typically clustered in squares or along truncated streets; these are quarters

Children dancing on the street, early twentieth century.

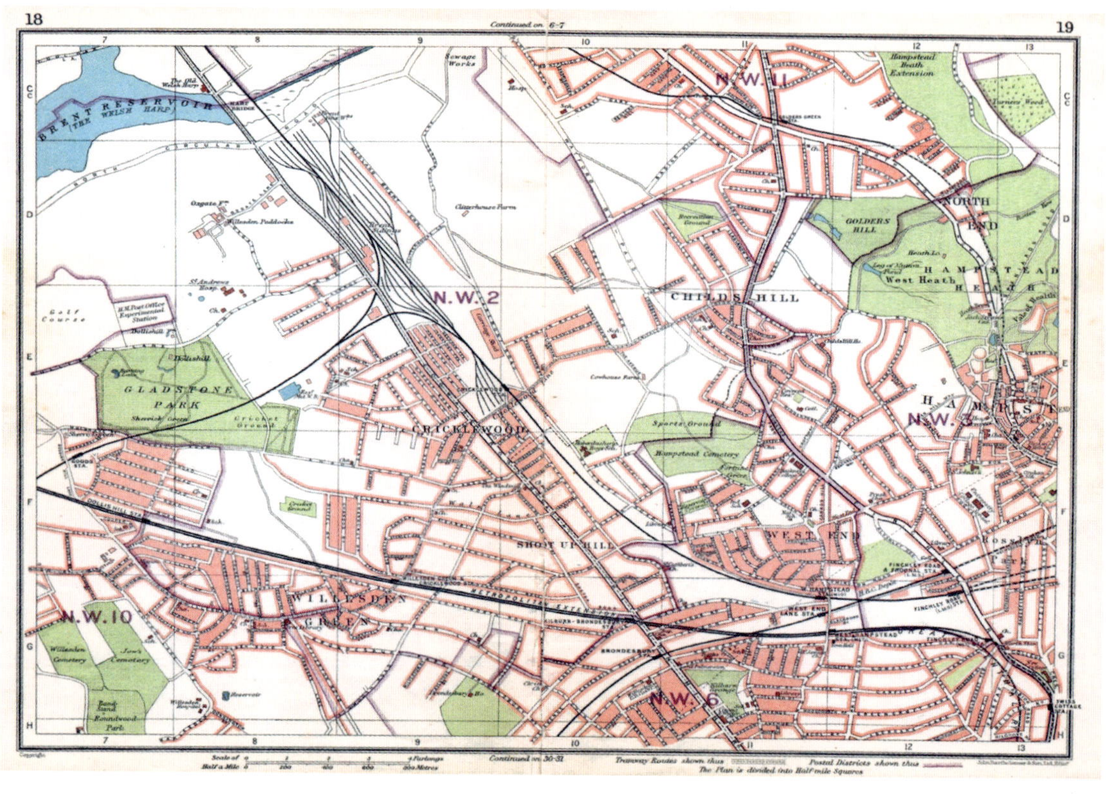

18
19
Continued on 6-7
BRENT RESERVOIR
THE WELSH HARP
Sewage Works
N.W.11
Hampstead Heath Extension
GOLDERS HILL
NORTH END
CHILDS HILL
HAMPSTEAD
WEST HEATH
N.W.2
GLADSTONE PARK
CRICKLEWOOD
N.W.3
Hampstead Cemetery
SHOOT UP HILL
WEST END
N.W.10
WILLESDEN GREEN
BRONDESBURY
N.W.6
Golf Course
Willesden Cemetery
Jews Cemetery
Roundwood Park
Continued on 30-31
Tramway Routes shown thus
Postal Districts shown thus
The Plan is divided into Half-mile Squares
Scale of
Half a Mile
Furlongs
Metres

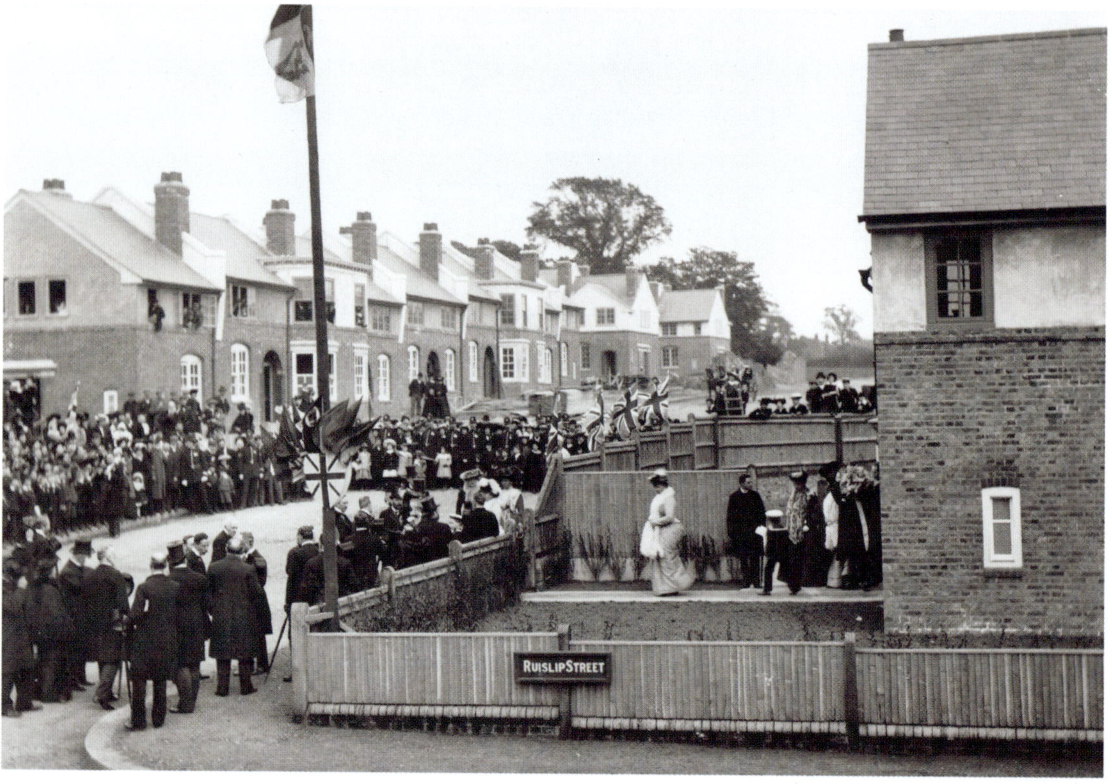

RuislipStreet

where the quick building of new dwellings is urgently required.
They accommodate terraces of two-storeyed houses, with small
gardens guarded by iron railings at the front and larger ones at
the back. The outer suburbs try more successfully to give the
impression of *rus in urbe*, with tree-lined streets and houses set
back from the road. The new dwellings here are given names like
'Fairview', 'The Prospect' and 'The Laurels'. Nearby there will be
a park, a bowls or tennis club, and a discreet row of shops. The
householder can live undisturbed by their neighbours, with whom
they might exchange no more than a few words. Young mothers
push perambulators, without nurses or maids accompanying them,
and boys from the grocer or butcher make their deliveries. Few, if
any, children play outside. That is one of the great changes since,
for the ordinary children of London, the street is their playground.

No street singer or street seller disturbs the general quiet of the
suburb. You will not see street urchins or vagabonds of that kind.
Nor will you see any drunken men, the plague of the metropolis,
or evident signs of misery. The suburb represents a life of security,
a life of sedentary occupations and a life of respectability. Men
in dark suits and bowler hats leave their houses with umbrella
and perhaps newspaper in hand. They work in small and crowded
offices, under artificial light, calculating immense sums while
doing other men's accounts and writing other men's letters.
They travel to work on electric trams and omnibuses, as well as
overground and underground trains. Trams are the cheapest means
of transport but, precisely because these trams are popular in the
lower class of suburb, the middling classes prefer to take the train.
Suburban estates of all kinds are still in their transitional stage,
a period of 'settling down' in which everything and everybody
is open to change, and we cannot yet predict their development.
When the years have matured them and made them part of the
future London, we may find that they adjust well enough to a new
scene. The busy little enclaves of shopping streets, tea shops, trams,
buses and massed houses may become as much part of the city as
Cornhill or Threadneedle Street.

In the more leafy and spacious suburbs, of course, the prices
of suitable dwellings are higher. It is reported that a house in the
green southern district of Balham may cost as much as £1,000 to
buy, and the enormous sum of 12s a week to rent. If you take a cab
from Cannon Street and drive to Sydenham, you will pass 5 miles
of houses, all indicative of an annual expenditure of £1,500 or
more. An advertisement for one of them may say, among other

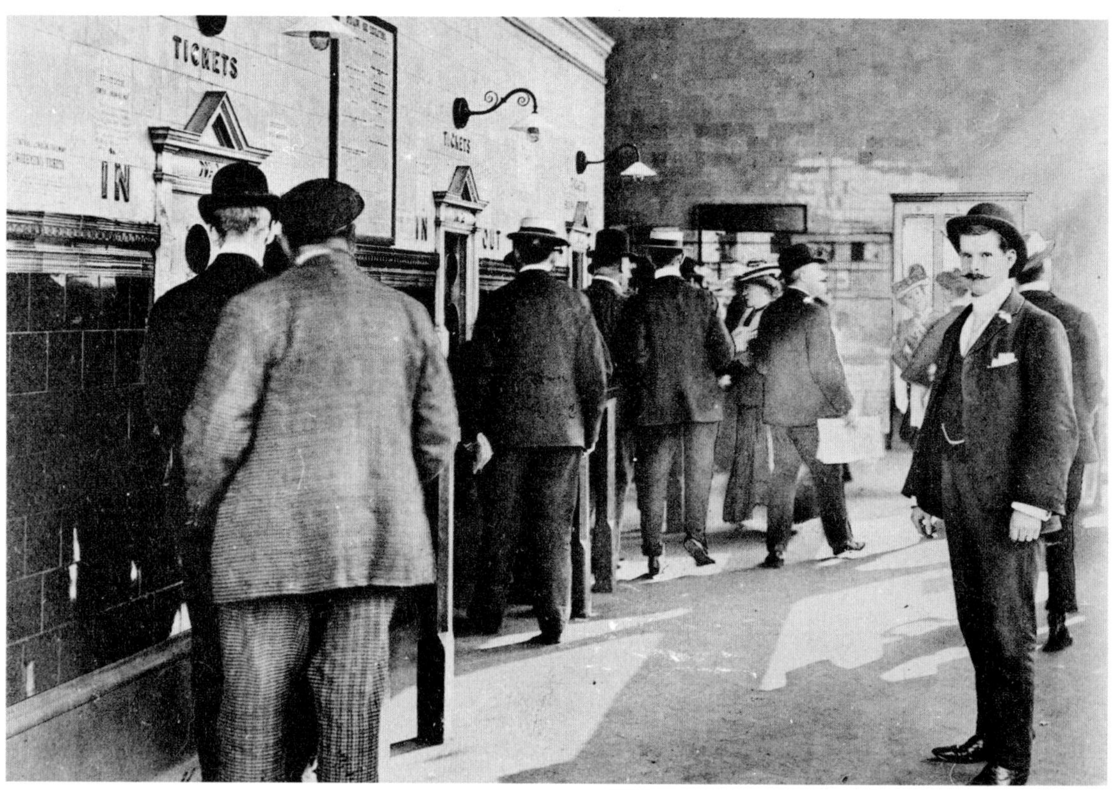

The booking hall at Shepherd's Bush station on the Central London Railway's Two Penny Tube, c.1900.

things, 'Seventy-five year lease; near trams; bargain; only wants seeing'. Whenever a new train station is built, the offices of estate agents will emerge at close hand, offering land to speculators, construction firms and private buyers. Within a few weeks the sound of continual hammering and sawing invades the area like distant thunder, and the new houses rise up among heaps of brick and of wood, of trenches and ditches. The suburban life is condemned by some, therefore, as a stain of red rust creeping over the countryside; it is considered to be a greater menace than other examples of modern life, such as the gramophone, bamboo furniture and secondary school education.

However, the suburbs are praised by others as clean and sweet, at least compared with the areas of London that have been left behind. Observe the Caledonian Road, a great channel of traffic running directly north from King's Cross to Holloway. It seems to have been forgotten or ignored. If you stand at the entrance to it, you gaze into a thoroughfare of supreme ugliness; every house front is marked with meanness and inveterate grime, and every shop seems to be breaking out in mould or dry rot; the people who walk here appear to be employed in a labour that soils body and spirit. Journey on the top of a tram-car, and you see the pavements half-occupied with the paltriest and most sordid wares. The population is dense and the poverty undisguised. This will never be seen in Ealing, known as 'queen of the suburbs', a mere 8 miles distant.

Consider also the children of the city. In the more affluent neighbourhoods the boys and girls have spinning tops and marbles. If you save up 6d, you can buy a 'whizzer' with a little metal propeller that flies through the air; and there is the 'scooter', made up of planks of boxwood with rubber tyre wheels. Both toys are considered dangerous by many parents, but the craze for them continues. The spinning top and the whipping top are considered to be safe both inside and outside the house, and marbles are always popular. In the poorer areas of the city, only cigarette cards and conkers are readily available. The game of 'flickers' must have been in play for at least half a century or longer, with the cards from packets of Player's Navy Cut or Wild Woodbines readily available. Conkers are now played with horse chestnuts, but older people will tell children that they once used the shells of snails and winkles with the little creatures still ensconced. Without them, of course, the shells are more fragile. This did not affect the hardy chestnut, which can be called a 'thirty-sixer' or 'ninety-fiver' according to the number of its victories. Pavement games such as Tig, Hopscotch, Hi Jimmy Knacker and Fivestones are popular. In recent days there has also been a craze for paper darts and other missiles that can be launched in the street or in the classroom. They are made more lethal by the attachment of a 'Jay' nib from a pen that acts as an arrow. It is not recommended. The children of the suburbs, however, are of course denied all of these cheap pleasures. They must be content with kites and bicycling outdoors, and card games like Pope Joan indoors. On the subject of city children, the sweet-stuff shops may also be mentioned, with their 'jujubes' of jelly, as well as the foot-long strips of hard toffee called 'hanky-panky', the sherbet dabs with a liquorice stick, the toffee apples, the tiger nuts and the 'Ally Sloper's lunch', which is a plate of 'meat and two veg' all made out of sugar.

*

The distinctive aspects of city living are also obvious in transport. The electric tram-cars and the motor omnibuses have appeared on the streets, together with modern bicycles. One of the earliest lines of the tram runs from the south side of Westminster Bridge to

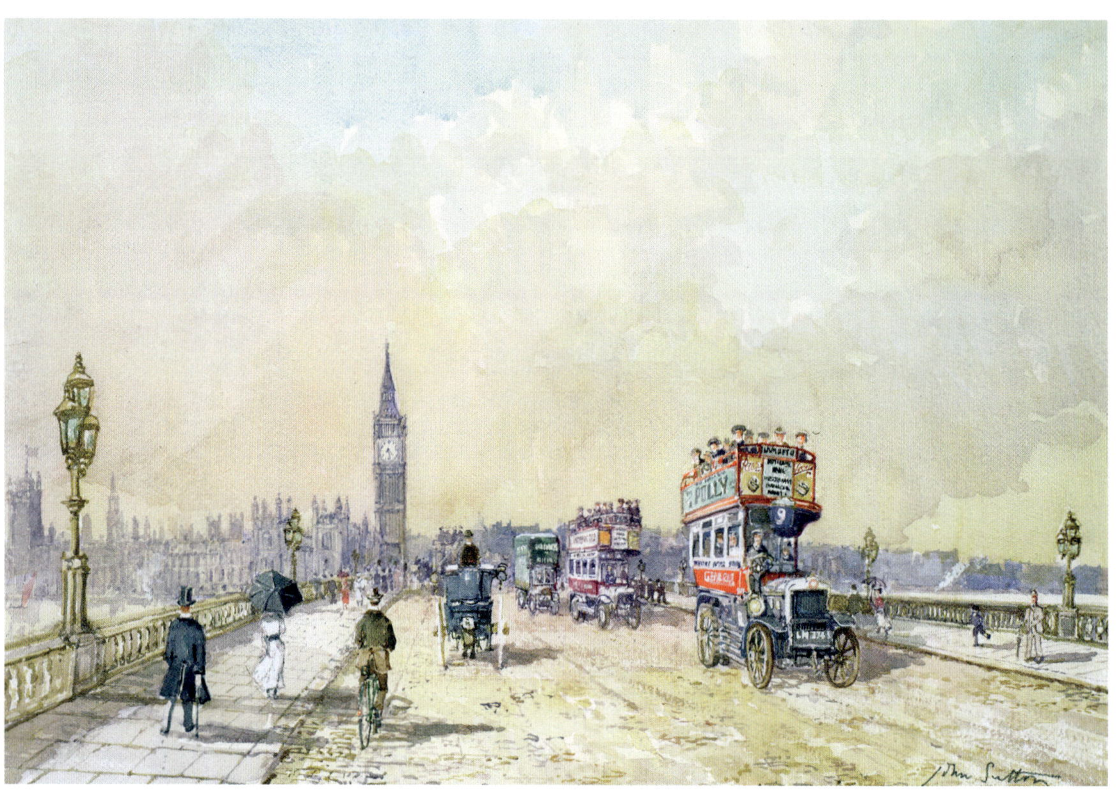

Traffic on Westminster Bridge by John Sutton.

Clapham Common and, at the cost of one penny per mile, is very popular. In some respects it rivals the workmen's trains, which are half-price in the early morning. The motor omnibus arrived on the streets at the turn of the century, and for a short time it vied for supremacy with the horse bus. At the very beginning the horses were familiar and reassuring, and the motor bus was seen as an unwelcome intruder. We can still remember the horses which pulled the dark green 'Favourites' from the Monster at Pimlico to the Angel at Islington, with their sound echoing along the narrows of Chancery Lane, and those which dragged the 'Royal Blues' through the traffic of Bond Street to reach King's Cross, or those which trotted the yellow buses to Camden Town. It seems just yesterday that Tilling's ran a four-in-hand service from Balham to the City every weekday morning. Within the last few years, however, it has become obvious that the horses will eventually go; they are still in general use, but they are beginning to clog the arteries of London. They no longer seem appropriate. Another absence has gone largely unremarked; donkeys have all but vanished from the London streets.

Two or three years into the new century, the petrol-driven taxi came along to scare off the hansom cab; by the end of that first decade, it had taken over. The hansom has still lingered on, outside a few fashionable restaurants and gentlemen's clubs, but the old clip-clop, clip-clop, jingle-jingle, is rarely heard. Showing its age, a hansom cab has just been donated to the London Museum! This has also been the period of the electrified trams; their first route lay between Shepherd's Bush and Kew Bridge, but they are now supposed to be the most efficient and cheapest means of street conveyance in many parts of the city.

The horseless buses, powered by steam, appeared in the last century, but they were considered to be ugly and, with their jolts and jars, alarming to pedestrians and passengers alike. The petrol-driven motor buses have taken their place, and are now indispensable. You see them in Cannon Street and Shepherd's Bush, in Maida Vale and Victoria, in Holloway and Highgate; they are generally painted in broad swathes of red, with their conductors in smart caps and uniforms. They are the behemoths of the road. A printed notice on their sides states that 'In the interests of cleanliness and the prevention of consumption, passengers are kindly requested to abstain from the objectionable and dangerous habit of spitting'. This was followed by a shorter injunction, 'DO NOT SPIT. PENALTY 40s'. Spitting has become a frequent habit, and is detrimental to the health of others, but it is hardly peculiar to the motor bus. Spitting on the underground trains, due to the steam and smoke, is still more frequent. It has also been determined that the routes under the ground are 10 degrees warmer than those above. Many return to the open streets with relief.

The noxious vapours on the Underground have, in fact, increased demands for the electric traction that has proved so successful on the City and South London Railway. It is rumoured that the days of the underground steam engine may be coming to an end. Change has already arrived in other forms. An inclined 'escalator' has recently been introduced at Earl's Court station, to unite the platforms of the green and yellow lines, with the promise that the traveller can step on it at once and be gently carried to his train. The boon that the male will appreciate is the fact that he is not prohibited from smoking, as he still is in the hydraulic lift, since the escalator is made entirely from fireproof material. In its very early days a porter was employed to shout out, through a stentorphone, 'This way to the moving staircase! The only one of its kind in London! NOW running! The world's wonder!' but innovation has its problems. Some travellers screamed

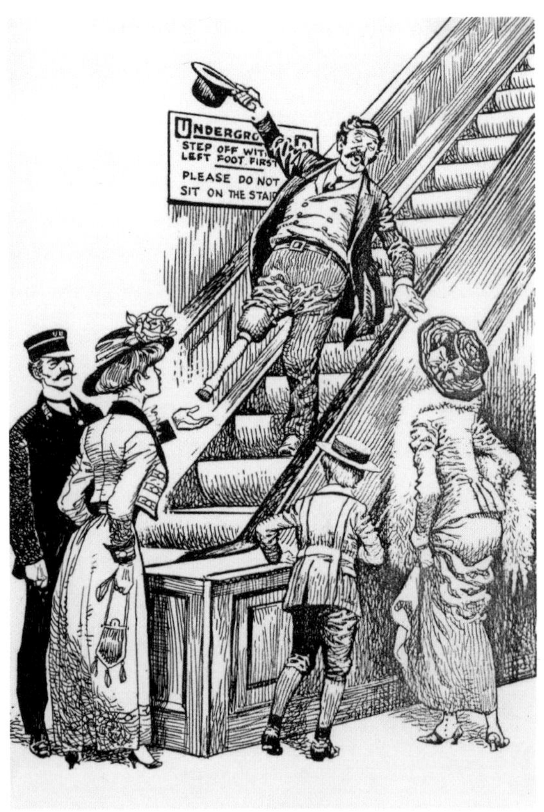

Above Guide to first London Underground escalator by Peter Jackson.

at the prospect of alighting from the moving steps, and placards invited them to 'step off with the left foot'. A man with a wooden leg was employed to ride up and down, in order to instil confidence in the nervous passengers. One newspaper stated that it was 'as good as a joy-wheel'. It was also reported that the owners of the various subterranean transport companies convened to find a general name for their joint enterprise. The choice was between 'Tube' and 'Electric' and 'Underground'. As we all know, the latter was the winner.

There was a short period when transport was only required for the journey from home to work, but now the custom of travelling has been extended to the leisure hours; for men this will include the pursuit of education or amusement, and for ladies the opportunity of visiting friends or shopping expeditions. As a result, the attraction of local entertainments and of local amenities has diminished, and the average man or woman will not be confined to one district. There has been a general levelling, upwards or downwards according to taste. Chokers and Derby coats are rarely to be seen, and the dress of the younger generation of working men and women no longer has a distinctive note of its own.

However, the future has really emerged in the shape of the automobile. There was a time when its progress was heralded by a man waving a red flag but that era has long gone. Those new cars were driven by steam, and their drivers were known as 'chauffeurs' because they had to stoke the fires to create the steam. Of course steam has now given way to the internal combustion engine. The motorcar has, in fact, become the most striking means of transport to have emerged in the last hundred years. Bicycles were once the fastest form of travel; their enthusiasts were seen riding in the parks, the men in suits and boaters, the ladies sporting loose knickerbockers under their billowy dresses, but that supremacy lasted a short time. The petrol-driven motorcar, intricate and peculiar as it seems, far surpasses the steam-powered vehicles that emerged on the roads in the last century. The sight of the motor driver, sitting high in his carriage just like an old-fashioned coachman, has now become familiar. People still sometimes shout at him from the side of the road or try to run beside him. Mischievous children hope to provoke an accident by throwing their flat caps in the path of the vehicle; they realize that if the driver brakes suddenly he may fall forward over the front of the automobile.

There is also trouble if he attempts to overtake a bicyclist. The two types of driver are always at odds. The owners of the motorcars, who think of themselves as a small and distinguished band, call their rivals 'cads on casters'. They wear heavy leather or fur-lined jackets, cloth caps with earflaps and rubber ponchos in the event of inclement weather. They sometimes refuse to pay the steep fines on the grounds that speed limits are 'unEnglish'. That limit was once 2 miles per hour but has now been raised to a generous 20 miles per hour, which cannot cause complaint from anyone except Mr Toad. The cramped economy of space in the motorcar has also led to the disappearance of the men's tall hat, the frock coat, the smart umbrella and even the buttonhole. The female passengers have also eschewed long skirts and flowered hats.

Below Oxford Circus (1905)
by Maxwell Ashby Armfield.

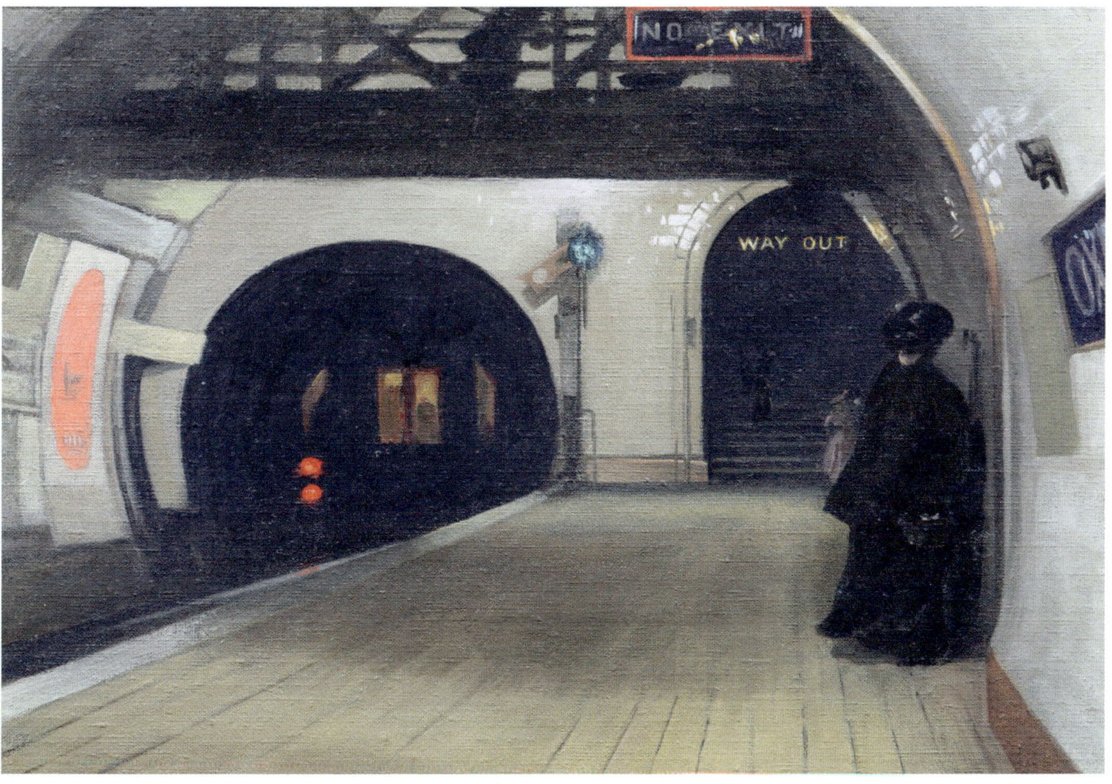

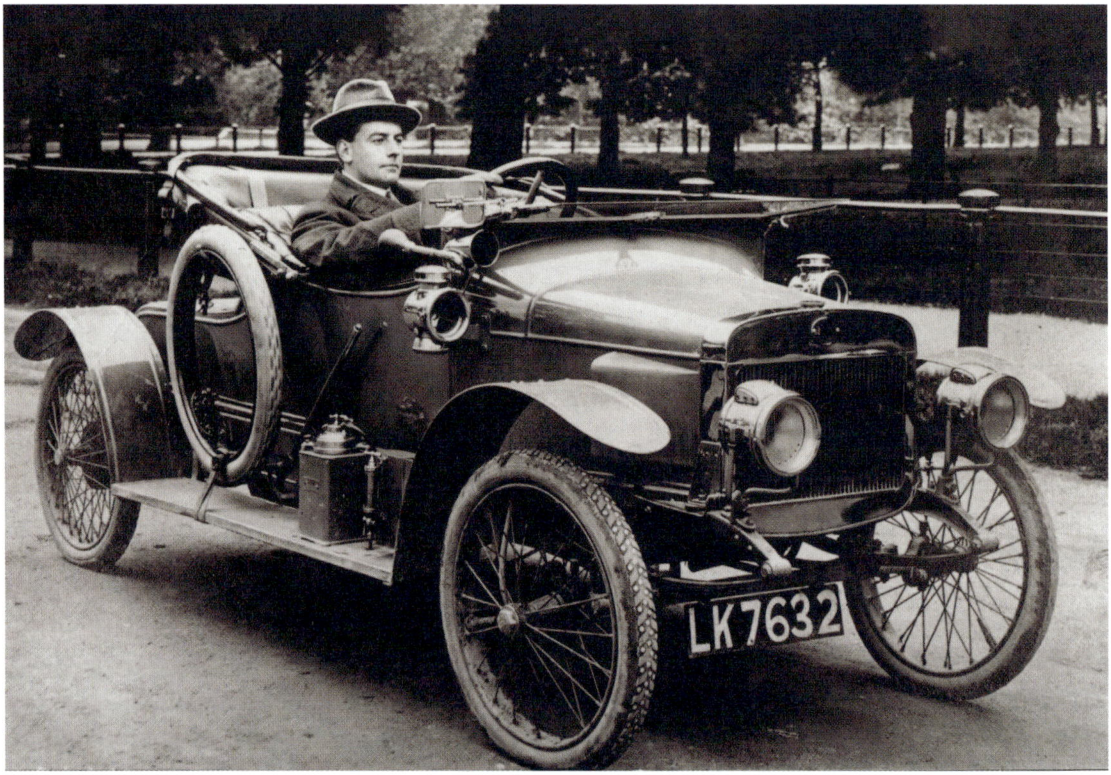

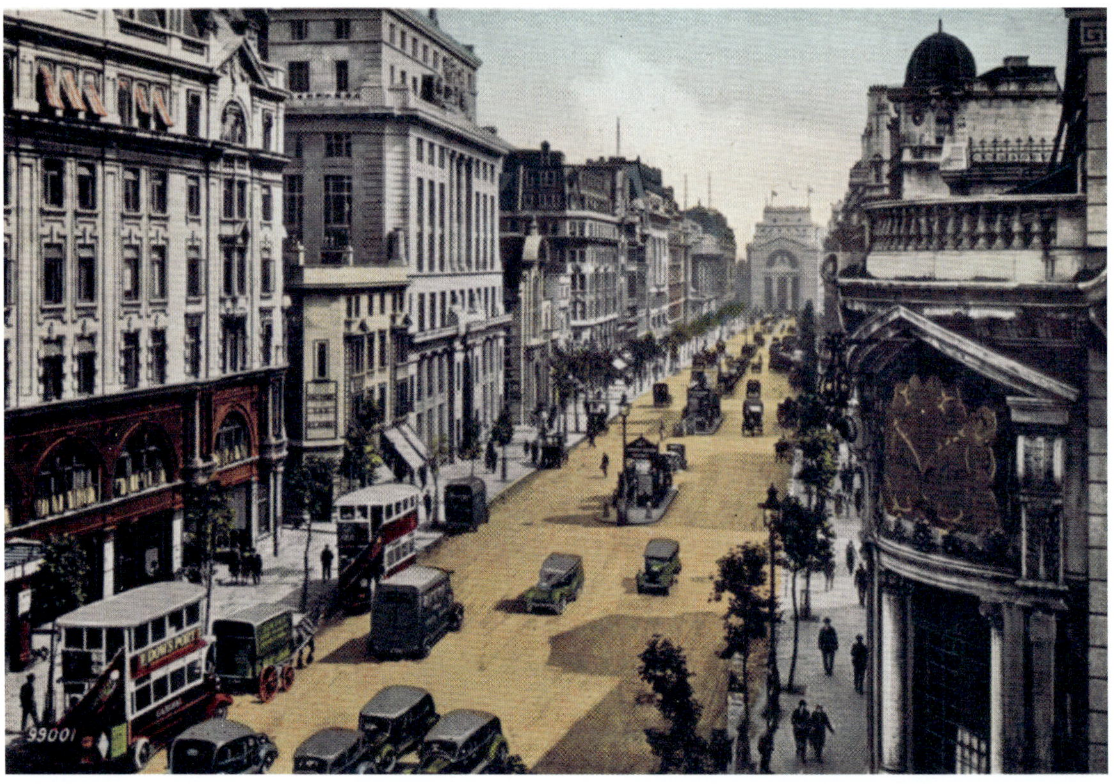

An increase in the number of accidents provoked a 'motorcar panic' for two or three years, but it has subsided. Improvements of models by companies such as Singer and Wolseley mean that motor vehicles are now complete with hood, screen, horn, headlights and tail-lamps. For the general public, however, these new vehicles only add to the mess and muddle of the streets. It has also become harder to calculate their speeds and sudden stops, so that the pedestrian will hesitate or dash or stand still. Motorized cabs may have largely taken the place of hansoms, but it is not yet clear that they have made a material difference in comfort or in quickness. The motor buses have also proved to be a nuisance, and their drivers are often prosecuted for dangerous driving. It is claimed that they wreak damage on roadways; their vibrations alarm pedestrians, cause serious annoyance to inhabitants and are a positive danger to premises along the route.

The frantic activity of the new transport compounds the experience of what has become known in every sense as a 'fast' city. Great hotels have grown up where slums existed before. Office blocks have become a familiar presence. New banks, new company headquarters and new insurance offices are being built on a massive scale and in a form designed to impress; they follow the example of the railway termini, the viaducts, the factories and public buildings of the last century. The style is called 'Edwardian baroque' because of its variety, even though it depends as much upon cast iron and reinforced concrete as brick or stone. Witness the new Central Criminal Court, Westminster Cathedral and the Ritz Hotel. What could be more fanciful and at the same time more solid? They speak of authority, but they impart a sense of progress. It is fitting that the boulevards of Kingsway and of Aldwych should be opened in this century. Harrods was one of the first great stores, but it has been followed in recent years by Debenham & Freebody, Selfridges and Whiteleys. Their vision of the future is complemented by the recent passion for merger and acquisition among the railway companies, the telegraph companies and the food manufacturers. Everything must be larger and more efficient.

Yet in London, the centre of business and the great capital of empire, the economic ills of society have of course left their mark. The irretrievably poor have always been with us, but changes in trade and in working practices have adversely affected those who live on the margin between want and relief. Some relief is now at hand. Those men without work can now visit the new 'labour exchange' where jobs can be exchanged for unemployment.

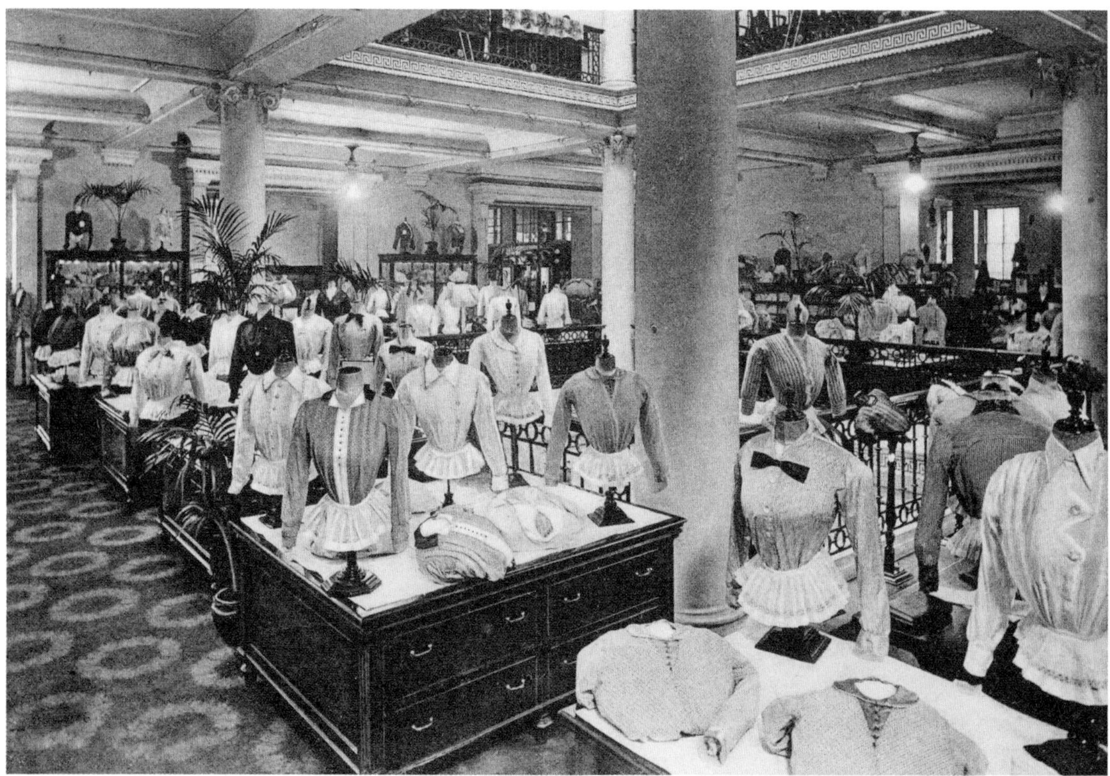

The right to work is now being advanced by social unrest in certain quarters of London, such as Limehouse and Stepney, and in protest marches through the centre of London. The placards tell us that the working people are starving in a land of plenty, which may give further proof for those prophesying revolution. Many of these demonstrations begin at Clerkenwell Green, which has for centuries been the centre of political disquiet. It is one of the tokens of London, just as Holborn has always been the home of astrologers and Clare Market, in similar style, is known for its generations of criminals and prize fighters.

Yet in truth London has grown too large to have any general civic consciousness. It is too accommodating and too callous to promote any political cause or struggle. Local self-government, which has now seemed to reach its peak of efficiency, has meant that it has become self-concerned. It does not reflect the interests of the rest of the country and, in turn, its own preoccupations and problems are quite different from those of any other town or city. Politics is a matter for jokes and gossip, and the plight of other areas is largely ignored. A march or a demonstration is really only noticed in the area in which it occurs. The rest of the city remains

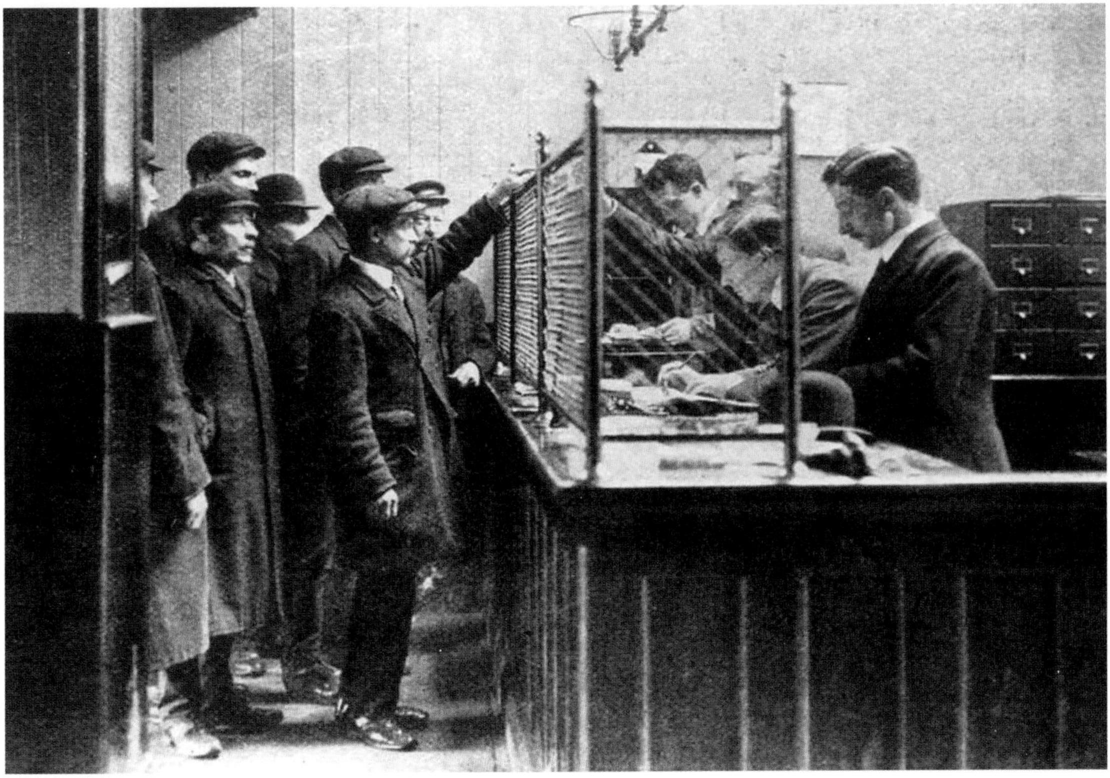

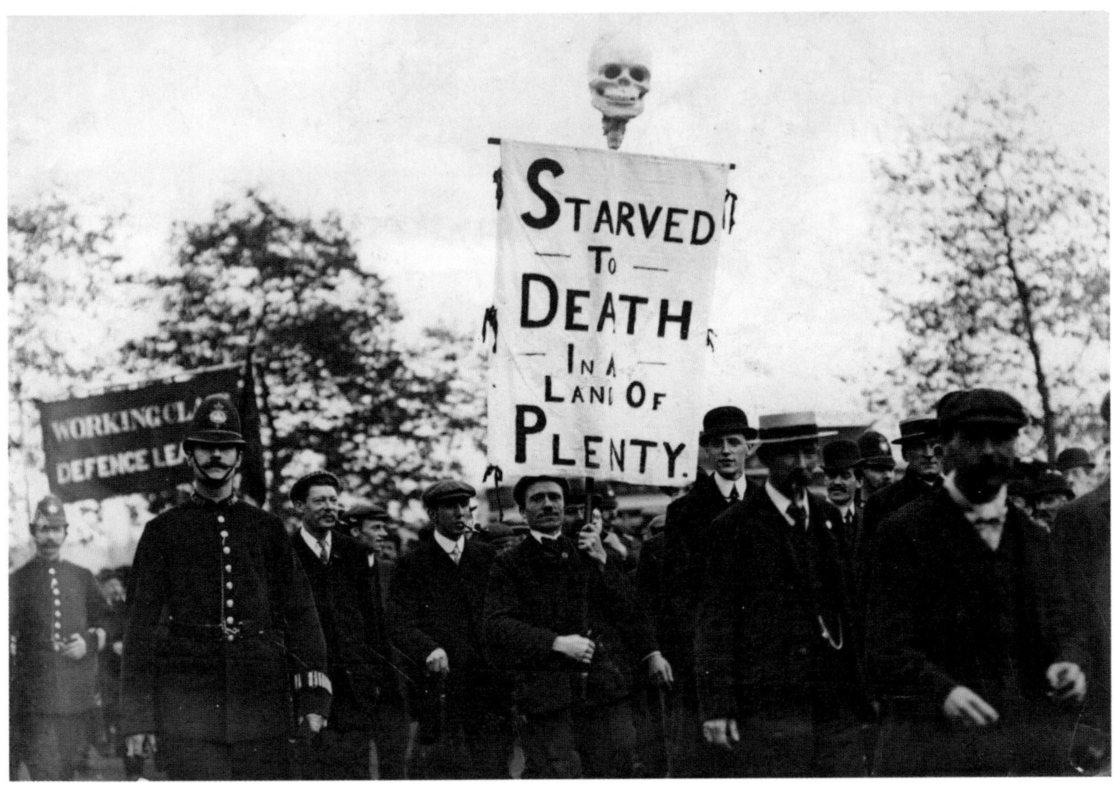

WORKING CLA
DEFENCE LEA
STARVED
TO
DEATH
IN A
LAND OF
PLENTY.

unmoved and, perhaps, indifferent. It takes most things for granted and discounts everything else.

There has been a particular concern, however, for what has been called social improvement within its own territories or, as perhaps we should now say, within its own domain. Many of the slums that disfigured London have now been replaced with healthy dwellings. Once familiar narrow courts, approached under archways from main streets, sorely lacking in light and air, have gradually disappeared from view; back-to-back houses have diminished very greatly in London. The city is becoming healthier in other respects. Various acts of parliament have strengthened the hands of the authorities in dealing with nuisances and offensive trades, and have led to a vast amount of work being done in connection with house drainage and scavenging, while common lodging houses, slaughter houses and cowsheds are subject to annual review; overcrowding and conditions of dirt and dilapidation in tenement houses have been vigorously dealt with, and great advances have been made in improving the conditions under which milk and foods of other kinds are being sold.

The tide of improvement has not stopped there. In the last 20 years the medical inspection of school children has been introduced, helping to remove ills from lice to rickets; the percentage of London children returned as 'badly flea-bitten' has been halved. As regards infestation by lice, three-quarters of the heads of older girls are now regarded as free from vermin. The cleansing scheme which played so great a part in this beneficent revolution was at first very unpopular with parents; great patience as well as tact were required on the part of teachers and nurses before the opposition could be overcome. However, as a result, recent years have seen a striking improvement in personal neatness and in carriage.

Since the turn of the century, attempts have also been made to eradicate tuberculosis and to prevent the spread of venereal diseases. The advance of knowledge has been combined with the humanitarian spirit to combat the filth diseases, like those which cause frequent or bloody stools, and the zymotic diseases such as typhus and scarlet fever. There have been, for example, no great epidemics of cholera or influenza in the last 30 years. Reference should also be made to the growth of nursery schools and open air schools. However, the spread of knowledge is still uncertain, and folk remedies are often applied. In London lore, if you see an electric ambulance racing past, you must hold your

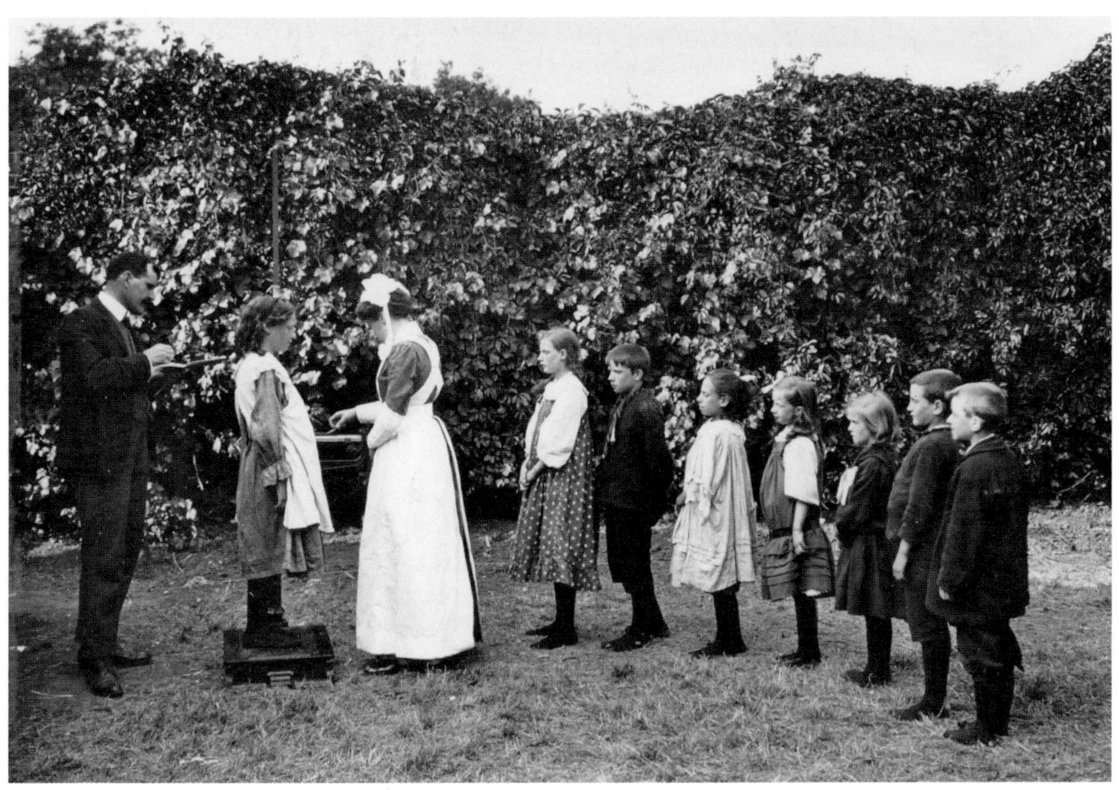

Children being weighed in the garden, Montpelier House Open Air School, 1908.

breath and pinch your nose until you see a brown or black dog. Alternatively, you must chant 'Grab your collar, don't swaller, never catch the fever.' Of course these measures, both scientific and traditional, have done nothing to mitigate the common problems of life. Many girls at work, for example, suffer from anaemia due to lack of fresh air and unsuitable food. Street remedies, for this complaint and others, are still used in many household; carts can be seen in the streets selling Sarsaparilla, a herbal drink which is said to possess valuable health properties. Young women are also warned not to wear low-cut or flimsy garments that are known as 'pneumonia blouses'.

These hazards have been increased by the continuing trend for young women to leave shop work or domestic work for office employment. It has become the new profession for females, and it is estimated that there are now one hundred thousand travelling into the central areas of the city. Women clerks will soon outnumber the male variety. The office world, spreading outwards from Finsbury Circus, from Houndsditch, from Fleet Street and other areas, has grown partly to accommodate this new female army. Girls of good education, who have been trained in

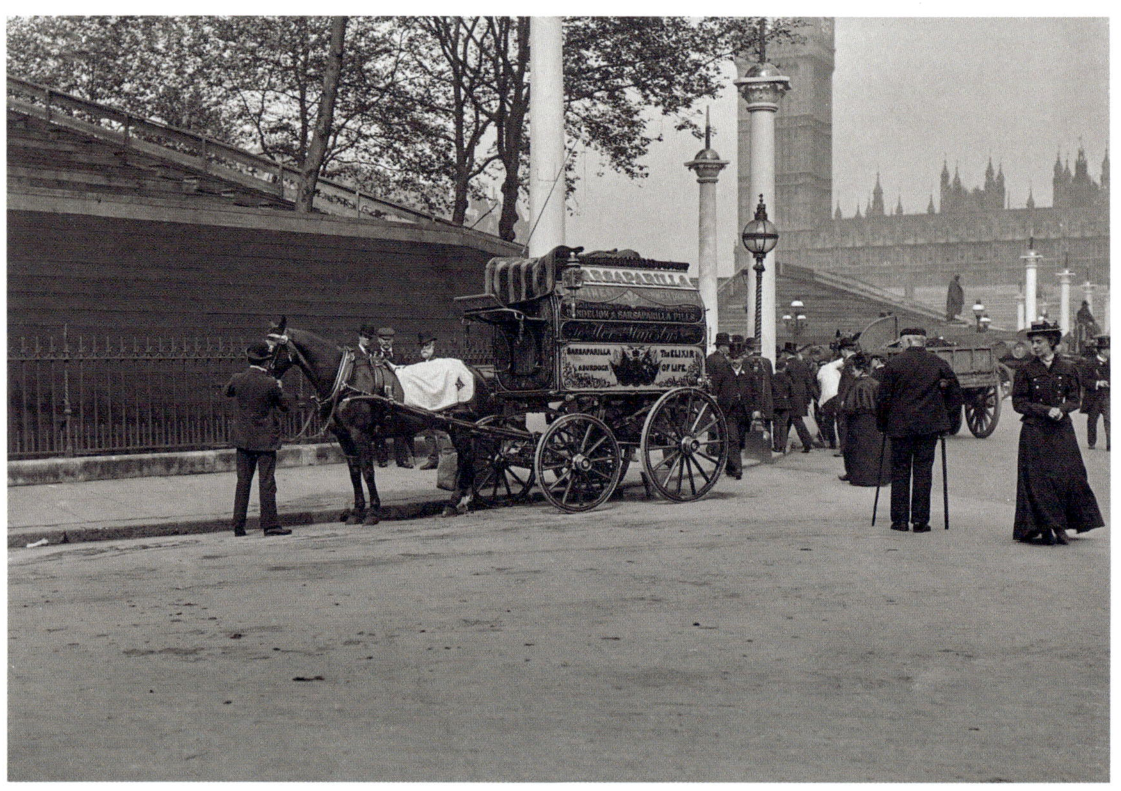

Above Pedestrians pass a
horse-drawn wagon selling
Dandelion & Sarsaparilla Pills
in Westminster, c.1905.

Right An advertisement
for the Royal Bar-Lock
Typewriter

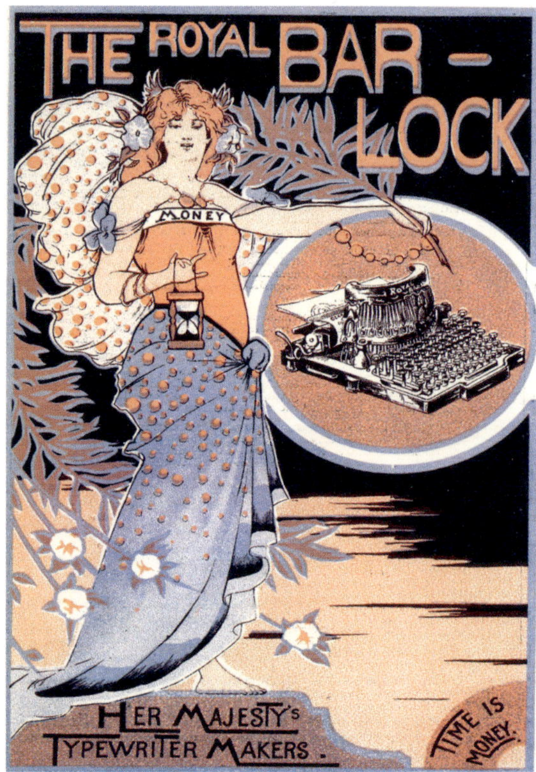

the skills of shorthand and typing, can now earn up to £2 or £3 a
week. They generally work from eight-thirty in the morning to six
in the evening, with a pause for lunch, but no tea or coffee 'breaks'.
It is important to be smartly dressed, and the girls are asked to
wear a good jacket and skirt. The typewriter itself is known to be
a machine especially suitable for women to use, as important as
the spinning wheel and the sewing machine once were. It is well
adapted to feminine fingers, and involves no more hard labour and
no more skill than playing the piano. There is also work available
for females in the new telephone switchboards, provided that they
have suitable voices. The companies recruit their operators from
the ranks of bright, well-educated, intelligent girls who are in
many cases the daughters of professional men – doctors, barristers,
clergymen and others. These 'hello girls' will work nine hours
a day, their salaries rising from 11s to £1 per week. They are of
course segregated from the male clerks and, as in other female
occupations, marriage will terminate an operator's employment.
However, it is undoubtedly true that the typewriter and the
telephone, available to the public in the closing years of the last
century, have revolutionized the life of women.

*

The demand for popular entertainment has greatly increased,
with new theatres and new music halls springing up almost
every year, promising variety from revue to water spectacle,
from French circus to Russian ballet. The actor-manager has also
come into his own with an efflorescence of new drama, from *John
Bull's Other Island* to *The Sins of Society*. However, the conventional
routine of a 'night out' is being altered beyond recognition by
the advent of the kinematograph theatre or, as it is now being
called, the picture palace. In the very first years of this century,
The Great Train Robbery caused an immense sensation, followed by
the films produced by the Biograph Company dealing with the
incidents of the Boer War. Gradually the film is taking its place as
the story teller of the people, and all over London picture shows
have appeared in old shops, sheds and disused halls. The audience
was at first mainly composed of men who paid threepence
for admission and sat on wooden benches to watch what are
sometimes still known as 'shakies' because of their movement.
The music was often provided by a phonograph, operated by the
ticket cashier.

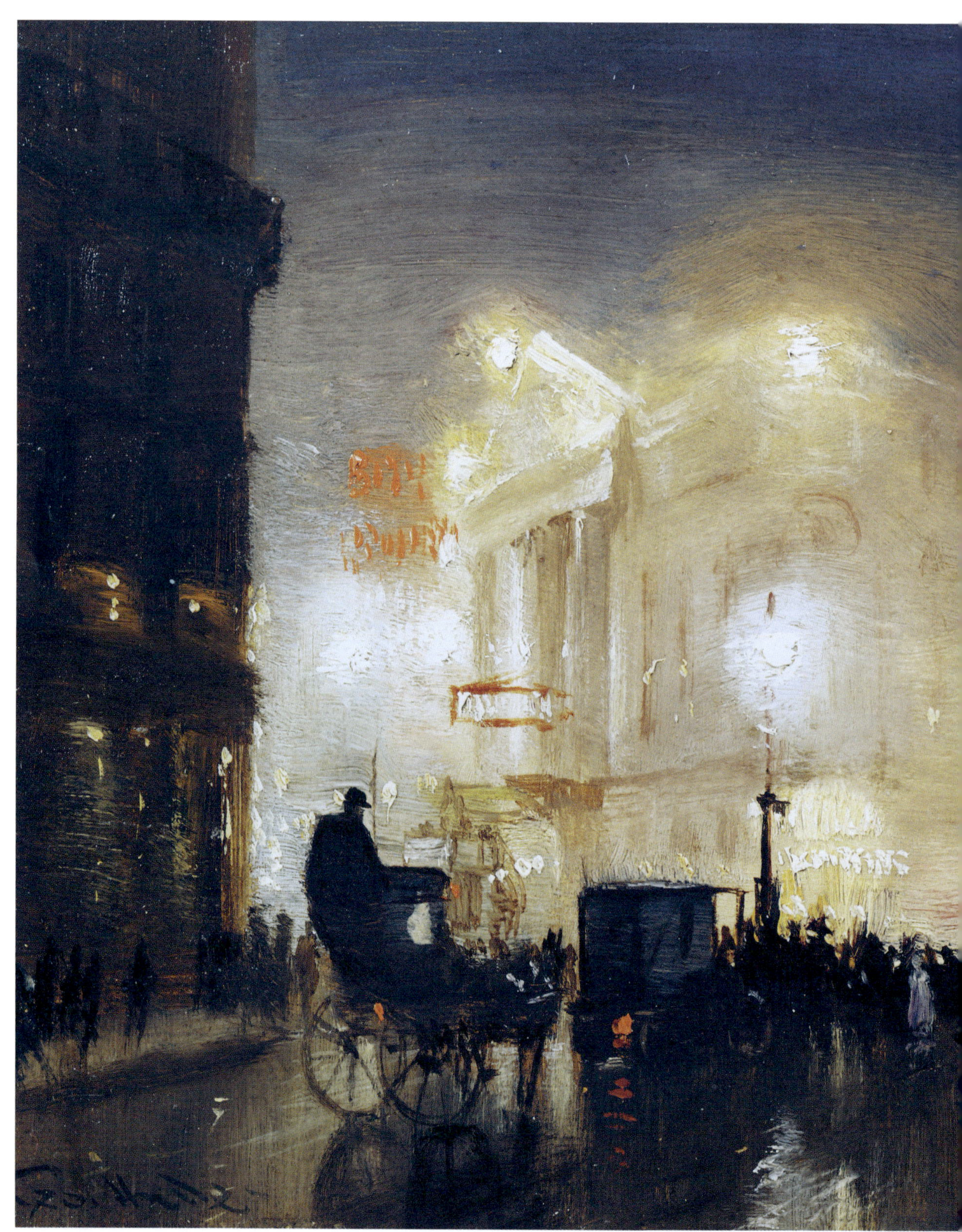

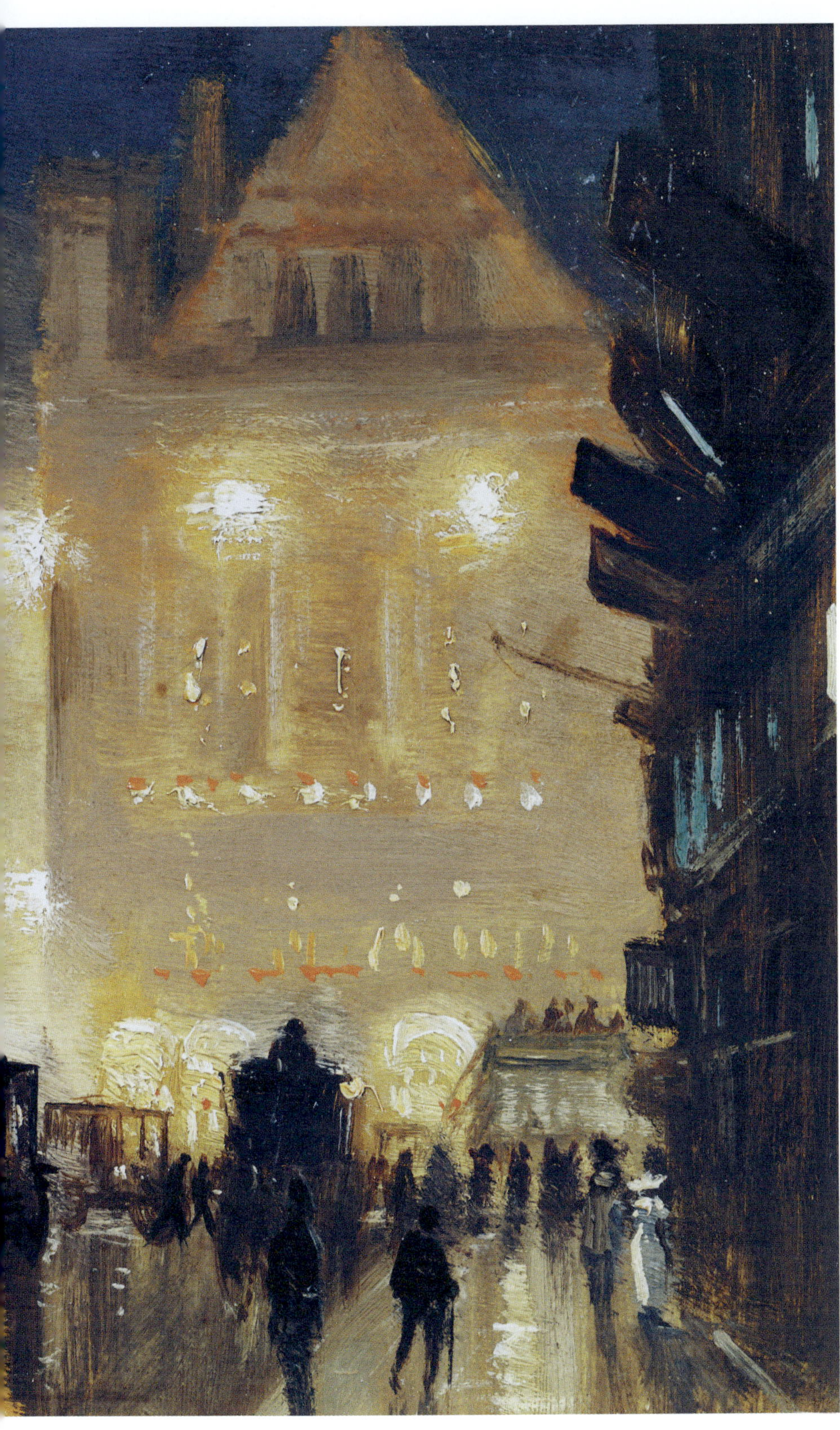

*Theatre Time at Drury Lane,
London* (c.1904) by George
Hyde Pownall.

The phonograph itself is a modern marvel, a veritable
voice machine and miniature orchestra all in one. The power
of the moving pictures seems likely to prevail over all other
entertainments, and they are now being shown in music halls,
fairs and suburban theatres. More than 400 of the new picture
palaces can be found in London, with 26 in Islington alone and
27 in Wandsworth. In 1906 the first of them, the Daily Bioscope,
was located on Bishopsgate Street Without, but in the last few
years they have spread to every neighbourhood. They provide
what are advertised as 'living pictures' in twice-nightly shows
of two hours, and many employ an orchestra to provide suitable
music. The famous Egyptian Hall in Piccadilly now displays
'Improved Animated Photographs', which attract improved and
animated audiences.

Short comedy films, often showing performers from the
music hall, have also appeared, but of course with none of the
coarseness and vulgarity of their stage acts; the 'blue bag', as it
is called, has been thrown away. News theatres have also been
introduced, so that the audiences can see the Derby race or the
King launching a ship. It is better than lifelike. It is life itself.

Façade of the Egyptian Hall
on Piccadilly, c.1890.

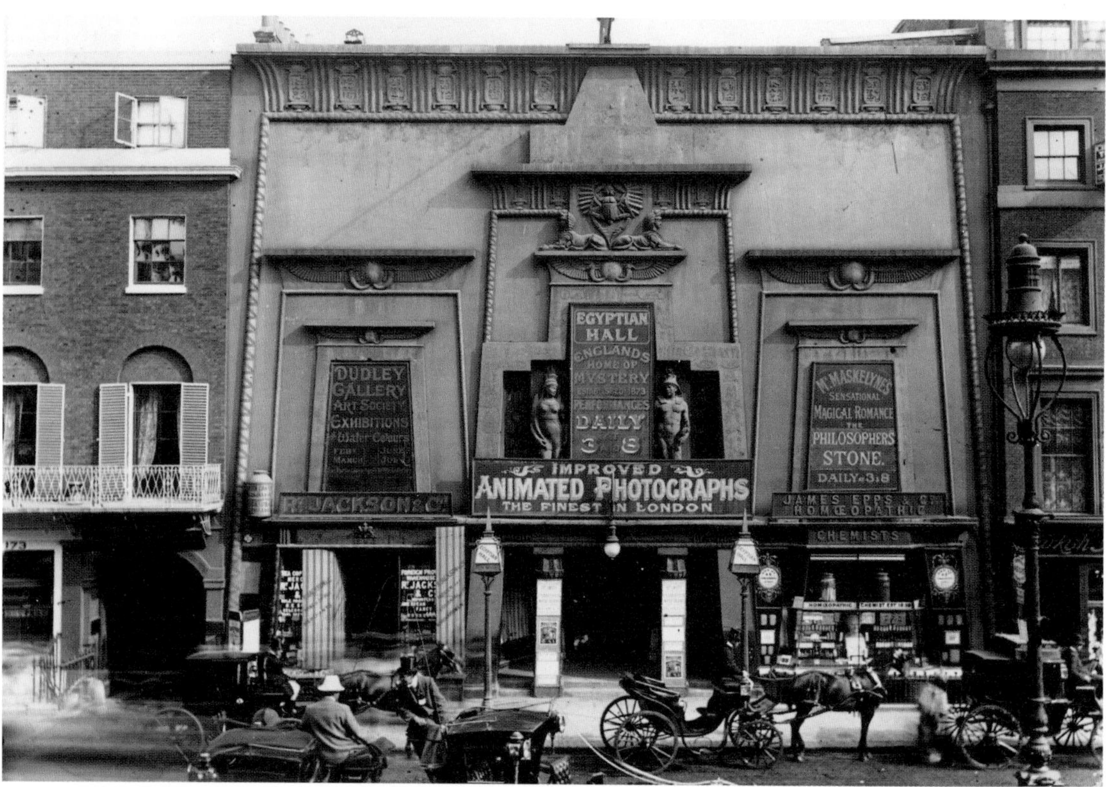

Great enjoyment has also been found in the use of the camera
and, in certain areas such as Holborn and Kensington, the shops
are offering Folding Pocket Kodaks and the Kodak Panoram. In
a similar spirit the newspapers now employ pictures as well as
type, and photographs of royalty and the aristocracy, of sporting
heroes and music hall 'stars' are sold in tobacconists, newsagents
and other local shops.

If they do nothing else, they add to the general sense of
change and speed towards an unknown but exciting future.
Yet, to some, everything seems to be going too fast. It has become
known as electromania. Even the chandeliers in the great London
mansions are now being wired for electricity. At night, the lights
are everywhere. At a touch the whole room is lit, and there are
no more lingering shadows and odd corners. Streets, hotels
and even churches are incandescent. The Edison Electric Light
Station on Holborn Viaduct has become a familiar sight. In the
stores for more prosperous customers, the variety of electric
lamps for sale is extraordinary. Some old-fashioned shoppers still
seem to believe that different forms of electricity are needed for
different equipment, and need to be reassured that it is always
the same force.

The revolution has also had less agreeable effects, since it
means that natural light is no longer required for daily tasks.
The city workers come to work in the darkness of a winter
morning and depart in the evening without once seeing the
sun. Is this a sign of the progress that everyone welcomes?
With the general introduction of hydraulic lifts, the buildings
themselves grow higher and higher so that, by the strange
alchemy of London life, the expansion of the available space
is matched by the increase in the number of people ready to
inhabit it. In the present century the number of working people
in the City has reached almost half a million. The ponderous and
elaborate London of the last century seems to have vanished,
and in its place has arisen an alert and active city for a new
century. We now have 'ragtime' music, tangos and even a Blue
Hungarian band. The shops and restaurants have grown in size
and popularity, with the same spirit of innovation as the vacuum
cleaner and the disposable razor. Once the city reeked of power
and wealth, but now it has become slick and snappy. The language
of the time has also changed. New phrases are heard in the street,
such as 'buck up', 'cut it short' and 'go it'.

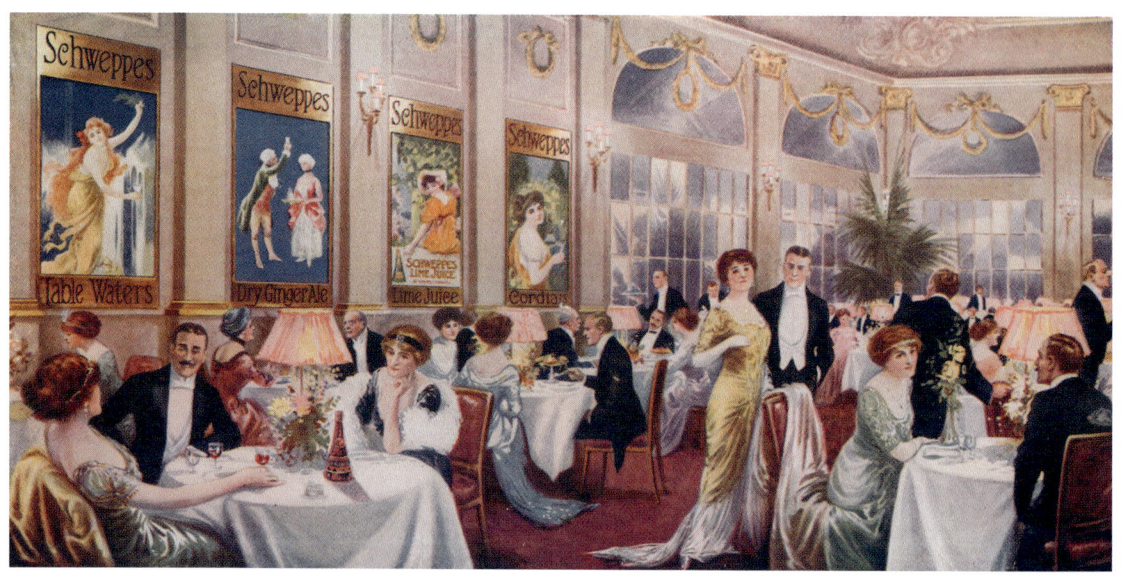

Schweppes
Schweppes
Schweppes
Schweppes
Table Waters
Dry Ginger Ale
Lime Juice
Cordials

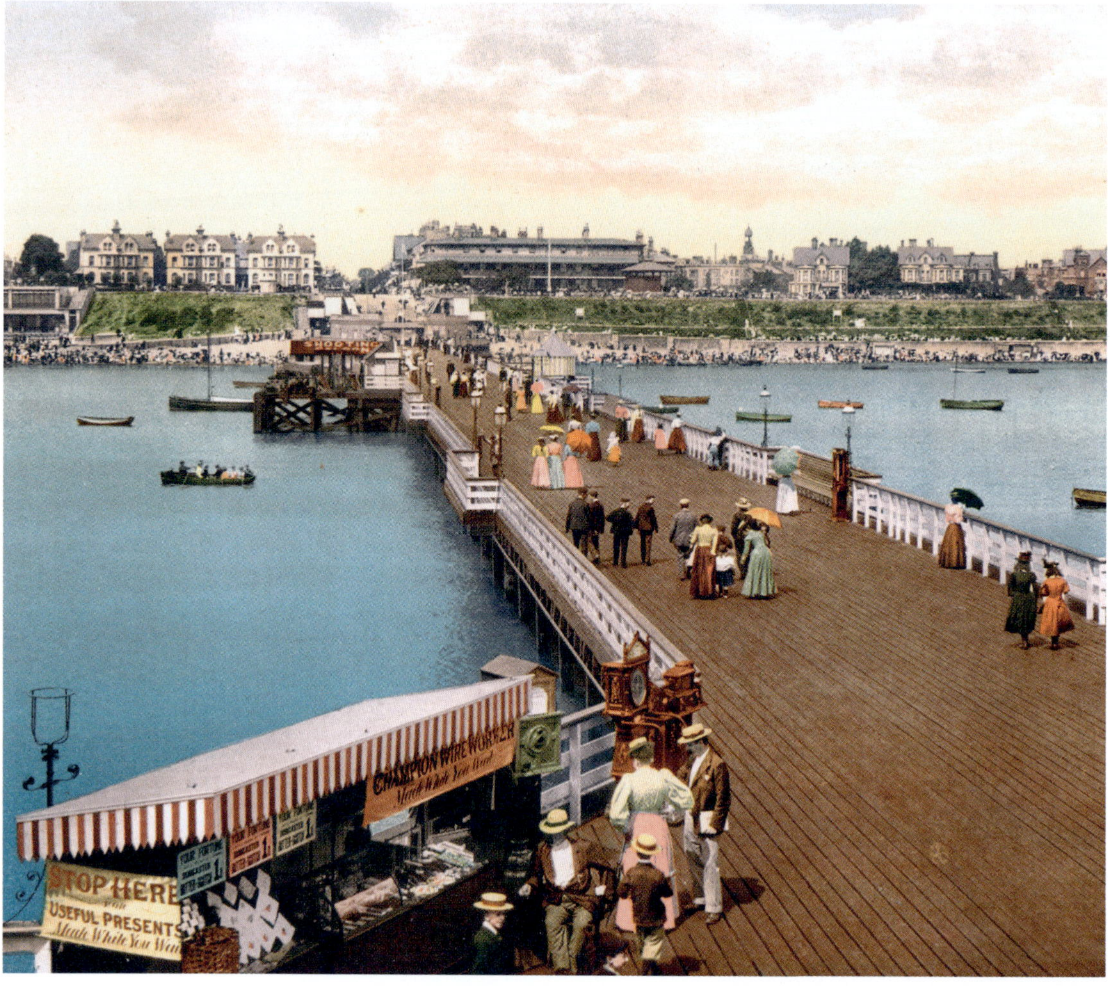

The expansion of the newspaper industry also plays its part in promoting the modern trends. In London the halfpenny *Star* was one among several evening newspapers, for example, but with its bold headlines and its vivid reporting it has now captured many hundreds of thousands of readers. The halfpenny *Daily Mirror* and *Daily Mail* are also in the vanguard of the popular press or what was once known as the New Journalism. They are intended to attract a female readership as well, but the principal reason for their success lies in the market for sensation in all of its forms.

Yet in many respects, of course, they reflect the same world that our parents and grandparents knew. Even for the born Londoner, the changes in domestic life are so stealthy and so minute that they are all but untraceable. There are few if any new bathrooms in the houses of the middle class and, instead, a galvanized bath is placed in front of the fire, replenished with water from a kettle on top of the stove; hip baths and slipper baths are also employed. Coal fires will always be considered important in most rooms. Cooking is still done in an open range, and on Sundays the joint is often roasted on a spit fixed to the mantelpiece. Old habits die hard. The middle-class family still play the piano and sing together. On Sunday mornings, they may take tram excursions to Dulwich or to Peckham Rye, and for special treats they may ride to Waterloo Bridge with bread to feed the gulls. The head of the household may save up his wages to enjoy two or three days at Clacton, or perhaps a day at the Crystal Palace. Excursions are always welcome, but women and children still need to be warned that country air is damp. This does not detract from the lovely quiet of the fields, the flowers, the white and dusty lanes undisturbed by motor roads. Others yearn for the seaside and for the bathing machines of Margate or Southend.

The old life of London goes on in its familiar ways. The cat meat man, the muffin man and the baked potato man do their rounds. The girls, wrapped in shawls, sit on the doorstep or on the kerb of the pavement. The men, standing in groups and smoking their pipes, gather by the doors of a public house. The poorer women, generally dressed in second-hand clothes, still come to clean the steps or do the mangling. The workhouses are in full operation, for better or worse. The female inmates make their daily walks to the local park, in single file, dressed in black coats and skirts, black straw hats and black buttoned boots, The male inmates march down the same streets in grey jacket suits, black cloth caps and open shirts. On a lighter note, costers still celebrate on bank holidays at the fairs in Greenwich, Peckham Rye and elsewhere. The women wear velvet dresses and huge hats covered all over with ostrich feathers, and their men have bell-bottomed trousers, full-skirted coats and caps, with the whole outfit covered by rows of pearl buttons. That is why they are known as 'pearlies'. Long may they continue.

An object of intense interest, in the popular press and elsewhere, has been the number of women who demand the right to vote. It is true that females are already permitted to serve on local councils and to vote in local elections, but this is considered to be an extension of their influence in domestic affairs. That is their natural sphere. It is also true that the women of the middling classes now have entry into higher education, despite their inability to graduate, and that they have gained access to such types of employment as teaching and nursing. However, for many this is not enough and 'go ahead' females claim that they have as much right to vote as the men. The *Daily Mail* has promptly described them as 'suffragettes', but just as promptly they have begun to call themselves 'suffra*gets*'. They do not necessarily desire to 'get' a vote for every woman, regardless

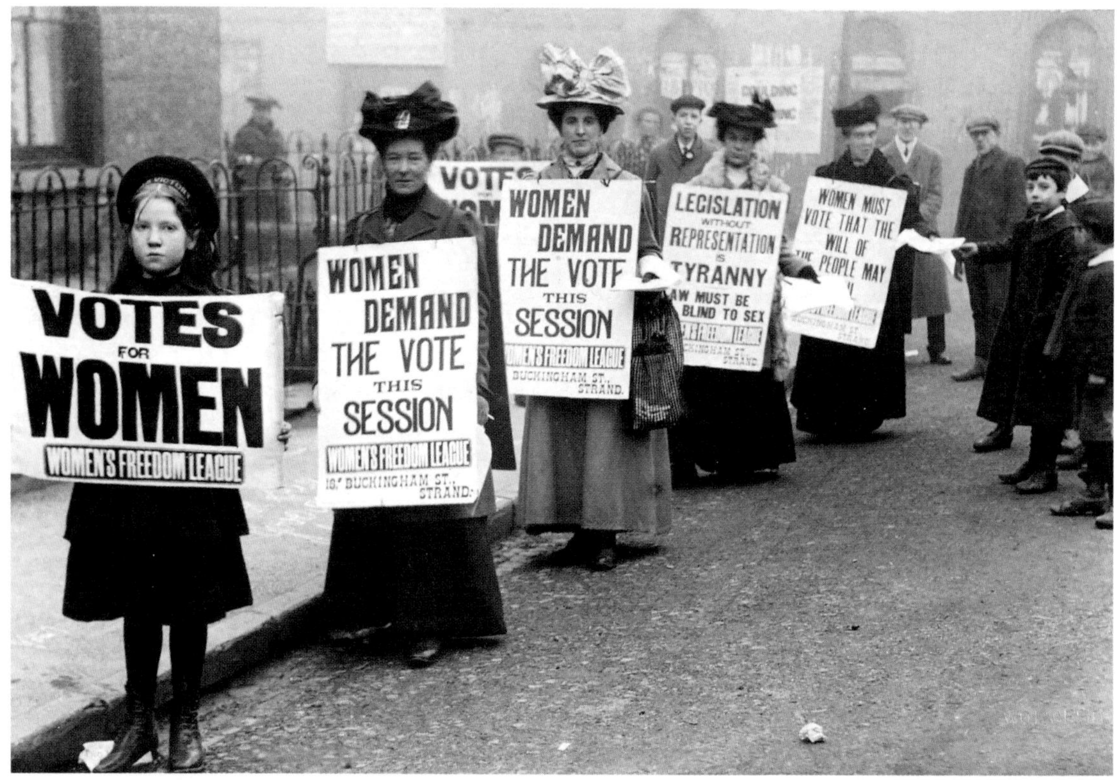

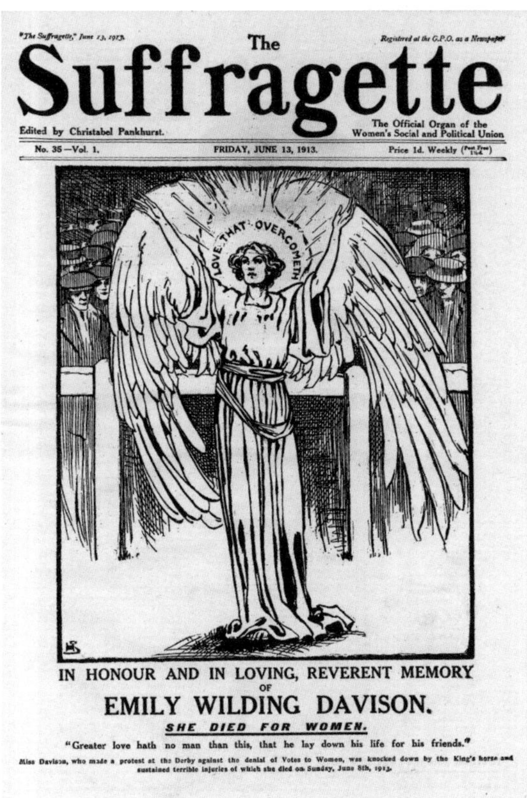

Above The Emily Wilding Davison memorial issue of *The Suffragette* newspaper edited by Christabel Pankhurst, 13 June 1913.

of class and property, because no such freedom is available to all men. Instead, they insist that their sex should not be a disqualification for the franchise. It is part of the rise in 'sex-consciousness' that occurred 30 or 40 years ago, in a period when all standards of taste and behaviour were being called into question. The scandals of that time, still fresh in most people's mind – including, notably the trials of Oscar Wilde and the post-office boys of Cleveland Street – stripped bare the pretensions of many leaders of society.

The principal spokesmen of parliament and press have derided these new women as exponents of 'petticoat politics' that threaten the whole of decent society. They are also denounced as 'desperadoes' or worse, and some believe that they dabble in revolutionary politics not unlike that of anarchists and Fenians. They have been described as females 'with hammers in their muffs'. The penny weekly, *The Suffragette*, is their bible and is read by women of the higher classes. In recent years, they have, in fact, become more active and more dangerous. They set postboxes alight and they chain themselves to railings. They break the windows of shops in Regent Street and of male clubs in Pall Mall. They destroy communal flower beds and slash cushions on trains. They write graffiti on public buildings and vandalize paintings which, they believe, portray females in a supposedly lascivious light. Some even resort to arson. Since they pose a threat to public order they have been arrested or imprisoned, and in some instances subjected to severe discipline, but it seems that their fervour is undiminished. Only recently a suffragette rushed onto the racecourse track of the Epsom Derby, and was killed by a horse owned by the king. It seemed to some to be a moment of symbolism. It is not at all clear where this fury will end.

'In a city of contrasts, the
bright exists beside the dark.'

1914–1931
WAR AND JAZZ

The war, despite all the dire prophecies, has not changed London to any marked degree. The city has always known death and destruction in many different forms, from plague to fire, and in any case war has always been popular with the London crowds. The city has, in fact, grown during the years of conflict. With so many young men detained elsewhere, full employment and higher wages have improved the general standard of living. The real damage is on the fields of battle. Only seven hundred Londoners have been killed during these four years of war, while almost one hundred and twenty-five thousand Londoners have died in warfare. There are, of course, obvious changes. Building work has been suspended, and the city is only partially illuminated by lamps, which are painted dark blue as a precaution against the Zeppelin raids. Parks and squares are used as kitchen gardens, and hotels have become hostels or government offices. But London emerged stronger and more dynamic after the war. New banks and office blocks are being erected, and the Bank of England itself is being rebuilt. Buildings which were once of two storeys have increased in height to eight storeys. The London County Council has embarked on initiatives for the education and welfare of its citizens, as well as schemes for the redevelopment of housing and of parks. Greater London has become the site of flourishing factories and of all the businesses that are attracted to what is called metropolitan prosperity. London is perpetually old but always new.

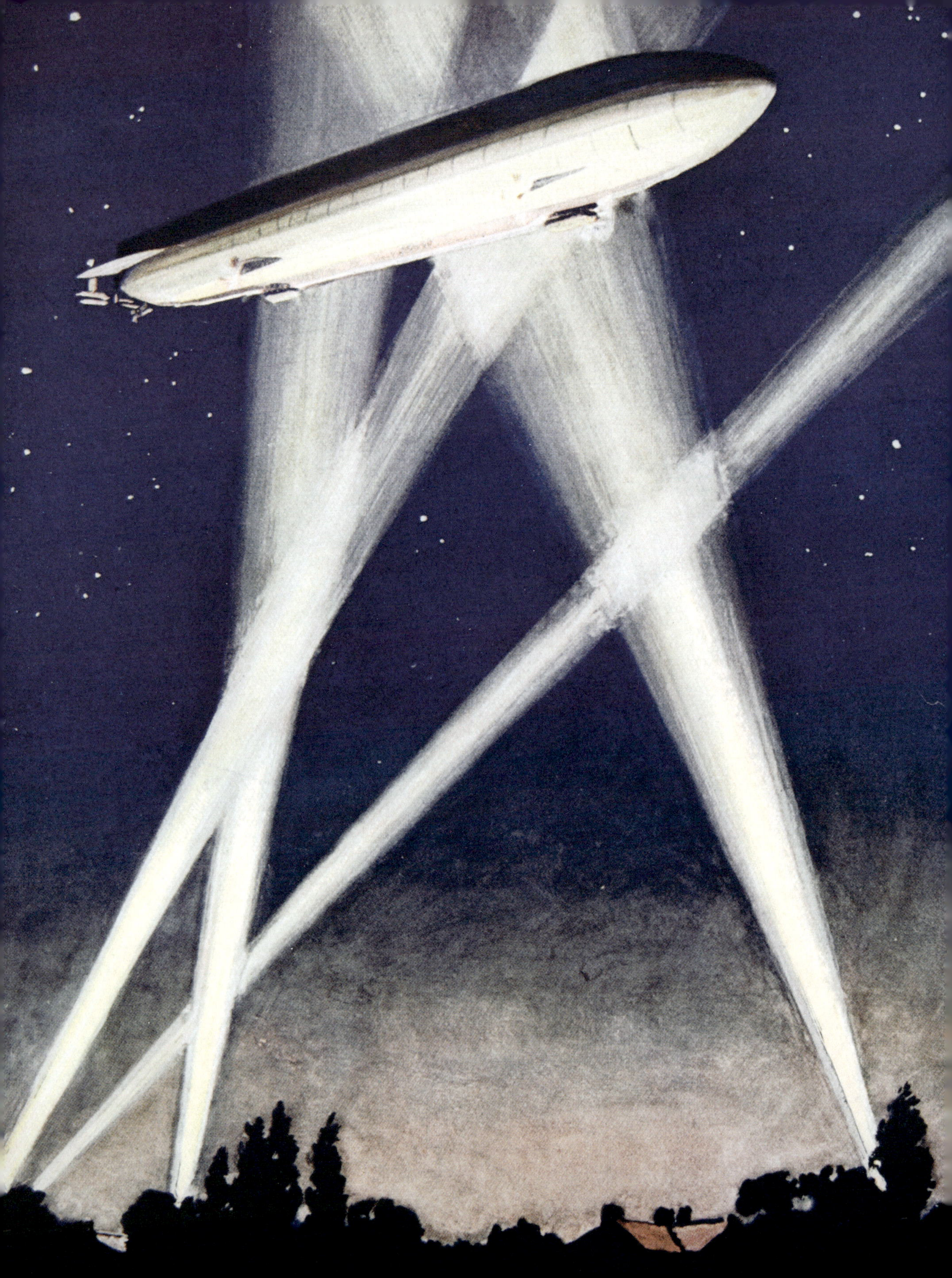

During the summer of the year in which war broke out, Londoners are in a nervous or at least uncertain mood. The suffragettes are still active, and the cause of socialism is advancing among the labouring classes; they both contribute to the elusive sense that the world is changing, even if its direction is still unclear. In fact, for many, the conditions of life are improving. The advent of cheap tram fares, the popularity of the picture palaces and, of course, the excursions to the seaside come as a welcome relief to those who are otherwise confined to 'out-of-the-way' streets and alleys.

The announcement of hostilities against Germany seem only to serve the mood of confidence. It has been open season against anything or anyone suspected of Germanic origin. Bakeries or confectioners bearing even the most innocuous 'foreign' names are looted or their windows smashed; children with the 'wrong' surnames are mercilessly bullied at their schools. The German and Belgian Jews of the East End are also looked upon with disfavour, and are not immune from the insults of the crowd. Some shopkeepers put out signs stating 'We Are Russians', but this is often taken to be a lie or a mark of cowardice. It is rumoured that German nationals are to be placed in large internment camps at Olympia, Alexandra Palace and elsewhere. This surge of patriotism, however badly directed, adds only to the general excitement, and it is confidently believed that the conflict will be short and successful. When the newspaper boys announce that war has been declared, people rush out of the shops and houses in order to cheer in the streets. The popular magazine, *John Bull*, sets the tone with its headline, 'The Dawn of Britain's Greatest Glory'. Fresh regiments march to the railway stations with bands playing and recruits sing as they are exercised along the Embankment. London buses, bearing the signs of 'To Berlin and Back', are filled with young men.

Yet, despite the optimism, Londoners have now been taught to fear the menace of the Zeppelin airships, for which crepuscular darkness seems to be the only efficient cover. The street lamps are dimmed, painted dark blue or black, so that Londoners are said to live and breathe in a murky haze, while the gaslights within the houses are also lowered or replaced by candles. They are turned down quickly, three times, when an air raid is deemed to be imminent. Perhaps, inevitably, these precautions have not proved to be sufficient; within the last year, a Zeppelin followed the trail of the Commercial Road towards the docks,

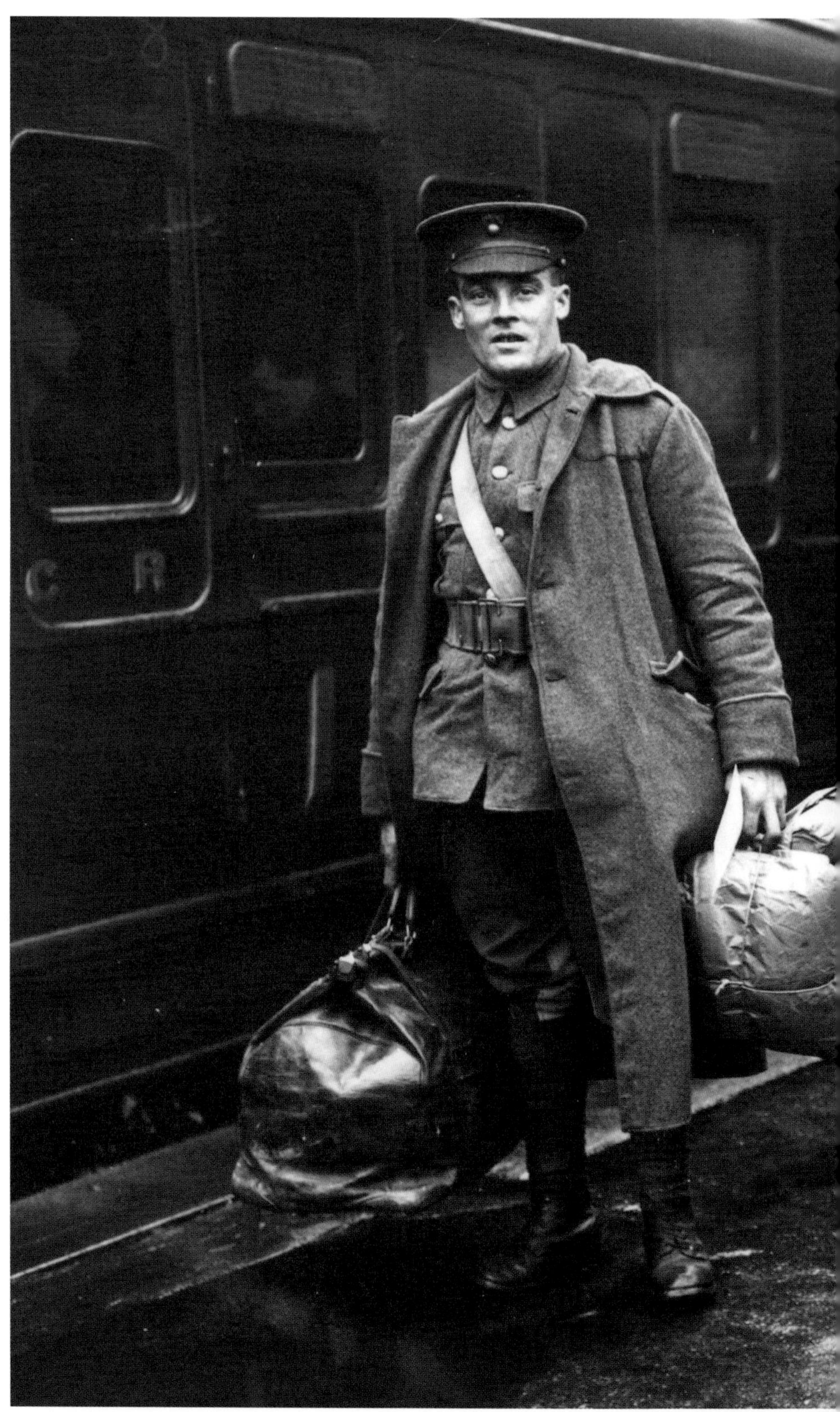

Two soldiers on the concourse at Victoria train station, carrying parcels full of provisions, about to leave for the front line, December 1914.

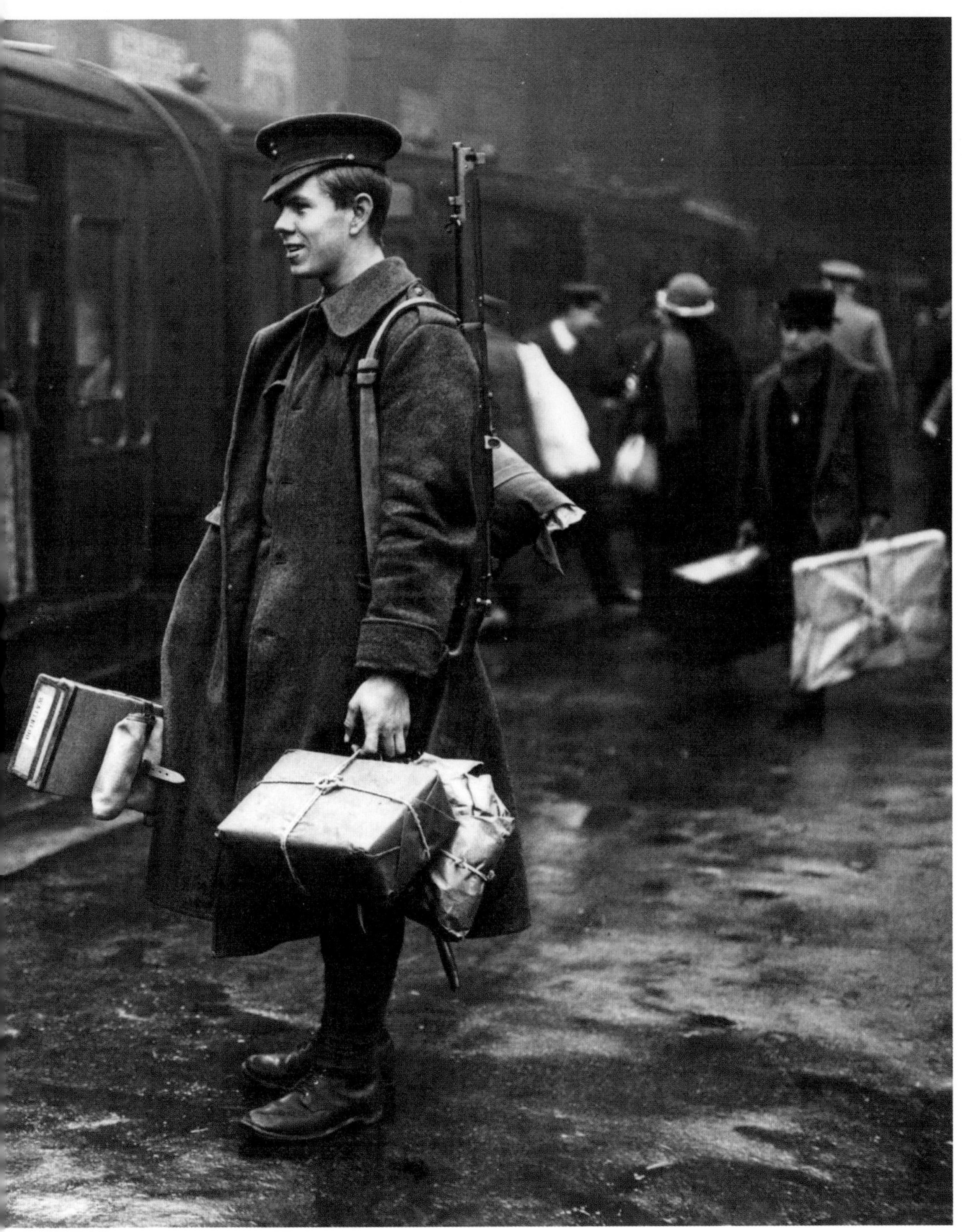

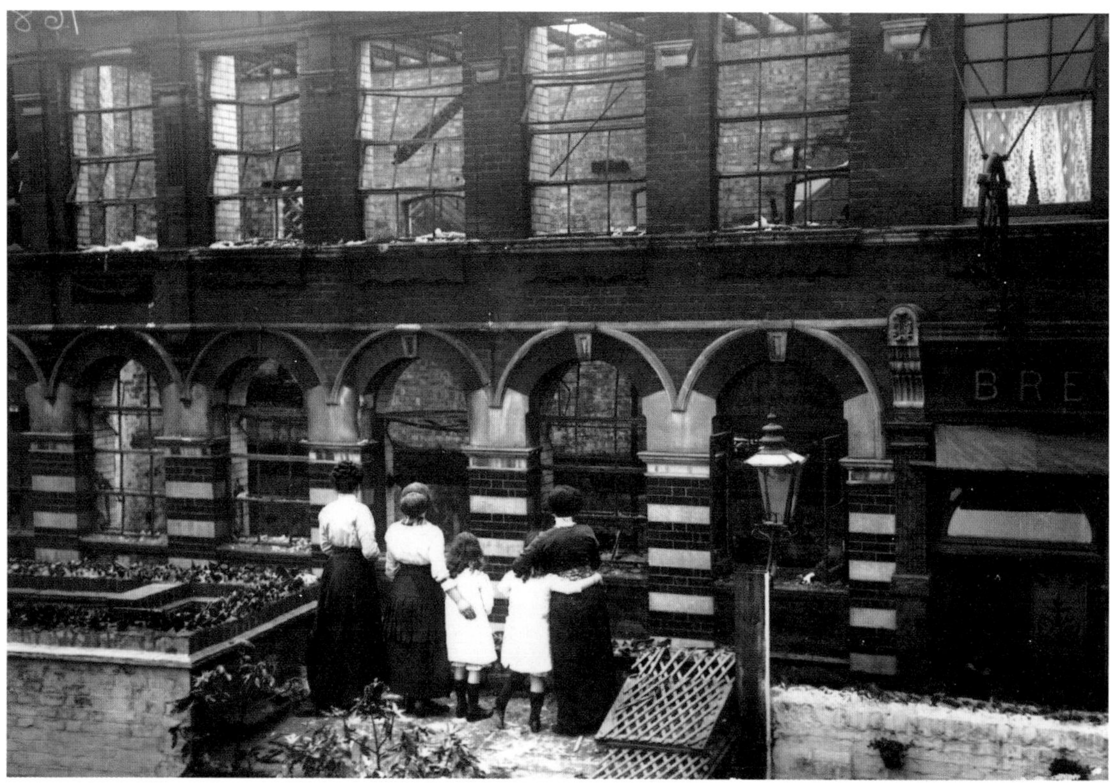

Above A group of women and children looking at a damaged building in Shoreditch, which was hit during a Zeppelin raid during the First World War, July 1915.

Right top People resting and sleeping on the platform and track of Aldwych Underground station, which was being used as an air-raid shelter.

Right bottom Women gardening in Finchley.

and 90 incendiary bombs fell on a wide area that included Stoke Newington, Whitechapel and Stratford. Seven people were killed in the first attack, and this unprecedented invasion from the air provoked anger at the state of national defences. Other raids from the airships have followed, and the see-saw battles between the opposing forces in Europe have only increased the anxiety. It has become clear that this may not be the short war that the government predicted and for which the people hoped, but this in itself has encouraged a mood of determination and endurance, just like that of the chirpy Cockney portrayed on the music hall stage.

In recent months, the news from the front has been accompanied by reports of domestic casualties. The attacks launched against London are only partly deflected by the system of searchlights, barrage balloons and anti-aircraft batteries that has been put in place. There seems to be no end in sight to the intensity of the enemy raids. Londoners in the worst affected areas, such as the East End, have sought refuge in natural shelters or in the basements of public buildings. A printed notice, fixed to a wall, might read, 'This House Contains a Fairly Good Sized Cellar. In the Event of an Air Raid, Passers-by Are Welcome to What Shelter

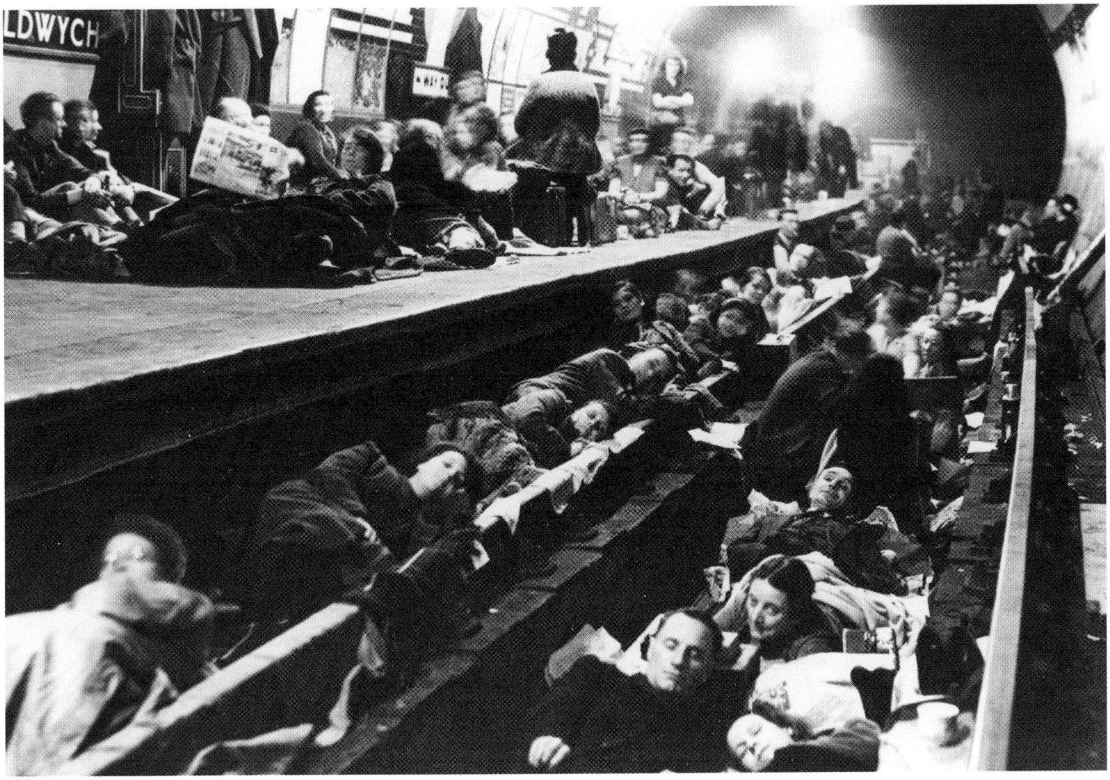

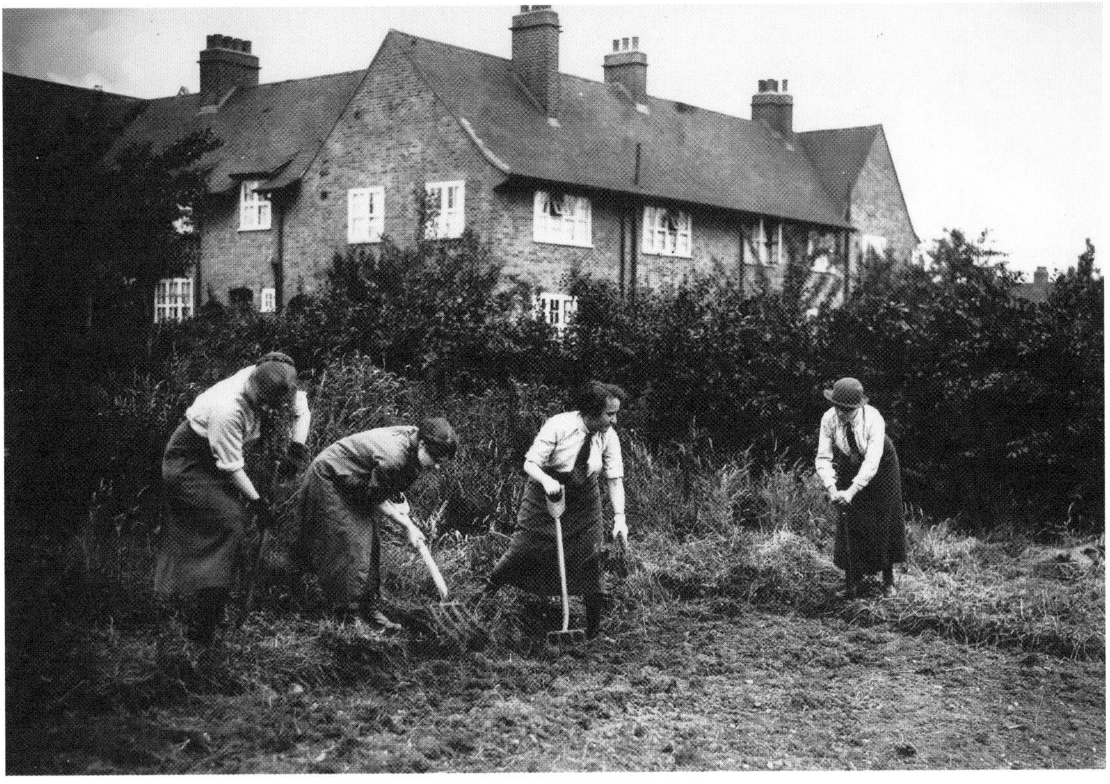

it Affords'. Of course large numbers of Londoners, estimated to be at least two hundred thousand, descend into the Underground system. It was agreed that that they could take refuge on the platforms if an attack was under way, but as yet there is little control or supervision.

Some cannot resist the spectacle of the silver-grey airships, spotlit and under attack, and stay by their windows to observe the scene. This is not encouraged. It is hoped that many more children will be sent into the neighbouring countryside or to the seaside towns. For the people who are obliged to remain at home, public kitchens have been established in order to provide staple foods at relatively low prices and all citizens are encouraged to cultivate, wherever possible, small garden allotments where vegetables and fruit can be grown. There are of course some shortages. A bottle of whisky costs 7/6d, four shillings dearer than before, and bitter beer has risen from 4d to 8d a pint. Twenty cigarettes now cost 1s rather than 6d! There are announcements in the newspapers that it may be necessary to ration paraffin oil and candles, together with jam, marmalade, syrup, treacle and honey. The pubs and shops are all closed by nine-thirty.

The threat from the air has not diminished in recent months and has menaced, in particular, the closely packed streets close to the river. The warning for these raids comes from 'maroons', bundles of fireworks which are launched from the local police stations or from other public buildings, but in the nature of things they can only be partially successful. They are, in fact, often mistaken for the German bombs themselves. The policemen race about the streets on bikes or motorcycles, calling out 'Take cover! Take cover!' Some carry signs with the same message, replaced at the end of the emergency with 'All Clear'. Of course there are many rumours of attacks and disasters even when, or especially when, the newspapers do not report them. Schools and hospitals have already been badly damaged, and many Londoners have lost their lives in the basements where they sheltered. Some Londoners were as much astonished as frightened. Middle-aged office workers, bankers and solicitors have taken off their customary dark suits and adopted blue uniforms to carry out fire-spotting or sky-watching. Of course, most importantly, women have been migrating in their thousands to the newly established munitions factories. The effort is unparalleled, and some female munitions workers, known as 'munitionettes', have decided to live in lodgings or in purpose-built hostels to be close to their

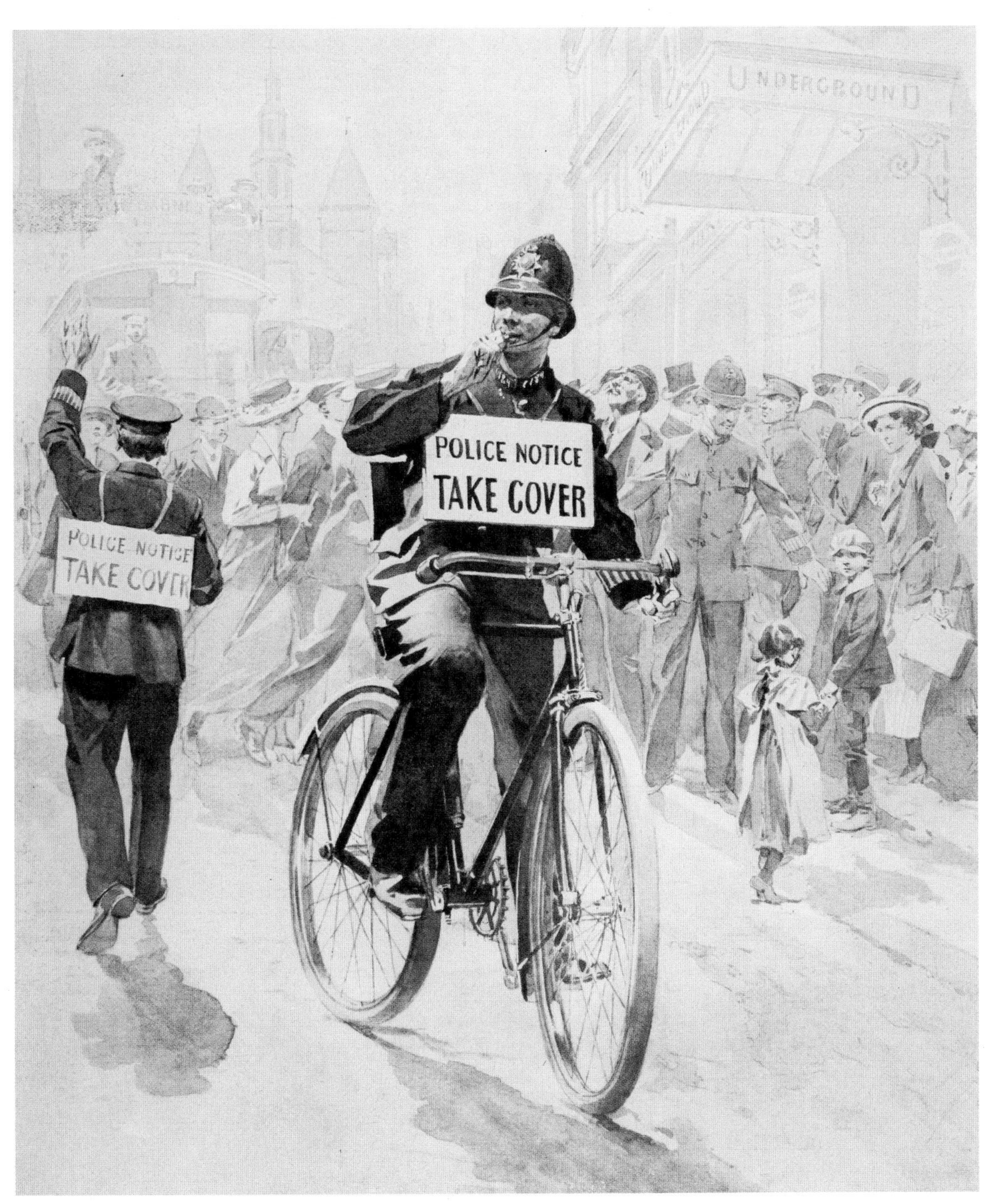

UNDERGROUND
POLICE NOTICE
TAKE COVER
POLICE NOTICE
TAKE COVER

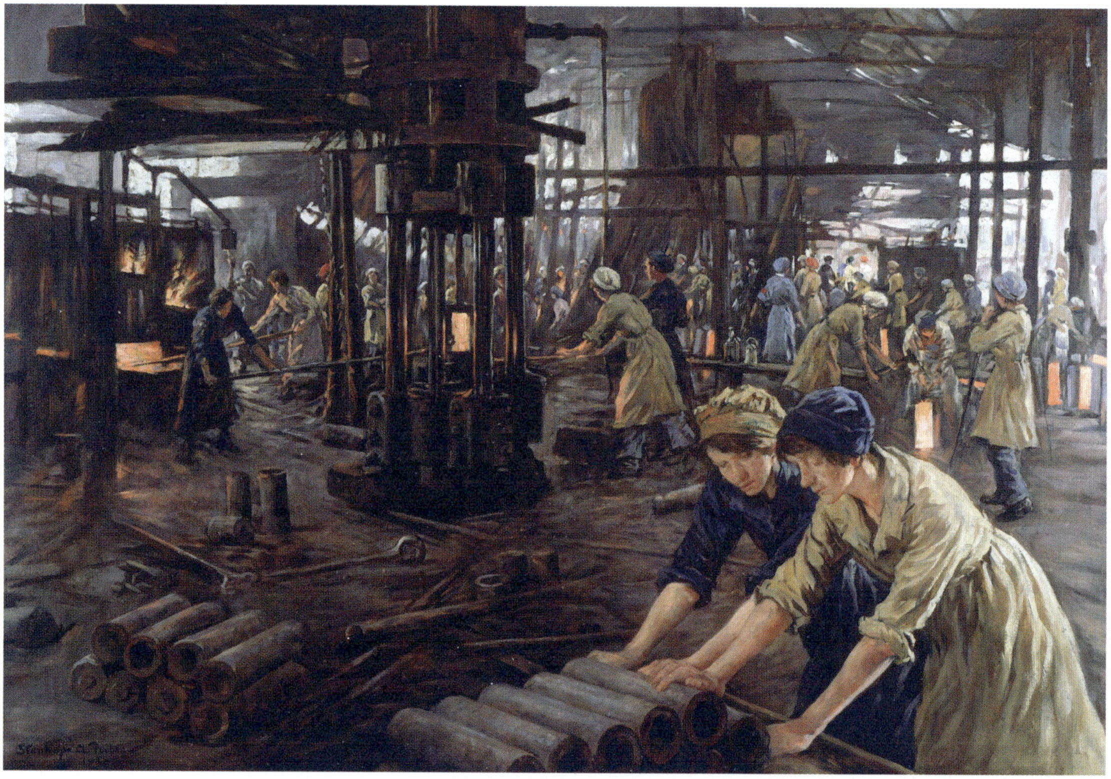

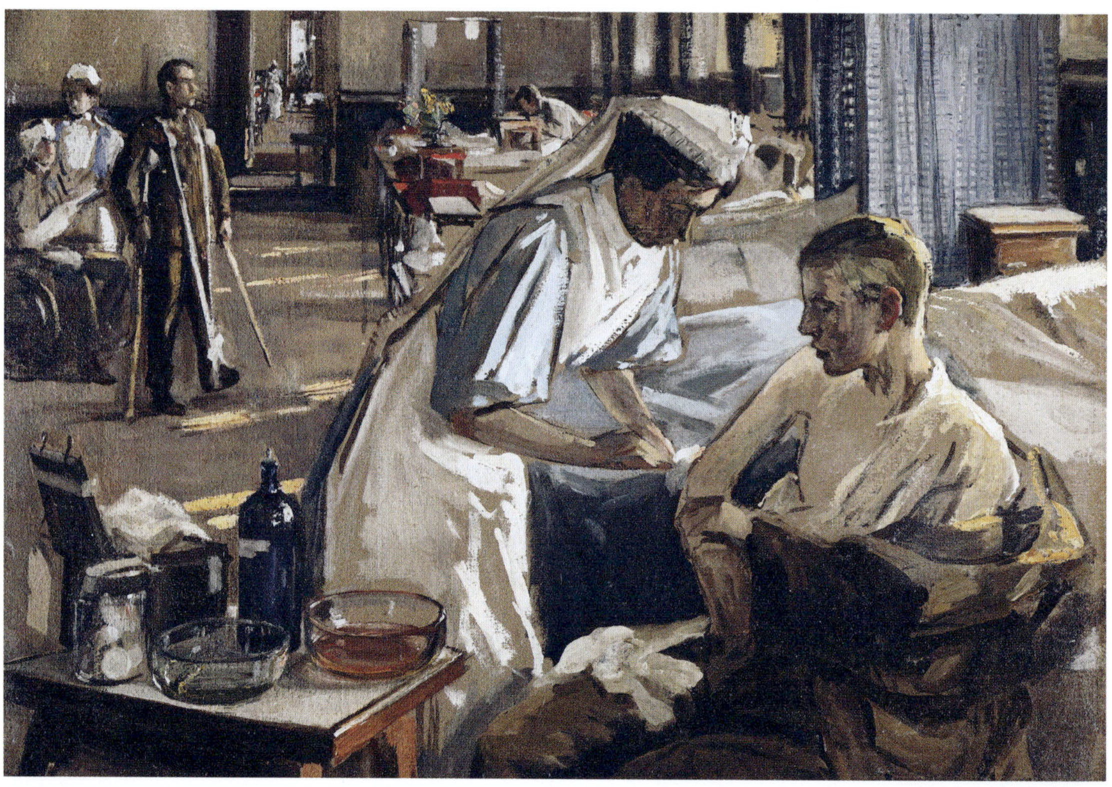

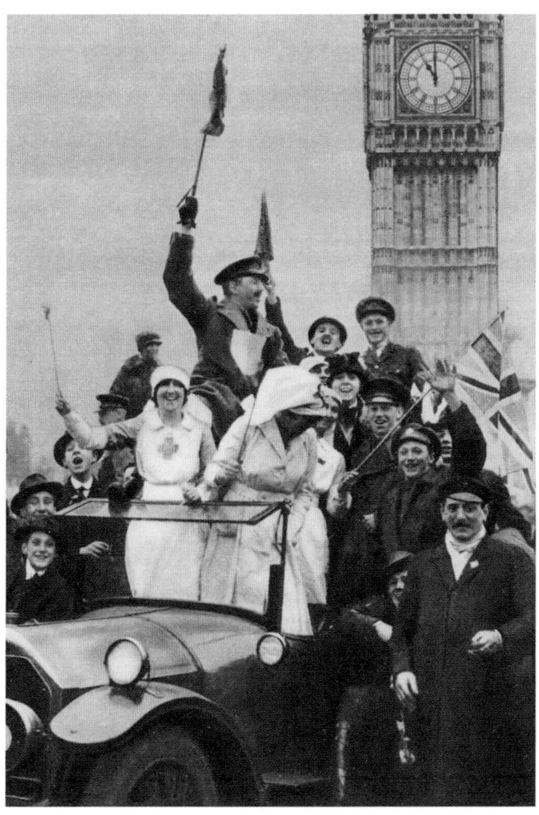

places of work. The figure on posters of the war-working woman is distinctive, with short hair, overalls and boots. Given the nature of their employment, and the fabric shortages, their attire has to be plain and practical. The frills and ribbons of Edwardian costume have been replaced by trousers or shorts. Not surprisingly, perhaps, women have begun to smoke in public.

Other social changes are also obvious. In the face of death and destruction, sexual license is a consolation if not a cure. It is said that some soldiers unbutton their flies on their way to disembarkation, and the dimming of London lights resembles the transformation scene in a pantomime when the familiar world vanishes in a trice. The unusual darkness seems to arouse feelings of restlessness and excitement, and has become a setting for unbridled lust. However, indulgence is only one response to danger. There has not been an invasion of London for hundreds of years and, as a result, it has produced panic or corrosive fear among certain sections of the population. The number of people who suffer from nervous collapse, rather than physical injury, cannot be counted. Some say that it is the first attack since the Norman Conquest or, as others argue, since the Civil War. Whatever the comparison, it comes as an all-consuming and terrifying ordeal. Newspaper reports of death and casualties at first provoked pity and fear but then, eventually, silent resignation. There were soon so many soldiers dying that there was no room in the newspapers to list all of the names. Over the city, women and children are dressed in mourning. Soldiers on crutches or in wheelchairs have become a familiar sight to everyone.

When it is announced that the war is over, and the Germans defeated, the people of London gather in the streets in triumph, many of them dancing on the pavements and in the roads. Drays, wagons and carts are filled with men and women from the East End and elsewhere, shouting and singing. People cling to statues and to lamp posts. Flags are everywhere, and a thousand motorcar horns sound along with a hundred bugles. They have been blown before to signal the end of an air raid, but now the sound represents something much more significant. The result is a pandemonium that only London can create. Five months earlier an epidemic of influenza broke out in the city and the 'Spanish flu', as it is called, has left many thousands dead. It is, of course, still with us. The church bells never stop tolling, and the undertakers are busy both by day and by night. Schools, churches and factories are forced to close for lack of staff. However, all this is forgotten on the day of triumph, Armistice Day. The girls put on their brothers' clothes as a sign that this day is different. Blinds are raised and the black paint is removed from the street lamps. Young children are carried outside to see the city light up for the first time in their lives. Strangers kiss and, linking hands, they dance like waves of the sea crashing against walls and buildings. It is not just the end of the war; it is believed to be the end of all wars. It is widely reported that the parrot in the Cheshire Cheese public house on Fleet Street drew with his beak a hundred corks without stopping, before falling into a dead faint. The celebrations, which some likened to a frenzy, lasted for three days and three nights.

*

In retrospect, this war has changed everything. It has accomplished those things which, in previous years, were only contemplated. The exigencies of warfare have demanded that the government take control of food production, shipping and the flow of labour; these measures are likely to have lasting consequences. Another significant change has been accomplished in the steady progress of mechanization. The enlargement of the industrial unit, the greater subdivision of labour and the increased amount of repetition work – all of which are direct consequences of mechanism – have opened up new possibilities for the employment of women and juvenile workers. The increase of factories, together with the decline of workshops, has been remarkable. A quarter of a million women, as well as unskilled men, have entered the workforce.

In order to keep domestic morale at a high level, working hours have been reduced and working conditions have improved. The demand for shorter hours has been satisfied with a 47-hour week which begins at seven-thirty or eight, so that for much of the year workers begin in daylight rather than darkness, instead of waking at five or five-thirty in the morning. A working day of eight hours has become normal. Only a few firms, however, grant an annual paid holiday to their workers. Wages are also kept at a high level, since it is believed that at times of crisis the working people and the unions are now the only barrier against domestic revolution. So has come the era of what is called by the newspapers 'war socialism'. What was once only considered, or urged by some of the political classes, is now at hand. This is also true of the woman question. Female workers are visible not only in shops and offices but on trams and trains, in banks and in schools. Women now go down mines, drive vehicles and work on the land. They are employed in the Civil Service as well as in factories. Along with their new jobs, clothes and freedom comes a new confidence, which may breed a new determination never to return to the old

A London Transport poster, c.1930s.

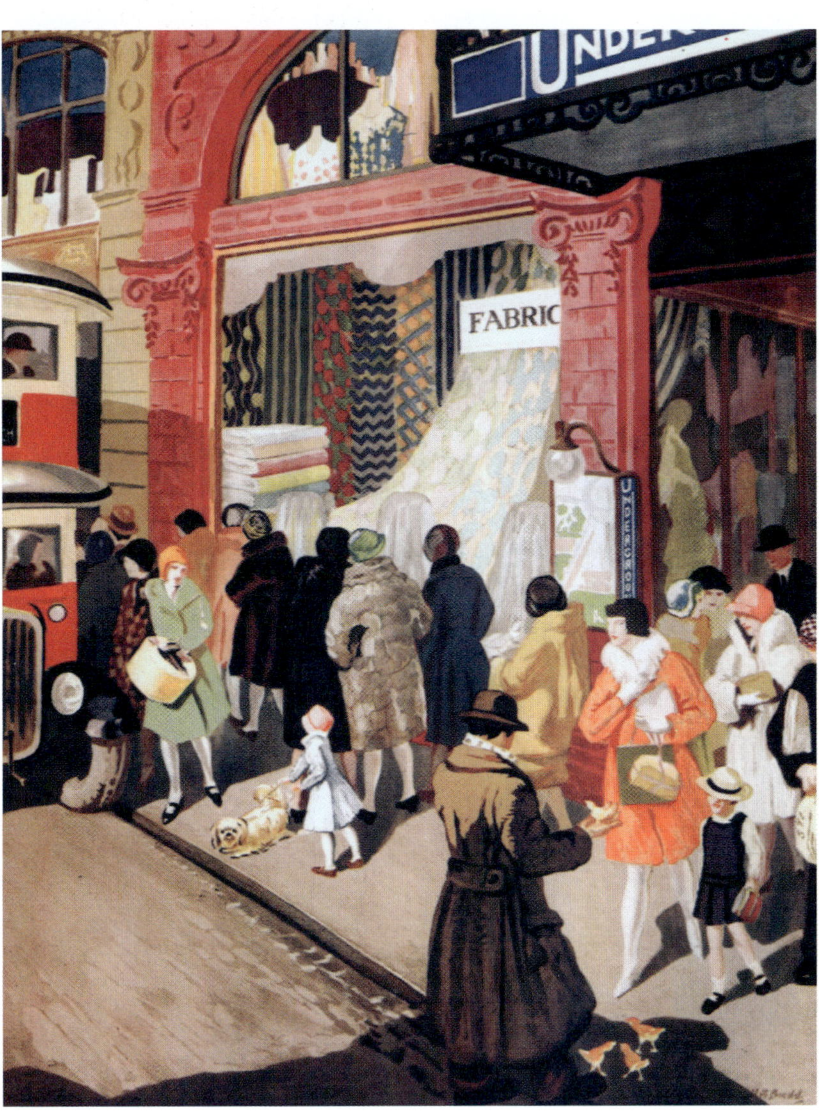

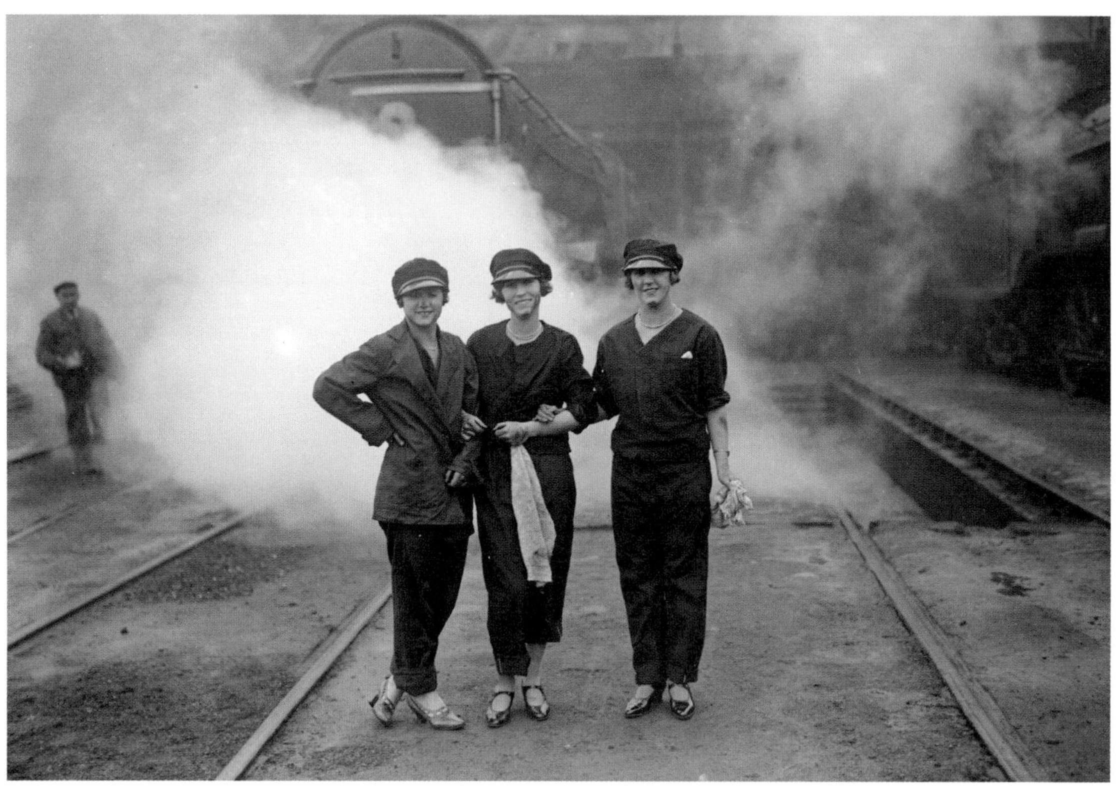

roles. Naturally enough, the demonstrations of the suffragettes had
all but vanished in the conditions of war, and it is widely believed
and hoped that females will gain the vote now that hostilities have
ended. The two great causes of public and political disquiet will
then have been removed. It seems to many observers that England
has broken with her past, and that we will soon be confronted by
the spectacle of a quite different nation.

That assumption is already proving to be correct. The two
or three years following the onset of peace have marked the
true introduction to the new century, with the old and familiar
terms of 'democracy' and 'democratic' reignited. The shared
experience of war has loosened social conventions to the extent
that a new spirit of equality seems to be abroad. It has become
evident, for example, that the old signs of wealth and privilege
are beginning to disappear. The extravagant life of private
households has moved to clubs or hotels; fewer servants are on
display and the aristocracy has left London's West End to cultivate
its country estates.

War rations are of course still in force for many provisions.
All Londoners, of whatever class, have become accustomed to

food queues for eggs and jam, for fruit and potatoes, for syrup and every kind of meat. The housewife is limited, for example, to 2 ounces of tea a week. If a queue forms, some people will promptly join it without knowing its purpose. They will even bring with them their own jars, canisters and tins. It is agreed that waste is at all times folly but, in these times, it is unpatriotic. Women are encouraged to place in their kitchen windows a pledge card stating that 'In honour bound we adopt the national scale of voluntary rations'. Voluntary or not, the force of popular opinion is in favour of this deprivation. It may be mentioned, in passing, that statistics reveal that there has been a marked increase in cigarette smoking, which has been accompanied by a considerable decrease in the consumption of alcohol.

In fact, the whole demeanour of the different social classes has changed. For men the pipe has given way to the cigarette and, where it persists, it is no longer a clay but a briar. The Cockney dialect and rhyming slang are slowly disappearing, while the Cockney twang is spreading to other Londoners far beyond the sound of the bells of St Mary-le-Bow. The general improvement in economic conditions, and the influence of the press, have been

Below From left to right, Chelsea footballers Andy Wilson, Jimmy Thompson and Willie Brown leave Euston station by train en route to a match against Wolverhampton in the Third Round of the FA Cup, 13 January 1928.

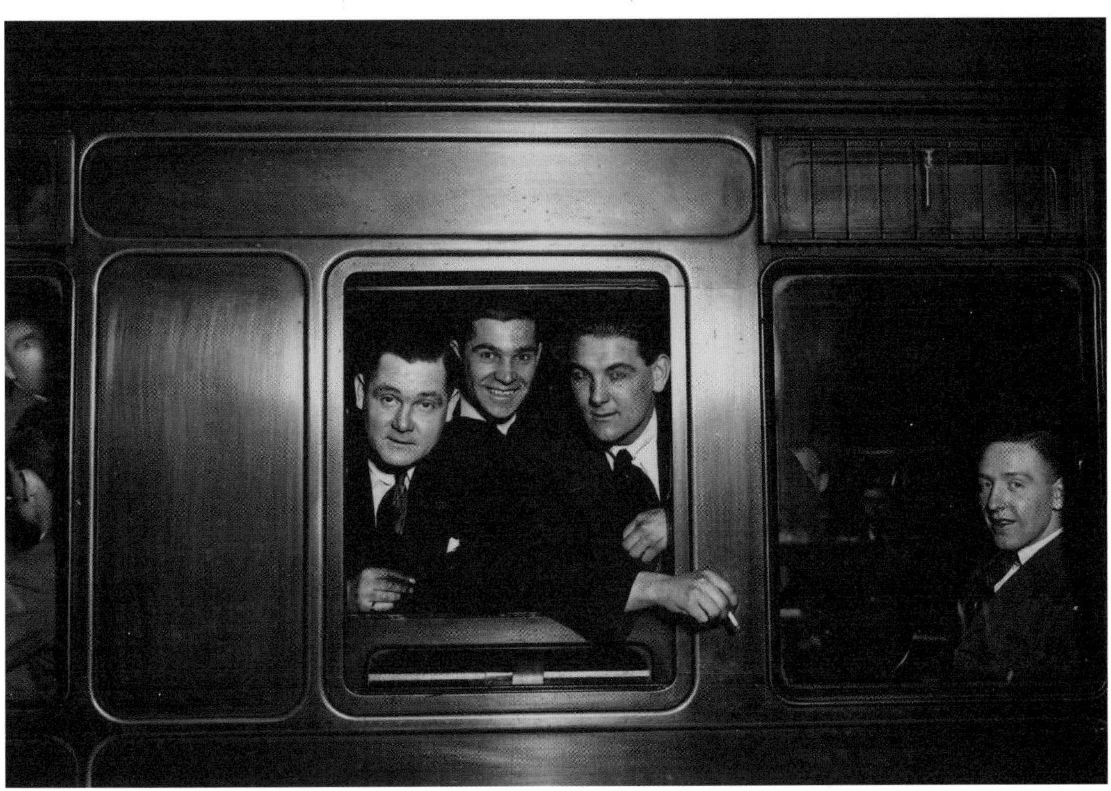

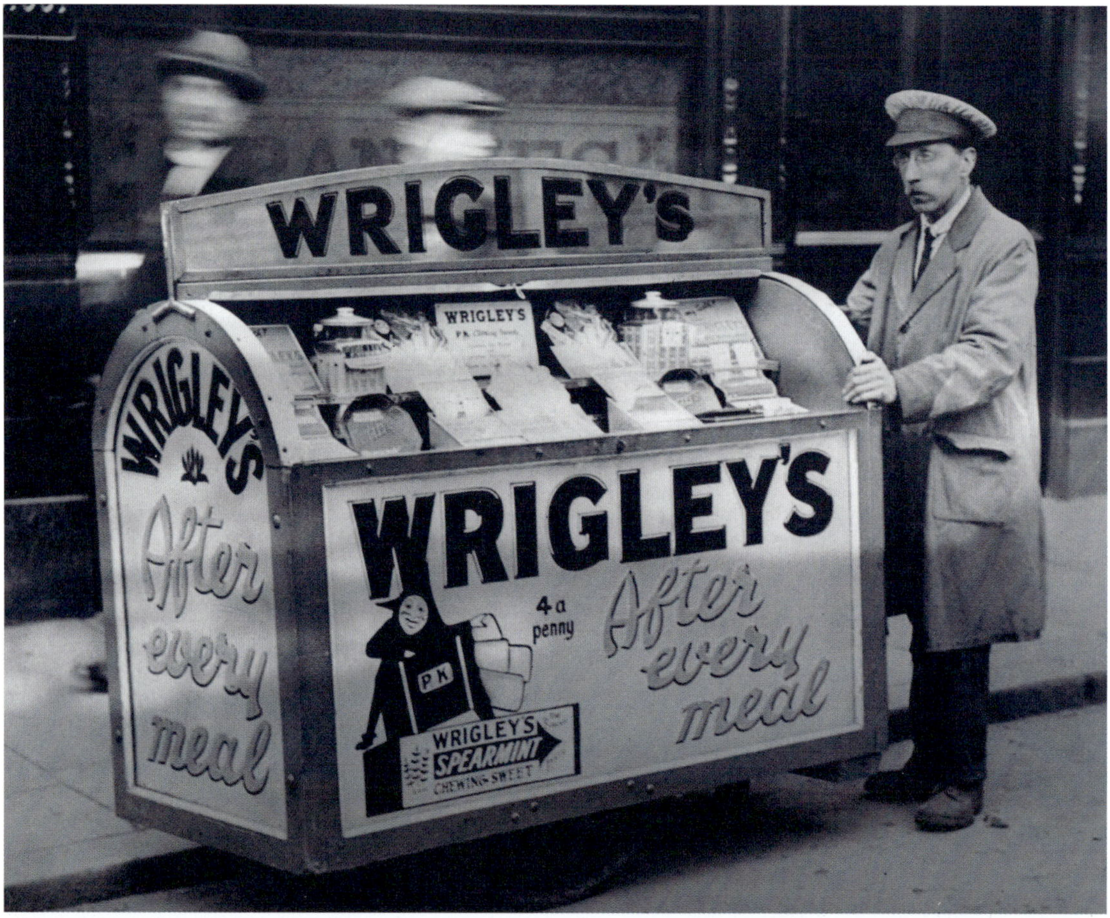

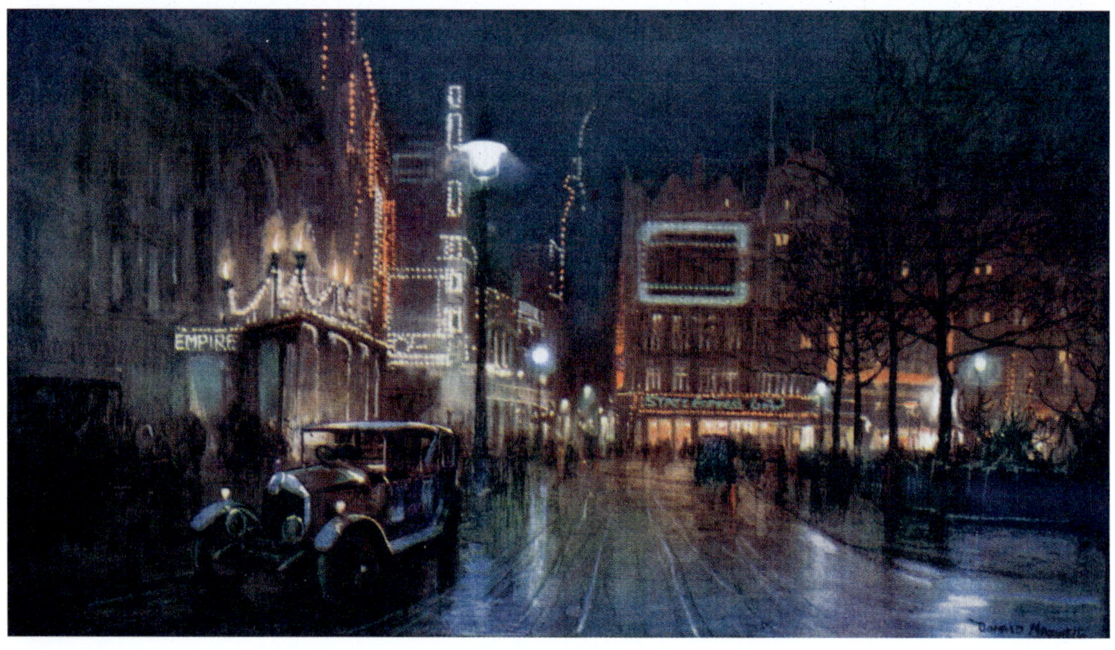
WRIGLEY'S
WRIGLEY'S
After every meal
WRIGLEY'S
After every meal
4 a penny
PK
WRIGLEY'S
SPEARMINT
CHEWING SWEET
EMPIRE

crucial in this regard. However, the much freer mingling of classes, resulting from the increase in travel and communication, has also been important. In so far as it represents a levelling up of opportunities and a breaking down of class barriers, it is to be welcomed, but perhaps a word of regret may be allowed to escape for the passing of something colourful in the old city customs and habits. The population of London is ever increasing, and the newspapers prophecy that it will soon reach nine million. Will this encourage a new uniformity?

*

Many believe, however, that the future can look after itself. In recent years, at least since the beginning of the 1920s, there has been a general relaxation of mood, manifest in all walks of life. Some ascribe this to the gradual Americanization of London life with the increasing popularity of snack bars and supper stands, of electric night signs and even of popular songs. The boys in the street – who include Post Office messenger boys, Theatre Agency boys, shoeblacks and street orderly boys – whistle tunes from such favourites of the musical theatre as *The Cabaret Girl* and *Chu Chin Chow*; tunes, such as 'Shimmy With Me' and 'Desert Song', are popular. Chewing gum, sold on the streets, is everywhere. In a similar spirit, young women, accustomed to smoking in public spaces, have also learned to frequent public houses. They embody, perhaps, the audacity and vitality of this new era. Some people still sigh, however, for the old days of wartime, when there were always vacant seats on the trams or on the Underground railway, and when a fine meal and a bottle of wine cost less than £1. Nevertheless, most Londoners look forward to a world of peace and plenty where clothes and travel will be cheaper, where theatres and restaurants will once more be vibrant and where every house will have a separate bathroom.

The syncopated beat of a nightclub band and the rattle of a cocktail shaker are now the required music for the young females known as 'flappers'. In the Victorian period a flapper had been a child prostitute, but now it refers to the high-spirited young woman, of slim figure, who will just as easily sit on the pillion of a motorbike as on a bar-stool. For the first time in history young ladies aspire to a boyish figure, with straight waists, flat chests and slender thighs, hips and buttocks. Where corsets had once accentuated the bust, breasts are now flattened by tight bodices

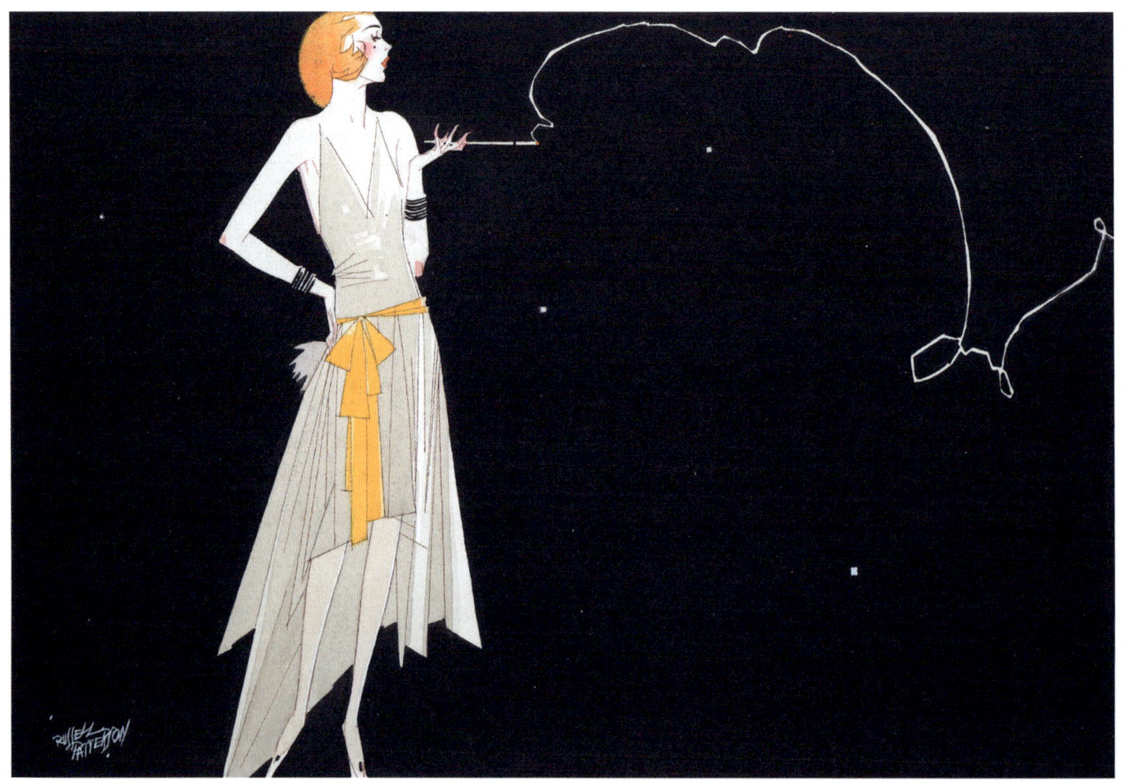

Above   Where There's Smoke There's Fire (c.1920s) by Russell Patterson.

Right   Three women dressed in the spring and summer styles of the flapper era, c.1920.

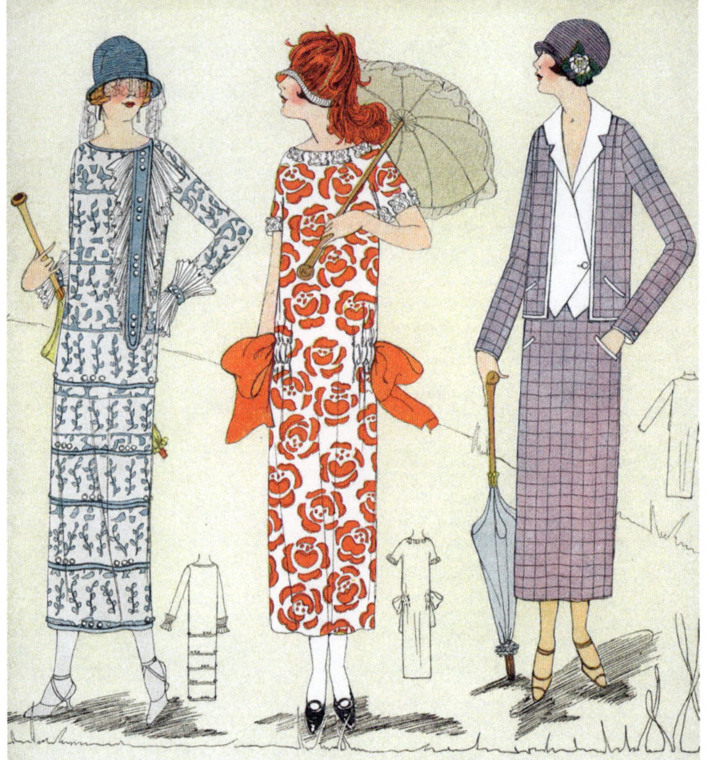

or brassieres. Waists have been eliminated, along with hips, by dresses that are straight, loose and cylindrical, or by baggy trousers. In donning trousers, some flappers seem to allude to the uniforms factory women had worn during the war; it may be a way of celebrating social and political change. They also use clothes to proclaim their pleasure in sex and fleshliness. Flapper dresses, often dipping low at the front and back, are sleeveless and short. Simplicity, lightness and comfort are the only standards of dress. The flappers also have their own slang. Older chaperones are called 'alarm clocks' or 'fire extinguishers'; terms of approval are 'the bee's knees' and the 'cat's meow' and, of disapproval 'Victorian', 'stuffy' and 'junk'. Boring men are 'pillow cases', while young men borrowed for the evening are 'umbrellas'. Young women eager for experience are 'biscuits', but if a girl steals a friend's partner she is a 'strike-breaker'.

The bright young man also ridicules pre-war customs and manners. Beards, moustaches and pipes have been discarded. The new males favour clean-shaven faces and brush back their oiled hair. They wear wide trousers known as 'Oxford bags' and high-necked pullovers. They wear 'underpants' with elastic tops rather than the old style of long woollen drawers. They prefer soft colours, and are said to be the first men ever to don pink shirts. They have even taken to brown suede shoes. They wear attractive wristwatches and constantly consult them with a flourish of the forearm. This is now considered to be a sign of effeminacy, and an invert may be called 'terribly wristwatch' or accused of having a 'wristwatch accent'. The bowler hat is being threatened by the homburg (but surely the bowler will survive?) and the double-breasted jacket is being replaced by the single-breasted, but all else remains in place.

Gin was until recently considered to be the drink of the lower classes but, mixed with vermouth, it has become acceptable in the highest circles. Martinis, Manhattans, Bronxes and White Ladies are in turn the cocktails of the moment. Jazz has also arrived from America.

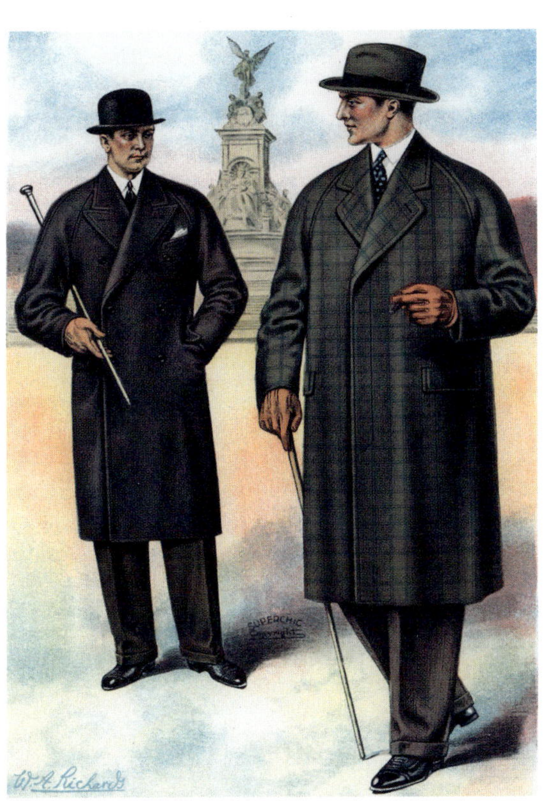

Below Two clean-shaven men, one wearing a long double-breasted town overcoat with bowler hat and cane, and the other in a single-breasted Raglan coat with cane. In the background is the Victoria Memorial on the Mall.

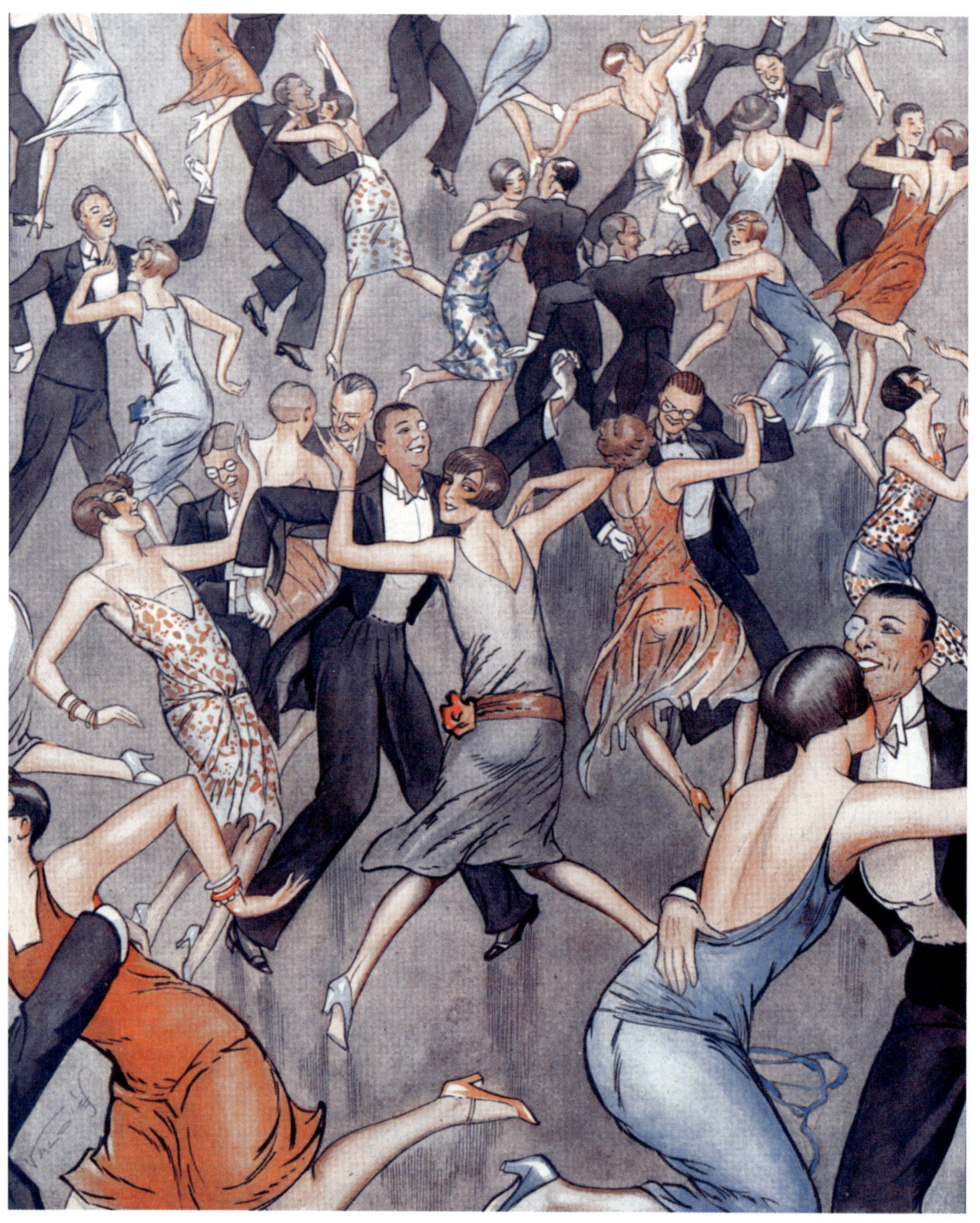

It is a restless, almost fevered, music. Young people are perhaps
too much disturbed by recent events to settle back into a former
and more tranquil life. They crave novelty and excitement. 'Jazz'
has become an adjective to describe bold clashes of colour or the
loud energy of traffic. Anything alien or shocking can be 'jazz'.
The fantastic music and dance of the newest jazzes have been
introduced, and within a short time have become, in the phrase
of the day, 'all the rage'. One tune bursts into life after another
tune, and a whole medley of notes soar to merge into one. It is the
melody of modern London.

One version of up-to-the-minute dance is known as the
'shimmy' or the 'shimmy-shake', and has become the latest craze.
The passion for this form of recreation was powerfully stimulated
by the psychological and emotional conditions generated by
the war; dances of every kind have emerged, with columns of
advertisements in the newspapers for tea dances, practice dances,
subscription dances and Victory dances. Public dancing is also
a frequent accompaniment to music in the London parks. In
more intimate surroundings, the Savoy restaurant was the first
to introduce dancing with meals, although many considered the
practice to be bad for the digestion. The new entertainment of
the cabaret has also emerged in the nightclubs; it consists of floor
shows featuring music, dance and song, with the performers
either on a small stage or moving between the tables.

Great Windmill Street has for long been known as a centre
of all-night pleasure. Just off this street is the entrance to a little
blind alley called Ham Yard, where you will find an open court
ringing with music and song. The taxi-cabs climb up Windmill
Street tooting and blaring, and deliver their passengers to the
Pavilion Club, the Last Club and the Ham and Bone Club, as well as
others. You can put your motorcar here for a few hours at the cost
of a shilling or so. Hawkers sell matches and the roast chestnut
men wheel up their barrows. The children gather outside these
clubs, and call out for coppers with 'Throw out your mouldy!' or
simply 'Thr-aoh!' and 'Mouldy!' When you leave these haunts, you
will always see a crowd on the corner of Piccadilly staring at the
advertising signs. Above the large cafés of the Circus, including
the Royal, the Imperial and the Monico, are glittering images of
a motorcar with silver wheels and of a red crystal bottle pouring
port into a glass, of the bright stars of Hennessy brandy and of the
baby who sucks a bottle of Nestlé's Milk. Fathers and mothers stand
with their children, pointing out the pictures.

The more fashionable quarters of London have been invaded by the Bright Young People; they used to roar around the streets in motorcars before discovering the perils and pleasures of the Scootamota, which is considered to represent an entirely new era in locomotion. They engage in games such as treasure hunts, and generally celebrate the lifting of old social conventions. The relaxed atmosphere of London after the war has also been captured in the fashion for impromptu parties, cocktail parties and, in particular, for fancy dress parties. This new generation enjoy arranging Wild West parties, Russian parties, Circus parties, Windmill parties and Swimming Pool parties. Naughtiness and excess are the keynotes, with the party-goers enjoying sexual intrigue, gin and little twists of cocaine which are known as 'uppies'. For a Bath and Bottle party, at St George's swimming baths in London, flowers and rubber horses floated on water illuminated by coloured spotlights. The guests, dressed in dazzling swimming costumes, drank 'bathwater cocktails' and danced to the strains of a Black jazz orchestra, sometimes breaking off to hurl themselves into the pool. It was a sure way of being reported in the Sunday newspapers. The young women,

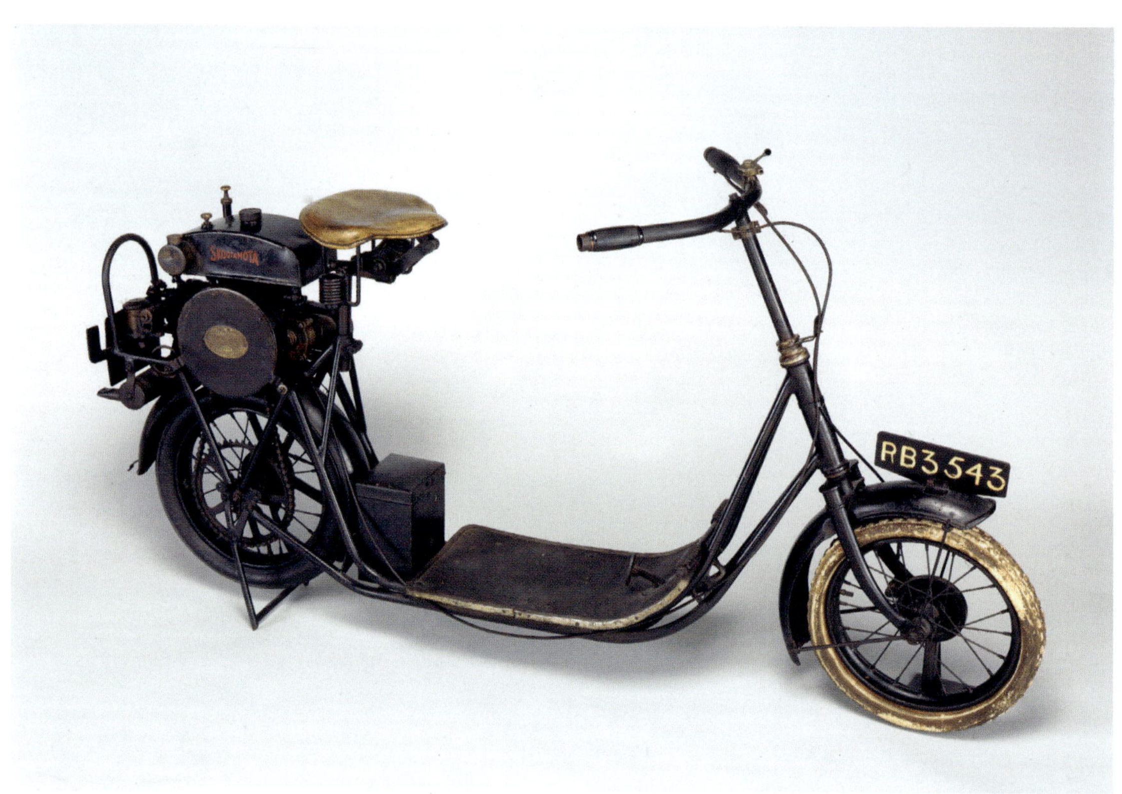

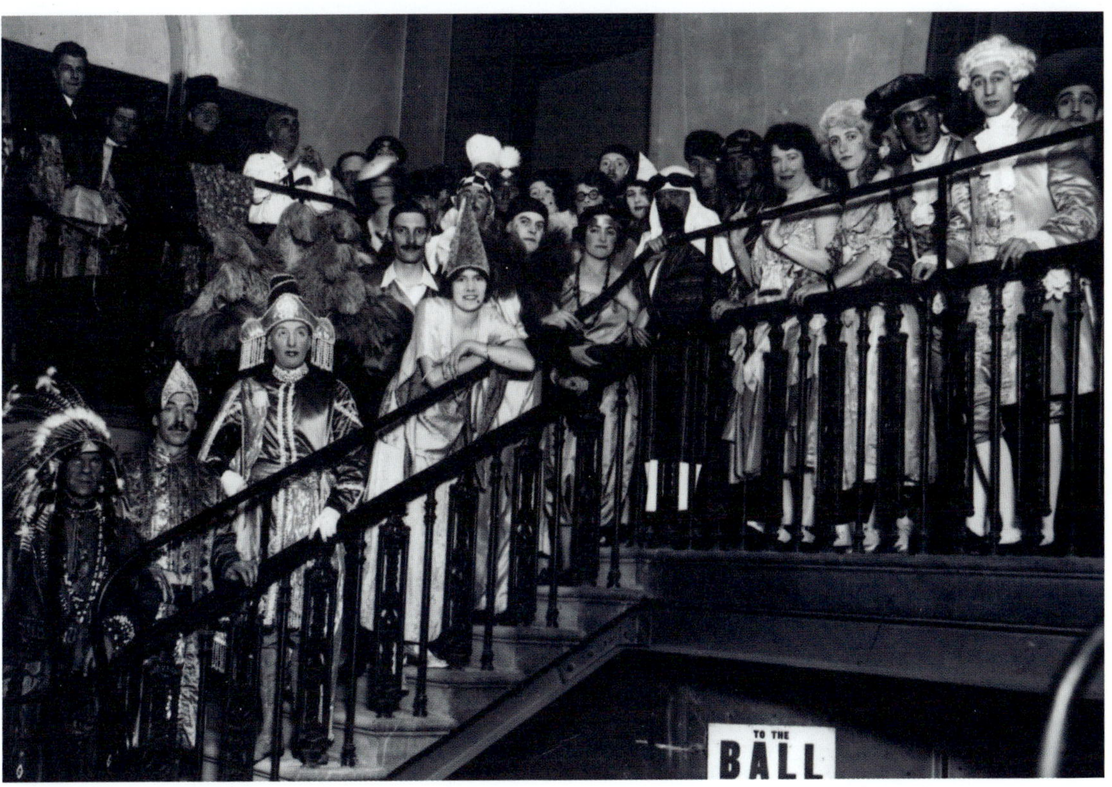

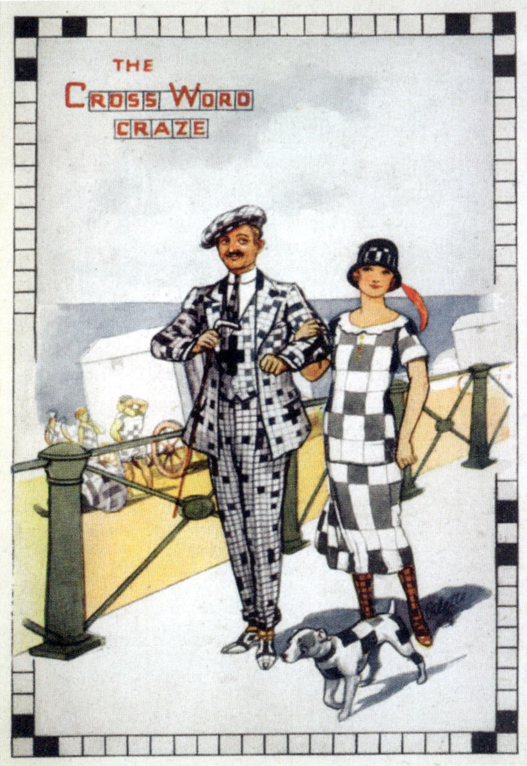

the 'It girls' as they are sometimes known, can also be seen at the racecourse, the greyhound races, the brasseries and even the wrestling bouts. One of their many 'crazes' is the pogo stick.

The older generation of Londoners seem to dislike these novel entertainments. They also disapprove of the Turkey Trot, the Bunny Hug or the Grizzly Bear; they hate the Charleston and cannot mention the Black Bottom. However, those of a quieter disposition, in these unquiet days, can partake in the new pastime of crossword squares. It is perhaps more than a pastime, since it takes time and ingenuity. It is maybe also a sign of the age, being both ingenious and harmless.

The working classes find amusement in more conventional entertainments, whether in boxing and wrestling matches,

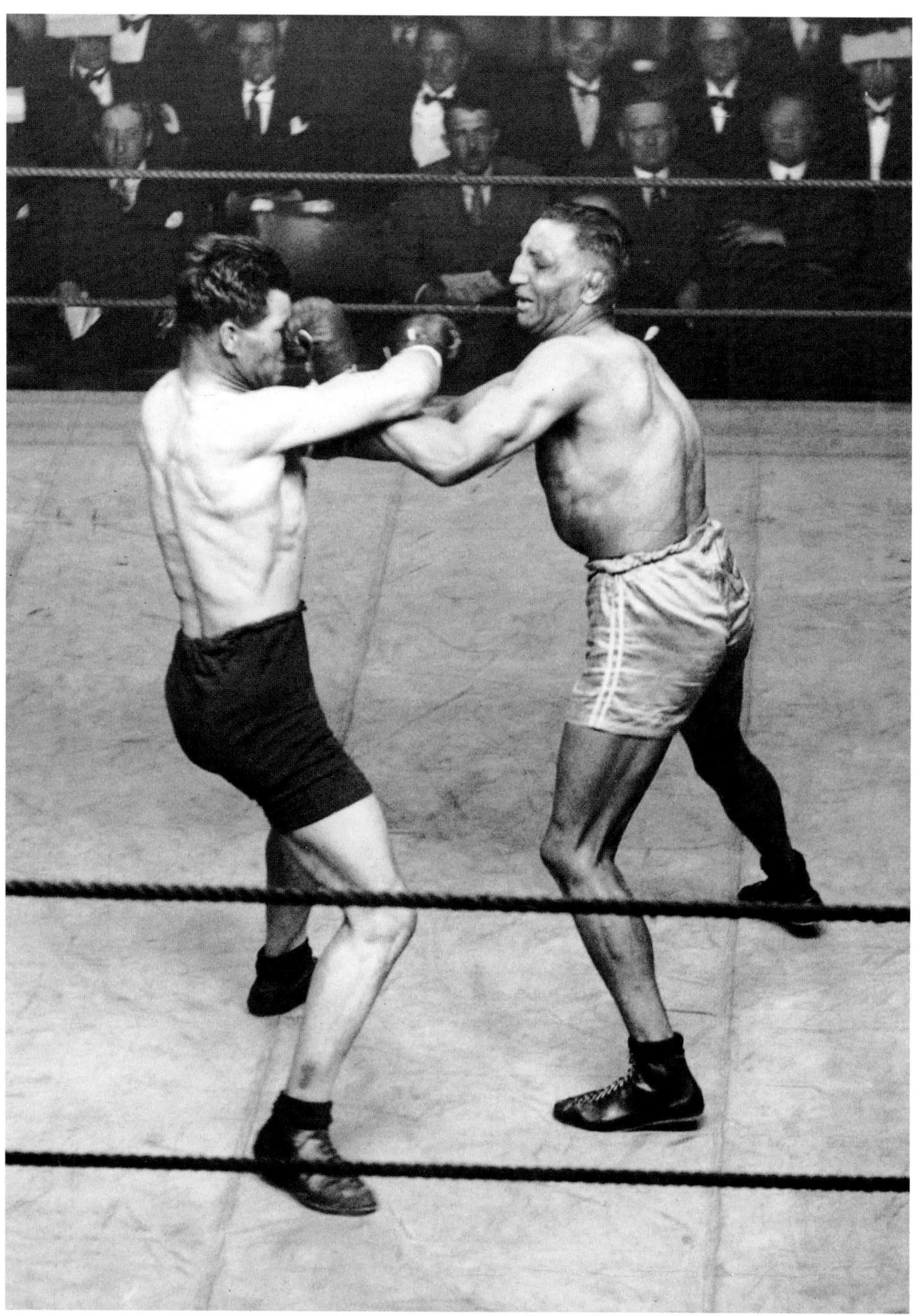

or in association football as played on a professional basis.
Other delights are now available. As one popular song puts it:

'I'll take her to the A-qua-rium,
I'll take her to see the Zoo,
She'll knock 'em I know
At the wax-work show
And the Crystal Palace too.'

Before the war it was considered bad form for lady to wear
'make-up' but now it is more than acceptable. It is the fashion.
Lipstick, rouge, eyebrow and eyelash colouring are taken for
granted among the faster set. It is not only considered acceptable
for a lady to apply powder in public places, but also at a private
dinner table. Short hair and short skirts are once more in evidence,
with the regularly stated rule that men will not dance with you
if you are all laced up. Stockings are now of all colours, and high
heels have come into more general use. Older ladies are more
cautious, on the understanding that the higher heel may cause
what the medical profession call 'uteral displacement'.

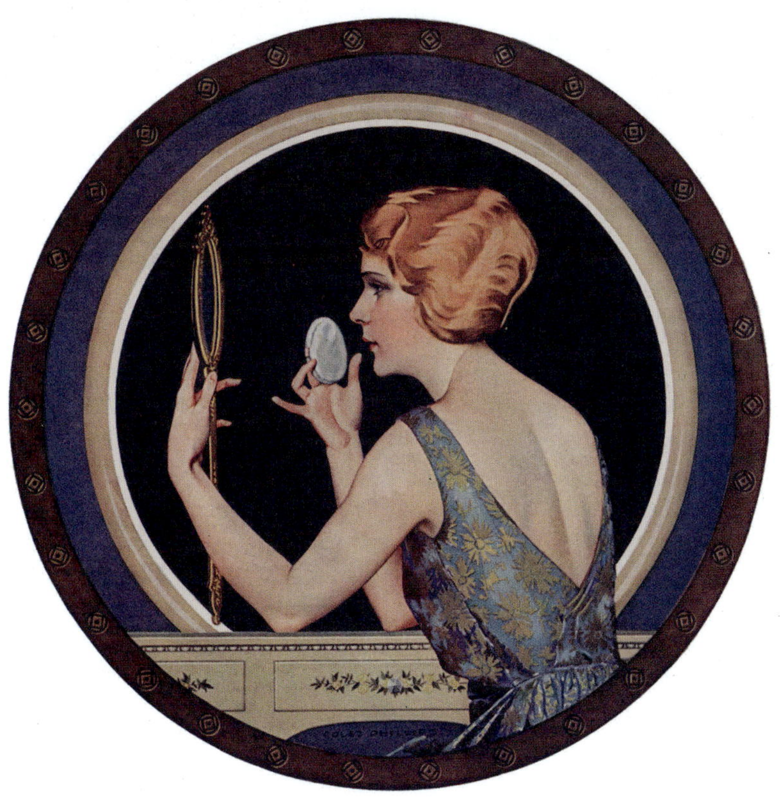

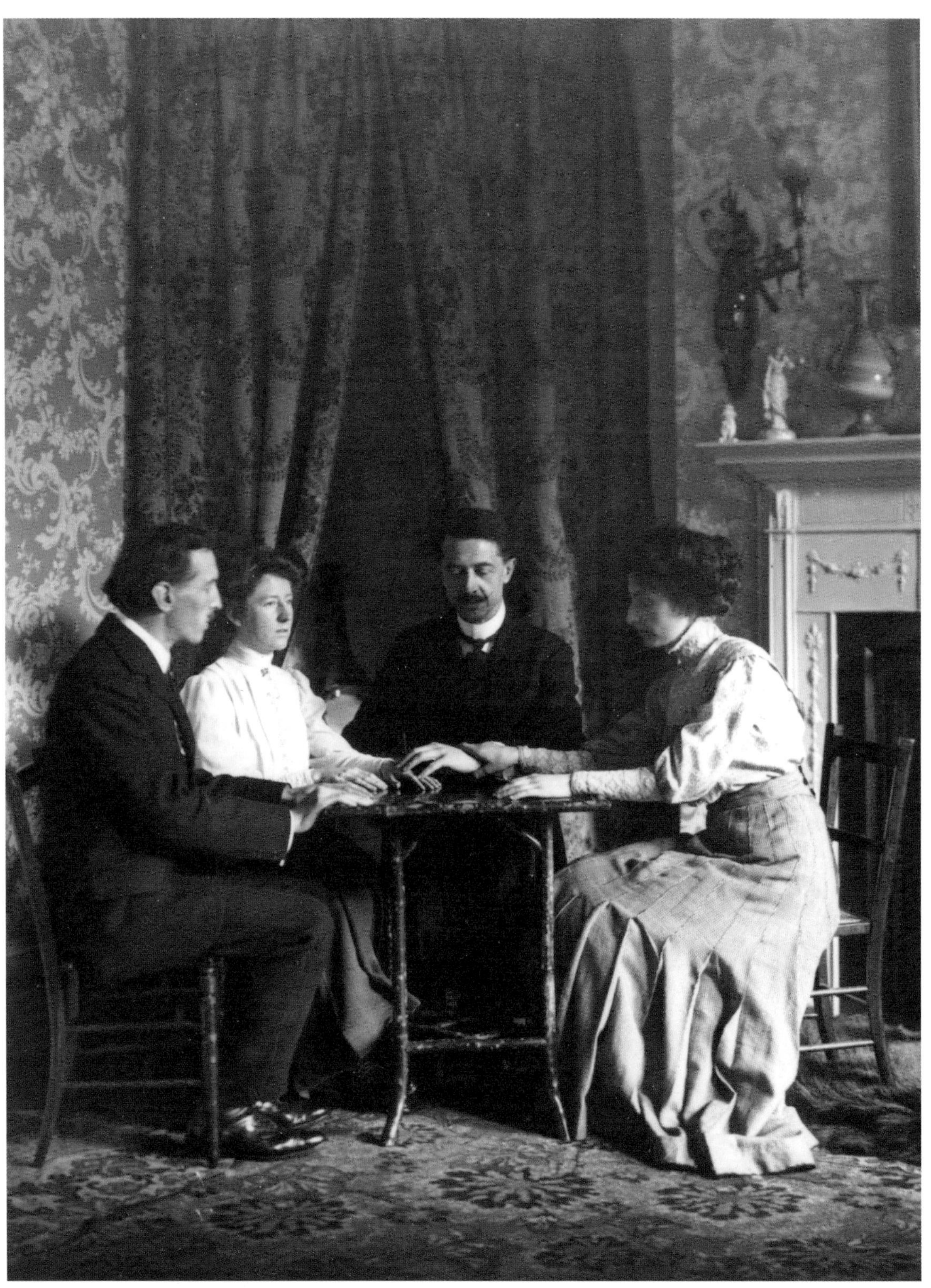

A curious consequence of that 'great catastrophe', as the late war is sometimes called, can be seen in the growing popularity of spiritualism, by means of which widows and mothers seek comfort in messages from the recently dead. Seances and Ouija boards have become familiar even in the suburbs. The Albert Hall was recently packed to capacity for the mediums who claim to convey news from 'the other side'. This has not promoted any particular religious feeling, however, since the widespread brutality of warfare has resulted in disillusion with the orthodox God and the established Church, many of whose members had once been enthusiastic about the war. There has in any case been a serious and obvious decline, both in church attendance and in church membership, over the last decades. It is estimated that at the end of the nineteenth century more than a third of the London population attended some form of religious service, but that figure has now been reduced to one-quarter. Londoners may not be irreligious, but they may be uninterested.

Other customs have not changed. The habit of swearing became most obvious in the war years and has been carried on, even by young women. 'This bloody fucking war' has been replaced by 'this rag-time fucking peace'. The Germans are still called 'the Huns', and nothing of German origin can be sold in the shops. Even German classical music is banned from the concert halls. The servant shortage is still acute, since many women who grew up in wartime conditions are no longer willing to take up the old roles of charwoman or chambermaid. As a consequence, perhaps, the ordinary housewife is now offered any number of appliances and materials for cleaning and washing-up, for cooking and laundering. Electric refrigerators and mass-produced clothes are two of the principal advantages of modern living. The phrase of the time concerning old-fashioned methods is 'too much bother'. Samples of American-style Corn Flakes or the new Rice Krispies are given out in the streets, and the range of hot bedtime drinks now includes Ovaltine, as well as the familiar Bovril and Horlicks. From the factories, too, come the tinned foods which are changing household diets. Canned peas, canned salmon, canned pilchards and canned ham – most notably produced under the auspices of Heinz or Crosse & Blackwell – are beginning to appear on London tables. This glut of artificial foodstuffs may account for the modern preoccupation with constipation of the bowels, evident in the advertisements for Bile Beans, Beecham's Pills

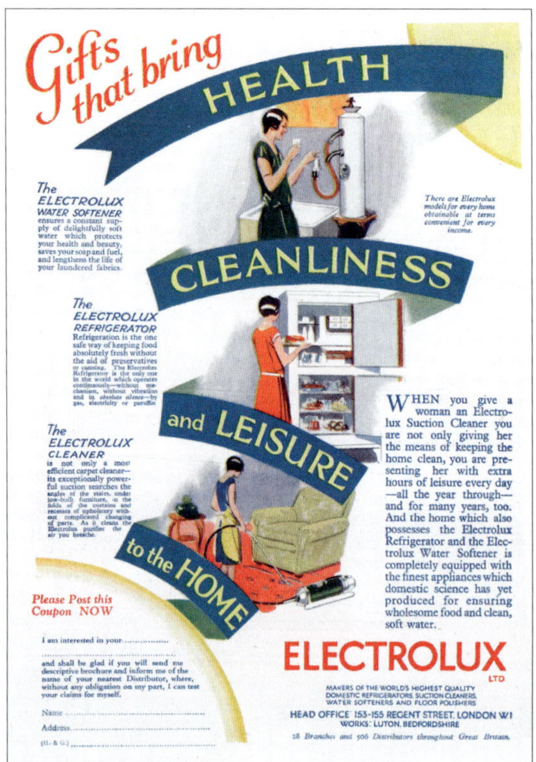

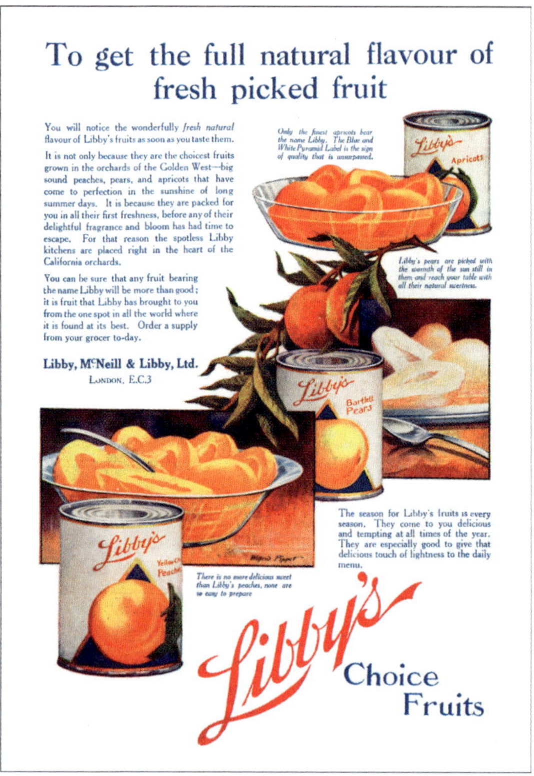

Above left An advertisement for Electrolux products, a fridge, a water softener and a vacuum cleaner, 1929.

Above right A magazine advertisement for Libby's tinned fruit, c.1920s.

and Eno's Fruit Salt. It can be compared with the vogue for all manner of health foods and for slimming pills which are paraded in the newspapers. The Women's League of Health and Beauty, just established in Regent Street, encourages dancing, dieting and indoor exercise for modern women who no longer regard marriage and motherhood as their only vocation. These pursuits can also be seen as part of the fashion for the boyish figure recommended to young women, which included the 'bob' and the 'Eton crop' in hair styling. Not all rely upon physical remedies for their well-being. Others place their faith in the theories of Professor Sigmund Freud and his followers since, as one newspaper has put it, we are all, or think ourselves to be, psychoanalysts now. Phrases such as 'wish fulfilment', 'inferiority complex' and 'persecution mania' are used even when they are not properly understood.

*

The war had taken half the omnibuses off the London streets for service in France and elsewhere, but there has now been a welcome return to normal service. A shift in population has made public transport all the more necessary, since the more congested metropolitan boroughs have become less populous, while the population of the outer boroughs has increased. It has also been observed that the further from the centre, the greater the proportion of women. The city is no longer so unbalanced, therefore, and has become more uniform. This is the case for many other aspects of London life. As a result of the change, the main services of train, omnibus and underground railway have been considerably extended. During the last 20 years, the route mileage of local and underground railways has doubled, and that of the tramway has increased by 50 per cent. The number of journeys per head of population has increased by similar rates, and on certain lines and routes it has quadrupled. One new Underground service that runs between Tooting and Camden Town has become known as 'Tootancamden' after the recent discoveries in Egypt.

If the modern electric train is more prone to sway than its steam predecessor, it is unquestionably very much cleaner

Below Members of the Women's League of Health and Beauty rehearse for an evening keep-fit demonstration to be given in Hyde Park, March 1933.

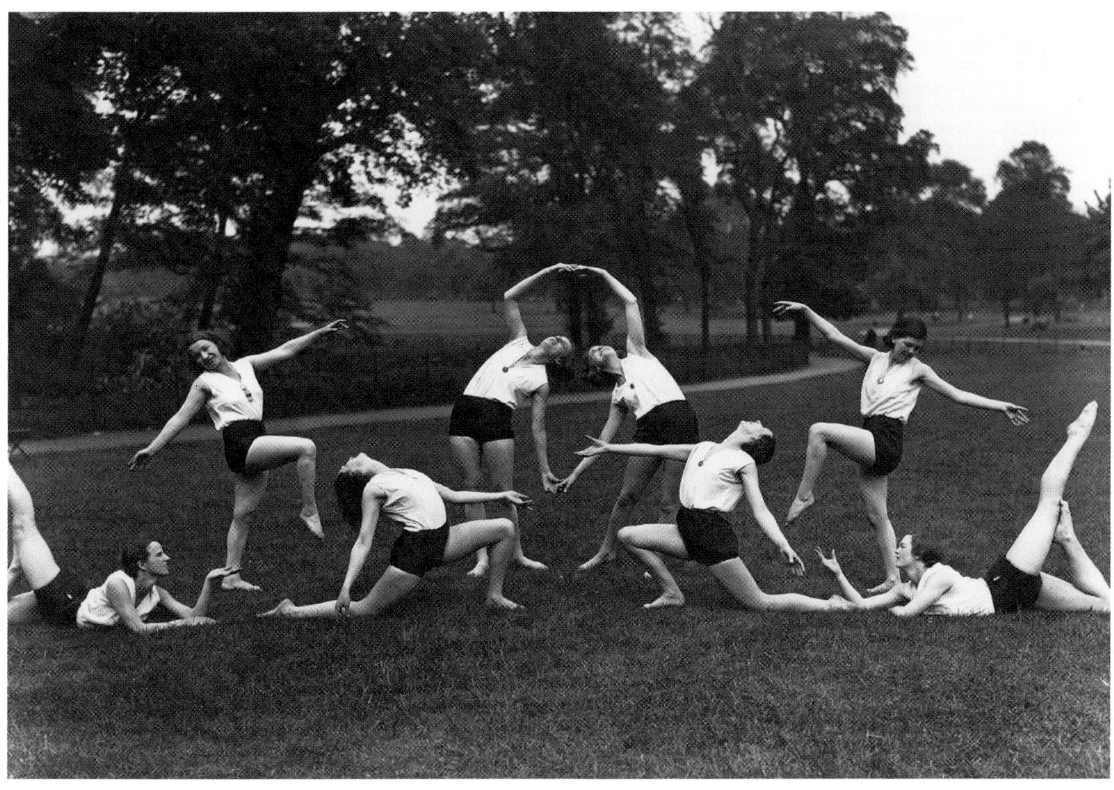

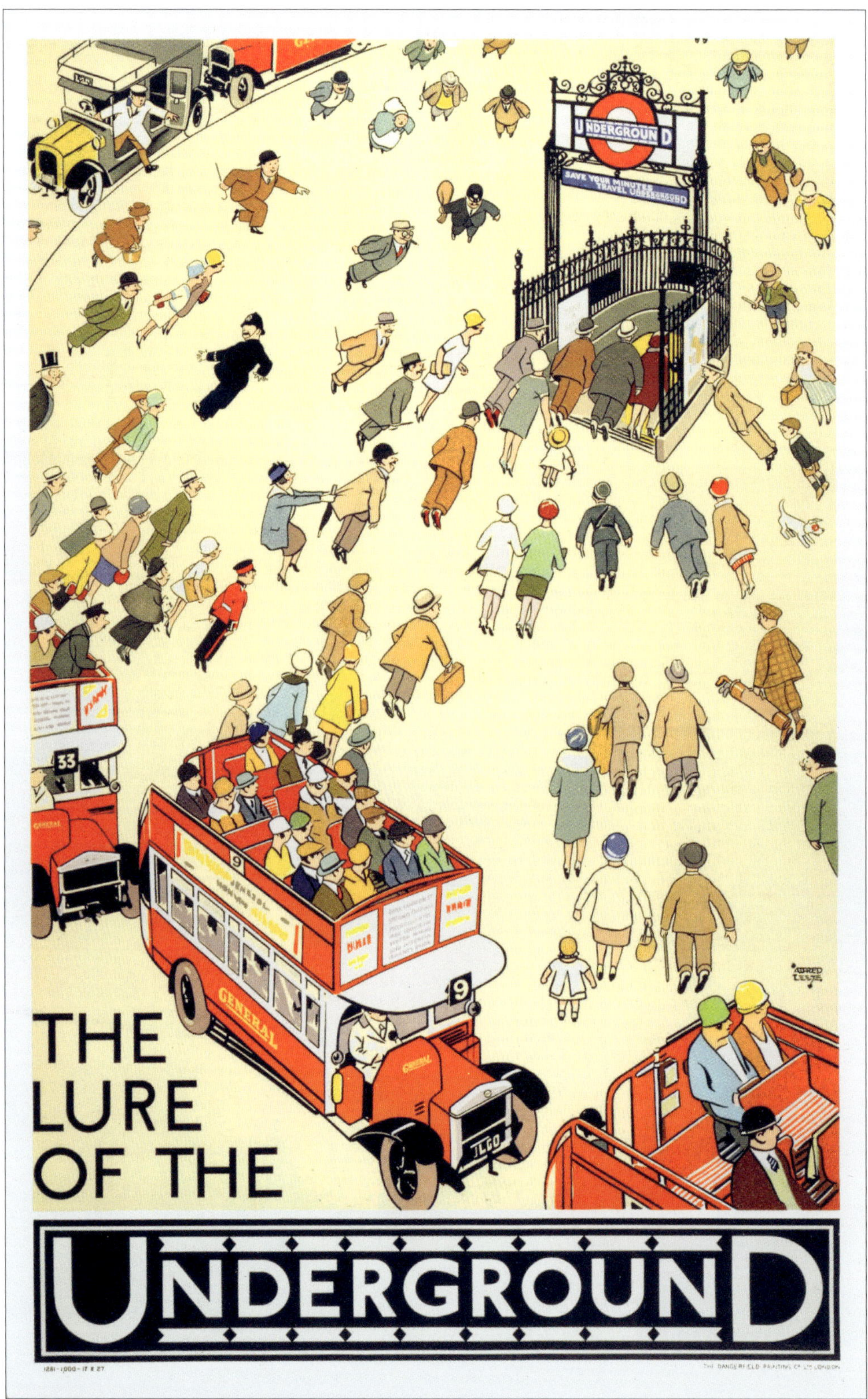
UNDERGROUND
SAVE YOUR MINUTES
TRAVEL UNDERGROUND
33
GENERAL
9
THE
LURE
OF THE
UNDERGROUND
ALFRED LEETE

and better lit. No longer are the unfortunate travellers nearly
asphyxiated in the neighbourhood of Baker Street or St Mary's,
Whitechapel, while their convenience and comfort are consulted
in numberless ways; automatic ticket-and-change machines, for
example, have been introduced. Trams and buses, which were
generally uncomfortable before the war, are now greatly improved.
Both services have the advantage of running covered-top or roofed
vehicles, and both now offer the passenger something approaching
an easy chair in place of the original hard wooden bench. Buses and
trams, which take up and set down passengers almost anywhere,
cater pre-eminently for short journeys. The underground railways
mainly serve for middle-distance transport of 2 to 10 miles. As a
result of the increasing swiftness of locomotion, the average London
workman now has an extra hour to himself, The almost universal
introduction in recent years of the eight-hour day has also left him
with more available free time, which may be taken up by sports or
gardening. It should be added that the cost of public transport, for
the average customer, has not greatly changed.

*

Left *Lure of the Underground*
(1927) by Alfred Leete for
the Underground Electric
Railway Company.

Below People using the
ticket machines at the new
Underground station in
Picadilly, 1928.

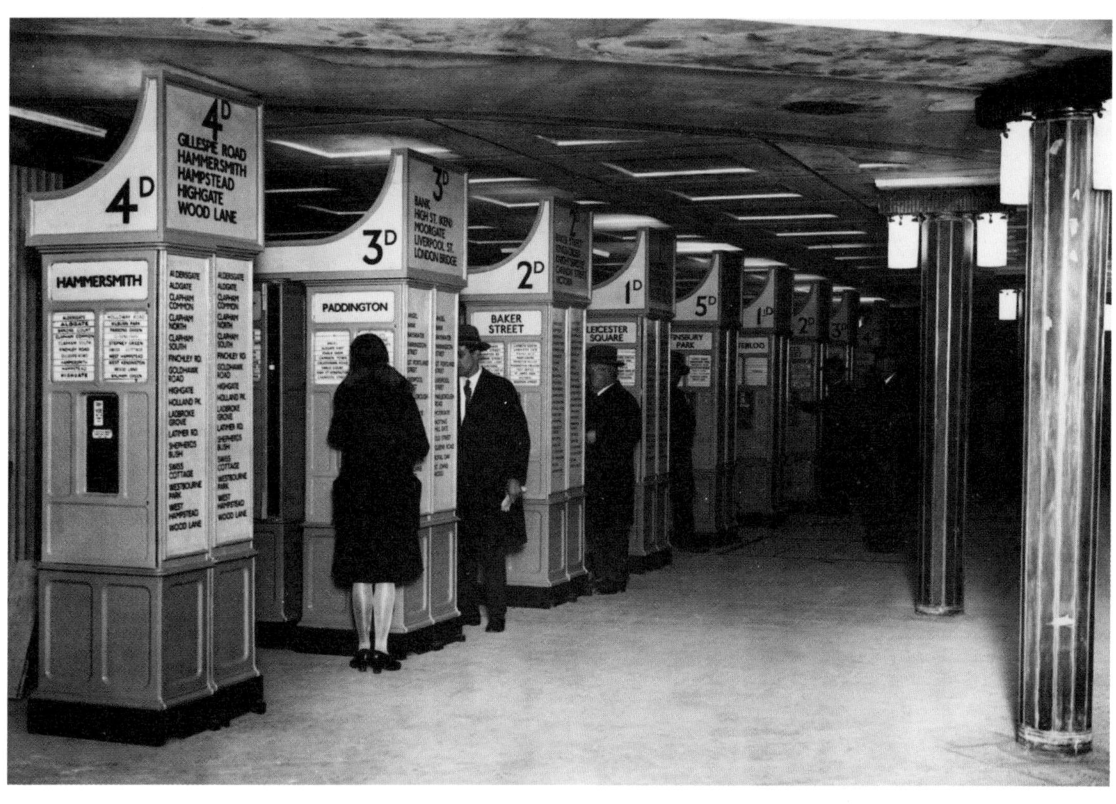

Height restrictions in London have meant that the American fashion for 'skyscrapers' has not been followed, but a tendency towards large office blocks, huge company headquarters and grandiose hotels, all based upon steel frames and concrete, is evident. This is also the age of the 'superstore', with large sheets of plate-glass windows at street level. Many buildings have risen from two and four storeys to six and eight storeys. The architectural style does not seem to matter, as long as it is grand and imposing: from Greek to Egyptian, from corporate classic to uncompromising modern. Everything has become larger. Omnibuses are bigger, railway carriages are wider and trams are longer. Newspapers have more pages, and even bus tickets are larger. Government departments have of course also increased in size. It is their nature. Restaurants are on several floors and the old Gothic heaviness, of décor and menu alike, has been lightened. Theatres have been expanded in a similar spirit of airiness. You might suspect that the world itself has been inflated.

As flat living has become more and more acceptable, so blocks of flats have risen where before there were once mansions and private houses. The stock of furniture has also increased. Ever since the British Empire Exhibition in Wembley Park, the shop windows have been filled with styles described as Tudor panelling, Georgian furniture or Jacobean textiles. The emphasis on 'tradition' in the modern world is clear. The headquarters of the Anglo-Persian Oil Company, recently completed, is called Britannic House. The Exhibition itself, although situated in the northwest of London, was the largest in modern times, and attracted some 27 million visitors, at a price of 1/6d for adults and 9d for children. It stretched over 200 acres, and was described as 'the first concrete city in the world'; it comprised numerous national pavilions and palaces, from Burma to Newfoundland, from India to the Falkland Islands, all uniting the mother country with its daughter states. The displays put on by British manufacturers were perhaps the most popular. Pear's Palace of Beauty, sponsored of course by the soap company, consisted of 10 separate, sound-proofed glass rooms, in each of which sat an actress impersonating a famous beauty of the past, such as Mary, Queen of Scots and Nell Gwyn.

There were other attractions. Fair rides in the entertainment park, such as the Chute, the Dodgem, the Racer and the Flying Machine, had signs above them reading 'Please Hold Your Hats'. Two miniature railways were in operation, one of them named

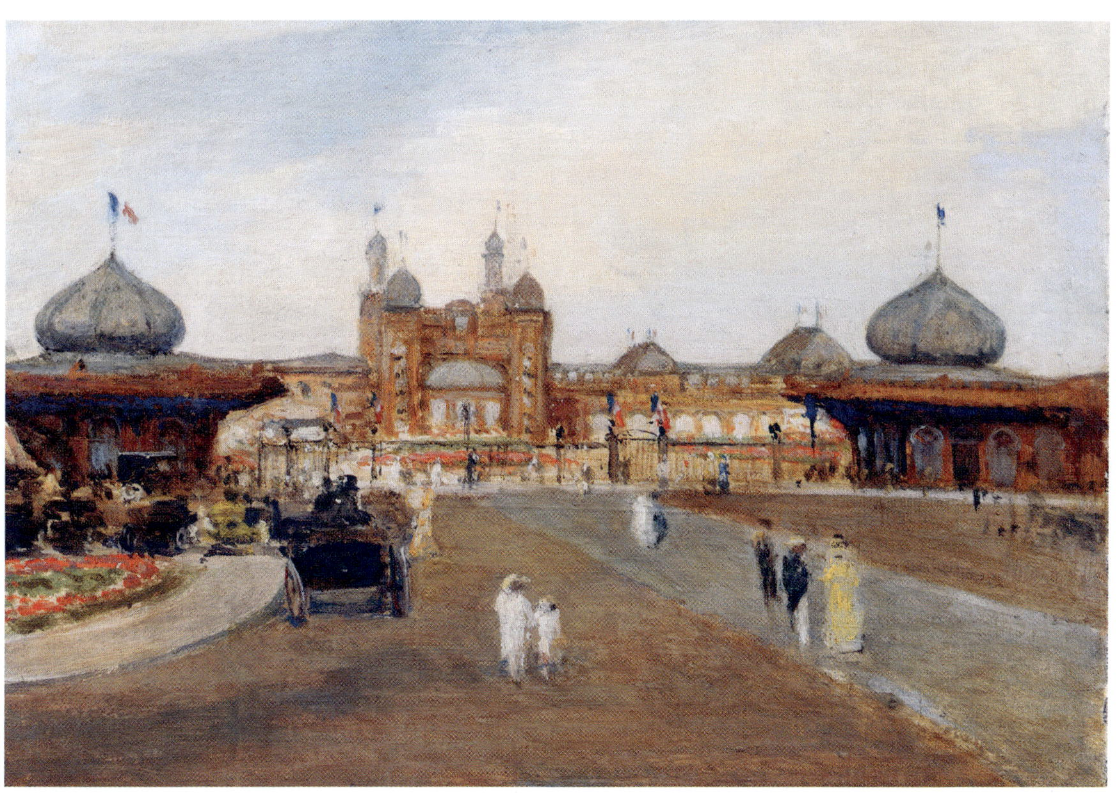

as the 'never-stop-railway'. When the King opened the exhibition on St George's Day, 1924, he pressed a gold button and dispatched a telegram that circulated the world in an astonishing one minute and twenty seconds before being given back to him by a Post Office messenger boy. Not all was lost when the exhibition eventually closed. Much of the concrete architecture and the sports ground that accompanied it have been used for the new national stadium now standing on the same site. Many of the buildings have also been transformed for commercial purposes. The South Africa Pavilion has become the headquarters of Claude-General Neon Lights Ltd, the India Pavilion is now Modern Kitchen Equipment Ltd, and the Palace of Arts is known as the Expanded Rubber Company Ltd.

The area itself is an example of the city spreading beyond its original boundaries. Everything is moving from the centre to the circumference. The new arterial roads, such as the Great West and the Great North roads, have become notable for the examples of splendid new building, such as the futuristic architecture of the Firestone Tyre Factory. The Great West Road also harbours facilities for such diverse products as toothpaste and potato

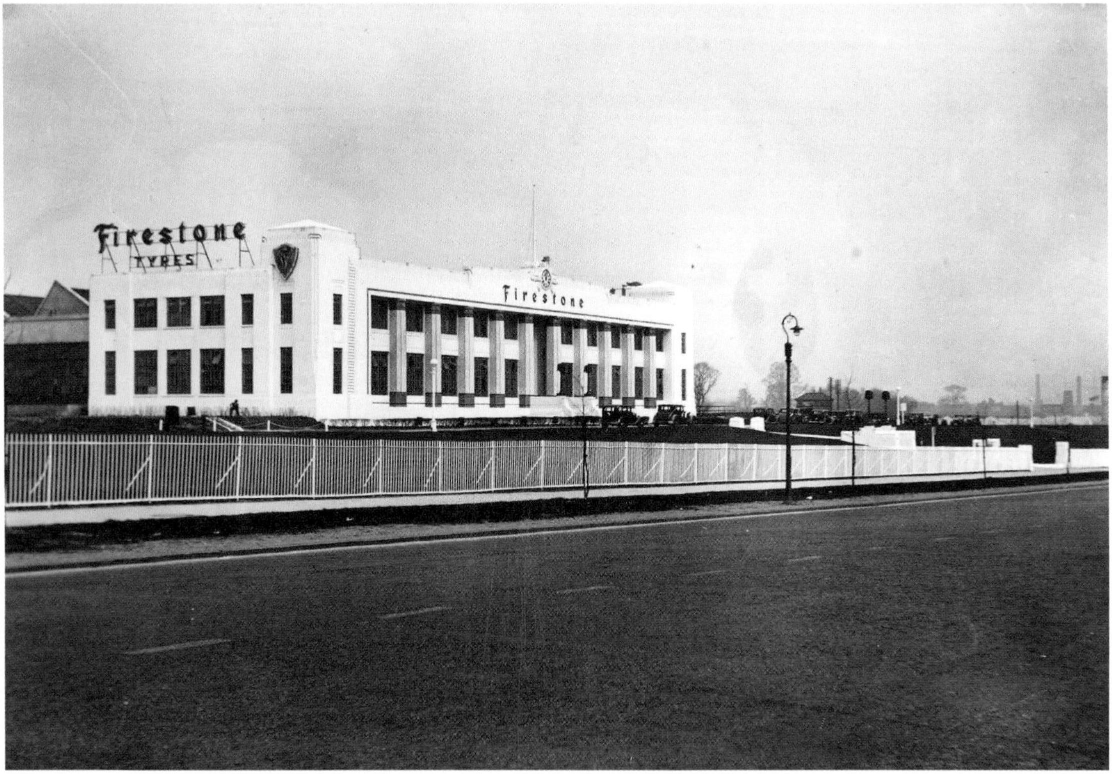

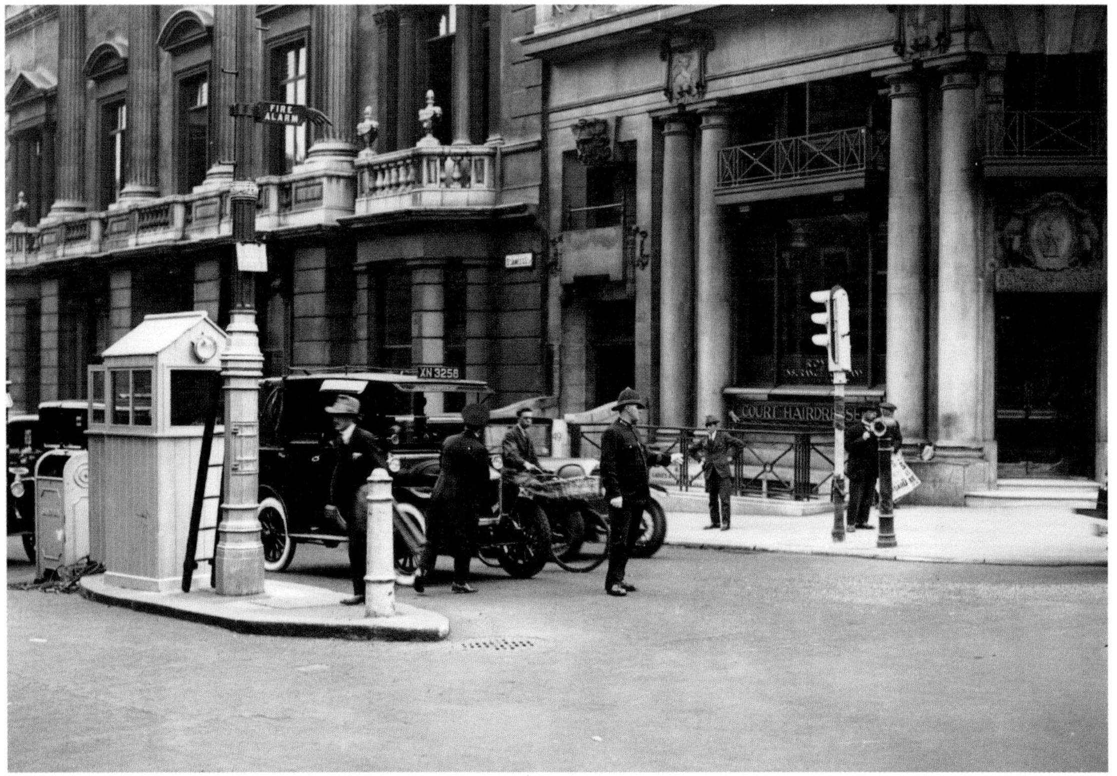

crisps, while there is more than room here for the manufacture of wireless sets, cosmetics, metal goods and the bodies of motorcars. Every office building and factory on the outskirts of London seems to be lighter and brighter than before. In the north and west of central London, the new roads, faster transport and the modern techniques of mass production, have meant that their economies are also racing ahead. This is evident in the number of new houses clustered around the principal roads, each of which might have been despatched from an Ideal Home Exhibition. It used to be said that to understand London it was necessary to visit Wapping. Now it is more important to see Park Royal.

The central parts of London itself, however, are still in a state of disrepair. All building and rebuilding came to a halt during the war, and only started again at the end of the conflict. Yet progress is still fitful. The number of builders, as well as the number of building apprentices, has been severely cut by the war effort; and the skilled workers that are left are fully occupied with the repair of damaged buildings. The great increase of traffic in recent years has meant that many streets are being widened and three-colour 'traffic lights', for the control of vehicles on crowded roads, are being introduced. So great is the congestion, it is proposed that Holborn and Oxford Street should both be enlarged by 150 feet on their south sides. The amount of disruption can only be imagined, since the spectacle of London in modern times already rivals that of Dante's *Inferno*. It may be appropriate to notice, in this context, that red has swiftly become London's colour. The telephone kiosks are painted red, no doubt to assert the city's imperial authority, and the vehicles of the London General Omnibus Company sport the same colour. Many of the Underground trains, and all of the pillar boxes, are red. Red was the Cockney word for gold. It is the colour of money and power, and but it has also become the emblem of war, bloodshed and victory. That is why it is London's true colour.

However, London at night is still a dark city. At certain times, and in certain quarters, it is no more than darkness visible. The night is most clearly seen and understood among the ruins of half-demolished houses, on the stairs leading from viaducts, in corners of the Blackwall Tunnel, in the recesses of massive buildings and in the porches of isolated churches. By midnight, the whole of Commercial Road is silent and deserted. You might be visiting a dead London, a hundred years hence. It is no less eerie in the west. To drive in an open car up Piccadilly is to see empty mansions and dark, closed shops. All the lamp posts, now painted to look like aluminium, have a processional aspect as if lifted from the *Book of the Dead*. They seem to lead to the great railway termini where, just before dawn, the first dark figures emerge onto the silent pavements of Cannon Street or Victoria Street; they resemble shadows pressing interminably at one another's backs. However, there is no more forlorn sight than the derelicts, male and female, sleeping on the benches of the Embankment. A drab, dressed all in black, is slumped inside a cab shelter. You cannot see her face, but a placard above her head invites you to inspect 'Fine Paintings in the Tate Gallery'. Another drunk leans against the stone wall and makes disgusting noises at the passers-by, who reply in the same coin. A constable on night duty makes his round and taps the sleepers, bidding them wake up and put their feet down.

The all-night coffee stalls are the lighthouses on this sea of darkness. The red-painted panels and gleaming urns attract the nightwalkers, the heavily muffled workmen on night jobs, the men and women who have drifted from a *palais de dance* or a nightclub. The stall at Marble Arch is known as the 'Hotel de Poosh-along', and 'Joe's stand' at Hyde Park Corner is called 'The West-End Eccentrics' Club'. A lady of the night 'mooches up' and is 'chivvied off'. A middle-aged man asks for some Oxo, and a younger man comes for 'a couple of woods' or 'woodies'. A sign above one coffee stall reads 'NO WOMEN SERVED HERE. BY ORDER'. However, in a city of contrasts, the bright exists beside the dark. The various Lyons Corner Houses, in Tottenham Court Road and elsewhere, can testify to the energy and vitality of the decade. They are staffed by the new brand of waitresses known as 'Nippies', wearing neat black and white uniforms. The food is clean and wholesome. The service is quick and precise. They are part of the new London.

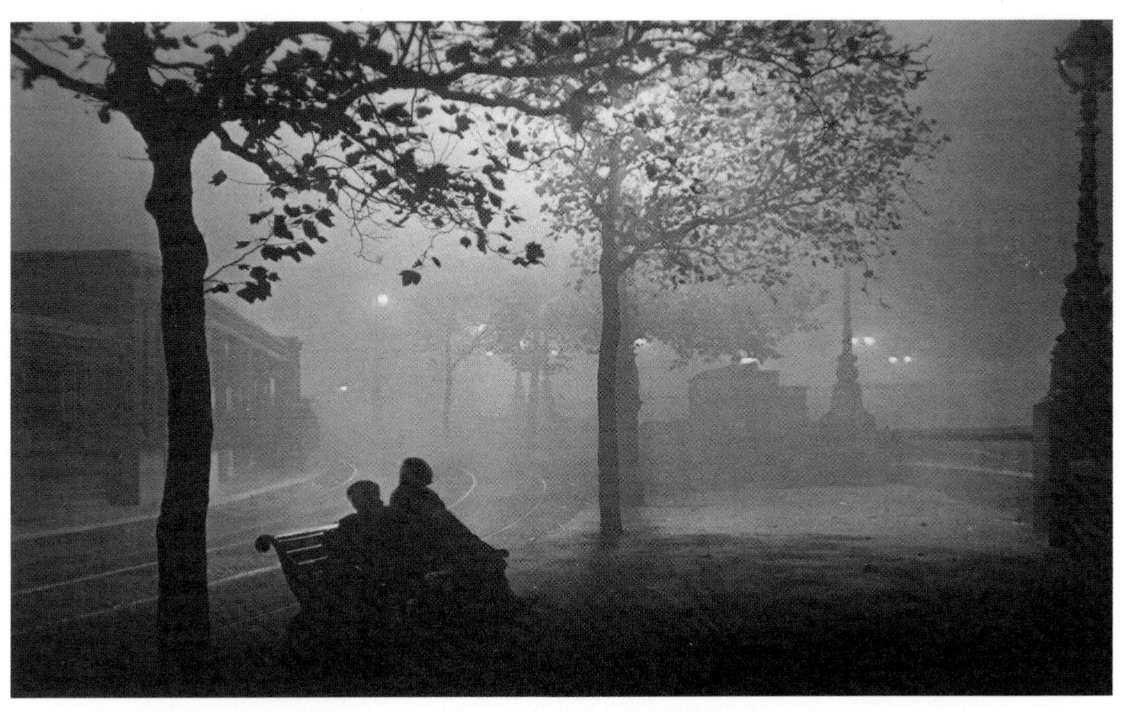

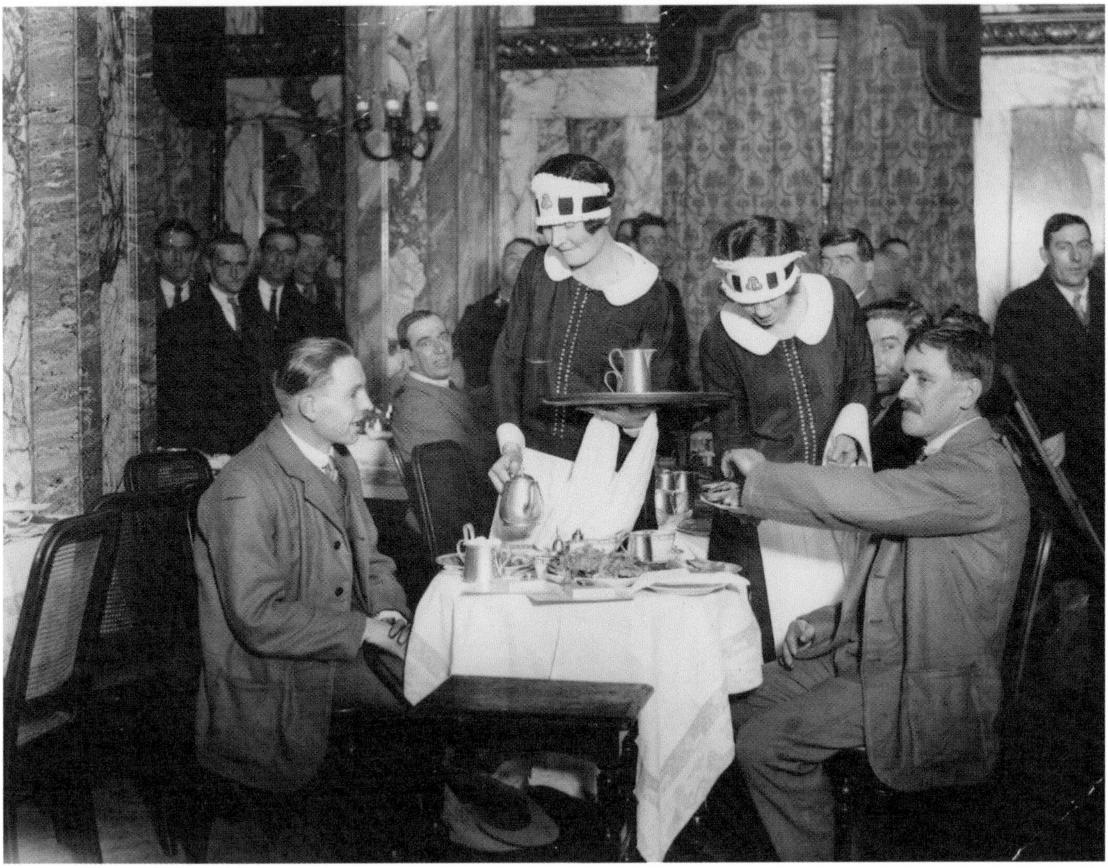

*' ... that sense of hopefulness, and of
expanding possibility, which is so
noticeable in the post-war world.'*

1932–1939
ON THE PRECIPICE

There is sometimes talk of a future war, but the city has not listened. It has just continued to grow. This is in fact the great age of expansion with the development of innumerable suburbs. Dagenham had been a small village in 1921; by 1931, twenty thousand houses had been erected to sustain the working-class population which has migrated from inner London. By the middle of the decade two and a half million people were on the move. This marked the emergence of 'Metroland' in order to describe the uniform and sprawling suburbs. The word itself was coined by the Metropolitan Railway Company and was taken up by the London Underground. It emphasizes the crucial importance of modern transport in the creation of the city. In the suburbs, London has once more created or harboured a new form of urban living, with shopping parades and cinemas and imposing Underground stations. The factories which lined the dual carriageways provided goods for a new class of Londoners with washing machines and refrigerators, electric cookers and processed food. A rejuvenated city, more dispersed and open, had arrived. It came just in time for the wartime Blitz.

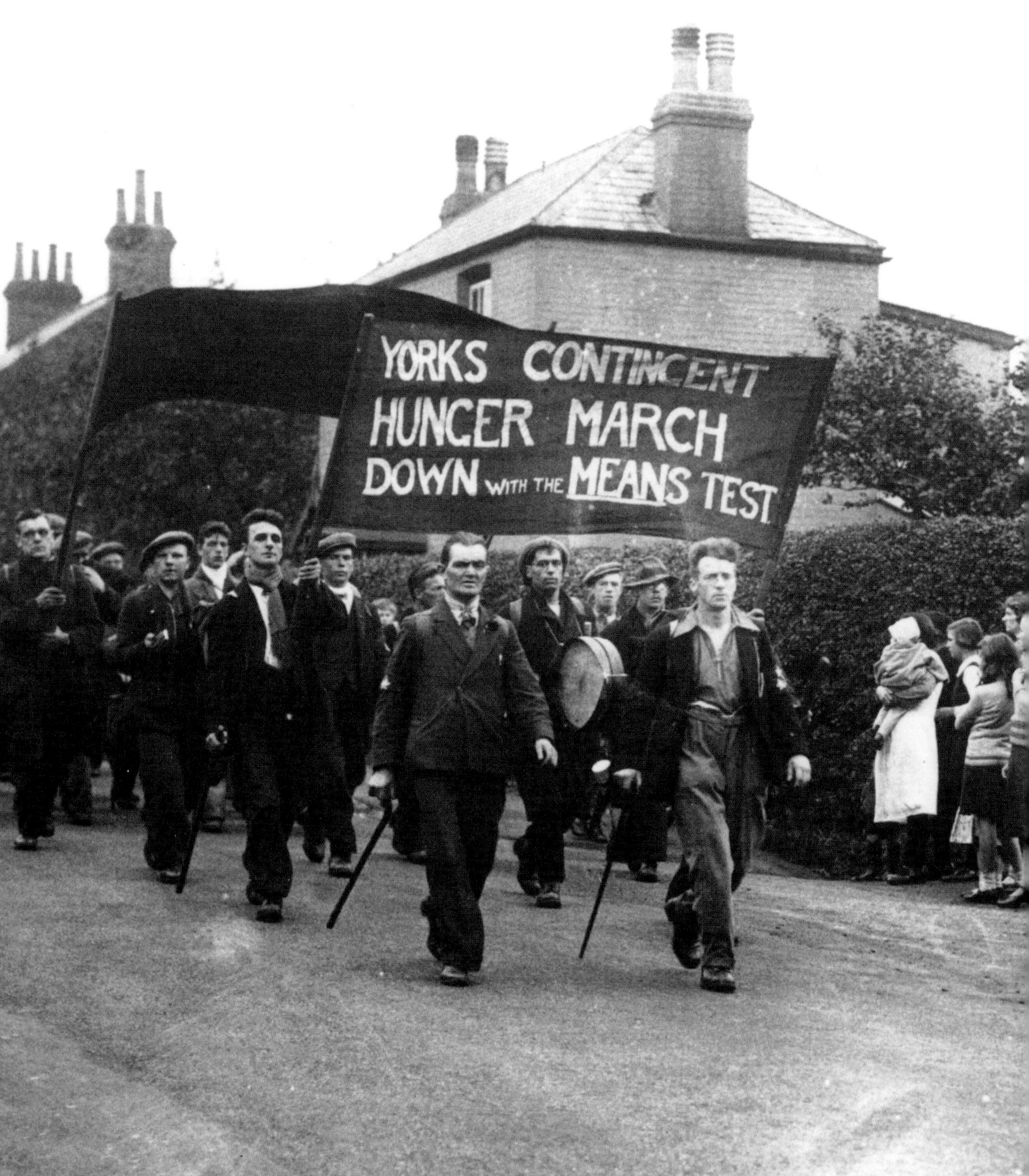

YORKS CONTINGENT
HUNGER MARCH
DOWN WITH THE MEANS TEST

The outbreak of the last war was responsible for the great disturbance of money values which is still with us, but the economic turmoil of the post-war world has now grown more dangerous. Witness the rising numbers of the unemployed and the steep increase in prices. Many journalists call it 'the crash' or 'the slump', and it is most visible in the numbers of men, young and old, who congregate at street corners or wait beside factory gates in the forlorn attitudes of complete idleness. Unemployed ex-servicemen can be seen in the corridors of the Underground with collection boxes. Women and children beg from passers-by in Oxford Street.

Hunger marches from other parts of the country have already reached their climax in London. In the late autumn of 1932, still of recent memory, the National Hunger March culminated in Hyde Park where its leaders harangued the crowd and, in particular, demanded the abolition of the new 'means test'. The police tried to suppress the marchers, which led to some severe clashes and even violence. Marches and demonstrations have also been organized by the National Unemployed Workers' Movement; the marchers try to maintain a military order, complete with banners, flags and bands, while some equip themselves with knapsacks and blankets. They sing national and sentimental ballads, and even pantomime refrains. They have gathered in Hyde Park and in Trafalgar Square but political meetings are also being held at Earl's Court, Olympia and the Albert Hall. The message is clear. They are attacking the 'means test' as an instrument of government coercion and are condemning the recent cut in unemployment benefit, or 'the dole' as it is commonly called. In the revised state unemployment scheme, the payment of 17s a week for a man has been reduced to 15s, from 9s to 5s for his wife, and from 2s to 1s for each child. For those unemployed living in London, this is close to the bare minimum by which they can live. As a result, their savings are gone, their furniture sold and even their clothes have to be pawned.

Yet, despite some accounts in the popular press, the city has not yet reverted to the conditions of Victorian penury. The material circumstances under which most Londoners live have improved over recent years, while the real privation, suffering and apprehension endured by those still living in poverty are partially reduced by the operation of various public services. Some of the worst of the toil and discomfort caused by the incessant need for cleaning and washing, for example, are alleviated by the provision

of municipal washhouses and public baths with the proper
facilities. Another aspect of institutional relief has been seen
in the more general use of the Poor Law hospitals.

The city has, in fact, been less troubled by the general
economic and social depression than the rest of the country.
The proportion of manual workers has diminished, but with
an accompanying rise in professional and clerical employment.
The increase in the number of 'white-collar workers', as they have
become known, has protected London from the worst effects of
unemployment. It is estimated that there are now more clerks
than artisans and labourers. That may or may not be true but, in
terms of London life and labour, there are far more office workers
than dockers. The professional classes of London, such as dentists
and teachers, have also increased, while the new industries of
outer London require engineers, draughtsmen, designers and
technicians. In the City, the expansion of banking, commerce
and insurance demands a huge growth in office employment,
required for management and administration, while the Civil
Service itself is an ever-expanding enterprise.

It is true, however, that changes in the nature of industry
and trade have led inevitably to the loss of jobs. In certain areas
the actual process of manufacture is performed by automatic
mechanism, while in most industries machines have also taken
over the work of sorting and packing the components of the
finished product. The progress of mechanization, or what is
termed 'rationalization', has resulted in some unemployment,
especially among skilled male workers and the floating population
of day labourers who were once required, but the change is
inevitable. A contrast can be drawn between the organization
of work in the scientifically laid-out modern plants and the old-
fashioned 'works' where a large amount of heavy manual labour
was necessary. It cannot be denied, however, that machines have
in turn been responsible for the proper development of industry.
They have led to an increased and standardized output, which is
of course the sole reason for their use.

The number of those now out of work is in part balanced by
the increasing employment of women who, provided that they
possess the all-important qualities of steadiness and reliability,
can easily master the few simple and repetitive movements which
they are needed to perform. They are no longer required to learn
special skills in the old-fashioned sense. (An exception must be
made here for bread baking, from which women are excluded

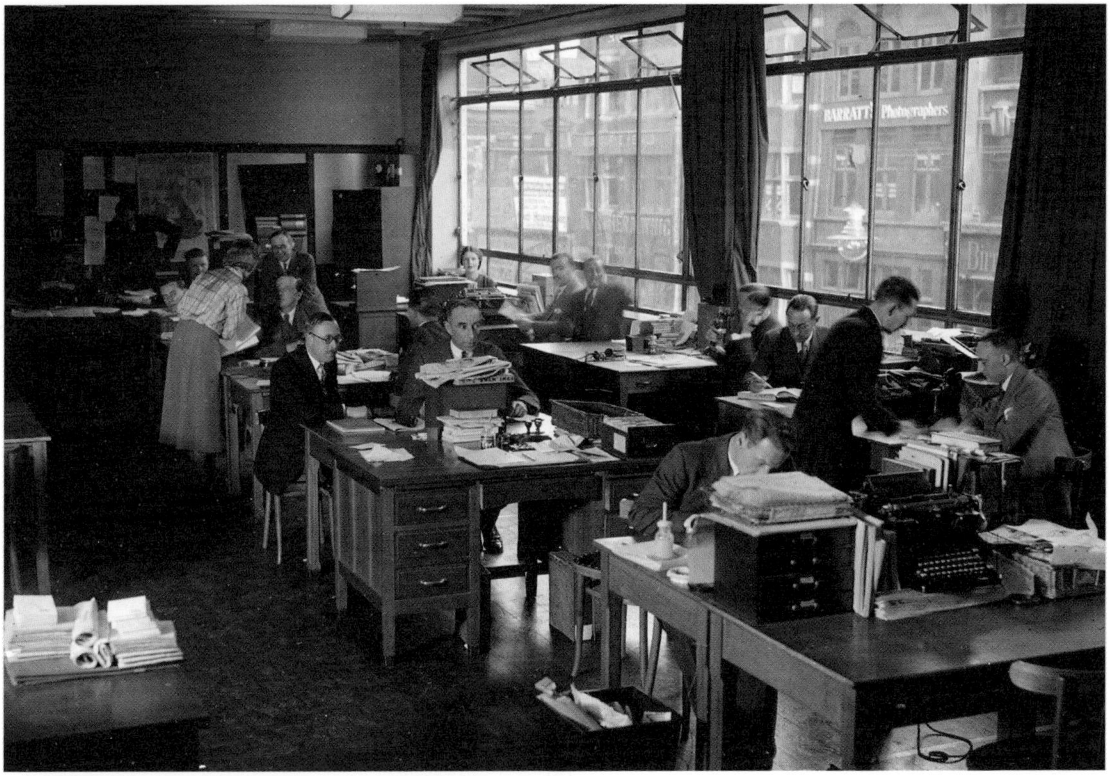

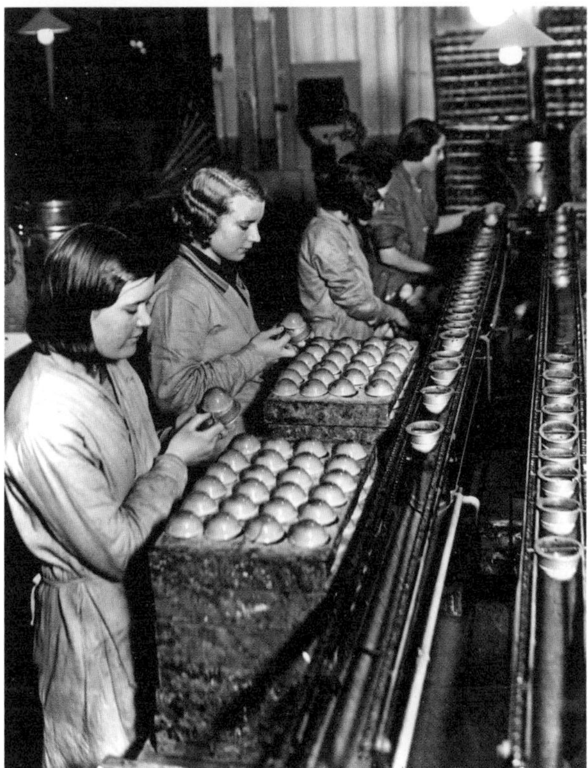

Above Busy office workers at the *Daily Express* building, Fleet Street, April 1935.

Left Female employees in a Putney factory, during the vulcanizing process of tennis balls.

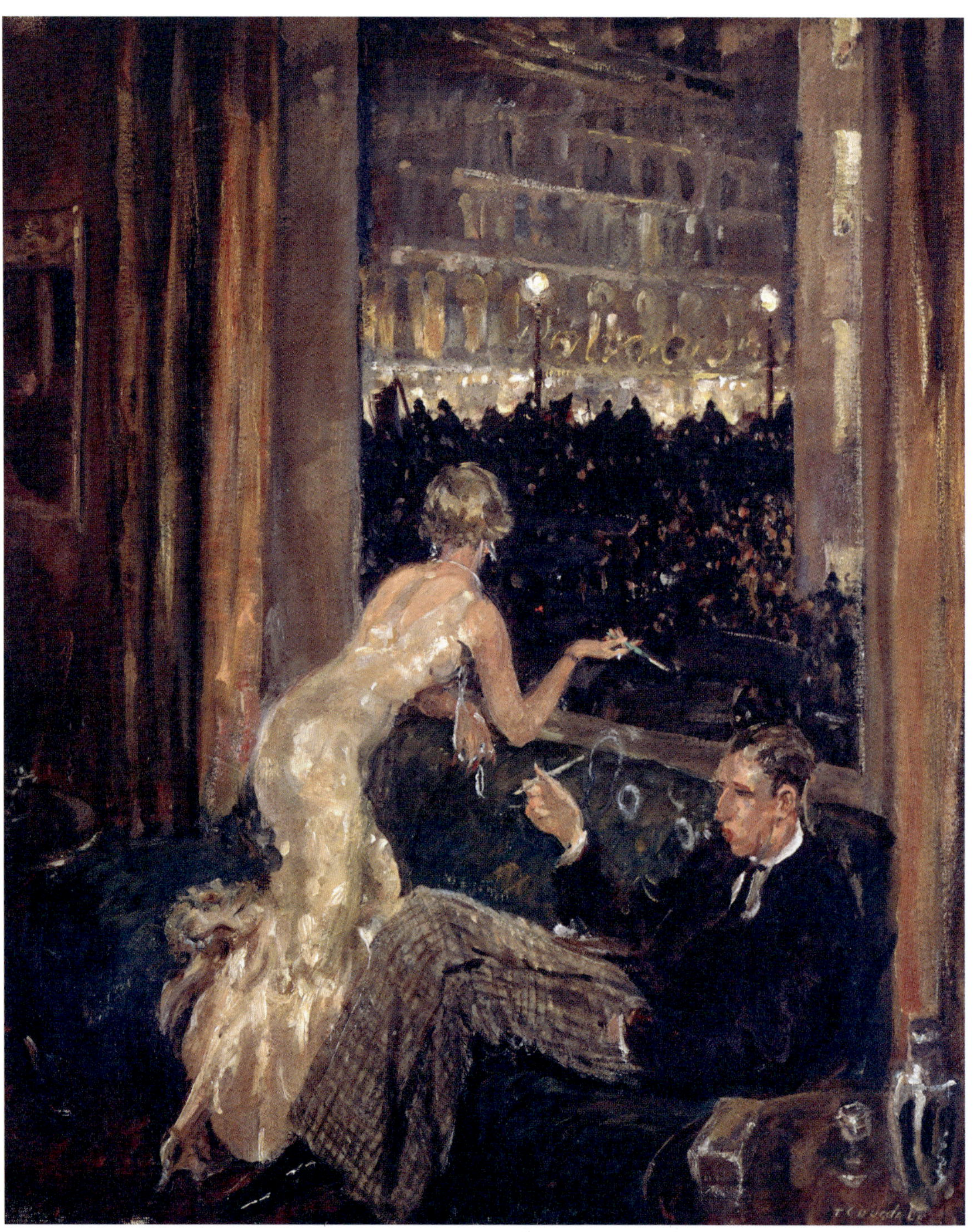

by their being prohibited from night work.) As a result of these welcome changes, the unit of trade organization is now based upon the new industrial process rather than traditional craft work. This has been matched by the general tendency towards amalgamation or absorption. In the case of manufacture, for example, standard methods of management are necessary, as well as the procedures of centralized control.

However, this need not imply any loss of concern for the workers themselves, as some commentators seem to believe. The group of industries involved with the preparation of food and drink, for example, are pre-eminently the centres of 'welfare' or as it is now commonly called 'labour management'. To take one prominent example, an annual holiday of a week with full pay is now considered to be normal. Holiday payments, like other 'amenities', are frequently regarded as a form of compensation for monotonous or disagreeable work. The earliest age at which boys can do night work has been fixed at 18 which is, in itself, a considerable improvement. The average working week is now levelled out at 47 or 48 hours, although there are variations. Laundresses and navvies, for example, work longer than clerks or telephonists.

So although Londoners may sympathize with the distress or chronic want present in many other parts of the country, they are not materially affected by it. The absence of communal feeling can be adduced in the national strike of recent memory. The effects of that mass action were scarcely felt in many parts of London. The members of the Stock Exchange, for example, took on the jobs of market porters and van drivers, while city clerks and office clerks volunteered as guards, conductors and signalmen. Single females managed the telephone and telegraph exchanges, while others boarded the omnibus as 'clippies', where they were greeted with affection.

Attempts have been made to reduce the housing shortage in London. Within the inner areas of the city, the slums and tenements of the past are slowly being replaced by housing built by the London County Council, and council house 'estates' have emerged in outlying areas such as East Acton. Building materials are now easy to obtain, and are of a uniform standard, so that new housing is relatively quick and easy. On one estate, 12 houses are being erected each week. The building company, Wates, has announced that in 15 'lovely districts', ranging from Catford to Streatham, new houses can be purchased for a weekly repayment of 8/11d. In certain respects, and in chosen areas, it really is a boom time for property. State intervention has also helped, with the creation of such bodies as the General Electricity Board. Among these beneficial public services can also be added the British Broadcasting Service and the London Passenger Transport Board.

The quality of the houses themselves has improved. Those of the middle class are of much the same standard and appearance as in the previous decade, but their furnishings have become a little bolder. The geometrical patterns of circles and rectangles can be found on a range of items, from cushion covers to garden gates; the fireplaces may be shaped in the 'Aztec temple' style and the sofas and armchairs decorated in 'jazzy' patterns. In the houses of the more affluent, chrome and coloured mirror glass will be supreme. No self-respecting home is complete without walnut veneer on desks, sideboards and tables. Ascot heaters have replaced the paraphernalia of copper geysers, and electric washing machines are becoming more popular.

There are still some problems with home heating, since the electric-bar fire has only a modest range, and lighting is often restricted to bare bulbs without a shade. Many houses were of course built in the Victorian period; they may be spacious and solid, but they lack new facilities which have become necessary for domestic ease. If they are not modernized, for example, they will be draughty. Running water is still unusual in bedrooms which now have a basin, and hot water can only be obtained by stoking the boiler. The recently built houses tend to be more modest than their predecessors, and are generally of two storeys in order to accommodate smaller families and lower incomes; they have no basement and few stairs, but the standard of real comfort has steadily increased. The most expensive of them may be purchased for as much as £2,000, but the majority will cost £600 or £700.

This has confirmed the appeal of the suburbs. It has become the age of 'Metroland', which began life with the Cedars Estate in Rickmansworth and spread outwards to include Ruislip and Wembley Park, Edgware and Finchley, Epsom and Purley. The importance of transport in effecting this mass dispersal is emphasized by the fact that the very notion of 'Metroland' in the leafy purlieus of London was created by the Metropolitan Railway Company and the London Underground. Their booklets and advertisements emphasize the bucolic, or at least non-urban, aspects of what are in essence great housing estates. They contain pastoral views of lanes in Pinner, of the brambly grasses of

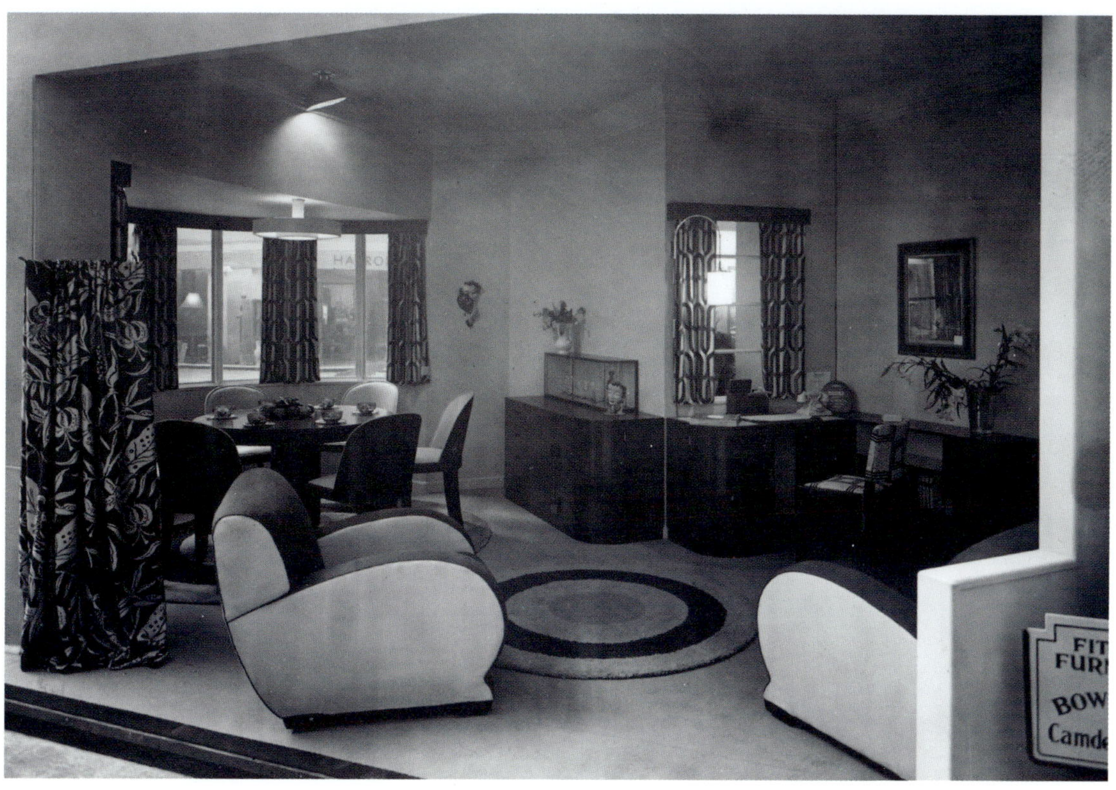

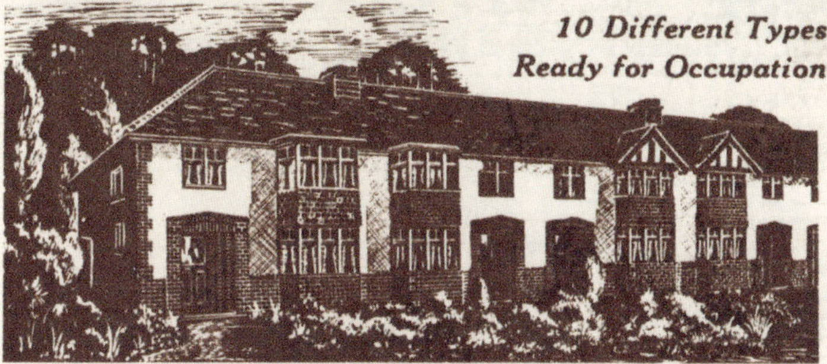

HERE'S A WONDERFUL HOUSE FOR £395!
10 Different Types
Ready for Occupation
FROM 10/4 PER WEEK
£5 secures any house
"Never before such value at this popular price."
Fine elevations—good square rooms, fitted with modern labour-saving devices planned for your convenience.
Two or Three Bedrooms, Lounge with Dining Recess and Service Hatch, or Two Reception Rooms, Modern Labour Saving Kitchen and Splendid Bathrooms, Large Gardens, Clean Finished Roads, Tree Lined, Delightful Country.
A few to be let from 20s. per week.
No Road Charges or Legal Costs
WOOD BLOCK FLOORS
CENTRAL HEATING
FITTED WARDROBES
DECORATIONS FREE
HOW TO GET THERE.—Book direct to RUISLIP by Metropolitan or Piccadilly Railway, or to RUISLIP GARDENS on the G.W.R. and L.N.E.R. Both Stations are facing the Estate Offices. Alight at RUISLIP or RUISLIP GARDENS (not Ruislip Manor). Weekly fares from Marylebone or Baker St. 5/1½. Telephone : Ruislip 378 for our private car to take you to Estate.
Please send for Brochure to :—
RUISLIP Gardens Estate
WEST END ROAD, RUISLIP
Please send me your brochure of Ruislip Gardens Estate, post free.
Telephone: Ruislip 378
NAME ....
ADDRESS...
P.O.M. Oct.

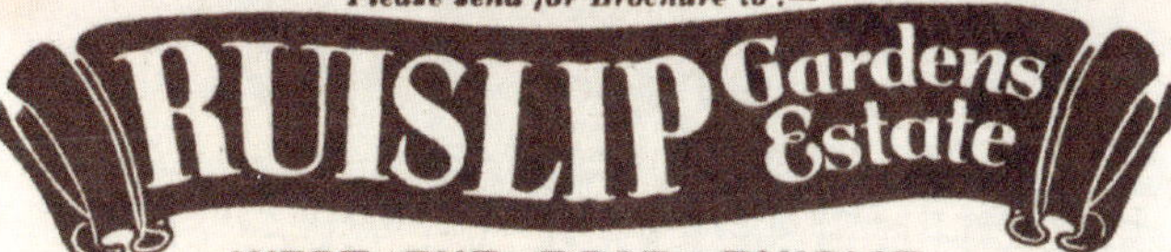

Chertsey where the nightingales sing, of the lost Elysium which is rural Middlesex. One advertisement for the Underground shows three rows of grey and mournful terraces, with the words 'Leave This and Move to Edgware'. Now the suburban Gardens, Drives, Parks, Ways and Rises are as much a part of London as the old Rents and Lanes and Alleys.

The social effect has been of the utmost significance. Before the war it was unusual for the middle-class man to be the owner of his home. Today the number of householders grows consistently and rapidly. It would be difficult to exaggerate the influence of this silent revolution on the habits and outlook of the population. The ownership of property cultivates prudence and encourages thrift.

What of those who cannot afford to buy their own homes? The average 'council house', in the outer areas of London, consists of a living room, kitchen and bathroom on the ground floor with three bedrooms upstairs; there will be a small garden which will accommodate a lawn and a patch of ground for flowers or vegetables. It may not be large, but for those who live in them it is a welcome relief from the squalor of London's poor districts, and soon enough the house becomes 'home'. Some local authorities, however, have decided to rehouse tenants in or near the areas where they had previously lived. The number of people involved, and the space available, oblige them to build blocks of flats rather than housing estates. They are characteristically of five storeys, with concrete stairways and narrow balconies, and contain public spaces paved with granite. They are perhaps not ideal homes, but they seem to be the only alternative to filthy and diseased surroundings. What were once termed 'poor streets' are rapidly disappearing.

The mechanization in private homes has been matched by that of the public services. Moving stairs are now familiar on the London Underground, and self-propelling luggage trucks are available for the porters at the terminal railway stations. Other influences have included the development of cash registers, automatic

Below A poster advertising London Underground to Ruislip, c.1920s.

Right Leicester Square Underground station showing the longest and deepest escalators in the world, 1935.

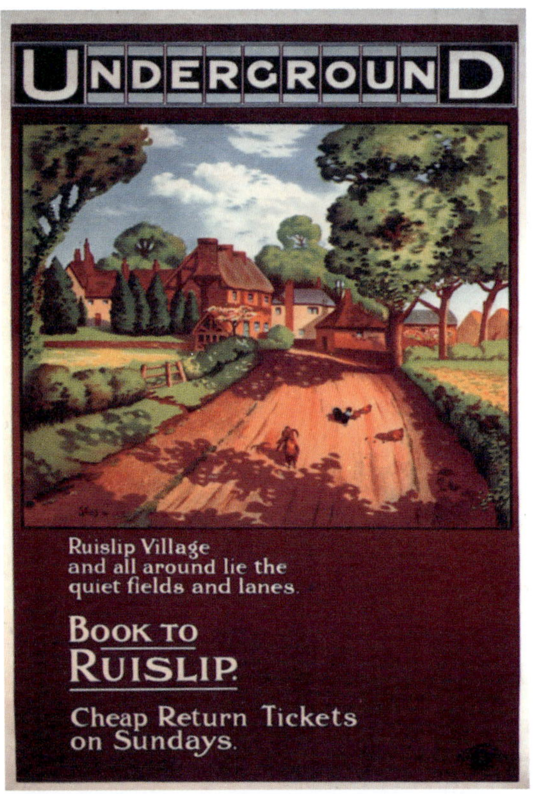

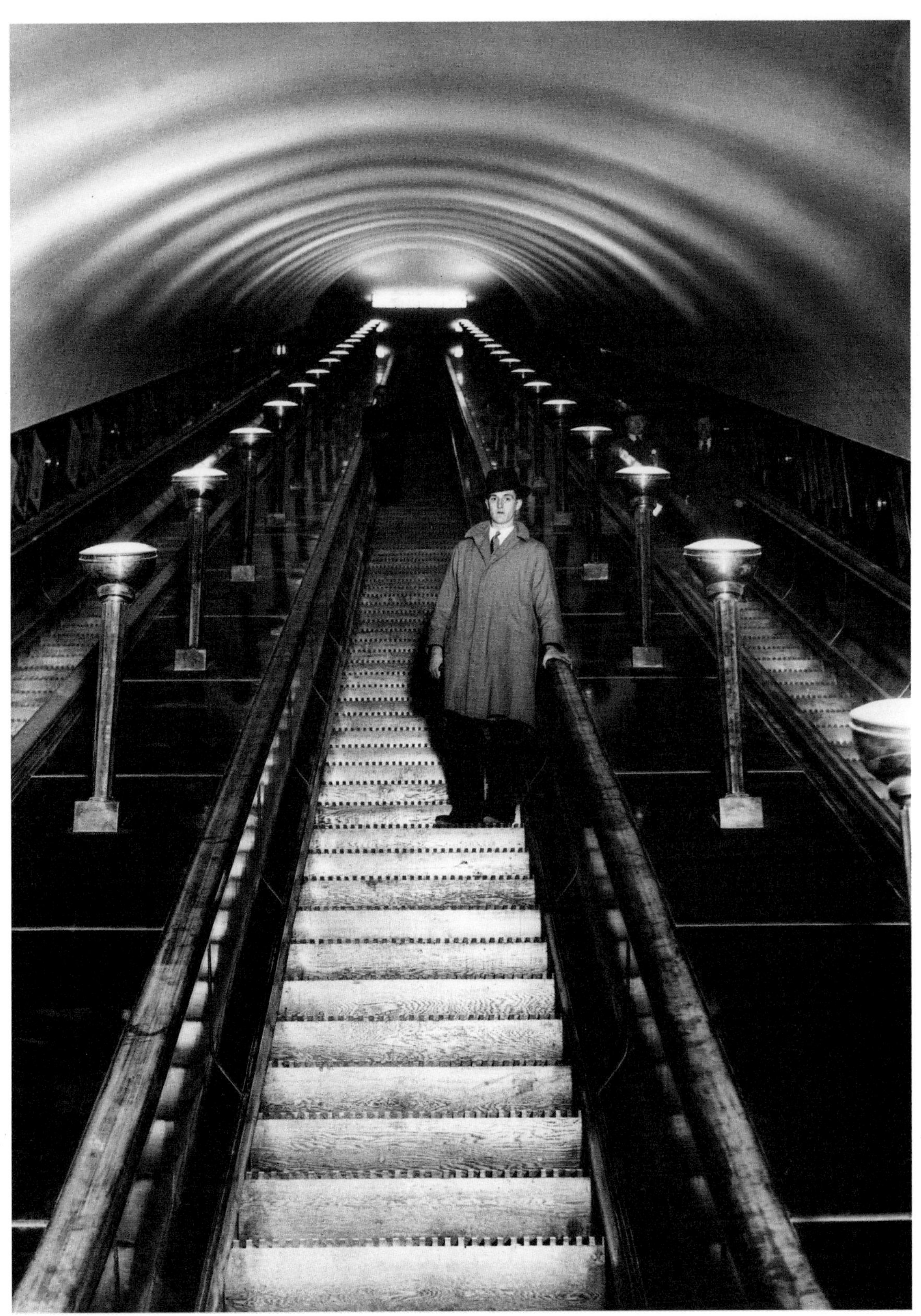

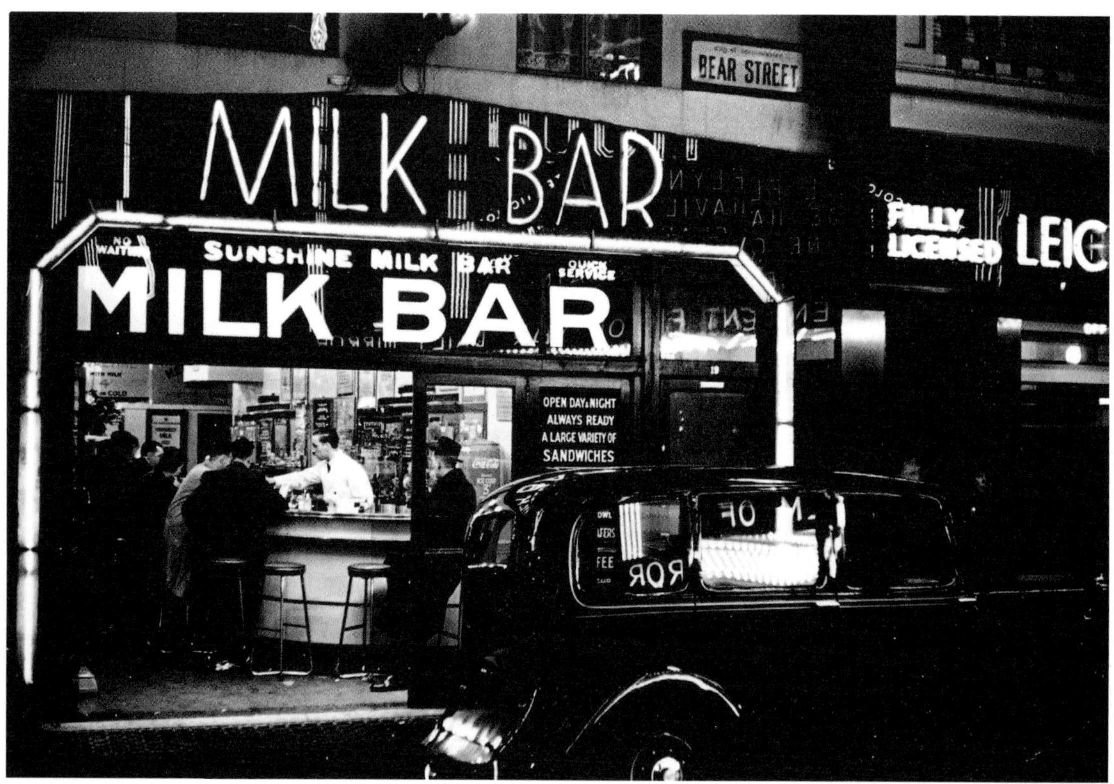

Above A milk bar in Bear Street, near Leicester Square, c.1936.

scales and the like. In the streets outside you can find cigarette machines, lunch machines and fruit machines; mechanized restaurants have also appeared in the shape of American-style cafeterias. They are rivalled, however, by the popular milk bars which take on a thoroughly modern appearance with areas of gleaming glass and chromium, with high counters and high stools, and with machines for mixing milk drinks. Some customers say that it must be like drinking on the moon. There has, in fact, never been a better range of establishments designed for catering. The high-class licensed restaurants are situated within a quarter-mile radius of Piccadilly and a number of sandwich bars, usually managed by ladies, have been set up in the central areas of London. They compete here with coffee stalls and the public houses. The tea shop has a middle-class clientele, while the fried fish shops and small eating houses predominate in working-class districts. These last have linoleum-covered tables arranged in rows and served by the proprietor and his family. They sometimes act as the meeting place for the local branch of a trade union, whose sign or initials they display. They often bear the legend, 'Good pull-up for carmen', by which are meant of course the drivers of horse-drawn lorries, wagons or vans. The carmen have halved in number over the last 10 years, while the number of motor drivers has doubled. This disproportion can only increase.

*

In the last three or four years 'talkies' have taken over the town. They are called 'vocal films' or 'dialogue films' and are beginning to supersede their silent predecessors commonly known as 'dumbies'. It is reliably estimated that eighteen million people visit the moving pictures, or 'the flickers', each week, and of course the numbers have been increased by the novelty of the 'talkies', which has satisfied the increasing demand for realism. The advertisement for Mr Hitchcock's *Blackmail* announces 'The First Full Length All Talkie Film Made In Great Britain. See & Hear Our Mother Tongue As It Should Be – Spoken … Hold Everything Till You've Heard This One!'

The motion picture has improved immensely since the days of the bioscope, and now most picture palaces are fitted with a 'talkie' apparatus as well as new tip-up seats. Their customer capacity is calculated, in fact, to be double that of the theatre and music hall combined. Wartime conditions no doubt intensified this popularity, together with a general recognition of the actors on the screen. At first all such figures had been anonymous, since no one seemed to care about the caricatures who went through the simplest motions. But then they acquired nicknames of the crude schoolboy sort, such as 'Fatty' and 'Skinny' or 'Lofty'. Kisses on the screen were greeted with whistles from the audience. Slowly the actors became acknowledged and even welcomed, their names widely known, until gradually favourites emerged who have become box-office 'draws'.

While the problem of combining speech with moving pictures may be said to have been technically solved, it is not yet possible to forecast the influence of this novelty on the future popularity of the medium. It is

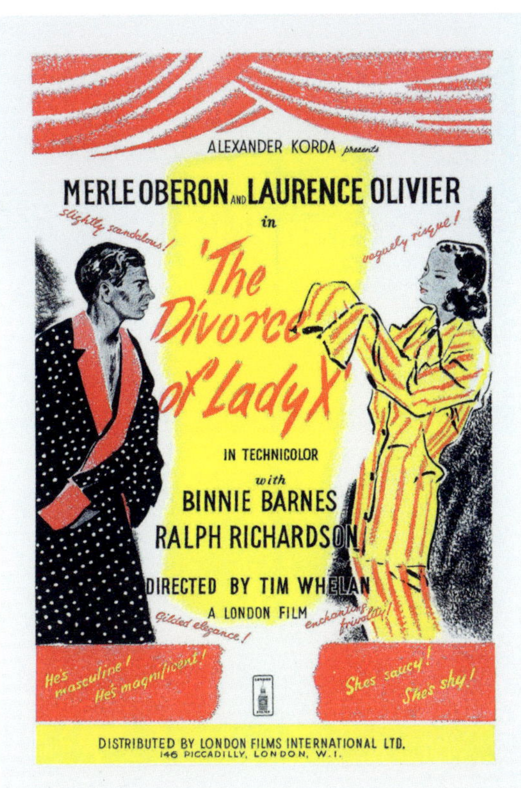

Below A poster advertising Laurence Olivier and Merle Oberon in *The Divorce of Lady X* (1938).

impossible to be satisfied with the present standard of achievement, and it is greatly to be hoped that the advent of the talking picture will not divert attention from the importance of improving the quality of the cinema film both as a branch of the dramatic art and as a means of rational entertainment.

The application of 'mass production' to film technology, however, enables a much cheaper article to be put upon the market; the least expensive seats cost 6d, and provide a formidable competitor to the public house and the streets. However, there is a significant difference. In a public house, or in the street, the people are together, often packed tightly beside each other. In the old music hall, too, the members of the audience could hear each other, observe each other and even speak to each other. In the modern picture palace that sense of community has gone. The spectators gather in the dark and, however full the place may be, there is no feeling of kinship. In the same way, perhaps, London itself has become more public and less intimate. It is not yet clear that the talking picture represents a healthy development, but it is to be hoped that new forms of entertainment will provide new means of instruction.

One modern example provides a clue. The wireless or radio has been with us for almost a decade, and has attracted so large an amount of interest and enthusiasm that it is now an important part of popular entertainment. Yet it could also become an avenue for greater education as well as indoor diversion. It was at first a hobby for young men building crystal receiving sets in their home workshops or garden sheds, but now large general stores like that of Harry Selfridge have set up loudspeakers so that their shoppers can 'listen in' to concerts or opera productions. Listening-in sets have also been added to the amusements of some public houses, although various temperance societies have objected to them. Nevertheless, the number of wireless licences issued in the London postal district has risen by two hundred thousand over the last three years, and the magnitude of this figure makes it certain that it has taken a firm hold on the working class as well as the middle-class population of the city. The cheapening of wireless sets and the improvements in reception have created an entirely new means of adult pleasure. The morning hours are generally devoted to the entertainment of the housewife, and the evening to the general public, while the late hours are reserved for the leisured and the cultivated. The terms of 'highbrow' and 'lowbrow' have become commonplace.

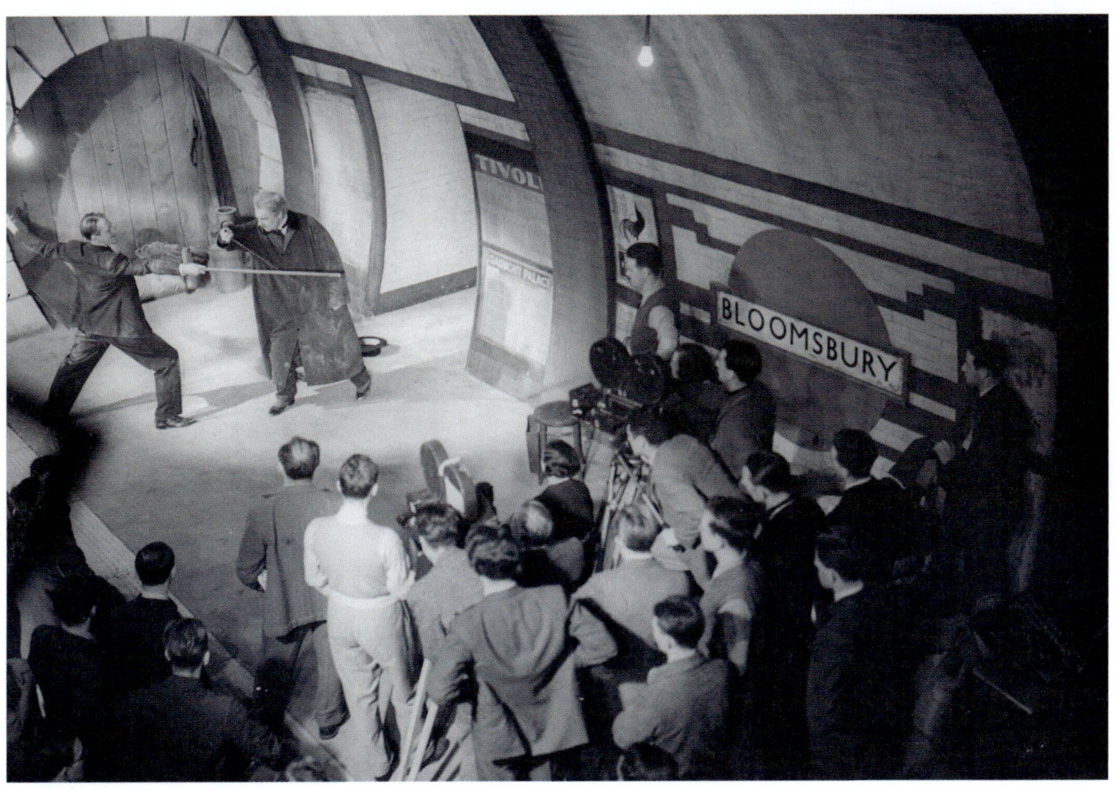

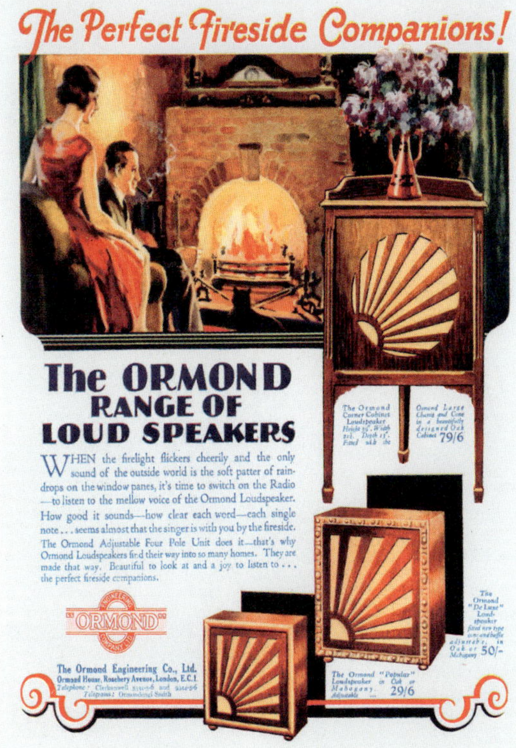

Although overshadowed by the phenomenal development of wireless, the invention and gradual improvement of the gramophone have also been noteworthy features of recent years. Since Edison invented the phonograph in 1876, there has been an astonishing revolution in the mechanical means of performing music, the end of which is not yet in sight. Note also the appearance of 'photomatons' in the large stores; at a cost of 1s they produce in a few minutes a strip of developed photographs of a sitter taken from various angles. It is another amusement.

In more general terms, there are some who observe with misgiving the growing influence of the vast mechanical organizations of wireless and cinema, as tending not only to foster a habit of passive receptivity of entertainment at the expense

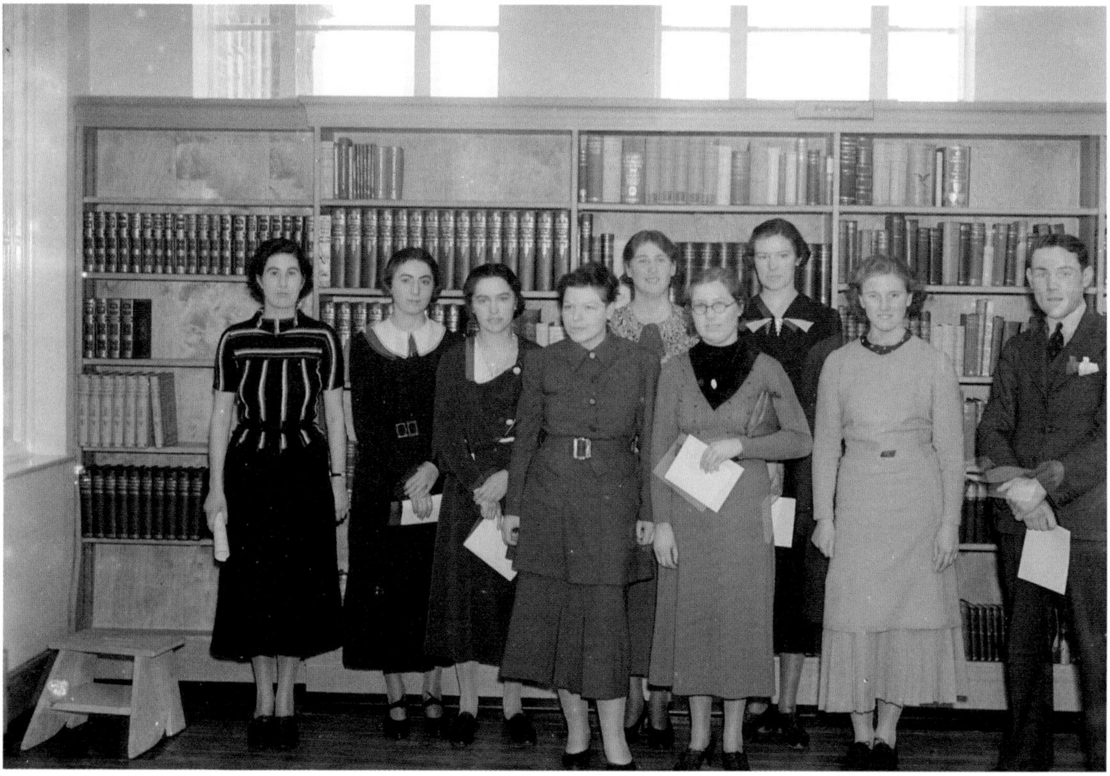

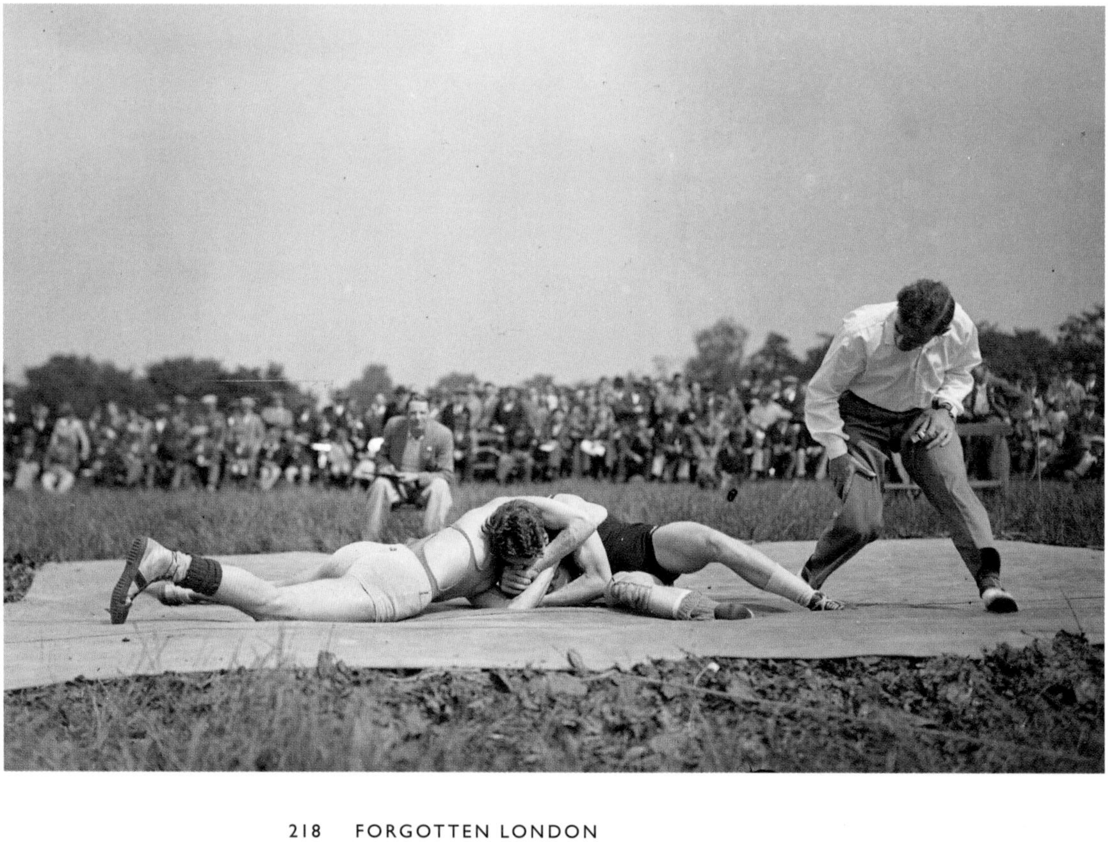

of more active and energetic uses of leisure, but also possibly to establish something in the nature of a dictatorship of amusement and even of opinion. Yet, in spite of the ominous experience of some foreign countries, there seems to be no immediate risk of mechanized entertainment being employed for the purposes of propaganda or what is called 'mass suggestion'.

A contrast is found in the growth of the rate-supported public libraries and of the reading public who resort to them. It is now estimated that the number of borrowers has risen four times in this decade, and that the number of separate libraries in London has doubled. This increase is of the greatest interest in any consideration of literacy and education. The public library authorities have also taken an increasingly broad view of their functions. Some librarians are keenly interest in the Workers' Educational Association, while others arrange University Extension courses, wireless listening groups and study circles. Perambulating libraries on street barrows can be seen in some of the poorest parts of London, which call weekly from door to door to exchange and lend works of fiction at 1d per volume. These books may be below the standard of the public library, but they represent the first steps of a literate community. The advances in the provision of compulsory education have wrought a transformation of the London working population from a semi-educated to an educated community, and no backward movement can be contemplated.

There can be no question that the potentialities of the average working-class life are fuller than ever before. If there are no books, most families possess a banjo and a gramophone to amuse them in inclement weather. Some have a homemade portable wireless. Some will go to sports meetings or picture palaces, while for others good music or a little gardening form most of the recreation. Others, too, will dismantle their beds to make room for dancing or games that might be played. The famous Wonderland in Whitechapel has gone, but the sports of wrestling and boxing in south London and east London still provide extremely lively and violent entertainment. An interlude in the regular programme of boxing might be filled, for example, by female wrestlers in an exhibition of 'Catch-as-catch-can' where they will issue a challenge to any man or woman in the audience. An old bruiser will be matched by a girl of 25, with sometimes surprising results. Some rings are well worth the visit just to see the local heroes 'scrapping', encouraged shrilly by their girlfriends and mothers.

The vogue for the motorcar has increased in intensity, and the new mass-produced vehicles are of course the most popular. After the war, tens of thousands of young men, who had become used to motorcars and motorcycles, came back to civilian life with great expectations. More and more people have also taken to the road, now that motoring has become less expensive. The Ford 'Tin Lizzie' has gradually been replaced by the Morris Cowley and the Austin 7 for family driving, and the small car has become as much a prized family possession as the wireless set. These smaller and cheaper cars are also equipped with four-wheeled brakes and corded tyres, which encourage much inspection and tinkering by the new driver. No suburban home is considered to be complete without a garage or drive. Weekend driving has, in fact, become part of middle-class life and as a result the 'Baby Car' or 'Mighty Miniature' is supreme. The Morris Cowley, for example, costs just under £200, and is so well-designed that it can be used throughout the winter by drivers who in the past did not dare to risk their vehicles from October to March. It is used for sport and entertainment, with forays into the countryside and expeditions to the coast. The roads are relatively clear and, although the speed limit has now been set at 30 miles per hour, it is generally ignored in the thrill of speed. The new drivers like to race against one another or roar down country lanes with a cloud of dust in their wake. As a result, some country people will urge their children to throw mud or stones at the passing vehicles. The term 'road hog' has come into use for reckless or fast drivers who insist on 'cutting in'.

The great increase in car ownership has had more immediate consequences, since in the last 10 years the risk of being killed in a street accident has doubled. Hand signals have been made compulsory for turning and stopping, while the driver is expected to blow his car horn when approaching a bend or coming close to a pedestrian. Nevertheless two-thirds of road fatalities are pedestrians, mostly killed in trying to cross the roadway and primarily due to mechanically propelled vehicles. It is said that walking through the streets of London is now a more perilous occupation than coal mining, but the proposal that a driving licence should be granted only after a driving test was recently rejected by the House of Commons.

A licence can, in fact, be obtained at the age of 16, which allows you immediate access to the road. The local distribution of danger spots is well-illustrated by a map of central London

Such roadworthy
cars in *every* way . . .

They're as snug as you please in dirty weather, these Morris cars. But never stuffy (thanks, of course, to the clever work of the Air Cleaner). Neat, built-in direction indicators do your signalling for you; no need to stir a finger outside. You feel so very secure; brakes smooth as a cat on a thick pile carpet; roadholding and cornering a miracle of steadiness. Every advantage . . . speed, comfort, power . . . All are included yet none is overstressed.

In fact, for the first time you discover what Balanced Motoring really means—that carefully planned combination of perfectly matched qualities found in every Morris car.

MORRIS
The Car you're proud to own

MODELS FROM 8 TO 25 h.p. PRICED FROM £110 - £395 ex WORKS.

MORRIS COWLEY SIX SALOON (SLIDING HEAD) £220

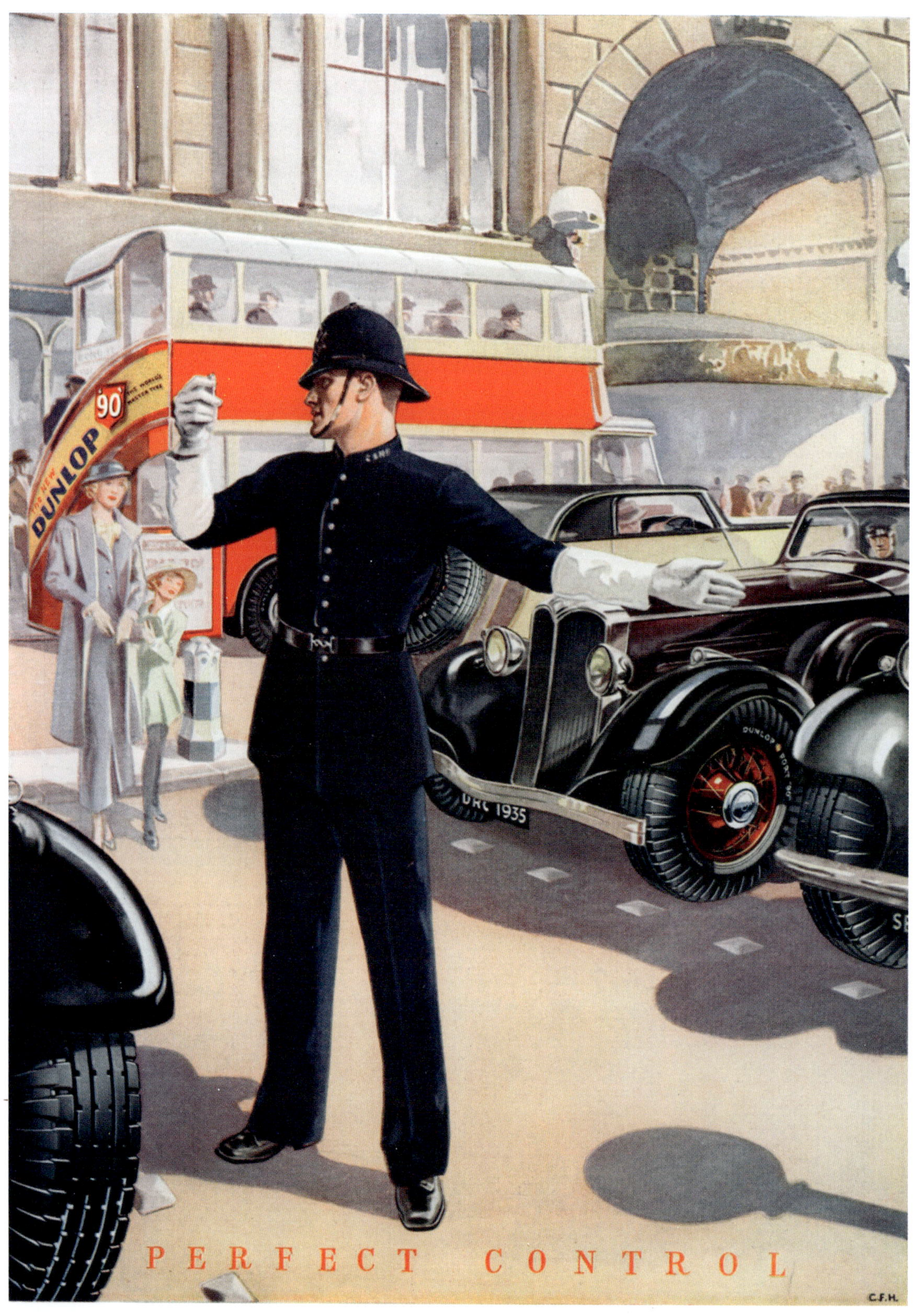

DUNLOP
90
THE NEW
THE WORLD'S
MASTER TYRE
DRC 1935
DUNLOP FORT 90
PERFECT CONTROL
C.F.H.

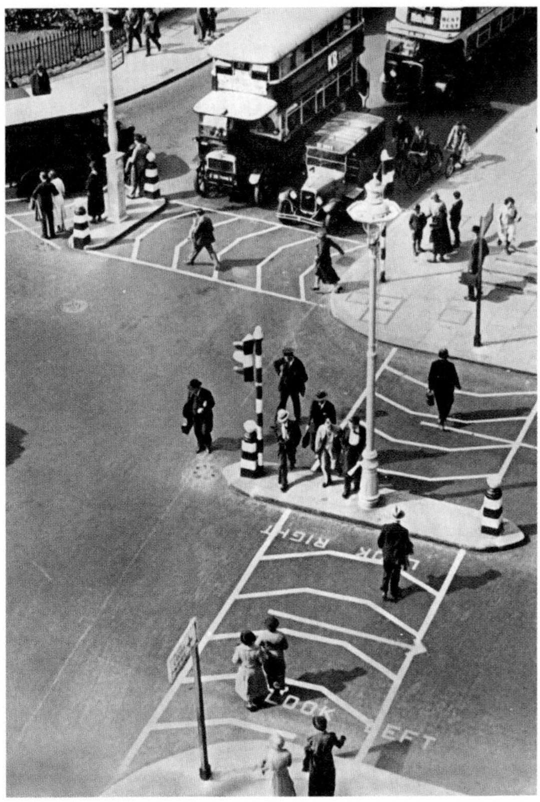

Left 'Perfect Control', a 1930s magazine advert for Dunlop tyres, with a policeman directing traffic.

Above Traffic and pedestrians in Trafalgar Square, 1935.

Overleaf Hyde Park in Summer (1931) by Stanley Lewis.

published by the Ministry of Transport. The most dangerous locations in recent years are Charing Cross, Newington Butts and High Street, Camden Town. The startling growth of such accidents, together with the noise and vibration due to motor traffic, are at present a considerable offset to the advantages of increased mobility.

Some precautions have been taken. Ten thousand pedestrian crossings have been introduced to the city, marked by black and white posts topped by orange globes. It has also become illegal to sound a motor horn after dark; this is a measure designed to end the practice of driving 'on the hooter', which produced a continual barrage of sound on the streets of London. It is hoped that the motoring public, ranging from the millionaire to the artisan, will become less noisy. Yet there is still an alternative. Although there are now estimated to be more than a million owners of private cars, ten times that number are pedal cyclists. The bicycle is predominantly the vehicle for the young, and a second-hand one can be picked up for no more than a few shillings. A new Raleigh model, however, will cost as much as £4 or £5.

The attraction of the London County Council parks, in fact, has been attributed to the growing volume of traffic on the roads. The use of parks and open spaces as the means for restful recreation is more apparent in this fast moving age. It is also noticeable that in the smaller open squares and gardens, which are typical of the central London area, more attention has been paid in recent years to the provision of seats and to the care of flower beds. The construction of ornamental gardens, rookeries and aviaries have all added to the attraction of the parks, while more consideration of physical comfort is shown in the provision of refreshment kiosks and conveniences. Band concerts and Pierrot concerts have also been introduced, but the most important change has been in the provision for outdoor sports and active physical exercise. The facilities for bathing, boating, gymnastics, running and cycling are being continually increased or improved, while undoubtedly the

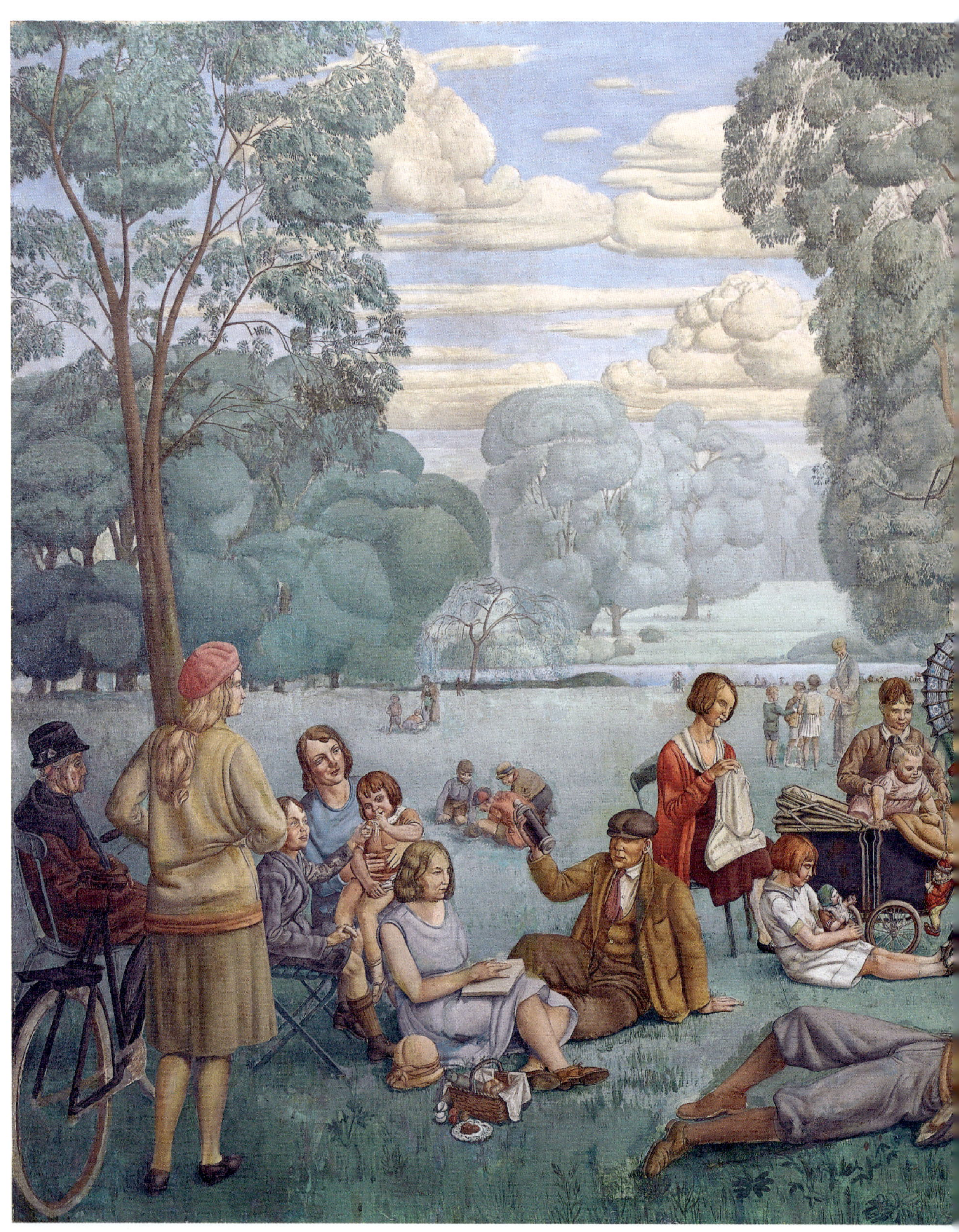

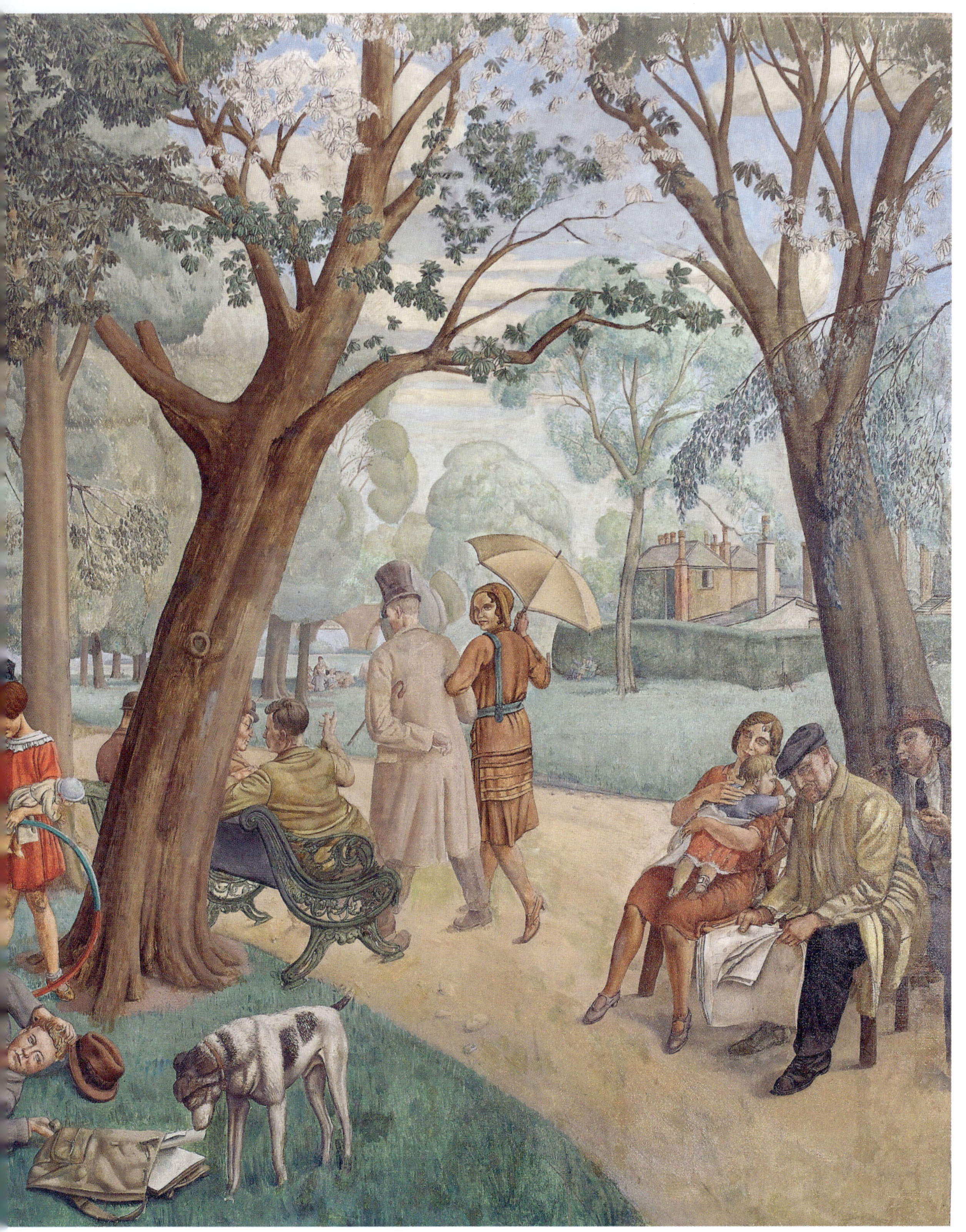

chief advance has been made in such generally popular team games as cricket, football and lawn tennis. Hockey, bowls, golf-putting and netball have not been neglected, to the extent that London may now be regarded as a sporting city. The decline of roller-skating in recent years has not altered that description.

*

It has been demonstrated that the purchasing power of the average London workman has risen by one-third over the last 40 years, largely as the result of higher wages and reduced prices. All of the new domestic appliances and furnishings can be bought by the means of 'hire purchase' or 'instalment buying', which promises the best of both worlds. What seems to be a trifling weekly payment enables many to acquire dress suits, bicycles, dentures, dictionaries – all of which they would otherwise lack. This has encouraged the growth of publicity to sell such items. A legion of copywriters has been drafted to compose slogans for particular commodities and artists are employed to illustrate them. Celebrities are able to augment their income by acknowledging their taste in face cream or in cigarettes. Art and science are used to persuade the public to eat more, drink more, smoke more and to wear more.

The new products have brought a number of shops and amenities into being. These include the wireless shops and the gramophone shops (usually combined with music shops), the lingerie and silk stocking shops (known in the trade as 'Madam shops'), the camping shops and the shops dealing in motor accessories. The consumption of such popular items as tinned fruit and canned meat has doubled and redoubled. Baked beans, tinned peas and Spam are now everyday household items, while new methods of refrigeration have guaranteed the sale of cheap oranges, apples and pears. This in turn has fostered the rise of great enterprises devoted to the packaging and branding of processed food. They include Unilever, United Dairies and Tate & Lyle, whose products are now sold by shopkeepers small and large. Bird's Custard

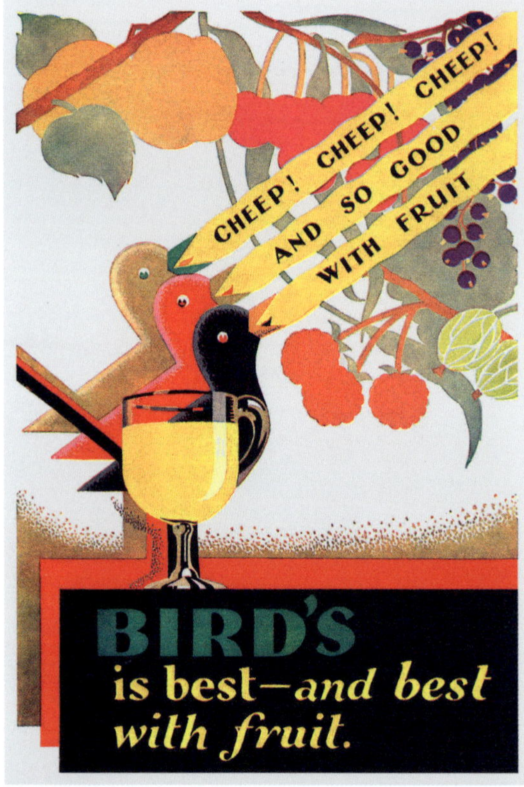

Below An advertisement for Bird's Custard Powder, 1930.

Right A woman displaying stockings at the International Laundry and Allied Trades Exhibition, at the Royal Agricultural Hall, Islington, 1938.

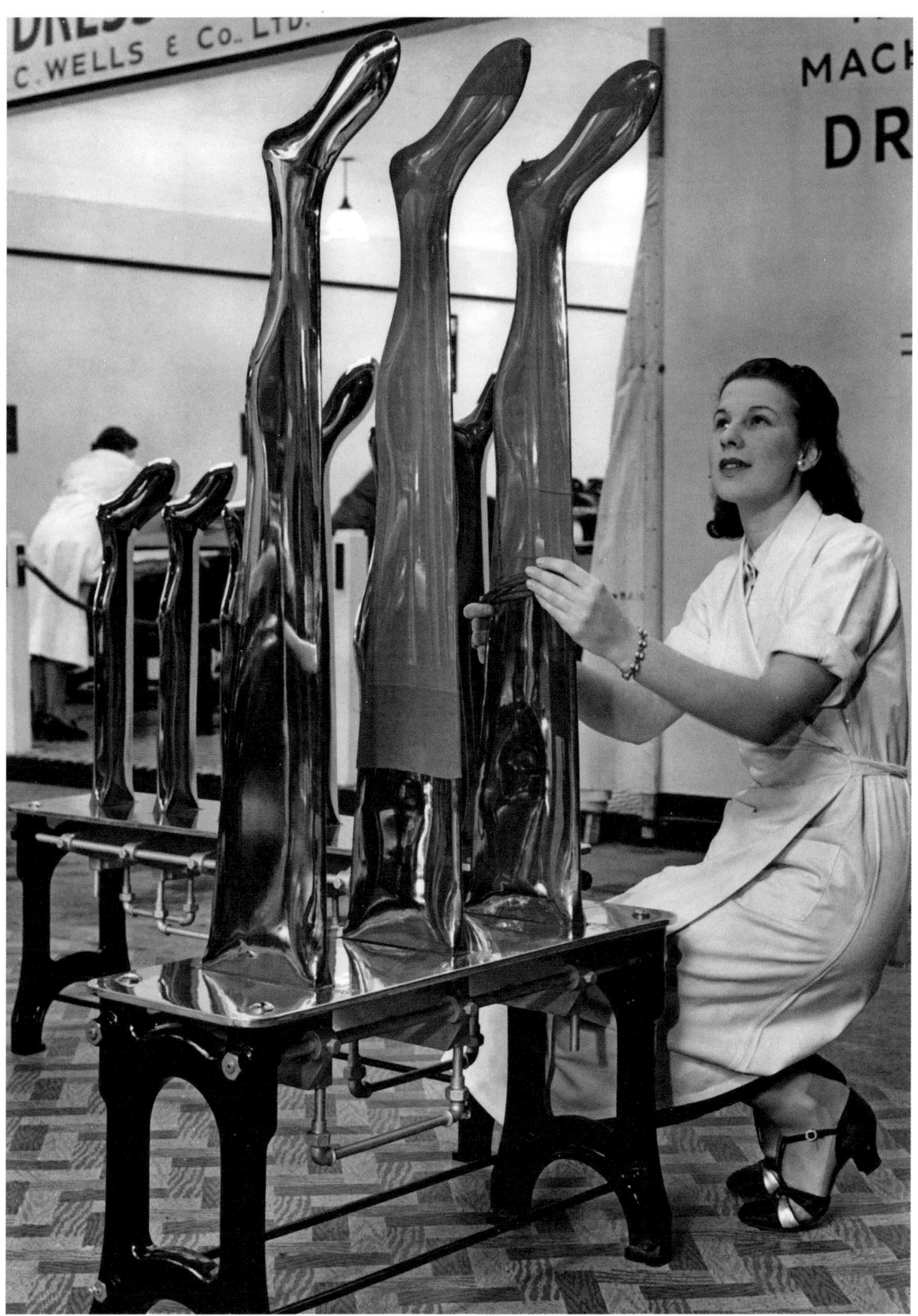
DRESS
C. WELLS & Co., LTD.
MACH
DR

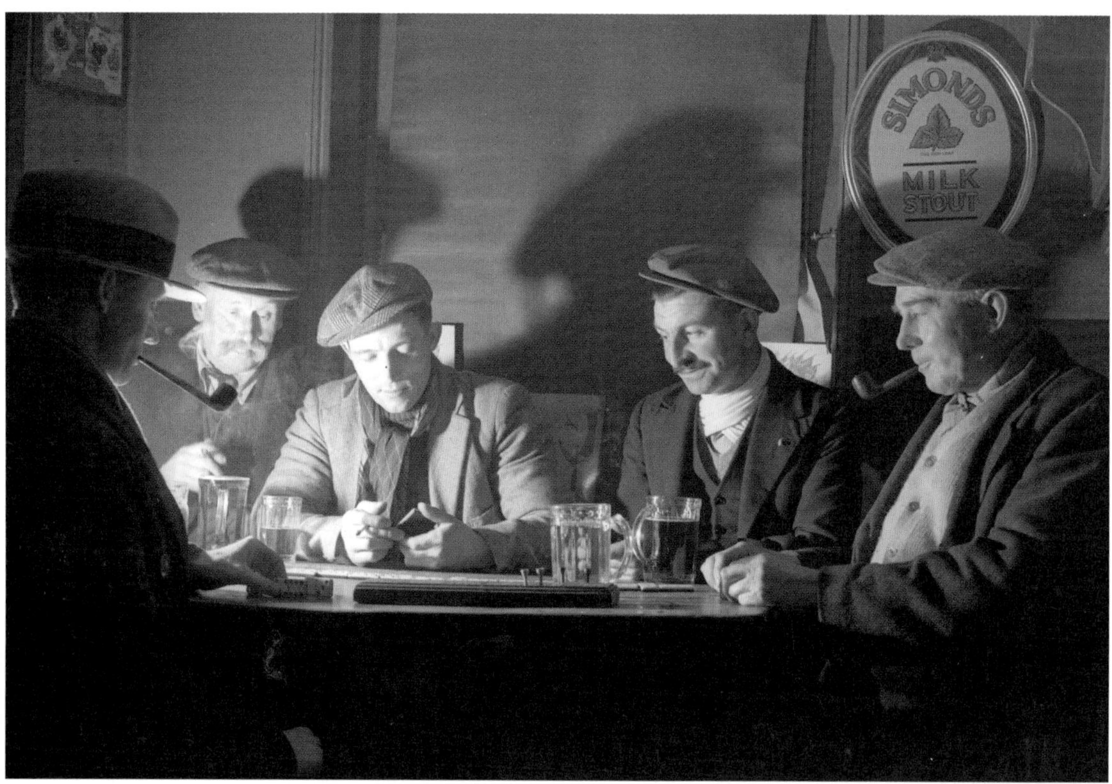

Above Regulars at the King George V Inn playing dominoes, c.1938.

Right top *Market Day outside the Old Red Lion at Greenwich* (1938) by Thomas Rowlandson.

Right bottom An advertisement for Guinness with the slogans, 'Guinness is good for you' and 'Nothing takes its place'. Originally published in *The Illustrated London News*, 1932.

Powder and Quaker Quick Oats are now as familiar as Pears Soap and Beecham's Pills. It is perhaps not necessary to state that the sale of ice-cream, chocolate and general confectionery has reached unprecedented heights. In a further sign of the times, the old ice-cream barrow has been largely replaced by a moving vendor on a tricycle, whose slogan is 'Stop me and buy one'. It is worth noticing, however, that in a survey organized by the Ministry of Agriculture, only one-half of the population achieved an 'optimum' diet and that a third lived upon a 'seriously deficient' diet. The old slogan, 'Homes Fit for Heroes' should be replaced by 'Food Fit for Everyone'.

For the less necessary forms of expenditure, let us look into the modern public house, protected as it is from the street by panes of frosted glass. There are three bars labelled 'Saloon', 'Private' and 'Public', with the most noise coming from the 'Public'. The brown or peeling walls are bare except for a dartboard and its scoring slate, a few display cards for selected drinks and a notice forbidding gambling or the passing of betting slips. There is sawdust on the floor and two spittoons. Everyone is standing up. The dart players have pints of beer standing on the counter and the barman is leaning over to watch the game. He

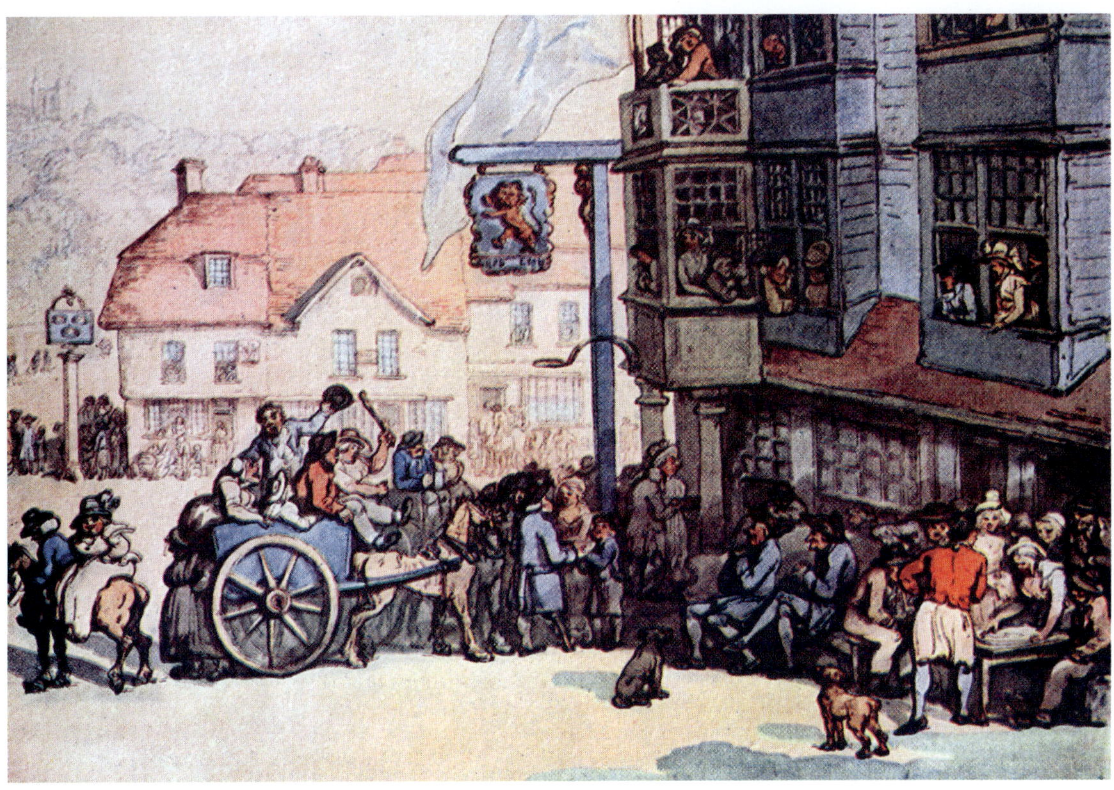

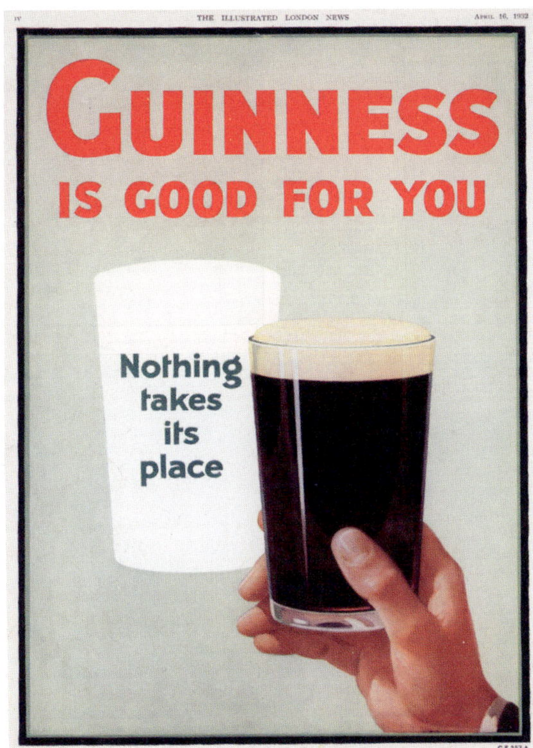

comes to take your order and then goes back. Darts are the main game, shove-ha'penny being rare compared with it. 'Pin-tables' are more often to be found in the largest public houses, sometimes known as road houses.

There is a comforting fug of beer and tobacco, mixed with the odour of unwashed bodies. A group of middle-aged men, most of them in cloth caps, are continuing an argument about football teams with much swearing but with no ill humour. Another small group is discussing, quietly and intently, the sport of pigeon-racing. In the corner of the saloon bar a group will gather each evening, out of habit and conviviality. They call one another by Christian names or even by nicknames. Their conversation is concerned mainly with minor matters of their individual trades, jokes about

Scotsmen and Jews, together with desultory discussions on drinks, motorcars, tobacco, the latest murder, old popular songs, music halls and the horse-races. A young man comes in alone, orders a half of bitter, drinks it while smoking a cigarette and goes out again with a nod. An older man takes his place at the counter.

'What's it for you sir? Is anyone attending to you?'
'I won't have a glass of bitter tonight. I'll have a whisky.'
'That's right. Your usual. A double whisky and some soda.'

Mr Wells and other illustrious writers have painted the city of a hundred years hence as a glittering world of skyships, spaceships, silver towers and domes. What are the chances that it will be more like the one we already know?

The men found in the public bar are often poor but rarely poverty-stricken. The poorest of them tend to order pints rather than half-pints, not only because they get the cheapest beer, but because a pint can last out an evening. The unemployed regard the public houses as closed to them, and will admit to being afraid someone will stand a drink they cannot return. There are perhaps three times as many male customers, of all ages, as female. Women drink stout more than ale, sometimes adding gin to it while their husbands are not looking. 'Just slipped into the saloon,' is a typical example of the wife's excuse. Young people drink less at a visit and go away sooner than the older ones. Some selling and buying goes on, for example through tallymen and the local agents of mail-order stores. In some areas pornographic postcards or 'medical apparatus' may be hawked around, but this is rare.

American coloured cartoon-strip papers are sometimes sold in the East End. On an average evening, match-sellers and newspaper boys enter, musicians play outside and then pass the hat round, and so on. On the whole, however, the selling and the begging are very severely discouraged. The generally expressed opinion of the trade is that street music also 'lowers the tone of the house'. In the private and saloon bars hard-boiled eggs, potato crisps, twopenny bags of nuts, cigarettes, matches and proprietary breath-sweetening cachous are often available. Children standing outside public houses are still a fairly common sight, although drink never appears to be supplied to them, and they display in fact no interest in it.

Even if the incidence of drinking is still immense, the actual volume of drinking has declined over the last 30 years. The latest statistics reveal that the individual consumption of beer at the

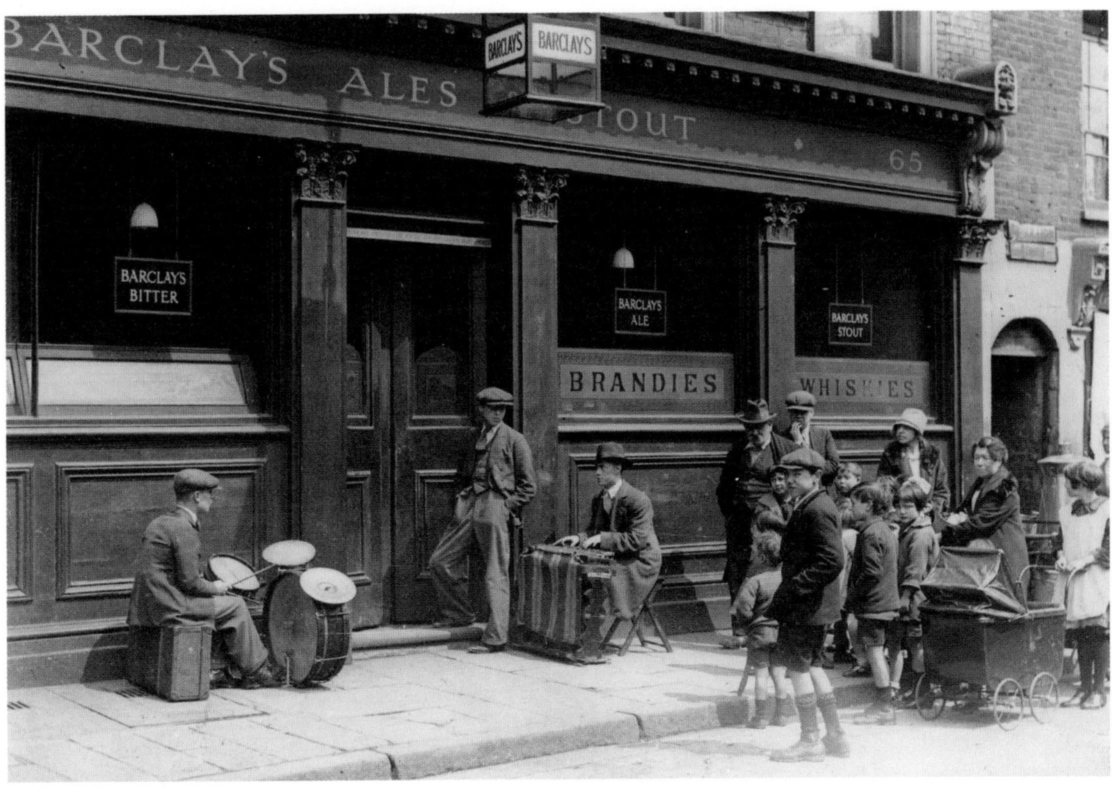

A street band in front of a pub, c.1930.

turn of the century was 45 gallons, and is now only 23 gallons. It is also determined that a smaller percentage of the London population habitually frequents public houses. Just before the late war one-quarter of a very poor family's income was spent by the husband and wife on drinking, but that figure has now been reduced to one-sixth. Before the war, too, the consumption of spirits entered into the normal drinking habits of even the poorest families. It has now virtually disappeared.

There are fewer women to be seen in the public houses, and the average age of the customer is as much as 10 years higher than before. However, the relative absence of women may be due to the habit of drinking at home rather than in public. Rings of stale beer are frequently to be observed on the tables of working-class households. You will notice, if you look at a ticket, that most journeys on the London bus end at a public house. Yet it is possible that the old association of drink and the city may at last have been broken. Certainly the social status of drunkenness has steadily fallen in the eyes of the population. It was once half-admired as a token of virility but it is now regarded, on the whole, as rather squalid and ridiculous. Other amusements now compete with the bottle. More importantly, working conditions have been lightened by the new shorter working week and, with the recent improvements in housing, the need to take refuge in alcohol is not so pressing. It should be admitted, however, that even the poorest type of public bar sometimes compares favourably with the customers' own home accommodation.

Although the volume of drinking has decreased over the past 30 years, that of gambling has grown during the same period. The sense of insecurity which the war engendered, and the instinctive search for a narcotic against its graver anxieties and perils, inclined men to this kind of relief. It is said that a nation in arms is almost inevitably a gambling nation. Work and money, for the civilian population, were plentiful then as they never had been before; there was always enough to stake something on the chance of winning, and so to shut out the consciousness of surrounding menace. Now that the war is over, gambling provides some faint aroma of the spice that is now lost. It gives a sense of fortune and adventure which has otherwise been dispelled.

Gambling takes many forms in the city. The fate of a pontoon during the racing season, and still more during the football season, affords an unfailing topic of conversation. For those not of the gambling fraternity, a pontoon consists of betting on choices in six different events. In many factories and workplaces, too, the sweepstake is well-established. A stake of 6d a week, in a place where 20 or more people are employed, will mount up to a respectable winning. In more private circumstances a gang of men will retire to a favourite house, or some secluded spot out-of-doors, and 'run' a pack of cards. In many quarters of poorer London are to be found obscure premises which are known locally as 'spieling houses', from the Yiddish word for 'play', which people frequent for gambling purpose, usually in the familiar forms of dice or card-playing.

Of late years a new factor has made its appearance in the betting field. This is the sport of greyhound racing. It consists of the pursuit of an electric hare by the hounds around a stadium, and has become a firm favourite with Londoners. It provides cheap entertainment in the open air, easily available to the working man after his day's work, and one in which both sexes and all ages can share. Gambling today is as extensive as it ever was in London. It may be responsible for a certain amount of distress and corruption in the capital, but it is also a source of harmless enjoyment and interest among diverse sorts of people. It is doubtful whether it is so damaging as its more extreme opponents claim, or as the

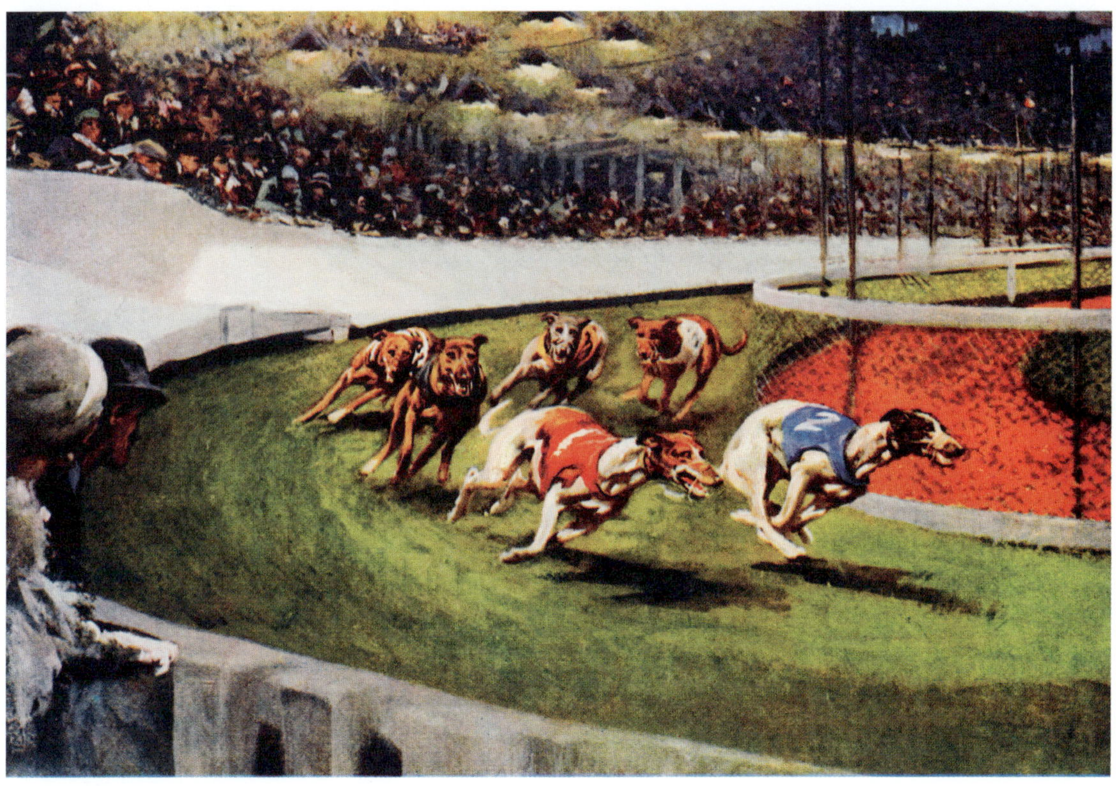

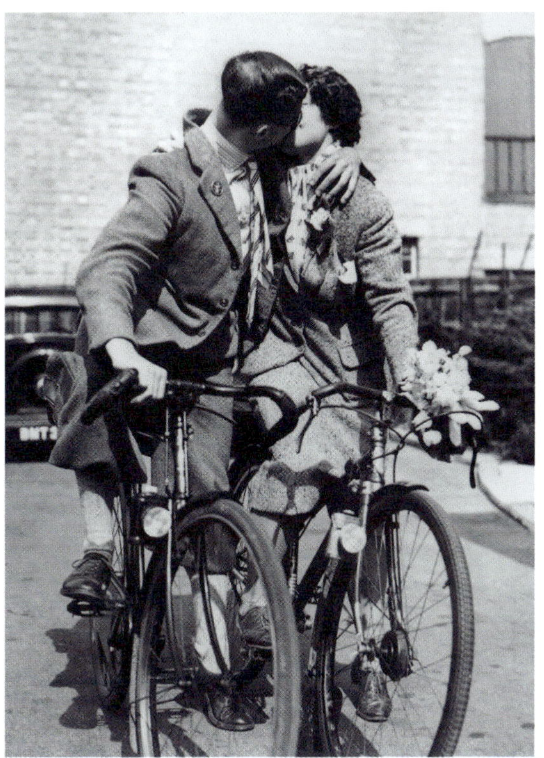

drink habit was a generation ago. It also gives a fillip to that sense of hopefulness, and of expanding possibility, which is so noticeable in the post-war world.

On another note, the relationships between the sexes are now maintained with a higher standard of conduct and consideration. The abnormal conditions of war had brought about the relaxation of conventions, and the prevailing psychological conditions led to widespread intercourse of a non-commercial type. For that generation, the loss and disablement of a large body of adult men seriously disturbed the balance of the sexes at marriageable age. As an aftermath of the Great War, too, a significant number of women were forced into the labour market to become economically self-supporting and with no opportunity of marriage.

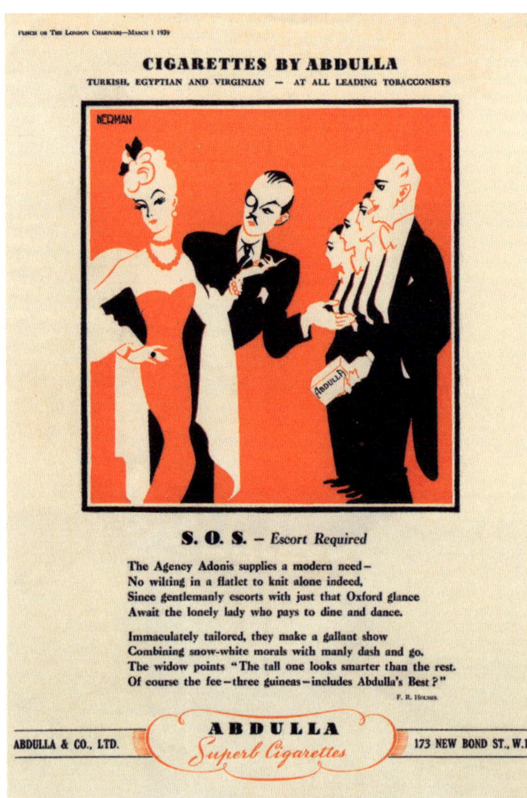

Above 'Cigarettes by Abdulla S.O.S. – Escort Required'. From *Punch* magazine, 1 March 1939.

This may have promoted independence, but it also encouraged restlessness and uncertainty.

Thirty years ago, a girl of whatever class was seldom without the guardianship or assistance of a responsible person. Today, in every social class young women, both at work and at leisure, are free of any supervision. The majority, for example, have had little positive education on sex behaviour. The knowledge that contraception can be practised is widespread, but accurate information as to methods is not. Yet there are signs of progress. It is hoped and believed that the improvement in the general standard of education will raise women's social status, while at the same time it will increase the sense of self-respect and personal responsibility in both men and women. Already the new mobility of youth and the early economic independence of women have led to changes in behaviour that have resulted in far greater freedom of companionship between the sexes.

The number of women following prostitution in a systematic or professional manner seems to have declined since the war, and is believed to amount to less than three thousand. These common prostitutes frequently have men known as 'bullies' attached to them, living as parasites on their immoral earnings. Some hundreds of girls are calculated by the social agencies to have been 'lost sight of' in any year. In addition there is a fringe of 'casual' or occasional prostitutes, such as the married woman from the suburbs seeking sex adventure and an augmented dress allowance. She plies her trade discreetly, particularly near Victoria station and in the afternoon cinemas. Motoring has introduced a new factor, and both men and women solicit from cars in the West End and in the suburbs. However, there is no hard and fast line today between those places in which a respectable women or an unmarried girl may and may not be seen without loss of character, provided she does not go alone. The nightclub, the dance hall and the hotel lounge are cases in point. All the evidence, however, indicates that domestic service is still by far the most prolific occupational source of sex delinquency.

However, there is a brighter and more interesting side to female independence. This may turn out to be yet another decade for celebrating the achievements of women. Amy Johnson, for example, has recently become the first female to fly solo to Australia; she trained herself to travel such a vast distance by studying meteorology and by learning jujitsu in case she fell into the hands of Arab sheikhs or African head-hunters. It may be worth mentioning that she was sponsored by the *Daily Mail*. This guaranteed her wide publicity and, for the newspaper, larger readership. It seems, in more general terms, that women are vying to be on equal terms with men. They no longer wish to appear boyish, with the Eton crop and the slim figure, but to be much more feminine. Cosmetics are back in favour. The skirt has been lowered, and the backless evening dress has come back in fashion; the cloche hat has been discarded, and a narrow waistline is accentuated with wide, padded shoulders. In addition, the availability of ready-to-wear clothing in the larger department stores has widened the range of choice. Rayon is now used, and is regarded as a cheap alternative to silk. The metal zip-fastener, copied from military uniforms, has also appeared on items of female clothing.

Below The pioneering pilot Amy Johnson CBE seen here adjusting the engine of a de Havilland DH60 Moth, c.1930.

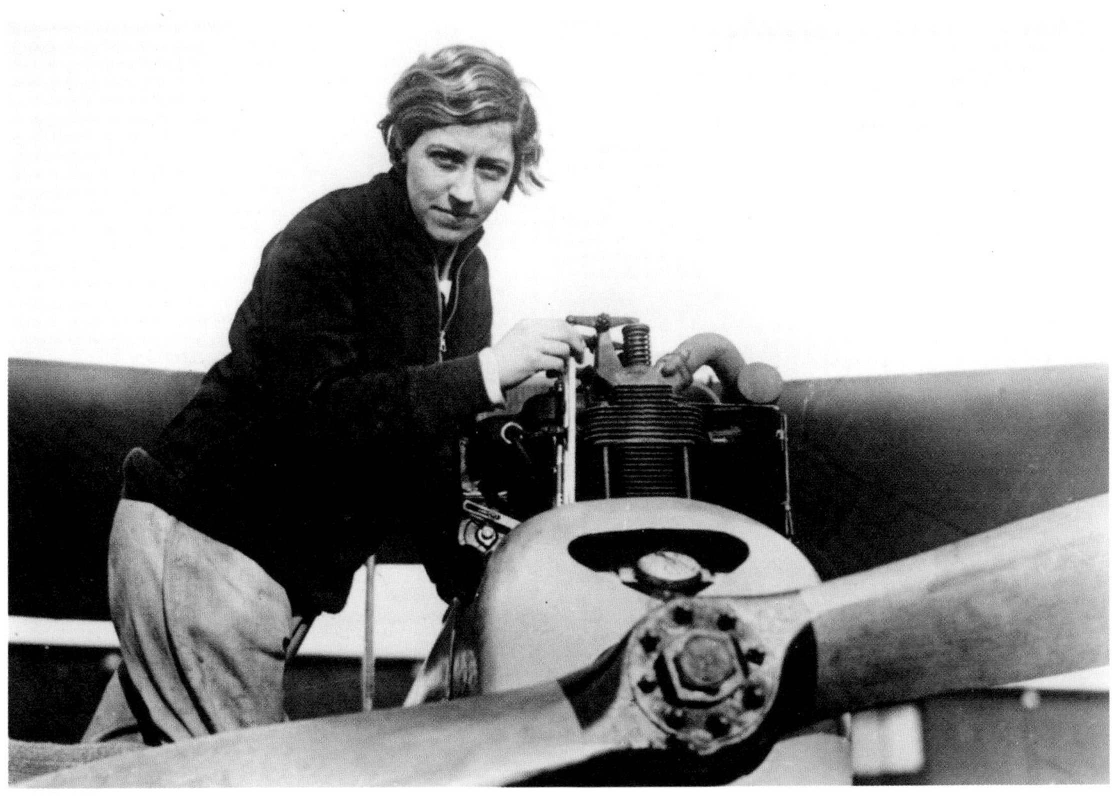

Two magazines designed exclusively for women are now being published, *Woman* and *Woman's Own*. They are designed to address the interests of married women and, in particular to those who are in their own words 'worth their salt' and aspire to be 'the best housewife ever … and then some'. Another new periodical, *Housewife*, declares that 'happy and lucky is the man whose wife is house proud … who likes to do things well, to make him proud of her and her children'.

It is hard to explore any individual marriage, since enquiries into the private manners of the people are always difficult. All great cities have the gift of anonymity for those who seek it, but in London it is granted to you without any choice in the matter. Its districts are so widely separated, and the English character so reticent, that most Londoners of the middling classes do not know the names of their neighbours. The maxim that 'my home is my castle' discourages any but the most superficial attempts at cordiality. You may know a man for years without learning whether he is married or single, let alone whether he has children or goes boating on Sundays. The main exceptions to this are among the very rich or very poor. Understatement, the humour of the Londoner, is really a form of self-defence. London is the only city in the country where a large number of people with telephones will not allow their names to appear in the telephone book. Few houses in inner London have the names of the householder on the door, and there are many districts in which it is impossible to learn the names of its residents. It is perfectly easy to observe a clerk arriving at his office in Leadenhall Street, but anyone who expects to acquire his address from that place of business will draw the blankest refusal.

*

There has been a mania for health and fitness. The advertisements extol the virtues of the latest health foods and health pills, and many groups have emerged to encourage outdoor sport and indoor exercise. The women are advised on matters of diet and slimming, while the newspapers lecture the men on the need for what is called the vigour of the body. The preoccupation is not confined to adults, and it is hoped that free school milk will soon be introduced throughout the country. At the beginning of this decade a league of 'youth hostels' was established in order to encourage rambling and bicycling as well as walking, so as

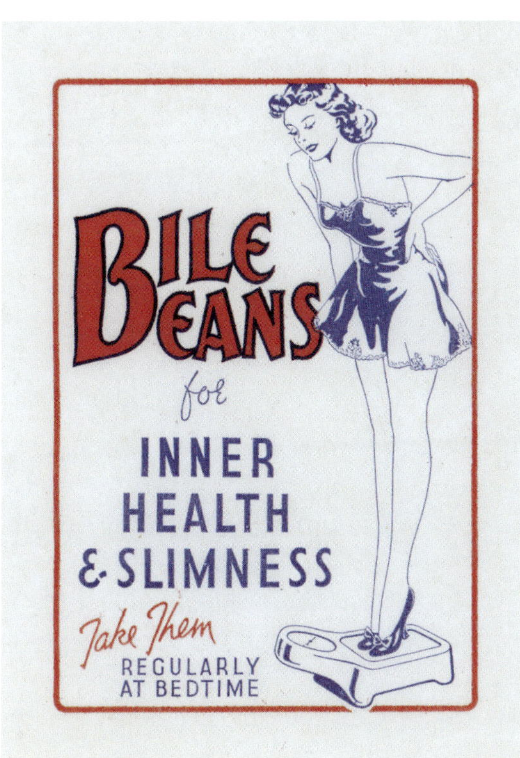

to improve the stamina and vitality of the young. Less energetic pastimes have emerged in yo-yo, started in South America, and midget golf, begun in the United States. There is also the new indoor game of Monopoly for those who do not wish to exert themselves.

In pursuit of health, emblems of the sun and sunshine are everywhere; so are hikers and people in shorts. The heroes of the period include the helmeted airman and the muscular worker, both representative of the 'truly strong man' – to use a phrase of the day – who is always being cited. In this same period, the pleasures and entertainments of the people have grown almost beyond comprehension. Smoking, for example, has become habitual and almost universal. It is estimated that 80 per cent of males

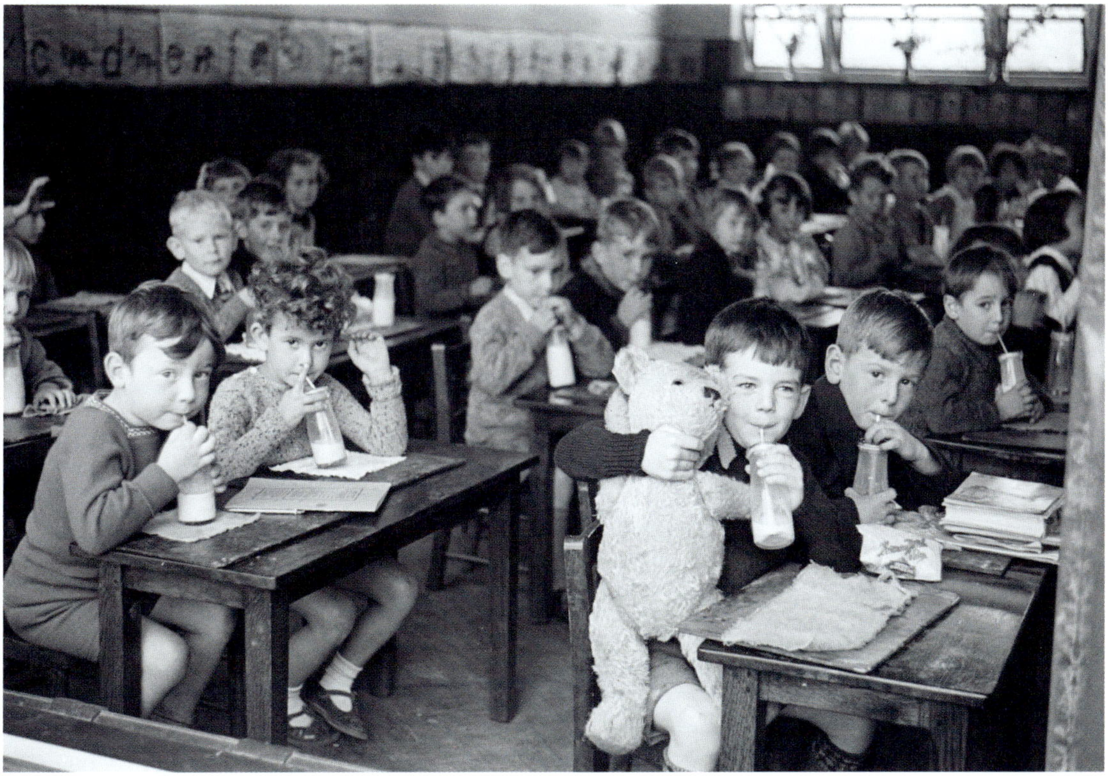

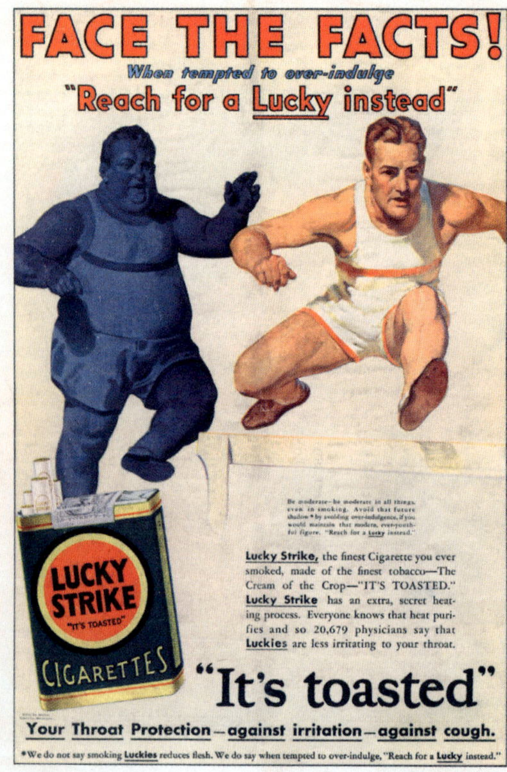

Above A magazine advert for Lucky Strike cigarettes, c.1930s.

Right Advertising posters on a Fleet street building, above a London barber's shop called Sweeney Todd. Among the products advertised are Guinness, Andrews Liver Salts, Nestlés Milk, Diamints peppermint sweets and Yardley Lavender perfume.

and 40 per cent of females now smoke, with cheapest cigarettes selling at 2d for five and the more expensive at 6d for ten. Woodbines, Capstans, Navy Cuts and Kensitas are circulating everywhere. Smoking is considered to be an essential part of masculinity. Their health-giving properties are advertised, while the heroes and heroines of the cinema screen all seem to smoke.

It is clear also that the circulation of newspapers has immensely widened in the last few years, with discounts and gifts multiplying sales. You can receive a full set of the novels of Charles Dickens, for example, if you subscribe to one popular daily. Certain newspapers have adopted very large headlines and very short sentences to cater for a new public; they use photographs and cartoon strips to add variety and, as a result, some of them have acquired millions of readers. That is why their proprietors, such as Lord Beaverbrook and Lord Rothermere, have become eminent public figures. These two men have even created a new party, called the United Empire Party.

The success of the press is aligned with its ever-present advertisements. London suffers from the wanton disfigurement of some of its finest streets and squares by unsightly advertisement hoardings erected over the entire upper floors of many houses. These have now completely marred the appearance of the reconstructed Piccadilly Circus, which would otherwise be the finest open space of its kind in Europe; they have also ruined the stretch of the Strand, next door to Somerset House, and facing Bush House, as well as the noble buildings on the north side; other hideous hoardings are to be found facing the Law Courts and St Clement Danes Church. No sort of protest is ever raised against this wanton vandalism.

It ought to be noted, in stark contrast, that great improvements have been carried out in other parts of the city. Most of the new streets of London were constructed in the Victorian era, but the present reign of George VI has witnessed the greatest amount of rebuilding that has ever taken place

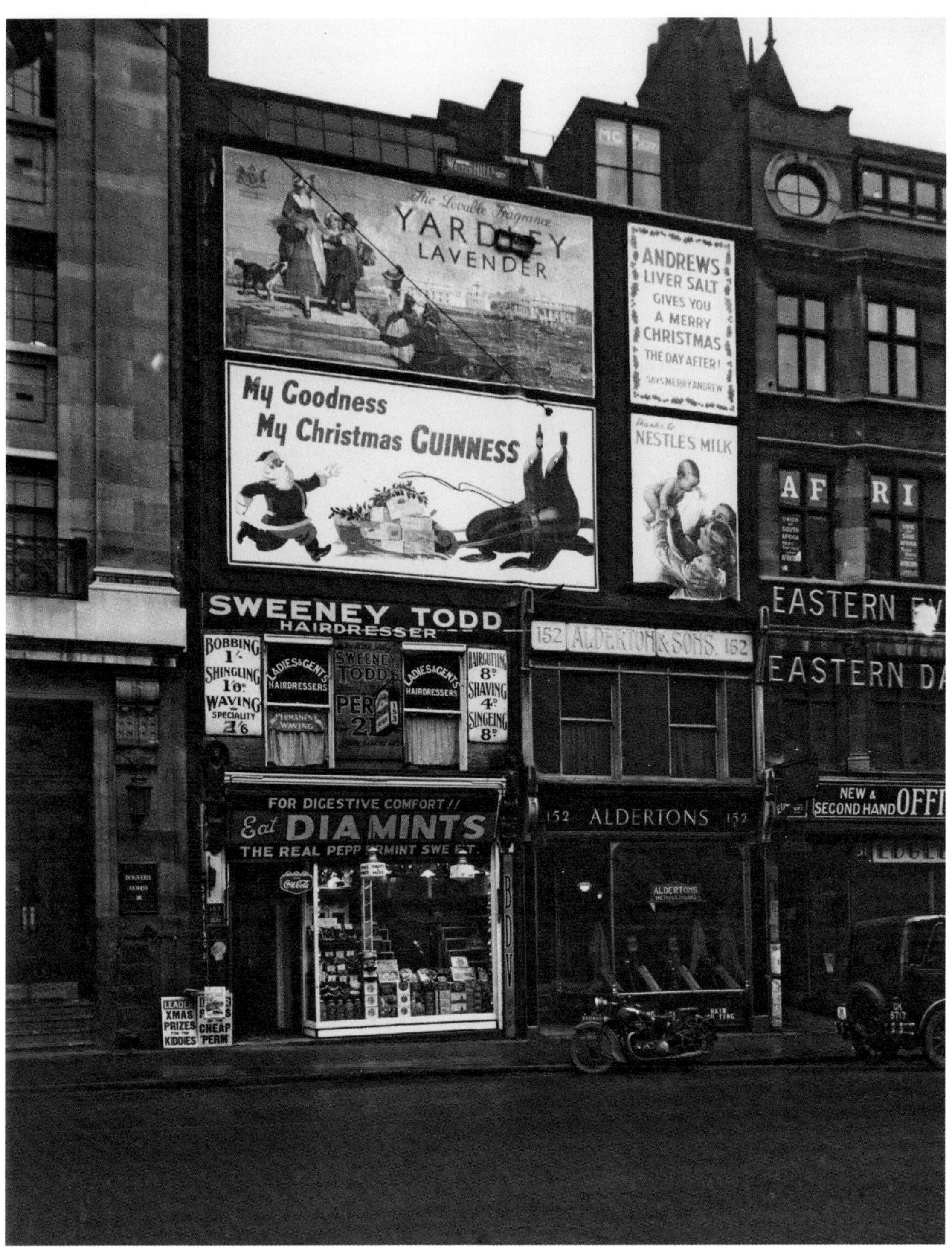

The Lovable Fragrance
YARDLEY
LAVENDER
ANDREWS
LIVER SALT
GIVES YOU
A MERRY
CHRISTMAS
THE DAY AFTER!
SAYS MERRY ANDREW
My Goodness
My Christmas GUINNESS
thanks to
NESTLES MILK
AFRI
UNION
SOUTH
AFRICA
EASTERN E
EASTERN DA
SWEENEY TODD
HAIRDRESSER
152 ALDERTON & SONS. 152
BOBBING
1/-
SHINGLING
1 0°
WAVING
SPECIALITY
2'6
LADIES & GENTS
HAIRDRESSERS
SWEENEY
TODD'S
PER
2/-
LADIES & GENTS
HAIRDRESSERS
PERMANENT
WAVING
HAIRCUTTING
8°
SHAVING
4°
SINGEING
8°
FOR DIGESTIVE COMFORT!!
Eat DIAMINTS
THE REAL PEPPERMINT SWEET.
ALDERTONS 152
ALDERTONS
NEW &
SECOND HAND OFFI
LEADER
XMAS
PRIZES
FOR THE
KIDDIES
CHEAP
PERM

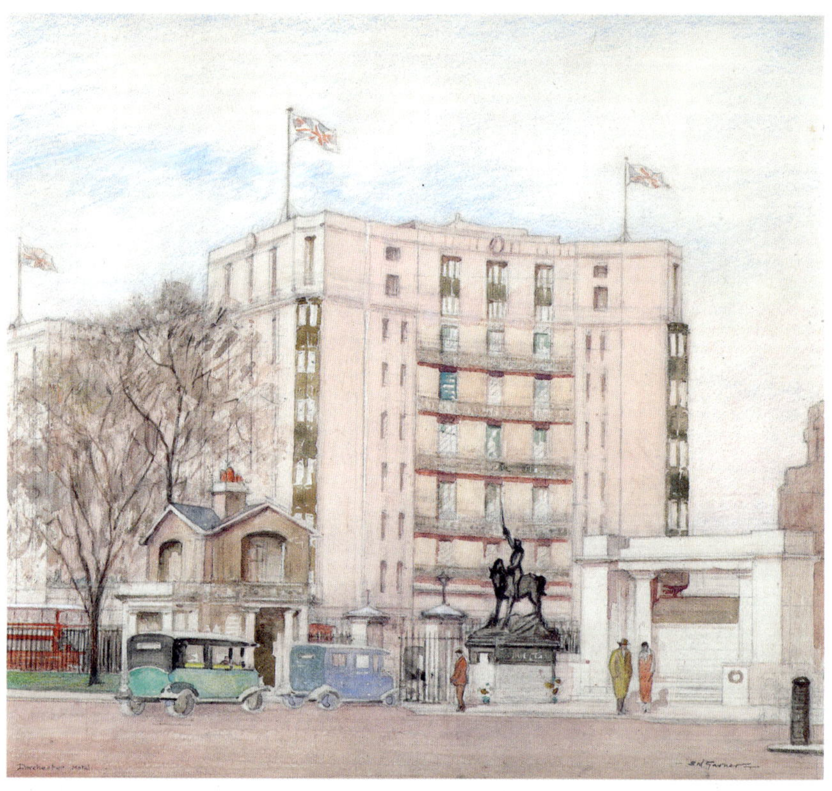

within so short a period of time since the Great Fire of London. Aldwych and Kingsway have been completely lined with stately buildings, the greater part of the Strand and the whole of Fleet Street have been widened, King William Street, Moorgate and Finsbury Circus have been rebuilt. The list, from Oxford Street to Leadenhall Street, is endless. In Mayfair great and famous residences, like Grosvenor House, Dorchester House and Devonshire House, have given way to huge new hotels and blocks of flats. County Hall has been completed. Park Lane is rapidly changing its former character from a street of private residences to one of hotels, shops and flats. In Great Queen Street the stately new Freemasons' Hall, with a tower some 200 feet high, has just been erected at a cost of £1,000,000. Splendid new by-pass roads have been constructed leading out of the metropolis in every direction. London has always been the place in which the wealth of the country has been spent, but it is also the place where the wealth of the country is gained.

*

Yet in London, ancient or modern, the poor are our constant
companions. The fight against urban poverty has not abated, and
in certain districts of London it has intensified. In the last years
of this decade 'hunger marches' have again become familiar.
Two hundred men marched into the grill room of the Ritz and
demanded to be fed; after some debate, they were eventually
served. A large number of unemployed men lay down in Oxford
Street and called for 'Work or bread!' and 'We want extra relief';
a sign was erected at the Monument stating that 'For a Happy New
Year the Unemployed Man Must Not Starve'.

In the area bounded by Limehouse Cut to the north and a maze
of railway lines to the east is the notoriously poor and degraded
area still known as the 'Fenian Barracks'. Slightly further to the
south are the poorest parts of Limehouse itself. Similar conditions
of poverty prevail in the district of West Ham which has, between
Canning Town and Custom House, one of the biggest areas of
crowded and poverty-stricken streets in London. Across the river is
a very poor area in Deptford, largely inhabited by casual labourers,
costermongers and pedlars. Social conditions vary. Poverty and
crowding are worse in Bethnal Green than in Stepney, although
the area south of Commercial Road is difficult. Shoreditch is even
worse, with its statistics of poverty and density of population
as bad as any other part of the city. Finsbury is quite as bad as
Shoreditch, in terms of poverty, crowding and delinquency, but
is a little better in the provision of social work. In passing from
Southwark to Bermondsey, one enters a district where living
conditions are bad but where the atmosphere is more hopeful.
Other reflections may be of interest in this context. Holborn is not
a very populous or crowded borough, but it has a high percentage
of juvenile delinquency. This may be the result of its proximity
to Oxford Street and Soho. In Battersea the poorer parts are near
the Thames; the further inland, the better conditions become.
Poplar, which is the poorest borough in London, has attracted a
considerable amount of social effort of all kinds.

It is clear enough, therefore, that certain areas of London
might have been coloured black or dark blue on the old poverty
maps, but even though many are still classified as 'poor' or 'very
poor', we no longer have to think of them as hanging on the brink
of destitution. It is also worth noticing that the number of people
below the poverty line has decreased by two-thirds over the last
four decades. The number of persons belonging to the common
lodging-house class in London, for example, has been halved

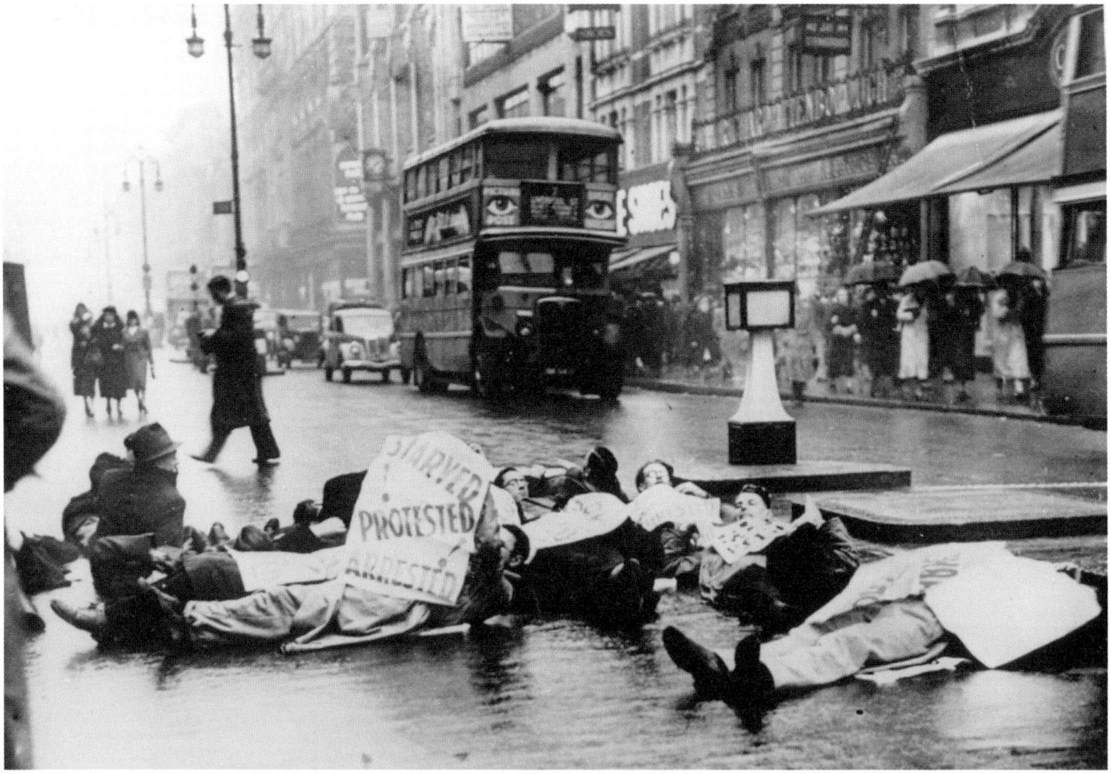

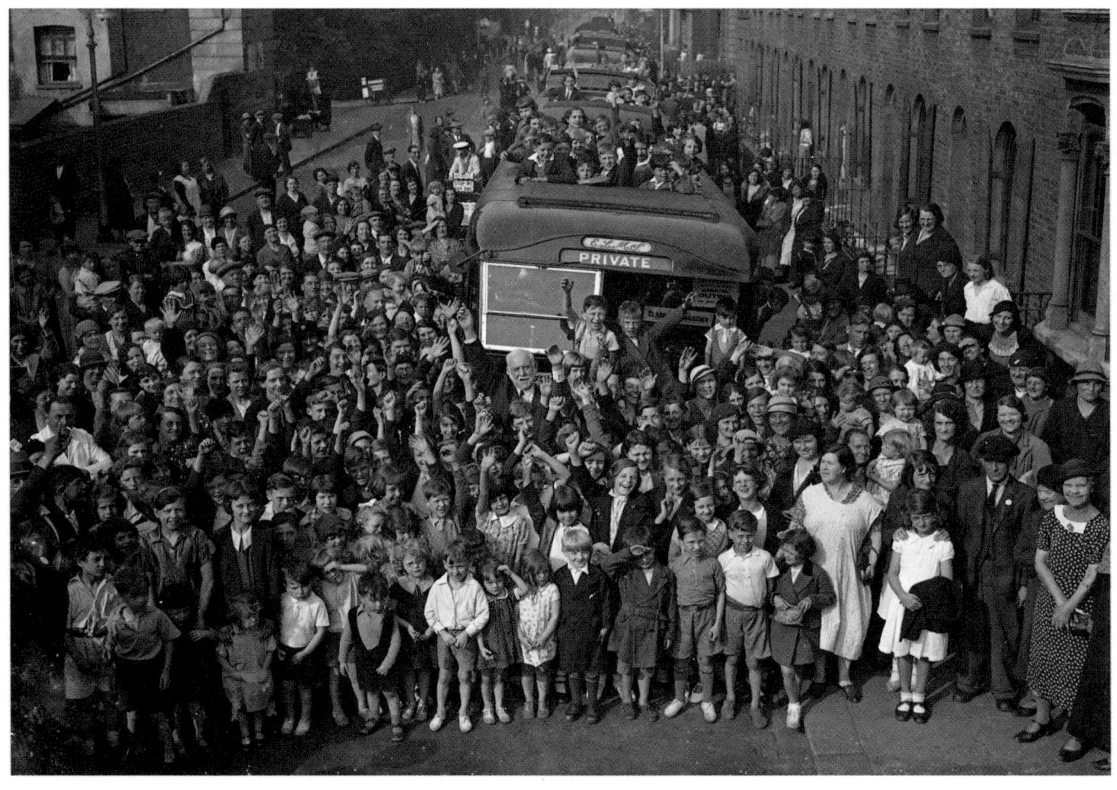

over recent years. There has also been a marked decrease in the numbers of poverty-stricken older men, mainly of the vagrant sort, who are attracted to the lure of London. The general provision for old age, sickness and unemployment has been greatly improved for the London workman and his family since the turn of the century, and the net addition to their standard of comfort tends greatly to diminish the dangers formerly associated with age, infirmity and bad times. Nevertheless, the unemployment among returning soldiers, and the difficulties of the peace settlement, have led some to wonder what in truth the war was fought for.

Boroughs such as Hackney, Stoke Newington and Islington are largely middle class and residential, but contain some very poor streets. Islington in particular suffers from much overcrowding and some criminal streets. In similar fashion St Pancras, Marylebone and Paddington contain some high-class residential areas along with some squalid streets in which property is deteriorating. In the case of Chelsea, middle-class and poor working-class streets are jumbled up together, while in the northern part of Kensington conditions are equalled only by the worst slums in the East End. The economic conditions of Paddington are growing worse; many of its large houses are given over to hotels and boarding houses, and in other parts there is much subletting with its own attendant evils. The listlessness of a deteriorating district and the lack of local feeling characteristic of a dormitory area are combined. Westminster remains, of course, the one area where the extremes of wealth and poverty meet, with the most noisome slums existing within yards of the Houses of Parliament. It may be regarded as the emblem and symbol of London itself.

In regard to other housing, the inmates of the cheaper type of lodging house (those under private management or controlled by the Salvation Army) appear to be hawkers, casual labourers, pedlars, news vendors, sandwich men, street singers, musicians and costermongers, with a few unskilled workers such as market porters and dock labourers. The inmates of Rowton Houses (which are not technically common lodging houses) appear on the whole to be of a higher grade, including clerks, artisans and waiters, as well as some old-age and service pensioners.

The occupants of the women's lodging houses exhibit less variety. Female laundry hands congregate in in Paddington and Kensington, but in the inner boroughs such as Holborn, Southwark and Islington there are a number of waitresses, washers-up in

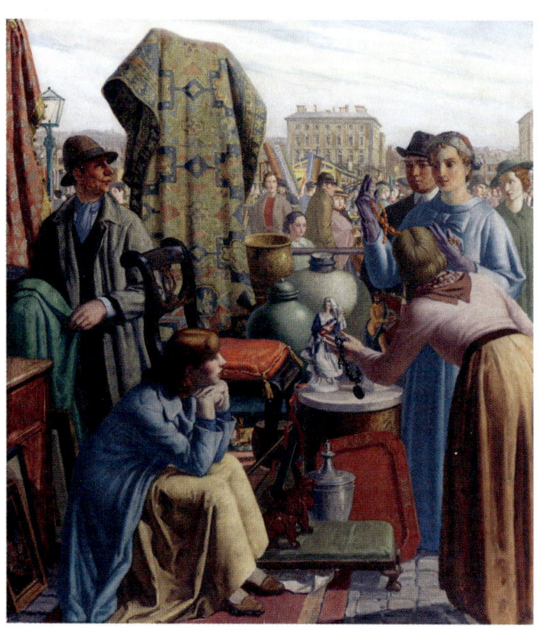

The Caledonian Market (1936) by Harry Morley.

coffee houses and restaurants, servants in hotels, office-cleaners and charwomen. Hawkers and old-age pensioners are found in practically all of the lodging houses; flower-sellers and match-sellers occur only here and there, while prostitutes reside in the great majority of the privately managed houses. There has been, however, a gradual transformation in the prevailing conditions of these places, shown notably in better standards of sanitary and washing arrangements, as well as a great reduction in vermin. As in all areas of social life, it seems that improvements continue.

Street traders are for the most part outside the benefits of unemployment insurance. In turn they cater mainly for the wants of the poor; they are situated in London's difficult areas and generally shun the residential suburbs. The number of traders has increased in recent years, and there are now more than eight thousand licensed stalls; the number of unlicensed cannot be estimated. However, the market for their goods has changed. The total number of stalls selling perishable goods has not altered, for better or worse, but there has been a noticeable decrease in the sale of fish and flowers. In the case of fish, this is certainly due to the increased popularity of the fried fish shop. There has been an increase, however, in the sale of toys and games, with the appearance of stalls selling gramophone records and wireless parts. There has been no falling off in the number of old clothes stalls, which affords evidence that the poorest classes are still largely clad in second-hand goods.

Foremost in London are the Caledonian Market and the Sunday market in Petticoat Lane (now Middlesex Street). Even more famous than the silks sold in Berwick Street and the cloth of Old Castle Street are the bookstalls of Farringdon Road, which is now also notable for its aggregation of wireless stalls. Sclater Street in Bethnal Green is renowned for a Sunday morning dog and bird market, and Bangor Street in Notting Dale for its Sunday morning 'rag fair'. The origins of the street traders are similarly diverse. One may have inherited a pitch, and exhibits a notice to the effect that his business has been established for 70 years, while another may have set himself up with his gratuity immediately

after the war. In addition to the street traders, there are in London
a considerable number of hawkers who seek out their own market
by pushing a barrow or driving a cart or even a car. The street
sellers of newspapers in London number, perhaps, two and a half
thousand. The most prosperous are those who have inherited
certain key pitches where pedestrian traffic is thickest. There is,
for example, a pitch by the Underground station in Westminster
which, it is claimed, has been in the possession of the same family
for over a century.

In the last years of this decade many of these same newspapers
have begun to print horoscopes, reflecting the fact that we live in
an uncertain time. In the carnage of the late war, perhaps, will be
found the origins of that loss of belief in religion, in government,
in tradition, in anything which was once solid and reassuring.
Many people have entered the British Union of Fascists, whose
incursions into the East End have caused so much damage and
consternation; others have joined the International Brigade of
the Spanish government forces. All of them manifest a desire to
recover some purpose and meaning in the contemporary world.
Theirs is not only a protest against immediate crises or local
distress. It is in part a battle of youth against age, of revolution
against tradition, of health against disease. It is all of these things,
and more. There are unsubstantiated rumours of apocalypse or
catastrophe, but most dismiss this as the anxiety of the neurotic or
the intellectual. Some people talk of 'the next war', even though
they have no idea of what the phrase might mean in reality.

An atmosphere of fear is somehow 'in the air' but that grave
mood has been countered, deliberately or spontaneously, by the
resurgence of popular dancing in the dance halls and on the dance
circuits. In the summer of 1937, the London County Council began
the experiment of 'open air dancing' in the city's parks. It has
been hugely successful. In some areas, such as Myatt's Fields Park
in Camberwell, more than three thousand dancers and spectators
have congregated. In Highbury Fields, the crowds have totalled
some twenty thousand.

The most energetic of these dances is undoubtedly the
'Lambeth Walk' which arrived in 1938. It is the first British dance
in a generation to challenge American supremacy, and is enjoyed
in Mayfair ballrooms and suburban dance halls, at cockney
parties and village hops. It began as a song, and then became a
song-and-a-dance accompanied by the famous walk. The dancers
face each other with linked arms, and they take jigging steps

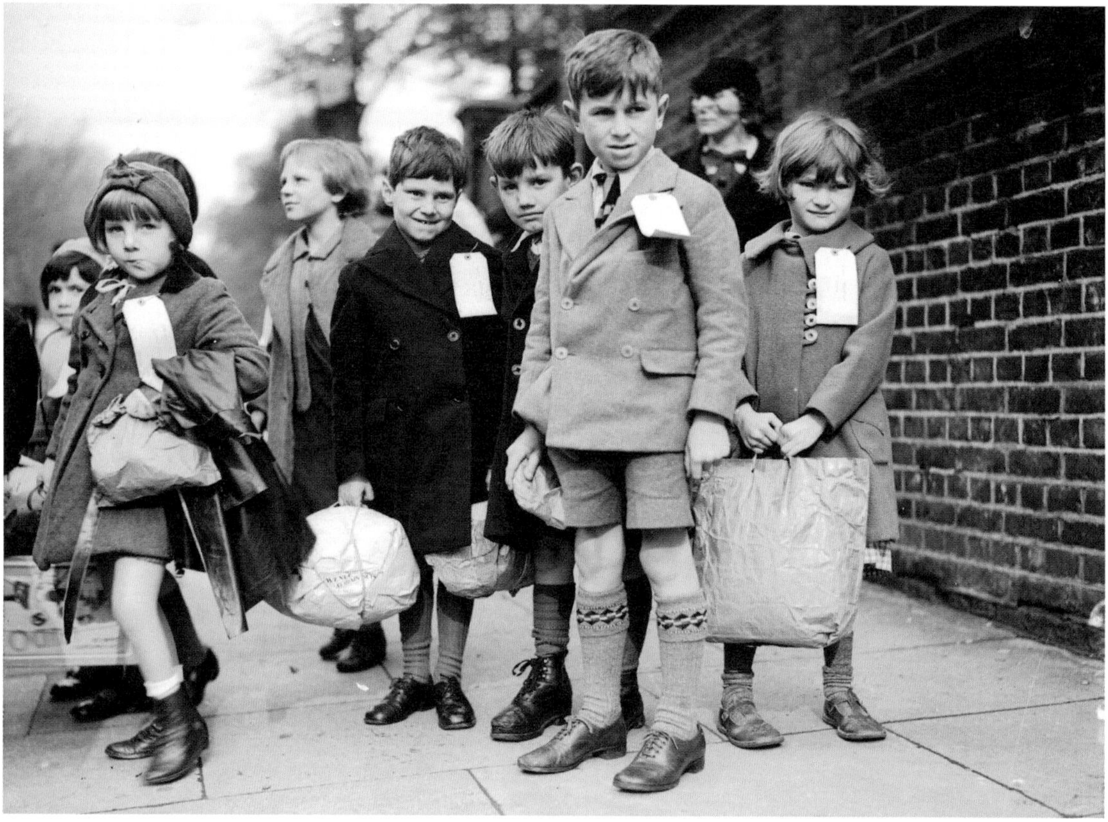

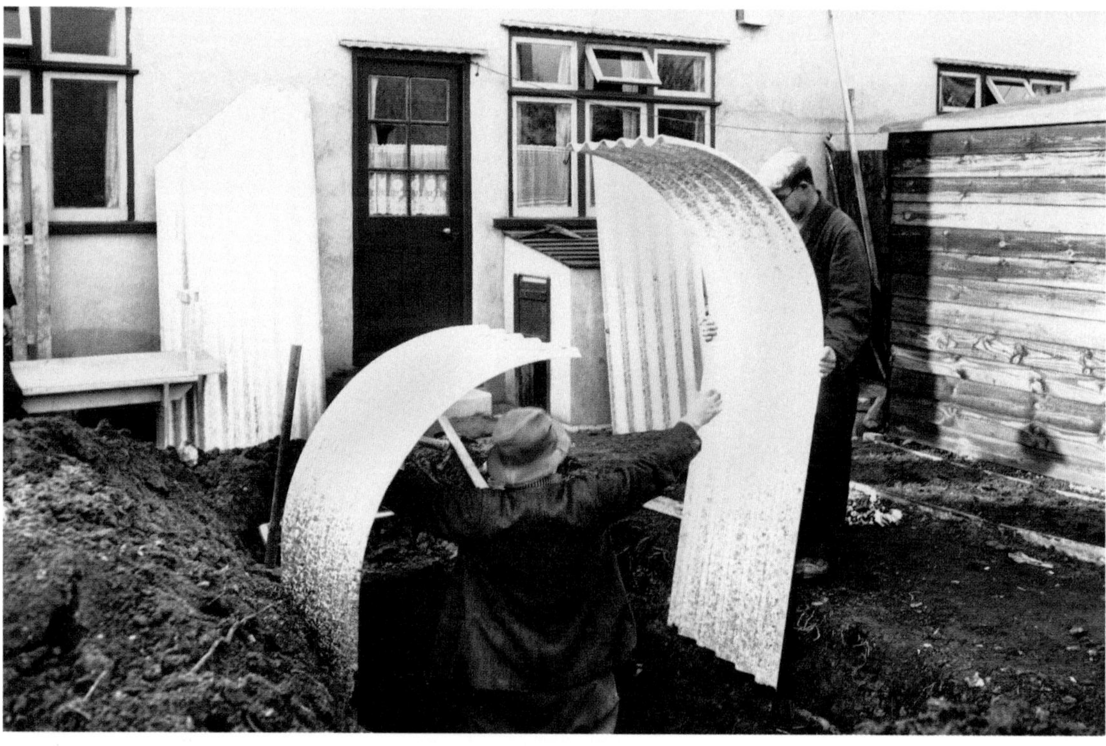

together with high kicking; then the two lines cross over, turn and then re-form. For the men it is a swagger, arms out from the sides like a boxer playing for position; for the women it is more of a lilt, with hips swaying, but all call out the customary 'Oi!' Men will dance with men, and women with women. In some cockney neighbourhoods the men will even dress as women, with false breasts and sometimes a 'pregnant' belly. It may be worth noticing that Lambeth Walk itself is a working-class shopping street, containing a street market, a cinema also used as a chapel, a street market and much condemned housing. So it is the dance of London in hard times.

In the same year that it became popular, 'Knees Up Mother Brown' was first published. Older people may recall that 'Mother Brown' was sung more than three or four decades ago and even further back, but its recent appearance in printed form, to be sold in the streets and shops, was an indication of the cheerful defiance with which Londoners always confront the nebulous future.

Yet, of course even the music has been silenced by the news of the last months and days. Factories have been established to manufacture gas masks and warning sirens are being tested. The widespread belief that reason will replace force in human affairs has been abandoned. We must all begin to live a day at a time and never think of any plans for the coming years. As a result of recent 'scares' in some of the newspapers, everyone hopes each night that there will not be an air raid. The digging of trenches is going ahead and the evacuation has begun, the children carrying one favourite toy together with a gas mask box and parcels of food and clothes. Street lights are extinguished and housewives are searching the shops for material to cover their windows. Many thousands of citizens have spent money on building back-garden trenches and on making rooms gas-proof. Public speakers, at the Albert Hall and elsewhere, issue warnings of an apocalypse and prophesy the end of Western civilization. The people are instructed to keep calm and stay cheerful, yet all are disturbed and distressed. They ask each other whether there will be a war, and dread to hear the answer.

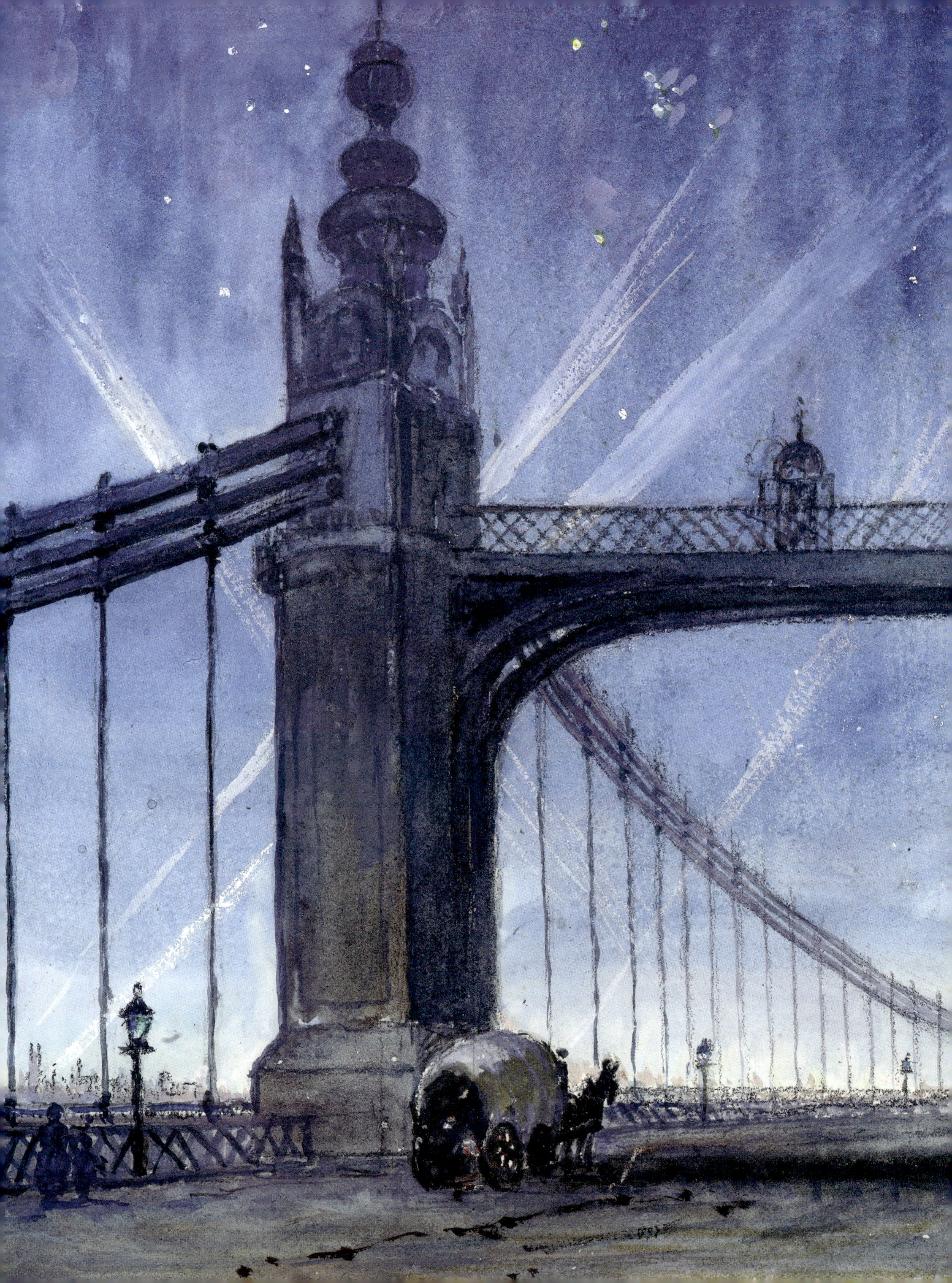

BIBLIOGRAPHY

Ackroyd, Peter, *London: The Biography*, Chatto & Windus, 2000.

Ackroyd, Peter, *Illustrated London*, Chatto & Windus, 2003.

Ackroyd, Peter, *Thames: Sacred River*, Vintage, 2007.

Ackroyd, Peter, *London Under*, Vintage, 2011.

Ackroyd, Peter, *London: The Concise Biography*, Vintage, 2012.

Ackroyd, Peter, *Queer City: Gay London from the Romans to the Present Day*, Chatto & Windus, 2017.

Ackroyd, Peter, *The Colours of London*, Frances Lincoln, 2022.

Beaumont, Matthew, *Nightwalking: A Nocturnal History of London*, Verso Books, 2015.

Grey, Drew, *Dark London*, Frances Lincoln, 2025.

Lond, David, *London's Secret Square Mile*, The History Press, 2023.

Porter, Roy, *London: A Social History*, Vintage, 2000.

Rees, John, *A People's History of London*, Verso Books, 2012.

PICTURE CREDITS

Jackson Collection / Bridgeman Images; **147** Photo
© The Fine Art Society, London, UK / Bridgeman Images;
148t Heritage Images / Getty Images; **148b** dpa picture
alliance / Alamy Stock Photo; **150** Chronicle / Alamy
Stock Photo; **151t** Pictorial Press Ltd / Alamy Stock Photo;
151b Topical Press Agency / Getty Images; **153** Heritage
Image Partnership Ltd / Alamy Stock Photo; **154t** London
Stereoscopic Company / Getty Images; **154b** Amoret
Tanner / Alamy Stock Photo; **156–157** Fine Art
Photographic / Getty Images; **158** Hulton Archive / Stringer
/ Getty Images; **160t** Look and Learn / Peter Jackson
Collection / Bridgeman Images; **160b** Niday Picture Library
/ Alamy Stock Photo; **162** IanDagnall Computing / Alamy
Stock Photo; **163** Lordprice Collection / Alamy Stock
Photo; **166** The Stapleton Collection / Bridgeman Images;
168–169 Topical Press Agency / Stringer / Bridgeman
Images; **170** Topical Press Agency / Getty Images;
171t Daily Herald Archive / Getty Images; **171b** Hulton
Archive / Stringer / Getty Images; **173** Classic Image /
Alamy Stock Photo; **174t** © Science and Society Picture
Library / © Estate of Alexander Stanhope Forbes. All rights
reserved 2024 / Bridgeman Images; **174b** Christie's Images /
Bridgeman Images; **175** Culture Club / Getty Images;
177 © The Advertising Archives / Bridgeman Images;
178 Fox Photos / Stringer / Getty Images; **179** H. F. Davis /
Stringer / Getty Images; **180t** FPG / Staff / Getty Images;
180b Bridgeman Images; **182t** GraphicaArtis / Getty
Images; **182b** GraphicaArtis / Getty Images; **183** Florilegius
/ Getty Images; **184** Prismatic Pictures / Bridgeman Images;
186 Science & Society Picture Library / Getty Images;
187t Hulton Archive / Stringer / Getty Images;
187b Chronicle / Alamy Stock Photo; **188** Trinity Mirror /
Mirrorpix / Alamy Stock Photo; **189** GraphicaArtis /
Getty Images; **190** Mills / Stringer / Getty Images;
192tl Chronicle / Alamy Stock Photo; **192tr** f8 archive /
Alamy Stock Photo; **192b** Hulton Deutsch / Getty Images;
194 Pictures from History / Getty Images; **195** Hulton
Deutsch / Getty Images; **197** Christie's Images / Bridgeman
Images; **198t** Hulton Archive / Stringer / Getty Images;
198b Hulton Archive / Stringer / Getty Images;
201t Chronicle / Alamy Stock Photo; **201b** H. F. Davis /
Stringer / Getty Images; **204** Central Press / Stringer /
Getty Images; **207t** London Express / Stringer / Getty
Images; **207b** - / Getty Images; **208** © Geffrye Museum /
Bridgeman Images; **211t** Hulton Archive / Getty;
211b John Frost Newspapers / Alamy Stock Photo;
212 Bridgeman Images; **213** Keystone-France / Getty
Images; **214** Science & Society Picture Library / Getty
Images; **215** Album / Alamy Stock Photo; **217t** William
Vanderson / Stringer / Getty Images; **217b** Lordprice
Collection / Alamy Stock Photo; **218t** Smith Archive /
Alamy Stock Photo; **218b** Smith Archive / Alamy Stock
Photo; **221** Universal History Archive / Getty Images;
222 Retro AdArchives / Alamy Stock Photo; **223** Print
Collector / Getty Images; **224–225** © Liss Fine Art /
Bridgeman Images; **226** Neil Baylis / Alamy Stock Photo;
227 © SZ Photo / Scherl / Bridgeman Images; **228** London
Express / Stringer / Getty Images; **229t** The Print Collector /
Alamy Stock Photo; **229b** Hulton Archive / Getty Images;
231 brandstaetter images / Getty Images; **233t** Lordprice
Collection / Alamy Stock Photo; **233b** Keystone-France /
Getty Images; **234** Print Collector / Getty Images;
235 Michael Nicholson / Getty Images; **237t** Look and
Learn / Valerie Jackson Harris Collection / Bridgeman
Images; **237b** Mirrorpix / Getty Images; **238** © The
Advertising Archives / Bridgeman Images; **239** Hulton
Deutsch / Getty Images; **240** Christie's Images / Bridgeman
Images; **242t** ullstein bild Dtl. / Getty Images; **242b** Smith
Archive / Alamy Stock Photo; **244** Photo © The Maas
Gallery, London / Bridgeman Images; **246t** Daily Herald
Archive / Getty Images; **246b** Associated Press / Alamy
Stock Photo; **248** Photo © Sarah Colegrave Fine Art /
Bridgeman Images

Quarto

First published in 2025 by Frances Lincoln,
an imprint of The Quarto Group.
One Triptych Place, London, SE1 9SH
United Kingdom
T (0)20 7700 9000
www.Quarto.com

EEA Representation, WTS Tax d.o.o., Žanova ulica 3,
4000 Kranj, Slovenia.
www.wts-tax.si

ISBN 978-0-7112-8764-8
eBook ISBN 978-0-7112-8765-5

10 9 8 7 6 5 4 3 2 1

Designed by Glenn Howard
Typeset in Gill Sans MT and Swift

Publisher: Philip Cooper
Editor: Isabella Toner
Editorial support: Laura Bulbeck
Senior designer: Isabel Eeles
Production Manager: Alex Merrett

Printed in Guangdong, China TT062025

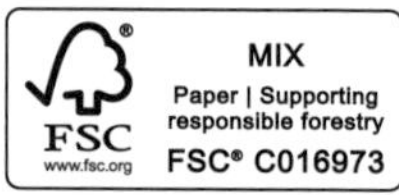

Page 2:
An engraving of Wentworth
Street in Whitechapel. From
London: a Pilgrimage (1872)
by Blanchard Jerrold and
Gustave Doré.

Page 4:
*Amongst the Nerves of the
World* (c.1930) by C. R. W.
Nevinson.

Page 248:
*Wartime Spot Lights from
Chelsea Bridge* (c.1917) by
Alice Maud Fanner.